D0583920

Merleau-Ponty's Existential Phenomenology and the Realization of Philosophy

Bloomsbury Studies in Continental Philosophy

Bloomsbury Studies in Continental Philosophy presents cutting-edge scholarship in the field of modern European thought. The wholly original arguments, perspectives and research findings in titles in this series make it an important and stimulating resource for students and academics from across the discipline.

Some other titles in the series:

Adorno, Heidegger, Philosophy and Modernity, Nicholas Joll
Between the Canon and the Messiah, Colby Dickinson
Castoriadis, Foucault, and Autonomy, Marcela Tovar-Restrepo
Deconstruction without Derrida, Martin McQuillan
Deleuze and the Diagram, Jakub Zdebik
Deleuze and the History of Mathematics, Simon B. Duffy
Derrida, Badiou and the Formal Imperative, Christopher Norris
Derrida and the Future of the Liberal Arts, edited by Mary Caputi
and Vincent J. Del Casino, Jr
Derrida: Ethics Under Erasure, Nicole Anderson
Emmanuel Levinas, Abi Doukhan
From Ricoeur to Action, edited by Todd S. Mei and David Lewin
Gadamer and Ricoeur, edited by Francis J. Mootz III and George H. Taylor
Heidegger and Nietzsche, Louis P. Blond
Immanent Transcendence, Patrice Haynes
Jean-Luc Nancy and the Question of Community, Ignaas Devisch
Kant, Deleuze and Architectonics, Edward Willatt
Levinas, Storytelling and Anti-Storytelling, Will Buckingham
Lyotard and the 'figural' in Performance, Art and Writing, Kiff Bamford
Michel Henry, edited by Jeffrey Hanson and Michael R. Kelly
Performatives After Deconstruction, edited by Mauro Senatore
Place, Commonality and Judgment, Andrew Benjamin
Post-Rationalism, Tom Eyers
Rethinking Philosophy and Theology with Deleuze, Brent Adkins
and Paul R. Hinlicky
Revisiting Normativity with Deleuze, edited by Rosi Braidotti
and Patricia Pisters
The Movement of Nihilism, edited by Laurence Paul Hemming,
Kostas Amiridis and Bogdan Costea
The Time of Revolution, Felix Ó Murchadha

Merleau-Ponty's Existential Phenomenology and the Realization of Philosophy

Bryan A. Smyth

B L O O M S B U R Y
LONDON · NEW DELHI · NEW YORK · SYDNEY

Bloomsbury Academic

An imprint of Bloomsbury Publishing Plc

50 Bedford Square	1385 Broadway
London	New York
WC1B 3DP	NY 10018
UK	USA

www.bloomsbury.com

Bloomsbury is a registered trade mark of Bloomsbury Publishing Plc

First published 2014

© Bryan A. Smyth, 2014

All rights reserved. No part of this publication may be reproduced or transmitted in any form or by any means, electronic or mechanical, including photocopying, recording, or any information storage or retrieval system, without prior permission in writing from the publishers.

Bryan A. Smyth has asserted his right under the Copyright, Designs and Patents Act, 1988, to be identified as Author of this work.

No responsibility for loss caused to any individual or organization acting on or refraining from action as a result of the material in this publication can be accepted by Bloomsbury Academic or the author.

British Library Cataloguing-in-Publication Data

A catalogue record for this book is available from the British Library.

ISBN: HB: 978-1-7809-3705-2
ePDF: 978-1-7809-3786-1
ePub: 978-1-7809-3787-8

Library of Congress Cataloging-in-Publication Data

Smyth, Bryan A.

Merleau-Ponty's Existential Phenomenology and the Realization of Philosophy/Bryan A. Smyth.

pages cm. – (Bloomsbury studies in continental philosophy)

Summary: "An original re-reading of Maurice Merleau-Ponty's existential phenomenology by way of a critical investigation of its crucial yet enigmatic references to 'heroism'"– Provided by publisher.

Includes bibliographical references and index.

ISBN 978-1-78093-705-2 (hardback) – ISBN 978-1-78093-787-8 (epub) –
ISBN 978-1-78093-786-1 (epdf) 1. Merleau-Ponty, Maurice, 1908-1961.
2. Phenomenology. 3. Heroes. 4. Courage. I. Smyth, Bryan A. II. Title.
B2430.M3764S58 2014
142'.7–dc23
2013039128

Typeset by Deanta Global Publishing Services, Chennai, India
Printed and bound in Great Britain

Contents

Acknowledgments

The ideas in this book have been brewing for many years, and as is often the case, they stem from much wider explorations. This means, among other things, that a large number of people have contributed helpfully to them in various ways over the years. For their particular forms of assistance, I would like to thank Alia Al-Saji, Renaud Barbaras, Robert Bernasconi, Ronald Bruzina, Philip Buckley, Anna Carastathis, Françoise Dastur, Duane Davis, Bernard Flynn, George di Giovanni, Wayne Froman, John Hellman, Richard Holmes, Jonathan Kim-Reuter, Don Landes, Len Lawlor, Mary Beth Mader, Iain Macdonald, Darian Meachum, Arsalan Memon, David Morris, Stephen Noble, Richard Nutbrown, and Michel Rybalka. I would also like to thank Suzanne Merleau-Ponty for kindly making available to me her volume of Merleau-Ponty's unpublished personal notes from the late 1940s (*Notes inédites de Merleau-Ponty, 1946–1949*), and Kerry Whiteside for having transcribed these notes and for conveying copies of the originals to me.

Very special thanks to Anne Quinney for her patient support and encouragement, and to Fyntan and Aurélia for making everything so much more intensely rewarding. It is to my parents that I owe the greatest debt—the book is dedicated to their memory.

Parts of the Preface and Conclusion are reprinted from "The Meontic and the Militant: On Merleau-Ponty's Relation to Fink," *International Journal of Philosophical Studies,* 19:5 (2011), 669–99, with the kind permission of Taylor & Francis Ltd.

Parts of Chapter 5 are reprinted from "Heroism and History in Merleau-Ponty's Existential Phenomenology," *Continental Philosophy Review,* 43:2 (2010), 167–91, with kind permission from Springer Science + Business Media.

Abbreviations Used in Text

See bibliography for complete bibliographic information. Where applicable, page references are given in the form "original/translation." Translations are, however, frequently modified.

Works by Merleau-Ponty

AD   *Les aventures de la dialectique* (1955)/*Adventures of the Dialectic* (1973).

CR   "Christianisme et ressentiment," in Merleau-Ponty (1997), pp. 9–33.

EP   *Éloge de la philosophie* (1953)/"In Praise of Philosophy," in Merleau-Ponty (1988), pp. 3–67.

HT   *Humanisme et terreur* (1947)/*Humanism and Terror* (1969).

NI   *Notes inédites de Maurice Merleau-Ponty, 1946–1949.**

PhP   *Phénoménologie de la perception* (1945).

PNPH   "Philosophie et non-philosophie depuis Hegel. Cours de 1960–1961," in Merleau-Ponty (1996b), pp. 269–352.

Pros.   "Un inédit de Maurice Merleau-Ponty," in Merleau-Ponty (2000), pp. 36–48/"An Unpublished Text by Maurice Merleau-Ponty: A Prospectus of His Work," in Merleau-Ponty (1964b), pp. 3–11.

PrP   "Le primat de la perception et ses conséquences philosophiques," in Merleau-Ponty (1996a), pp. 41–104/"The Primacy of Perception and Its Philosophical Consequences," in Merleau-Ponty (1964b), pp. 12–42.

Signs   *Signes* (1960)/*Signs* (1964d).

SC   *La structure du comportement* (1942)/*The Structure of Behavior* (1963).

SNS   *Sens et non-sens* (1948)/*Sense and Non-Sense* (1964c).

TT   "Titres et travaux: Projet d'enseignement," in Merleau-Ponty (2000), pp. 9–35.

VI   *Le visible et l'invisible* (1964a)/*The Visible and the Invisible* (1964e).

* Unpublished notes from the late 1940s. Collated, paginated, and transcribed by Kerry Whiteside (see Whiteside 1988, 312ff). I would like to thank Suzanne Merleau-Ponty and Kerry Whiteside for making copies of the originals as well as the transcription available to me. Original assigned pagination is followed by transcription pagination in square brackets. At Mme. Merleau-Ponty's request, it should be noted that these materials were never intended for publication.

Works by others

Carnets Saint Exupéry (1975), *Carnets, édition intégrale.*

EG Saint Exupéry (1982), *Écrits de guerre.*

EN Sartre (1943), *L'être et le néant*/Sartre (1956) *Being and Nothingness.*

ES Roger Caillois, (2003), *The Edge of Surrealism: A Roger Caillois Reader.*

FTL Husserl (1969), *Formal and Transcendental Logic.*

HCC Lukács, (1967a), *Geschichte und Klassenbewußtsein*/Lukács (1971), *History and Class Consciousness.*

KrV Kant (1998), *Critique of Pure Reason* (standard A/B pagination).

KS Fink, "Die phänomenologische Philosophie Husserls in der gegenwärtigen Kritik," in Fink (1966), pp. 79–156/Fink (1970), "The Phenomenological Philosophy of Edmund Husserl and Contemporary Criticism."

KU Kant (2000), *Critique of the Power of Judgment* (*Akademie* pagination).

MAM Saint Exupéry (1981), "Le marxisme anti-marxiste."

MH Roger Caillois (1938), *Le mythe et l'homme.*

PG Saint Exupéry (1942c), *Pilote de guerre* (Gallimard).

SCM Fink (1988a), *VI. Cartesianische Meditation*, Teil 1/Fink (1995), *Sixth Cartesian Meditation.*

SV Saint Exupéry (1956), *Un sens à la vie.*

SZ Heidegger (1957), *Sein und Zeit*/Heidegger (1962), *Being and Time.*

TD Lukács (2000), *A Defence of History and Class Consciousness: Tailism and the Dialectic.*

TE Binswanger, "Traum und Existenz," in Binswanger (1994), pp. 95–119.

TH Saint Exupéry (1939), *Terre des hommes.*

ÜP Binswanger, "Über Psychotherapie," in Binswanger (1994), pp. 205–30.

Preface: Rereading *Phenomenology of Perception*

As with other figures of like stature, there is a vast amount of secondary literature devoted to the thought of Maurice Merleau-Ponty. The last decade or so in particular has seen the publication of numerous new books. Why one more?

A critical glance at the situation in recent English-language Merleau-Ponty scholarship may be instructive here. For we see that the vast majority of recent volumes fall into one of the following two categories: (1) general introductions and reference works,[1] including several edited collections of a general nature,[2] and (2) applications of Merleau-Ponty's work to specific topics or problems.[3] Many of these contributions are, in whole or in part, of significant scholarly value. But nonetheless, a clear pattern emerges: in recent years little new basic interpretive research on Merleau-Ponty's philosophical work itself has been accorded book-length treatment, and what has been published has invariably tended either to adopt an overall view of his corpus that emphasizes his later works, or else to focus exclusively on the latter.[4] In other words, even though recent years have seen a marked upsurge in the level of interest in Merleau-Ponty's work, both within and beyond the disciplinary boundaries of philosophy, and even though *Phenomenology of Perception* remains, by all accounts, his *magnum opus*,[5] there has been no new book-length scholarly contribution aimed principally at coming to terms with the formulation of existential phenomenology that this text epitomizes. There is, rather, an overwhelming tacit consensus that this early stage of Merleau-Ponty's work has, over the last 60-plus years, already been sufficiently studied, such that there is really nothing new (of any philosophical consequence) to be said about it.[6] It might be expounded or elucidated or spun or summarized or applied in this or that new way, but the standard working assumption is that with regard to Merleau-Ponty's existential phenomenology in the immediate postwar period, there remain, so to speak, no unturned stones.

Methodological questions

There can be no denying that Merleau-Ponty's later works are of immense philosophical interest, and this is especially true of the recently published and as-yet still unpublished materials from his lectures at the Collège de France. Be that as it may, however, it is fundamentally mistaken to maintain that critical scrutiny of Merleau-Ponty's early reinterpretation of Husserlian transcendental phenomenology as expressed primarily in *Phenomenology of Perception* is, for all intents and purposes, an exhausted project. There may be several reasons for this, but one aspect stands out quite prominently—to wit, the question of *method*. It would be very difficult for any Merleau-Ponty scholar to disagree with the claim that Merleau-Ponty's work from the early postwar period, and *Phenomenology of Perception* in particular, is (or at least appears to be) rather elusive with regard to conveying the underlying methodology on the basis of which its claims unfold. Such methodological elusiveness or unforthcomingness may also be found in some of Merleau-Ponty's later works too, and no doubt something similar is true of many (or even most) other philosophers as well. But reticence of this kind is particularly problematic in the context of phenomenology, and of *transcendental* phenomenology especially. For here, methodological issues concerning the nature of the phenomenological reduction—in general terms (including the *epoché*) and in its various possible modes (e.g. eidetic reduction)—are of paramount importance. As a distinctive approach to philosophical problems, transcendental phenomenology stands or falls with its conception of the reduction for at least two related reasons. First, the reduction is indispensable for any genuine phenomenology to get off the ground. As Eugen Fink once put it, "There is no phenomenology that does not pass through the 'reduction.' Anything calling itself 'phenomenology' while renouncing the reduction would in principle be a mundane philosophy, which is to say, a '*dogmatic*' one (in the phenomenological sense)" (KS 105n1/146n11, translation modified).[7] Second, whatever philosophical insights to which phenomenology may lay claim are unavoidably conditioned by the manner in which the reduction is performed, since those insights can only be based on the evidence of the phenomena that are thereby disclosed. It is thus simply not possible to overstate the extent to which the philosophical coherence and viability of transcendental phenomenology depend essentially upon its methodological self-understanding. And yet this self-understanding is not easily achieved. As Merleau-Ponty himself noted, even Husserl struggled at length with the "problematic of the reduction"—"there is probably no other question on which Husserl spent more time trying to understand—nor one to which he returned more often" (PhP v).[8] Consideration of these points—namely, the vital indispensability of the reduction, and the importance of getting clear about it—cannot but render the apparent elusiveness of Merleau-Ponty's early work with regard to methodology all the more puzzling and frustrating.[9]

Take, for instance, the well-known and oft-cited remark made in the Preface to the effect that "the best formulation" of the reduction was given by Fink "when he spoke of a 'wonder' [« *étonnement* »] before the world" (PhP viii; cf. 341f).[10] This was a point that Fink made in all of his important summary expositions of Husserl's project that he produced in the 1930s, articles which had a crucial formative impact on Merleau-Ponty's understanding of phenomenology: "the origin of philosophical problems is *wonder*" [*Verwunderung*] (Fink 1966d, 182; cf. Fink 1966c, 168.).[11] Such is, of course, a venerable sentiment, one that may be traced back at least to the Socratic claim that "wonder [*thaumazein*] is the feeling of a philosopher, and philosophy begins in wonder."[12] And Fink's connecting this to phenomenology is by no means an eccentric claim peculiar to him. Beginning with Husserl himself, phenomenologists have often conceived their work as rooted in something like that ancient sense of wonder.[13]

Yet, surely the *best* formulation of the phenomenological reduction cannot simply amount to a reiteration of a traditional notion, and one to which, needless to say, phenomenology has no proprietary claim. Fink himself was more specific. For him, philosophical wonder concerned the being of the world itself, and he claimed that the philosophical uniqueness of phenomenology lies in its effort radically to inculcate and operationalize this wonder methodologically. Phenomenological inquiry begins with the phenomenological reduction which, through the suspension of the natural attitude, brings about "the awakening of an immeasurable wonder over the mysteriousness" of the state of affairs [*Sachlage*] confronting philosophy at its beginning [*das Erwachen einer maßlosen Verwunderung über die Rätselhaftigkeit dieser Sachlage*] (KS 115f/109).[14] This wonder involves the loss of naïve obviousness, the disconcerting astonishment of which "displaces man from the *captivation* [Befangenheit] in everyday, publicly pre-given, traditional and worn-out familiarity with existents." It "drives one from an always already authorized and expressly laid-out interpretation of the sense of the world," with the result that the phenomenologist "once again opens himself primordially [*uranfänglich*] to the world, finding himself in the dawn of a new day of the world [*in der Morgendämmerung eines neuen Welttages*] in which he, and everything that is, begins to appear in a new light" (Fink 1966d, 183).

As we shall see, Fink had much more to say about the reduction. But Merleau-Ponty may have been echoing these general ideas in glossing as follows his own view of the reduction in terms of wonder: "reflection does not withdraw from the world toward the unity of consciousness as the foundation of the world; rather, it steps back in order to see transcendences surge forth [*jaillir*] and it slackens [*distend*] the intentional threads that connect us to the world in order to make them appear" (PhP viii). It is in this way that, for Merleau-Ponty, "true philosophy is a matter of learning to see the world anew [*rapprendre à voir le monde*]" (PhP xvi).

Merleau-Ponty thus concurred with Fink's main criticism of Kantian philosophy, namely, that it is not genuinely transcendental but rather remains "worldly" [« *mondaine* »], in that it ultimately takes the world for granted and makes use of it, rather than, as Merleau-Ponty put it, "*wondering* about the world and conceiving the subject as a transcendence toward it" (PhP viii). But he also self-consciously deviated from Fink—and, indeed, from everyone, including Husserl himself—inasmuch as he took this interpretation of phenomenology decisively in a particular existential direction that emphasizes what he called the "paradoxical" nature of the world.[15] By this, Merleau-Ponty meant that the being of the world does not simply present a "mysterious" state of affairs, the resolution of which could be achieved through the insights of transcendental phenomenology. Rather, his point was that the world *is* a mystery, that it is "defined" by its mysteriousness, and that therefore "there can be no question of dispelling it [the mystery] through any sort of 'solution'" [*il ne saurait être question de le dissiper par quelque « solution »*]—it is "below the level" of any solution [*il est en déça des solutions*] (PhP xvi). Thus, according to Merleau-Ponty, not only is it necessary to "break" [*rompre*] our familiarity with the world, but moreover—and this is what's crucial—what this rupture can teach us is "nothing but the unmotivated upsurge [*le jaillissement immotivé*] of the world" (PhP viii). This is crucial because from it follows immediately the most famous and celebrated claim regarding the phenomenological reduction in *Phenomenology of Perception*, namely, the claim that "the most important lesson of the reduction is the impossibility of a complete reduction" (PhP viii).

The point of this well-known assertion is to emphasize the spatial and temporal inherence of phenomenology in the world, such that the "radical reflection" it undertakes by way of the reduction is inescapably dependent upon pregiven layers of "unreflective life." Most readers of Merleau-Ponty who incline favorably toward his project view this claim as a concise expression of the way in which he takes up Husserlian phenomenology without succumbing—as Husserl himself supposedly did—to idealism or "intellectualism" and all its concomitant philosophical deficiencies. In other words, it is taken as an expression of how Merleau-Ponty goes Husserl one better methodologically.

Leaving aside the question as to whether or not this is fair with regard to Husserl, there is, on the face of it, something suspect about Merleau-Ponty's assertion. For even if it is granted that the reduction as envisioned by Husserl is indeed something that cannot in all strictness be completely carried out, it still doesn't quite make sense to say that the reduction *itself* could supply us with this lesson. The underlying point is a general one: how could any methodological procedure all by itself indicate its own limitations in an epistemically reliable way? To be sure, one may take up the phenomenological reduction in an attempt to do what Husserl had supposedly hoped to do and then find that it always comes up short. But in that case, the conclusion that would be warranted is *not* that the reduction is all well and good up to that point but no further, that is, in an incomplete form, but rather that the reduction is inherently flawed and should simply be discarded altogether. Just as archers, for example, may not legitimately claim technical mastery when they move their targets to wherever their arrows happen to land, no philosophical method that fails to achieve its own ostensible goals can be simply retained—that is, retained with further ado—as a successful way of reaching whatever unexpected results at which it chanced to arrive. Absent a sound and lucid methodological self-understanding as to how they were reached, and why any further targets are illusory, those results are, technically speaking, meaningless noise—or, in phenomenological parlance, they are transcendentally naïve. In short, if the phenomenological reduction grinds to a halt before attaining the goal it was designed to achieve, then the immediate implication is one of failure, with the result that no putative insights at all, whether with reference to the intentional objects under consideration up to that point or to the reduction itself *qua* method, could be considered reliable.

The point here is that while it is no doubt true that a complete reduction in the sense intended by Merleau-Ponty is indeed impossible, it makes no sense to say that one could learn this as a truth from an incomplete performance of that same reduction—a truncated implementation of a misguided procedure is not a recipe for insight. Pending further methodological elaboration, then, it remains entirely unclear as to why and how the reduction would be retained at all.

As mentioned above, the idea of an incomplete reduction is widely held and even celebrated as a positive virtue of Merleau-Ponty's reinterpretation of transcendental phenomenology—an existentially modified version of an originally idealist procedure that nonetheless remains methodologically central. But what exactly this means and amounts to has not been fully examined. In particular, the consequences that would follow in terms of the status of *Phenomenology of Perception* as a work of philosophy, if it is allowed that its central methodological procedure is necessarily incomplete, have been left unscrutinized. For while it may be clear enough how a complete reduction would (*per impossibile*) yield definitive philosophical truth, it would seem that on its own, an existentially limited performance of the same procedure could never attain any comparable degree of philosophical conclusiveness (including, of course, with regard to metaphysical claims concerning "ambiguity," since these would be pointless if they themselves were ambiguous). For it could never achieve the sort of determinate epistemic closure that is necessary to make compelling truth claims. That is, unless it borrows covertly the principles of verification or claims of apodicticity, for example, from the idealism it vigorously rejects, an existentially modified version of the reduction can never find itself in a position to make *bona fide* philosophical claims.

This is not to say that such is in fact the case with *Phenomenology of Perception*. Rather, it is to suggest that the incomplete reduction is not the whole methodological story here. Surely no one is prepared to draw the scandalous conclusion that "one of the great texts of twentieth-century philosophy" (Carman 2012, vii)[16] is actually—and even by its author's own admission!—*methodologically incomplete*, that is, lacking in rigorous methodological completeness of any kind. To be sure, such is a *possible* outcome. Before it is conceded, though, it strongly behooves anyone who holds that *Phenomenology of Perception* is indeed a text that makes vitally important philosophical claims to first make some concerted effort to disclose and to come to terms positively—rather than by privative reference to an impossibility[17]—with how it is that this work might indeed be considered methodologically complete. There is no room for ambiguity here— *Phenomenology of Perception* either is or is not methodologically complete, and only one option would allow us to take its results seriously.

Philosophical scholarship on *Phenomenology of Perception* has yet to settle this question. More specifically, those who appreciate the work as a major contribution to philosophy—as opposed to a very sophisticated contribution to psychology, say, or even to literature—have yet to render explicit the methodological completeness that they effectively assume is there, even if, as is not uncommon, they are unaware of making this assumption, or take no cognizance of the problem at all. It is first and foremost on this basis, then, that the idea, according to which there is fundamentally nothing new to say about *Phenomenology of Perception*, should be flatly rejected. This rejection opens up a space for genuinely fresh exegetical and interpretive work on this text related to issues of method, and it is in this space that the present book should be located.

■

This book thus aims at something like a rereading of *Phenomenology of Perception*. But if by *rereading* is understood an undertaking of comprehensive critical exegesis cover-to-cover, then a rereading as such goes well beyond its scope. Rather, the much more modest aim of this book is merely to do some of the groundwork for a critical rereading of *Phenomenology of Perception* by coming to terms with the problem of its methodological completeness. Its aim, in other words, is to articulate a previously uncharted angle of critical analysis which, by being based on the immanent methodological commitments of Merleau-Ponty's work, would be able to support insightful new approaches to the exegesis, interpretation, and ultimately the evaluation and, if possible, the further development and application of Merleau-Ponty's text.

In a certain way, though, this book does in fact deal with *Phenomenology of Perception* cover to cover. For there are two moments in the text that are of crucial importance to the overall discussion here, and they happen to fall—although this is anything but coincidental—on the very first and the very last pages. The first of these two moments is the reference to Eugen Fink's *Sixth Cartesian Meditation* that occurs in the first paragraph of the Preface (PhP i) and the second is comprised of the lines drawn from Antoine de Saint Exupéry's *Pilote de guerre* with which Merleau-Ponty's book, as is well known, ends (PhP 520). Neither of these moments has been the object of critical scrutiny in the scholarship devoted to Merleau-Ponty,[18] although their importance in terms of understanding *Phenomenology of Perception* is without parallel. The initial reference to Fink's *Sixth Cartesian Meditation*, a work devoted to "the idea of a transcendental theory of method," properly interpreted along with other explicit and implicit allusions made in the text, serves to indicate the basic methodological problem with which Merleau-Ponty had to grapple in composing *Phenomenology of Perception*, resolution of which was the *conditio sine qua non* for the wholehearted embrace of and identification with the phenomenological project, duly reconceived, that this book represents. The second key moment, the passage drawn from Saint Exupéry, manifests quite spectacularly Merleau-Ponty's resolution of this problem, and as such, it possesses superlative significance with regard to understanding the specific inner nature of Merleau-Ponty's reinterpretation of Husserlian phenomenology.

The present book focuses primarily on coming to terms with the second of these moments, that is, the Exupérian climax of *Phenomenology of Perception*. Although the cited passage is invariably given a warmly affirmative but inconsequential gloss whenever it is referred to in the scholarly literature on Merleau-Ponty, there is, as we shall see, actually much more going on than is readily apparent, and there are some unexpected interpretive difficulties that demand resolution.[19] Critical scrutiny will bring to light that, at least *prima facie*, it is deeply puzzling that *Phenomenology of Perception* concludes as it does. The main thrust of this book is devoted to dealing with this problem and its attendant difficulties by construing the end of *Phenomenology of Perception* in terms of Merleau-Ponty's solution to certain methodological issues concerning the reduction that had been posed by Fink—and more specifically, in terms of the solution that Merleau-Ponty had conceived as an *alternative* to that offered by Fink himself. In order to contextualize this in a way that will allow for a full appreciation of the nature of Merleau-Ponty's position and what is at stake in it, then, it is necessary to first discuss the relevant aspects of Fink's *Sixth Cartesian Meditation*.[20]

Eugen Fink and the idea of constructive phenomenology

In his capacity as Husserl's assistant, Fink drafted the *Sixth Cartesian Meditation* in 1932 as part of the project of systematically reworking the (five) *Cartesian Meditations* which, subsequent to their publication in French translation, Husserl had come to regard as still beholden to a certain transcendental naïveté.[21] For most of the time since then, this work led a sort of underground existence. In addition to Husserl, a small circle of others close to him were able to consult it shortly after its composition, including Gaston Berger, to whom Fink actually lent his (one) carbon copy of the text in 1934—a copy which apparently was never returned.[22] When he left Leuven in 1940, Fink retrieved the original typescripts from the newly established Husserl archive in Leuven (Bruzina 1995, xxxiii). Following the war, Fink submitted the work—as he had intended to do, with Husserl's support, in 1933, only to be thwarted for "political reasons" having to do with his connection to Husserl (Bruzina 1995, xx; cf. lxxv n63)— as his *Habilitationsschrift* at Freiburg (Bruzina 1995, xxxiv). As he noted at the time, Fink chose to submit the *Sixth Cartesian Meditation*, as opposed to newer and more substantial work, largely because it did carry that original endorsement from Husserl. The choice was thus more ceremonial than philosophical. Fink saw its submission as "an act of piety [*Pietät*]," a statement of critical allegiance to Husserl and to his project.[23] And as he noted in a letter to Hermann Van Breda, his *Habilitation* was in fact seen by the University as a case of "political reparation."[24] Unlike most, however, this *Schrift* faded from view. In part, this is because the work was somewhat extraneous to Fink's own emerging intellectual trajectory. But it is also the case that it had far-reaching critical implications for transcendental phenomenology that were easily liable to misunderstanding, for which reason Fink had never intended it to be widely available.[25] And this reluctance to disseminate the work did not change after the war. The text thus remained unpublished in Fink's lifetime—it did not appear until 1988, 13 years after his death.

These facts are significant for two reasons. First, it was only on account of Berger's extended possession of the carbon copy that Merleau-Ponty was able to read the *Sixth Cartesian Meditation*, which he did in 1942.[26] It has always been known that Merleau-Ponty had read this monograph, as he explicitly cited it three times in the Preface to *Phenomenology of Perception*, including—as mentioned above—on the very first page. Second, however, owing to its subsequent history, Fink's text was entirely inaccessible to anyone interested in Merleau-Ponty's book for over 40 years. It was thus never discussed, let alone established as an important point of reference, in scholarly commentary on *Phenomenology of Perception*. The references to Fink's text were simply passed over in silence.

Yet, despite the lack of attention that it has received in the literature, the impact that the *Sixth Cartesian Meditation* had on Merleau-Ponty's thought at the time of writing *Phenomenology of Perception* was singularly important.[27] This impact, however, had to do with the formal terms in which Fink posed the basic methodological problem faced by phenomenology, rather than with the actual solution that he proposed—for Merleau-Ponty disagreed quite sharply with that and offered a radically different solution. Fink's text was thus a decisively important methodological foil against which Merleau-Ponty worked out the basic terms of his own reinterpretation of phenomenological methodology.[28] In order to fully understand *Phenomenology of Perception* (and by implication any of Merleau-Ponty's subsequent work inasmuch as it represents either an extension or critique of *Phenomenology of Perception*), then, it is imperative to understand the salient aspects of "the idea of a transcendental theory of method" that Fink had developed in his *Sixth Cartesian Meditation*.[29]

To begin, consider Merleau-Ponty's initial reference to Fink. As is well known, Merleau-Ponty opened the Preface to *Phenomenology of Perception* by asking: "What is phenomenology?," and he motivated this question, insisting on its still being open, by noting several pairs of seemingly incompatible tendencies within phenomenology which would have led those of Merleau-Ponty's readers who were aware of them to doubt seriously the philosophical coherence of the project. Merleau-Ponty thus juxtaposed a search for essences with a concern for facticity, a standpoint of transcendental reflection with perspectives based in the pregivenness of the world, and the goal of rigorous scientificity with the relativeness of something like *Lebensphilosophie*. These points of contrast—or, as he put it, "contradictions"—roughly track idealist *versus* existentialist understandings of phenomenology, and they effectively boil down to the apparent opposition between a transcendental eidetic science and a concrete account of lived experience. It is within the final "contradiction" that the reference to Fink appears, and at issue here is methodology: Merleau-Ponty juxtaposed phenomenology construed as a project of "direct description" with two further developments: first, Husserl's reference to "genetic phenomenology" in his *Cartesian Meditations* (which, as it had been published in a French translation, was something that many of Merleau-Ponty's readers would have been familiar with) and second, the idea of "constructive phenomenology" that Fink discussed in the *Sixth Cartesian Meditation* (of which literally only a handful at most of Merleau-Ponty's readers in France could possibly have had any idea at all).

Merleau-Ponty's point here was that each of these developments is at odds with phenomenology understood as presuppositionless description of intuitional givenness in strict accordance with Husserl's original "principle of all principles."[30] For he implied that "genetic phenomenology" would take into account aspects of the "psychological genesis" of experience, in order to situate critically its intuitionally given content, and that "constructive phenomenology" would go further by introducing into consideration "the causal explanations [of experience] that the scientist [*le savant*], historian, or sociologist could provide," which is to say, broader third-personal or "external spectator" perspectives on human existence that would serve in turn to situate critically even "genetic" accounts of lived experience. In each case, it is a matter of reorienting phenomenological attention to the background of a given level of experience.

Merleau-Ponty did not elaborate in any detail in this opening paragraph. But he made it clear that he saw a profound tension between the idea of direct description and the sort of critical philosophical comprehension that phenomenology ideally aspires to achieve. For the latter demands a dimension of transcendental critique that straightforward description alone is incapable of providing. And if we admit "the unmotivated upsurge of the world," then how could it be otherwise? Direct description could not but reflect that opaque facticity naïvely. Merleau-Ponty wanted to insist, however, that this tension is not a shortcoming, but on the contrary, that phenomenology lives in and through it—and, in particular, that its "contradictoriness" is not extraneous to but rather fully present within Husserl's own work.[31] Merleau-Ponty's initial reference to Fink is thus ambivalent. On the one hand, the suggestion is that Fink's idea of constructive phenomenology implies a salutary openness to supplement first-person description with insights drawn from an external standpoint. On the other hand, however, the tone of the reference indicates unmistakably that Merleau-Ponty regarded Fink's idea with some suspicion, as being another one-sided expression of a particular metaphysical tendency internal to phenomenology. What is thereby suggested is that while there is something partly correct about the idea of constructive phenomenology, along with all the other "contradictory" aspects of the project, it too needs to be reconciled under the auspices of a genuinely phenomenological understanding of what phenomenology is.

Such is Merleau-Ponty's task, both in the Preface itself and beyond. In order to appreciate fully his efforts, it is necessary to lay out in some detail the account of constructive phenomenology that Fink developed in the *Sixth Cartesian Meditation*. To this end, I will unpack Fink's dense and technical text in terms of the problem of phenomenological self-reference, and the fundamental parameters of his own proposed solution. This will unfold as follows: I will provide (1) an account of Fink's construal of the phenomenologist as a detached theoretical "onlooker" [*Zuschauer*] that does not participate in the constitution of the world, and show (2) how this gives rise to a specific problem of transcendental "illusion" [*Schein*] which requires for its resolution (3) a speculative interpretation of phenomenology as the "absolute science" of the constitution of worldly Being [*Sein*] in terms of processes obtaining in the extraworldly dimension of "*pre-Being*" [Vor-Sein].[32] I shall then consider Merleau-Ponty's response to this, as well as some of the issues that it raises and how these serve to motivate taking a fresh look at *Phenomenology of Perception*.

The phenomenological onlooker

Fink's proposed revisions to the original *Cartesian Meditations* cut strongly against their "Cartesian" character, in particular by insisting upon the pre-givenness of the world as phenomenology's initial situation, and emphasizing that, just as much as it encompasses transcendent being, the world includes the sphere of human immanence. To deflect the common but mistaken view that performing the phenomenological reduction entails withdrawing into an inner domain of apodictic self-certainty, Fink locks human existence within the mundane world by circumscribing it ontologically, that is, by interpreting the "natural attitude" as a necessary *transcendental* fact of human existence. Rather than as any kind of psychological complex within the world, it is a matter of the constant world-apperception that is essentially constitutive of human experience. For Fink, world-belief is "the *primal happening* [Urgeschehen] *of our transcendental existence*" (Fink 1988b, 187), such that "existing-within-the-belief-in-the-world and believing oneself to be human are inextricably one and the same" [*Im-Weltglauben-sein und im Selbstglauben als Mensch sein sind untrennbar eins*] (KS, 115/109, translation modified). Hence, rather than as the "natural attitude," Fink preferred to denote the mundane predicament of human existence as *Weltbefangenheit*, captivation in/by the world (see Bruzina 1998, 57–60; Cairns 1976, 95). Human beings *as such* are imprisoned by ontic preoccupations.

Although familiar with the disagreements between Husserl and Heidegger over the being of transcendental and mundane subjectivity, in thus posing the "question of being," Fink was not following Heidegger (cf. Bernet 1989). For he rejects the "ontological priority" of Dasein. Instead, his move is to rethink Husserl's project on the basis of a sharper ontological difference between mundane and transcendental subjectivity, construing the former as the latter's worldly self-apperception, that is, as the constituted product of extramundane constitution. For Fink, *"the existent is only the result of a constitution,"* and *"constitution is always constitution of the existent"* (SCM 23/21; cf. 108/99). Key here is that the constitutive coming-to-be of an existent is not itself an existent (SCM 82/73), and thus cannot be understood in terms of worldly ontology. Fink argued that, pending a special reduction of it, our idea of being pertains exclusively to constituted objectivity of the natural attitude—hence the transcendental naïveté of the original *Meditations* (cf. SCM 78–84/70–5). As constitutive origination and becoming of the world, what we would call *transcendental* being *"is" "*simply and solely *in the process"* (SCM 49/45; cf. 107/97). Fink denotes this constitutive process as "enworlding" [*Verweltlichung*], or more precisely, as "primary" or "proper [*eigentliche*] enworlding" (SCM 108/99; cf. 23/21). And he refers to its "being-mode," which transcends the mundane idea of being, as *"pre-being"* ["Vor-Sein"]. Initially, at any rate, this is the central object of phenomenological investigation.

Radicalizing phenomenology's basic problematic in this way, however, it follows for Fink that, as *weltbefangen* entities, human beings are constitutively incapable of effecting the epoché, performing the reduction, and of carrying out the phenomenological investigation of primary enworlding. This could only occur outside the world; hence, the proper agency of phenomenological reflection must have transcendental status. Yet, at the same time, this agency must be separate from, that is, not participate in, the process that it is supposed to investigate. Consequently, in tandem with the ontological difference between mundane and transcendental, Fink further posits a radical "splitting" [*Spaltung*] within transcendental being—hence what Fink called the triadic "performance-structure" [*Vollzugsstruktur*] of the phenomenological reduction (KS 122/115). This splitting is the epoché, a "structural moment of transcendental reflection" (KS 121/115) whereby transcendental life "steps outside itself," producing the "non-participant" [*unbeteiligte*] "phenomenological onlooker" (SCM 26/23; Fink 1988b, 187; cf. Husserl, Crisis 285). The result is an antithetical duality at the transcendental level whereby the onlooker breaks with the *"innermost vital tendency"* of transcendental life (SCM 12/12), namely, the constitutive realization of the world, setting up a *countertendency* to it (SCM 26/24). As this countertendency, the onlooker's phenomenologizing is the becoming-for-itself of transcendentally constituting life. Fink describes the resulting dynamic in dialectical terms: "Split in this way, transcendental life turns upon itself, becomes objective [*gegenständlich*] to itself, and comes to itself through theoretical self-illumination" (Fink 1988b, 187; cf. SCM 163/147).[33]

Fink does not deny that the reduction is played out at the mundane level. But he insists that as "a theoretical self-surmounting [*Selbstüberwindung*] of man" (KS 134/126), the action it implies cannot be understood in worldly terms. For the reduction "de-objectifies, de-worlds intentional life by removing the self-apperceptions that enworld it, that situate it in the world," rendering wholly immanent the "depths of the intentional life of belief where the psychical life's self-apperception is first validly constructed" (KS 142/133). While a human subject may *undergo* such an experience, she is not the active reducing subject *per se*. Rather, the active element can only be the onlooker, the transcendental subject's tendency toward self-consciousness as it may happen to "awaken" in her. It is not any kind of human self-reflection, but rather transcendental subjectivity, "concealed in self-objectivation as man, reflectively think[ing] about itself" (SCM 36/32). In fact, on account of how he poses the basic problem of phenomenology, Fink is committed not only to denying that the reduction cannot be independently motivated in the natural attitude,[34] but moreover that "phenomenologizing is *not a human possibility at all*, but signifies precisely the *un-humanizing* [Entmenschung] *of man*, the passing of human existence . . . into the transcendental subject" (SCM 132/120; cf. 36, 43–4/32, 40; KS 110/104).

That the agent of phenomenology must be the non-participating transcendental onlooker is the guiding idea in Fink's attempt to redress the transcendental naïveté of Husserl's *Cartesian Meditations*. But what is also required is a "self-objectification" [*Selbstvergegenständlichung*] of the onlooker (SCM 14/13), a self-referential thematization of its phenomenologizing (SCM 25/23), lacking which a new naïveté would simply replace the old. For even if, through the onlooker's phenomenologizing, primary enworlding gains self-consciousness, the being of the onlooker itself remains a mystery. As Fink put it: "In the field of 'transcendentality' there remains . . . something still *uncomprehended*, precisely the phenomenological theorizing '*onlooker*'" (SCM 13/12; cf. 24–5/22–3). This is the focus of the *Sixth Cartesian Meditation* as a work of methodology. Taking up Husserl's own directive that transcendental phenomenology subject itself to rigorous methodological self-critique (Husserl 1969, 289; 1960, 29, 151f; see also Luft 2002, 8–22), Fink's aim is to clarify how the transcendental experience of the phenomenological onlooker could gain a complete self-conscious comprehension of its own activity and thereby establish itself scientifically. Phenomenological methodology is "the phenomenological science of phenomenologizing, the phenomenology of phenomenology" (SCM 13/12), in the sense of "submit[ting] the phenomenologizing thought and theory-formation that functions anonymously in phenomenological labors to a proper transcendental analytic, and thus to complete phenomenology in ultimate *transcendental self-understanding about itself*" (SCM 8–9/9).

The problem of transcendental illusion

The view of transcendental phenomenology presented in the *Sixth Cartesian Meditation* conspicuously reflects the structure of Kant's *Critique of Pure Reason* in a number of ways. For example, Fink distinguished the transcendental theory of method, as the dimension of phenomenology that thematizes itself, from what he called the "transcendental theory of elements," the dimension of phenomenology that thematizes transcendental subjectivity as primary enworlding. While *initially* the latter may be the central object of phenomenological investigation, it would be wrong to regard that as phenomenology proper, to which the theory of method would be a sort of appendix (as many readers of Kant's first *Critique* mistakenly regard *his* theory of method).[35] Rather, Fink's account of the phenomenological investigation of primary enworlding shows that its scientificity depends crucially on what the theory of method offers—in particular, on what he called, again echoing Kant, the "canon of phenomenological reason."[36] For while the ontological status of the onlooker makes transcendental cognition possible, it also presents phenomenology with certain paradoxes, such that its quest for transcendental truth is congenitally susceptible (here we hear Kant again) to "transcendental illusion." For Kant, this has to do with certain rationally necessary transcendental fictions which, if applied theoretically beyond the scope of experience, give rise to the dialectical fallacies of dogmatic metaphysics, but which are not necessarily deceptive (KrV A645/B673), as they possess indispensable heuristic value when employed regulatively (see Grier 2001, 268–88). In contrast, for Fink, transcendental illusion is not something that bears *directly* upon transcendental insight at all, but is a problem having to do with *how transcendental truth appears*, that is, with the fact that it can only appear in mundane form as "appearance-truth" [*Erscheinungswahrheit*] or "seeming truth" [*Scheinwahrheit*].[37] Whereas for Kant, then, there can be no canon of pure *theoretical* reason—there is a negative *discipline* for that, while he strictly limits the positive canon to reason's *practical* use (KrV A797/B825), as conceived by Fink, the canon of phenomenological reason is precisely that which enables us to distinguish between "mere appearance-truths" and "proper transcendental truths" with respect to phenomenologizing (SCM 111, 120f, 129f, 134/101, 110, 118, 121).

We can distinguish two levels within phenomenology's problem of transcendental illusion. First, there is the matter of communicating transcendental truth—*how it appears to others*. (Fink's *Kant-Studien* article is mainly limited to this level of the problem.) The issue here is that phenomenology faces profound, paradoxical difficulties when it tries to express its transcendental insights within the *weltbefangen* conceptual confines of ordinary language and formal logic (KS 153/142; cf. 155, 80/145, 75). However, strictly speaking, that is not a problem *within* phenomenology. Rather, it is a matter of others' limited understanding—a symptom of the growing pains of phenomenology at an early stage of its development.[38]

But the problem of transcendental illusion is not limited to the difficulties attaching to the *communication* of phenomenological truth. There is a deeper level to the problem, (upon which Fink deliberately held back from elaborating in his *Kant-Studien* article)—namely, *how transcendental truth appears at all* (KS 153/142). For in Fink's account, phenomenology is separate from enworlding. How then does *it* appear? How is it that phenomenology "*un*-performs" the reduction, as it were—how does it effect an *un*-un-humanizing—so as to avoid being stranded in transcendence?

The second level of the problem of transcendental illusion takes us inside phenomenology. There are two aspects to consider. First, there is the nature of transcendental cognition itself. In a sense, illusion obtains here germinally. For the onlooker's experience of enworlding necessarily involves a "transcendental ontification." That is, it necessarily reproduces the framework of mundane ontology at the "pre-existent" level (SCM 83/74). "[T]he theoretical experience of the phenomenological onlooker *ontifies the 'pre-existent' life-processes of transcendental subjectivity* and is therefore in a sense—a sense not comparable to any mode of productivity pregiven in a worldly way—'*productive*'" (SCM 85f/76). But because this "productivity" transpires at the level of apperception presupposed by any mundane experience, there is no "appearing," and therefore no *deception*—this is just the form that transcendental insight must take. And this will become progressively more suitable as the reduction of the idea of being that is required to properly understand primary enworlding gets worked out philosophically. It is just that this process starts in the natural attitude.

The natural attitude, however, "is not only the *wherefrom* [Wo-von-aus] but also the *whither* [Wo-für]" of phenomenology (SCM 109/99). Even if transcendental cognition is veridical in the "pre-existent" realm, what ultimately matters is how it surfaces in the natural attitude (SCM 109/99). The second—and more important— aspect of how phenomenology appears lies in what Fink called "secondary" or "non-proper" [*uneigentliche*] enworlding, by which he denotes "the summation of the constitutive process which places *phenomenologizing* itself *into the world*" (SCM 108/99; cf. 120, 142/110, 129). This is labeled "*secondary*" because it is the enworlding of the transcendental cognition of primary enworlding. But it is deemed "*non-proper*" because—significantly—it is a process with respect to which the onlooker is *passive*—it is a "being taken along" (SCM 127/116; cf. 125/113) that "does not rest *upon its own activity*" (SCM 119/109). Herein lies the real problem of transcendental illusion.[39]

Secondary enworlding results from what Fink describes as a "self-concealment, a self-apperceptive *constitution lying back over* constituting life" (SCM 120/109). He does not spell this out (SCM 120/110), but his point is that the transcendental acts of sense-bestowal in virtue of which a phenomenological cognition appears necessarily exceed its scope. Any rigorous science must grasp its own functioning, and so, this situation is potentially devastating for phenomenology. Unlike primary enworlding, the transcendental origins of which remain "anonymous" and are "forgotten," secondary enworlding is "precisely the worldly objectivation of *knowing* about transcendental origin," *including its own* (SCM 128/116, emphasis added). This must be the case not only with the transcendental "ontification" inherent in its (proper) phenomenological cognition, but *also* the mundane ontification brought about by its (*non*-proper) enworlding. The latter must therefore involve a *twofold transparency* with respect to transcendental constitutive essence: "transparency with respect to the transcendental process of *phenomenologizing*," and "transparency in the 'appearance' with respect to the constitutional processes that fashion that 'appearance'" (SCM 128/117).

This is crucial. For this twofold transparency announces nothing less than the canon of phenomenological reason. As Fink put it (envisioning phenomenology at a more advanced stage): "This twofold transparency provides the phenomenological cognizer with the possibility of forming at any time an insight-based judgment regarding that which is only a truth with respect to worldly appearance, and that which is a truth that forms the proper transcendental essence of phenomenologizing" (SCM 128/117). Nothing more is required to overcome the transcendental illusion of "seeming truth"— not to abolish it, since that is not possible, but rather to ensure that it is not deceptive. For inasmuch as we have gained this twofold transparency with respect to it, "seeming truth is itself 'sublated' ['*aufgehoben*'] in transcendental truth" (SCM 147/134). This means that the onlooker's self-understanding preserves the appearance-truths of phenomenologizing by accounting for their mundane one-sidedness in terms of transcendental truth. All distinctions between apparent and genuine truth made on the basis of the canon of phenomenological reason would be characterized by this sort of dialectical *Aufhebung* (SCM 129f/118).

This points to Fink's notion of the Absolute. To get to that, we need but ask: *Granting the first, how is that second transparency possible?* The answer lies in Fink's account of "constructive phenomenology."

According to Fink, phenomenology cannot limit its theoretical activity to regressive analysis of primary enworlding. This is because the onlooker cannot limit the scope of its investigation to the "internal horizon of constituting life"—which amounts to saying that it cannot adhere to Husserl's "principle of all principles." For regressive analysis of certain elements of the reductively given phenomenon of the world—for example, birth and death, psychological development, intersubjective relations, and world history—will necessarily founder, inasmuch as such phenomena prompt the onlooker to seek the transcendental sense of various forms of totality (SCM 71/63; cf. 12/11). But as transcendental constitution is *always already unfolding within them*, these totalities as such are not given (SCM 69f/62). This motivates a "*movement out beyond the reductive givenness* of transcendental life" to an examination of what Fink calls its "'*external horizons*' [*Aussenhorizonte*]" (SCM 7/7). The resulting investigation, insofar as it "abandons the basis of transcendental 'givenness', *no longer* exhibits things *intuitively*, but necessarily proceeds," as Fink put it, "*constructively*" (SCM 7/7).

Thus, it is not just that phenomenology is hampered by the difficulty of having an object that is *non-existent*, and thus mundanely *inexpressible*. It is also the case that its object as a whole is *non-given*, and thus even transcendentally *unintuitable*. Thus, in keeping with the structural echo of Kant's first *Critique*, Fink characterizes constructive phenomenology as "transcendental dialectic." For there is, he claims, a "material [*sachliche*] affinity" here, in that both deal with "the basic problem of the relation of the 'given' to the 'non-given'" (SCM 71/64). But with respect to transcendental knowledge, there is a profound difference. For Fink's construction is precisely meant to enable reason to go beyond the merely regulative role assigned to it by Kant, by granting it cognitive access to objects that are *in principle* non-given.

Although it belongs to one of the more provisional parts of the *Sixth Cartesian Meditation*, Fink's claim that regressive inquiry is inadequate to fulfill the aims of phenomenology, which is consequently required to pursue *constructive* inquiry— his calling into question, that is, "the *intuitional character* of phenomenological cognition itself" (SCM 29/26)—is certainly one of the most striking features of the work. At first blush, it might seem to be a phenomenological non-starter. But recall the problem of secondary enworlding: if it is the case that transcendental life is composed exclusively of constituting and phenomenologizing activity, then it follows that the constitutive processes of secondary enworlding—which *as such* are, in principle, non-given—belong to the "external horizon" of reductive givenness, and that the transparency the onlooker gains with respect to them—*and hence its own being*—must be achieved through phenomenological construction. This is consistent with the "'precedence'" ["*Vorhergehen*"] of the onlooker that distinguishes constructive from regressive phenomenology (SCM 72f/65f), and with the centrality of secondary enworlding to the "coincidence in Existence [*Existenzdeckung*] between the transcendental subject and its enworlded self-objectivation"—inquiry concerning which Fink explicitly placed in the province of constructive phenomenology (SCM 71/64).

We thus have the following: (i) the naïveté that the account of the transcendental onlooker is meant to overcome is transposed into the problem of the transparency of secondary enworlding. That is, that naïveté is solved by going outside the world, thus introducing the new problem of understanding how phenomenological cognition gets (back) into the world. (ii) Fink's solution to *this* problem would necessarily be "constructive." (iii) Constructive phenomenology thus plays a key role in *arriving* at the canon of phenomenological reason. But how would this be carried out non-arbitrarily *in advance* of the canonical distinction? Fink admittedly cannot shed much light on this. But we can glimpse where he was heading from his portrayal of phenomenology as "absolute science."

Phenomenology as "absolute science"

Fink's basic claim is that transcendental insights gained through the phenomenological reduction can be established scientifically only if the problem of transcendental illusion with respect to secondary enworlding is constructively overcome. A coherent system of phenomenological reason must be underpinned by a self-consciousness that comprehends completely the productive force of the project. The problem, however, is that the canonical distinction required *for* this constructive process can only come about *through* it. This circularity is redolent of the "dilemma of the criterion" attributed to Sextus Empiricus, and Fink proceeds in a way that situates phenomenology in close proximity to the speculative tradition of post-Kantian German Idealism, Hegel in particular (SCM 86, 173–9/77, 155–9; see also Bruzina 1986, 24; 1992, 279; cf. Westphal 1998). He does this by approaching secondary enworlding in terms of the complex "identity" of the phenomenologizing with the human and constituting "egos" (KS 123/116; cf. SCM 43/39)—within which, he noted, lie concealed "the most basic insights into the architectonic of the phenomenological system" (KS 123/116; cf. SCM 45–6/42). How is this "identity"—that is, the triadic "performance-structure" of the reduction—to be understood?

Fink answered this question in terms of the Absolute, understood as the inclusive, synthetic unity of the different moments of the performance structure of the reduction. Fink's Absolute thus straddles the boundary of worldly ontology: "the Absolute is not . . . a *homogeneous* universal unity of that which is *existent* . . ., but precisely the comprehensive unity of *the existent as such and the pre-existent*" (SCM 157/143). Since it thus includes being as a moment, this unity itself is beyond being. Fink thus characterized the Absolute as *meontic*—a notion that occupied a central place in Fink's thought during the period in question (Bruzina 1995, lv–lvii; 2004, 366f).

The unity of the Absolute can be thought of as joining world-constitution with both its being-for-itself (the onlooker as a moment of *knowing*) and with its self-apperceiving end-product (human being as a moment of *believing*). For there is an important sense even here—or *especially*, since world-constitution is teleologically directed at the world—in which knowledge implies belief. Yet, that is something the onlooker lacks.

This is why the style of the canon of phenomenological reason is one of dialectical sublation rather than simple supersession of appearance-truth. Transcendental insight is meaningless if not tied to that which it surpasses. Thus, not unlike in Hegel's *Phenomenology*, the appearance of phenomenologizing is recognized as a necessary constituent of the project. And the opposition between onlooker and human being is now comprehended as a "necessary antithesis *in* the synthetic unity of the Absolute" (SCM 166/150). The apparent contradiction in phenomenological agency is resolved through its being "*sublated in the absolute truth* that phenomenologizing is in itself a cognitive movement of the Absolute" (SCM 167/150; cf. 129/117f).

From the standpoint of the meontic Absolute, phenomenology can be seen as a "transformation [*Verwandlung*] of the 'self'": the reductive performance "doubles" the human ego by bringing its transcendental ground to self-evidence, and transcendental reflection reunites these at a "higher" level by realizing in self-consciousness the "identity" of the whole (KS 123/117). Thus, the "'*concrete*' concept of the 'phenomenologizing subject'" is the "dialectical unity" of the two "antithetic moments"—that is, "*transcendental subjectivity 'appearing' in the world*" (SCM 127/116; cf. 147, 157, 163/134, 142, 147). As the science of enworlding, phenomenology thus amounts to the theory of the appearance of the Absolute in being. This is, in a sense, the "self-cognition" of the Absolute, and phenomenology is, accordingly, "absolute science"—the absolute self-understanding of the Absolute (SCM 169/152).

The problematic circularity of the onlooker's self-understanding would be worked out within this absolute self-referentiality. The *Sixth Cartesian Meditation* is short on details, but the idea is that all metaphysical questions are answerable, and that transcendental illusion can, in principle, be fully mastered theoretically in a new dimension of transcendental philosophy which, surpassing intuitional givenness, would grasp the constitutedness of human worldly finitude on the basis of a speculative sort of "intellectual intuition,"[40] "thereby taking it back into the infinite essence of spirit" (KS 155/144f). Such is what the *Sixth Cartesian Meditation* anticipates as the only methodologically coherent form of phenomenology, and Fink glosses it as "a meontic philosophy of absolute spirit" (SCM 183/1).

Merleau-Ponty's response to Fink

Although the foregoing might seem to bear no resemblance to anything found in *Phenomenology of Perception*, there are, as we shall see, some important formal similarities. But at the same time, analysis of Merleau-Ponty's own conception of the "phenomenology of phenomenology" will show that his view of phenomenological methodology—or his own operative "idea of a transcendental theory of method"— differs radically from that presented by Fink in the *Sixth Cartesian Meditation*. For it becomes clear that it is based upon a fundamentally different orientation, one that sees phenomenology as participating actively in the ongoing historical realization of the world, rather than spectating passively upon a transcendental process that is always already determined from the empirical standpoint. But it is also the case that this raises some new methodological questions concerning the nature and possibility of the phenomenological reduction in *Phenomenology of Perception*—questions that are sufficiently important yet disconcerting as to motivate a certain rereading of that text.

Merleau-Ponty's phenomenology of phenomenology

When we recall that Merleau-Ponty's first book, *The Structure of Behavior*, completed by 1938 but published in 1942, concluded with the methodological desideratum to *"define transcendental philosophy anew* in such a way as to integrate with it the very phenomenon of the real" (SC 241/224, emphasis added), and when we take seriously Merleau-Ponty's claim that *Phenomenology of Perception* was "only a preliminary study," the intention of which was to *"define a method* for getting closer to present and living reality" (PrP 68/25, emphasis added), we can recognize that the latter work, far from exhibiting any sort of reticence about methodological issues, was, like the *Sixth Cartesian Meditation*, principally concerned with formulating the idea of a transcendental theory of method.

This claim may seem surprising and implausible. But some reflection upon the overall structure of *Phenomenology of Perception* can, at least to some extent, make it seem fairly unremarkable. Simply consider the way the text progresses through the different sections: in the Introduction, critical consideration of the "traditional prejudices" of "objective thought" [*la pensée objective*] in its empiricist and intellectualist forms serves to motivate a return to the "phenomenal field" [*le champ phénoménal*] (PhP 64–77; cf SC 222 n2/248 n40). Part I of the text is then devoted to investigating the paradigm of pre-objective experience, namely, experience of the body, that is, of one's own lived body, on the basis of which—or, more precisely, on the basis of the claim that "the theory of the body is already a theory of perception" (PhP 235–9)—Merleau-Ponty can then lay out in Part II his phenomenological account of "the perceived world" [*le monde perçu*]. This is not the place to discuss any of this in detail. For immediate purposes, the point is simply that while Merleau-Ponty may nowhere provide in *Phenomenology of Perception* a concise statement of his methodology, it could be the case that such a statement is in fact writ large and demonstrated across the structure of the work as a whole.

This sort of view makes a good deal of sense—at least up to the end of the second Part of Merleau-Ponty's book. But there is the matter of Part III (comprising the chapters on the *cogito*, temporality, and freedom). We need to ask: why is there another major section over and above the account of the perceived world?

That *Phenomenology of Perception* was ultimately concerned with phenomenological method, and moreover, that it was structurally conceived specifically in response to Fink's *Sixth Cartesian Meditation*, is evinced by the fact that, in contrast to "direct description," Merleau-Ponty refers to Part III of the book as a "phenomenology of phenomenology" (PhP 419). This is clearly set off as a distinct methodological project, its point being to use the phenomenological descriptions laid out in Parts I and II as an opportunity "for *defining* a more radical comprehension and reflection than objective thought" (PhP 419, emphasis added). This task of "second-order reflection" is explicitly announced at the end of Part II, but it is prefigured throughout the work, including at the end of the Preface (PhP xvi), and at the end of the Introduction (PhP 74–7). There, Merleau-Ponty reminds us that "the meditating Ego" is essentially situated within the perspective of a particular concrete subject, and that radical reflection must take this into account. "We must not only adopt a reflective attitude," therefore, "but also reflect on this reflection, understand the natural situation which it is conscious of succeeding, and which therefore belongs to its definition" (PhP 75).

The aim of Merleau-Ponty's "phenomenology of phenomenology" is thus to validate the descriptive account of Parts I and II as a *philosophical* contribution, rather than a mere "psychological curiosity" (PrP 55/19). For on its own, that account does not rule out there being a realm of pure thought over and above perception, and hence, the possibility of establishing a system of truth capable of disambiguating perceptual experience and resolving the contradictions and paradoxes that Merleau-Ponty had described. In other words, the point of Part III—developed in and through the chapters on the *cogito*, temporality, and freedom—is methodological: to show *the impossibility of an absolute science in Fink's sense*.[41] Whereas Fink had claimed that "to know the world by returning to a 'transcendence' which once again *contains* [einbehält] the world within it signifies the realization of a *transcendental* knowledge of the world [*bedeutet eine* transzendentale *Welterkenntnis realisieren*]," and that "in this sense alone is phenomenology 'transcendental philosophy'" (KS 106/100, translation modified), for his part, Merleau-Ponty made the very contrary claim that "a philosophy becomes transcendental, that is, radical . . . not by postulating the total making-explicit [*explicitation*] of knowledge, but rather by recognizing this *presumption* of reason as the fundamental philosophical problem" (PhP 76).

Although he agreed with Fink about the methodological limits of regressive phenomenology, it was not the intuitional but rather the cognitive character of phenomenology that Merleau-Ponty restricted. His interpretation of phenomenology is therefore radically different. Tellingly, he took his bearings, not (like Fink) from the speculative and systematic Hegel, but rather from the young Hegel—whom Merleau-Ponty viewed in decidedly existential terms (SNS 109–21/63–70) and conflated rather freely with Marx. He thus regarded the emergence of phenomenological philosophy— Fink's problem of secondary enworlding [*Verweltlichung*]—as a special case of the emergence of self-conscious historical collectivities in general, which is essentially the idea of the "realization" [*Verwirklichung*] of philosophy that Marx proposed in his early critique of (the "older," i.e., speculative and systematic) Hegel.[42] Both are matters of transformatively overcoming the silence of a "multiple solipsism" [*solipsisme à plusieurs*] by establishing "effective communication" between isolated individuals (PhP 412; cf. 76). *Merleau-Ponty thus dismissed Fink's problem of secondary enworlding.* For in saying—as he repeatedly did, including at the end of *Phenomenology of Perception*— that philosophy "realizes itself by destroying itself as *separate* philosophy [*se réalise en se détruisant comme philosophie séparée*]" (PhP 520, emphasis added),[43] he embraced the claim that philosophy cannot be realized without being "transcended" [*aufgehoben*], that is, without being integrated with reality through transformative praxis (cf. Marx 1975b, 181, 187). In other words, Merleau-Ponty founded the scientificity of phenomenology on the same "productivity" that makes historical agency in general possible (cf. SNS 229/129). It is thus a *praxiological* idea of method that Merleau-Ponty developed in response to Fink, a view based on the claim that transcendental subjectivity *is* intersubjectivity—a claim upon which he repeatedly insisted[44]—and hence that *the nexus of concrete intercorporeal praxis is itself the absolute.*[45]

Ultimately, it is this claim that Merleau-Ponty's phenomenology of phenomenology was intended to substantiate. For this is what underlies the method that he was aiming to define, which involves a sort of "plunge" into "present and living reality."[46] As he says in no uncertain terms, "the solution of all problems of transcendence is to be sought in the thickness of the pre-objective present" (PhP 495). That is, it is here that all philosophical problems will be resolved, *insofar as they are legitimately resolvable.* This qualification is crucial, for Merleau-Ponty did not maintain that all philosophical problems that can be posed are resoluble (the world itself is, recall, *en déça des solutions*). In an especially important footnote at the very end of Part II of *Phenomenology of Perception*, he presented a dilemma with respect to Husserl to the effect that either second-order phenomenological reflection clarifies the world completely, in which case first-order description would be superfluous; or else second-order reflection can at best only remove some *but not all* obscurities left by description (PhP 419). Inasmuch as it is agreed that phenomenology must begin in the natural attitude, then, first-order description is *not* superfluous, and we must opt for the latter prong and accept a certain degree of opacity. This has the implication that Merleau-Ponty rejected *in principle* the possibility of complete theoretical transparency with respect to the enworlding of phenomenology—precisely that for which Fink sought a "constructive" solution.

This is crucial. The Merleau-Pontian absolute is insuperably ambiguous, yet it is here that the problems of transcendence are to be resolved (PhP 418f). According to Merleau-Ponty, it is precisely the "contradictory" nature of human intercorporeal involvement, our being constituted and (*contra* Fink) constituting, that enables phenomenological achievements, and so, this must not be ontologically written off or sublated away. What we see, then, is that by aiming to "discover time beneath the subject [and to] link the paradox of time to those of the body, the world, the thing, and others," Merleau-Ponty's phenomenology of phenomenology poses a deflationary argument against Fink. The idea is to dissolve the dilemma of *either* "believing our descriptions" *or* "knowing what we are talking about" by showing that, beyond the paradoxical intercorporeal involvement revealed through descriptive analysis, "there is nothing to understand" (PhP 419). Phenomenology in Merleau-Ponty's account thus leaves no "uncomprehended residue" (cf. SCM 25/23)—none, that is, that could be comprehended *theoretically*. It thereby upholds Husserl's contention that phenomenology provides an "ultimate understanding of the world"—an understanding behind which "there is nothing more that can be sensefully inquired for, nothing more to understand" (Husserl 1969, 242)—while also obviating the need for constructive phenomenology as conceived by Fink.

Merleau-Ponty's aim is to maintain the intuitional basis of phenomenological insight. But recognizing its essential perspectivity, he decoupled intuition from apodictic truth. This decoupling is tied to his notion of "*le préjugé du monde*"—the naïve assumption, upon which objective thought is based, that a *fully determinate* world obtains (PhP 11, 62, 296, 316). For Merleau-Ponty, there is no such world—not yet, anyway—and therefore, no such determinateness is being constituted. As an active intervention into an "unfinished world," phenomenology has no privileged epistemological guarantee. The world and truth are *à faire*—to be made. For Merleau-Ponty, the philosophical validity of phenomenological claims accrues from their intersubjective appropriation and ratification—prior to which they are, strictly speaking, non-sense (SNS 32/19; PhP 491, 509).[47] Even—or especially—in the case of a theoretically detached onlooker. Thus, whereas in Fink's meontic interpretation, phenomenology's basic methodological problematic is structured in terms of the relation between *Sein* and *Vor-Sein*, Merleau-Ponty framed it in entirely human terms, such that "the question is ultimately one of understanding . . . the relation between *sense* and *non-sense*" (PhP 490).

Though considerable, such differences do betray some important formal affinities underlying the respective positions of Fink and Merleau-Ponty. This is particularly true with regard to outdoing the uncritically limited transcendental approach characteristic of Kantianism by ceasing to take the world for granted and inculcating a pathos of philosophical wonder that effects a certain kind of *extramundane* standpoint, that is, a standpoint that is *without* the world. Such is the core of their respective views of the reduction. Yet, there is at least one substantive claim on which Fink and Merleau-Ponty would agree entirely: that a complete reduction is not *humanly* possible. They agree on this point, but diverge completely with respect to its implications, with Fink retaining the possibility of the complete reduction and Merleau-Ponty insisting conversely on phenomenology as a human practice. The respective ways in which they understand what it would mean to adopt an extramundane standpoint thus differ drastically, since for Fink, there *is* a fully determinate world, albeit one whose origins remain shrouded in mystery, whereas for Merleau-Ponty, such a determinate world is the object, not simply of a naïve belief, that is, a true belief naïvely held, but of a naïve prejudice, that is, a *false* belief naïvely held, the placing in abeyance of which is the key to the reduction and thus to a truly transcendental standpoint. He thereby implies that *even with regard to the world*, Fink has an insufficiently radical sense of philosophical wonder.[48]

Inasmuch as it denies the existence of a fully determinate world, then, there is no basis for reading *le préjugé du monde* as understood by Merleau-Ponty as bearing any substantive similarity to Fink's notion of *Weltbefangenheit* (cf. Bruzina 2002, 194). We are not imprisoned, ontologically or otherwise, in the world. Merleau-Ponty had already shown in *The Structure of Behavior* that the nature of human existence is to project itself beyond given situations, that it fundamentally involves an orientation to the possible, even if this lies "*beyond the world*"—indeed, "*beyond any milieu*" (SC 189f/175f, 245n97, emphasis added). Thus, whereas for Fink, *Weltbefangenheit* is a *necessary* condition of human existence, for Merleau-Ponty, it could at most be taken as describing the natural attitude in *normal* cases. Nor did Merleau-Ponty agree with Fink's claim that the phenomenological reduction represents the first breakthrough (SCM 124/113). Rather, it is precisely the capacity of going "beyond any milieu" exhibited by certain forms of *non*-phenomenological activity that phenomenology itself relies on. Interestingly, what these have in common is a certain structural (but not etiological) filiation with schizophrenia. Concerning phenomenology, therefore, whereas Fink posited an *Ich-Spaltung* (splitting of the I) at the transcendental level,[49] Merleau-Ponty held that such is precisely what can and must occur in the concrete.

Hence his claim, for example, that "the highest form of reason borders on madness [*déraison*]" (SNS 9/4; cf. 121/70).

This is why Merleau-Ponty will describe the suspension of *le préjugé du monde* as a venturesome staking of one's life. It requires the capacity for a kind of selfless engagement which, not unlike death, imposes distance from vital egoic particularity in the direction of human universality (SNS 115ff/67). As we shall see, this is the standpoint of "the living subject, *man as productivity*" (PhP 171, emphasis added; cf. SNS 328f/185f; HT xli/xlv), that affords the transcendentally disclosive experience of the indeterminacy of the pregiven world.

This kind of selfless engagement clearly bears a formal similarity to Fink's idea of "un-humanization." But in substantive terms, it differs markedly. For Merleau-Ponty's radical emphasis on the contingent emergence of the world is more phenomenologically consistent than Fink's overarching Absolute. This is because even though Fink does not take the world for granted, he does take for granted *that there is a world to be taken for granted*. That is, he does not say uncritically that the world *is* there. But in taking for granted its determinacy, he does thereby presume that *the constitution of the world* "is" there (i.e., "pre-existently"). In an important way, then, Fink just shifts the locus of uncritical dogmatism. In contrast, for Merleau-Ponty, *le préjugé du monde* is just that—a prejudice. The determinate world *is* not, but rather is *à faire*, to be made, and the philosopher interested in truth is therefore required to engage in normatively-oriented creative activity that is necessarily fraught with uncertainty and possible failure.

This is the sense of Merleau-Ponty's alternative to the Finkian onlooker. Rather than severing from the mundane, the phenomenologist plunges into its thickness. In contrast to Fink's ideal of non-participation, for Merleau-Ponty, phenomenology involves an *intensification* of constitutive participation. In terms of productivity, he thus associates phenomenology with activities of *creative transgression*, those which generate from within themselves the ability to push the bounds of sense and expand the domain of reason,[50] albeit without any pre-given metaphysical guarantees of success.[51] Although he also refers to revolutionary politics, in general, the kind of activity Merleau-Ponty had in mind can best be termed *art*. Thus, whereas Fink had stated in no uncertain terms that the productivity of the phenomenological onlooker is "*not comparable to any mode of productivity pregiven in a worldly way*" (SCM 86/76, emphasis added), Merleau-Ponty replies—unmistakably—that "philosophy is *not* the reflection of a pre-existing [*préalable*] truth, but, *like art*, the realization [*réalisation*] of a truth" (PhP xv, emphasis added). There could not be a more concise statement of Merleau-Ponty's methodological departure from Fink.

But he goes further. Consider how Merleau-Ponty glosses the upshot of *Phenomenology of Perception*. In explicit and unequivocal opposition to the *Sixth Cartesian Meditation*, Merleau-Ponty wrote that "[t]he phenomenological world is *not* the making-explicit [*explicitation*] of a pre-existing being [*un être préalable*], but the laying down [*la fondation*] of being" (PhP xv, emphasis added). Directly challenging Fink's view, Merleau-Ponty claimed that "the meditating Ego, the 'impartial spectator' [*le « spectateur impartial »* (*uninteressierter Zuschauer*)] do *not* return to an already given rationality [*une rationalité déjà donnée*]." Rather—and here Merleau-Ponty quotes Fink again but slightly out of context (see note 33) —"they 'establish themselves'

[« *s'établissent* »],[52] *and establish it* [rationality], through an initiative which has no guarantee in being, and whose justification rests entirely on the actual power that it gives us for taking responsibility for our history [*le pouvoir effectif qu'elle nous donne d'assumer notre histoire*]" (PhP xv, emphasis added).

As a human endeavor in an unfinished, indeterminate world, phenomenology is fittingly dramatic—and dramatically different from Fink's portrayal of the onlooker's theoretical experience: "We take our fate in our hands, we become responsible for our history [*notre histoire*] through reflection, as well as through a decision whereby we commit [*engageons*] our lives, and in both cases what is involved is a violent act that proves itself in practice [*un acte violent qui se vérifie en s'exerçant*]" (PhP xvi).[53]

Rereading *Phenomenology of Perception*

Madness, art, violence—such is how Merleau-Ponty depicted the methodological basis of his existential reinterpretation of transcendental phenomenology. The above statements, and many others like them, are familiar to readers of *Phenomenology of Perception*. But they are usually not read in quite the way they were intended nor with the full gravity that they possess in the context of this work. For they are typically taken as rhetorical flourishes redolent of certain impetuous aspects of the immediate postwar atmosphere in Paris They add a certain polemical spice to the text, but nothing of philosophical substance—the dish can, it is assumed, be served more blandly. This view is, however, quite mistaken. Consideration of "the idea of a transcendental theory of method" that Fink had outlined in the *Sixth Cartesian Meditation*, and recognition that Merleau-Ponty's encounter with it was the pivotal moment on the philosophical trajectory through which he overcame the methodological impasse with which *The Structure of Behavior* concluded, make it clear that what Merleau-Ponty was expressing in these claims was nothing less than his own meta-theory concerning the possibility of the transcendental phenomenological reduction. An account, that is, not so much of the reduction *per se*, but of the transcendental conditions of its performance—for example, the nature of its agency, and of the "productivity" that makes it possible— and hence of the possibility of the reduction serving in a viable way as the central methodological maneuver of genuine philosophical inquiry.

It is far from clear, however, how we are to square this fundamental and high-minded aim with the heady and provocative content of Merleau-Ponty's statements. It is unclear, in other words, precisely how to understand the existential alternative that Merleau-Ponty posed to Fink's conception of the reduction's "performance-structure" [*Vollzugsstruktur*], and to the role played in his account by a form of "intellectual intuition" that goes beyond any sort of phenomenal givenness. If not the theoretical experience of a non-participating onlooker, then upon what exactly are the phenomenological results of *Phenomenology of Perception* based, who or what is responsible for them, and how are they justified? What secures their rational epistemic status? What are the methodological commitments concerning the agency of existential phenomenology that ensure its veritable philosophical credentials? How, in short, is philosophy realized within the terms of this project? Lacking tangible answers to these questions, it remains unclear whether any genuine philosophical insight is, in fact, achieved in this text—and this, not in some ahistorical idealist sense of philosophical insight that Merleau-Ponty rightly rejected, but precisely in the sense that he did intend—a sense which still implies a progressive movement toward truth understood in universal terms, and which as such, by "bringing rationality and the absolute down to earth," would supply "the remedy for skepticism and pessimism" (PrP 43, 70/13, 26).

The purpose of this Preface has been to motivate provocatively paying renewed interpretive attention to *Phenomenology of Perception* by showing that central methodological questions remain unanswered, and that this situation places a serious question mark over the work as a whole. To dispel this questionableness, we need to come to terms with the idea of "*the realization of philosophy*" as implied by Merleau-Ponty in his claim that "philosophy realizes itself by destroying itself as separate philosophy." We need to understand, in other words, the dialectical conception of phenomenological method that enabled Merleau-Ponty to overcome transcendental phenomenology's need for what Fink had termed "secondary enworlding."

In the chapters to follow, I take up this task by approaching *Phenomenology of Perception* from its very end, problematizing the textual fact of its culminating with a set of lines drawn from *Pilote de guerre* and offering a methodological explanation for it. This amounts to investigating Merleau-Ponty's idea of "heroism" and its role in his existential reinterpretation of transcendental phenomenology, an undertaking that will shed valuable light on the methodological commitments operative in *Phenomenology of Perception*—light which will reciprocally illuminate and corroborate the claims sketched out in the foregoing discussion of Merleau-Ponty's critical encounter with Fink.

∎

A final word or two before taking the plunge. It may be wondered how it could possibly be the case that issues of the significance and magnitude that I am suggesting have evaded scholarly attention for so long. To this sort of worry, there are three main replies. First, as mentioned, the simple fact of the publication history of the *Sixth Cartesian Meditation* goes a long way toward explaining the absence in the literature of any serious discussion of Merleau-Ponty's response to it, and of the deeper stakes of his own phenomenology of phenomenology. Although that text has now been available for over two decades, as far as Merleau-Ponty scholarship is concerned, the significance of its appearance was obscured by the tacit assumption, alluded to earlier, that all significant avenues of research on *Phenomenology of Perception* had already been explored.

Second, but not unrelated to this first point, it is also the case that the lines drawn from Saint Exupéry's *Pilote de guerre* with which *Phenomenology of Perception* ends have never elicited any critical scrutiny within Merleau-Ponty scholarship. It is, as we shall see, very perplexing that the book ends as it does, and some scholars over the years may well have felt this perplexity. But without access to Fink's text and the methodological problematic that it posed, it is very difficult, if not impossible, to formulate a compelling philosophical explanation. Thus, along with many other methodological statements, even the very zenith of *Phenomenology of Perception* has typically been wrongly discounted as a philosophically inconsequential rhetorical flourish (more on this below).

The third reply by way of assuaging the doubt that what I propose to say about Merleau-Ponty's project of existential phenomenology could possibly have been overlooked hitherto has to do with a more general feature of the relevant scholarship. And this point will invoke the political dimensions of Merleau-Ponty's thought—specifically, the existential form of Marxism that he espoused in the postwar period, and the fact, broached above, that this is the source and inspiration for his idea of "the realization of philosophy." Although in earlier years it was more common for commentary on Merleau-Ponty's work to address both its philosophical and political aspects, it is currently the case, and has been for some time, that Merleau-Ponty scholarship is marked by a crisp division of labor between those who study Merleau-Ponty as a phenomenological philosopher and those (far fewer) who study him as a political philosopher. By way of illustration, consider that neither of the two most widely-cited philosophical treatments of Merleau-Ponty's work (Dillon 1988; Barbaras 2004) make any significant reference to Marx or to Marxism at all, while the two most important studies of Merleau-Ponty's political philosophy (Whiteside 1988; Coole 2007) are both written by political scientists who do not have a specialized understanding of Husserlian phenomenology. In other words, although his works receive a considerable amount of scholarly attention, the intimate connection between Marx and Husserl, or more generally between Marxism and phenomenology, that was fundamental to Merleau-Ponty's postwar position tends to fall systematically between the cracks.

As with the idea that there is nothing fundamentally new to say about *Phenomenology of Perception*, there is a widespread tacit assumption at work here to the effect that, however strong his Marxist proclivities may have been, especially in the immediate postwar years, for Merleau-Ponty, Marxism was nonetheless *theoretically secondary* to phenomenology. This assumption does not imply that for Merleau-Ponty Marxism was entirely separate from phenomenology—there is no question that he brought the latter to bear upon problems facing the former, that is, that he explored the idea of a phenomenological Marxism. But it is the point of that assumption to deny the converse claim, that is, that Merleau-Ponty brought Marxism to bear upon problems facing phenomenology. And this denial has the implication that any references to Marxism found within his phenomenological work are philosophically inconsequential, however interesting they might be from the perspective of political theory, say, or intellectual or cultural history.

It is, however, a corollary claim of this book, albeit a major one, that this denial is incorrect, and that the assumption in question is consequently false. For in considering the outstanding methodological issues surrounding *Phenomenology of Perception*, and approaching them by way of the exegetical problem of Exupérian heroism, what we shall find is that alongside his efforts to give Marxism a phenomenological reinterpretation, *Merleau-Ponty also drew from Marxism in his reinterpretation of transcendental phenomenology*. In particular, as we will see, certain of the methodological commitments operative in the latter are based in a philosophy of history of Hegelian-Marxist inspiration. Contrary to the assumption of the theoretical secondariness of Marxism, then, at least in the immediate postwar period, Marxism and phenomenology stood on a roughly equal footing in Merleau-Ponty's thought as *essentially* interdependent and complementary projects. It was within the terms of this intersection with Marxism that Merleau-Ponty sought to solve the methodological problems of phenomenology. Just as his Marxism was phenomenological, then, there is a specific sense in which Merleau-Ponty's existential phenomenology was—at its core and not merely in a superficial way—"Marxist."

The resolution of the methodological questions concerning *Phenomenology of Perception* can thus be achieved only on the basis of a unified comprehension of Merleau-Ponty's postwar philosophical and political thought. Inasmuch as attempts at such a comprehension tend to predate the availability of the *Sixth Cartesian Meditation*, the claim that such questions could indeed be real and important yet still outstanding is far less implausible than it may initially seem. Had Fink's text been available to earlier generations of Merleau-Ponty scholars, the situation may well have been different. But given the artificial isolation from his Marxist concerns in which Merleau-Ponty's phenomenological work tends to be approached nowadays, plus the fact that Fink's text is still not a major point of reference for philosophical commentary, it is actually not at all surprising that the issues in question remain unexplored and even, so to speak, off the radar of most contemporary Merleau-Ponty scholars.

Going against this trend by recovering the essential and vital connection between Merleau-Ponty's philosophical and political thought, only now with a full appreciation of his response to Fink, the following investigation of the methodological significance of Exupérian heroism will serve to disclose and foreground the praxiological understanding of transcendental philosophy that is implicated in Merleau-Ponty's existential reformulation of phenomenology. It will thus begin to recover what I shall call the "militant" dimension of his thought, a dimension that has been lost or overlooked by virtually all scholarly commentary.[54] The new perspective that results will thus cast important new light on how Merleau-Ponty initially oriented himself in the transcendental tradition. But this light will not necessarily be philosophically flattering, and it may expose certain problematic or contentious aspects of Merleau-Ponty's early phenomenology that are typically unrecognized or glossed over—often with palpable obsequiousness—in existing scholarship. The following discussion is therefore intended to motivate and lay some of the interpretive groundwork for a critical rereading of Merleau-Ponty's work. This applies first of all to *Phenomenology of Perception* itself, in particular with respect to the methodological commitments to which the phenomenological descriptions therein presented are inescapably bound. But it also meant to play a prolegomenal role with regard to a critical rereading of the Merleau-Pontian *oeuvre* as a whole, inasmuch as its development was driven by a self-critical attempt on the part of Merleau-Ponty to work out more satisfactorily the philosophical and methodological grounds of his phenomenological project.

Introduction: Flight From Phenomenology?

As readers of *Phenomenology of Perception* are aware, Merleau-Ponty concluded this work (PhP 520) with the following series of enigmatic sentences selectively excerpted from Antoine de Saint Exupéry's 1942 book, *Pilote de guerre*:[1]

> Ton fils est pris dans l'incendie, tu le sauveras. . . . Tu vendrais, s'il est un obstacle, ton épaule contre un coup d'épaule. Tu loges dans ton acte même. Ton acte, c'est toi. . . . Tu t'échanges. . . . Ta signification se montre, éblouissante. C'est ton devoir, c'est ta haine, c'est ton amour, c'est ta fidélité, c'est ton invention. . . . L'homme n'est qu'un nœud de relations, les relations comptent seules pour l'homme.[2]

> Your son is caught in the fire, you will save him. . . . If there is an obstacle, you would give your shoulder to knock it down. You live in your act itself. Your act *is* you. . . . You give yourself in exchange. . . . Your true significance becomes dazzlingly evident. It is your duty, your hatred, your love, your loyalty, your inventiveness . . . . Man is but a knot of relations, relations alone matter to man.

It is, however, a remarkable fact about Merleau-Ponty scholarship that these lines—which, coming at the very end of his most important work, occupy, so to speak, the single most prestigious piece of textual real estate in his entire corpus—have received virtually no critical attention whatsoever.[3] Many otherwise comprehensive philosophical commentaries on Merleau-Ponty (e.g. De Waelhens 1951; Kwant 1963; Dillon 1988; Barbaras 1991; Priest 2003), even those whose explicit *raison d'être* is to examine *Phenomenology of Perception* in detail (e.g. Marshall 2008; Romdenh-Romluc 2010), simply make no reference to the way the book ends.[4] To be sure, many others do refer to it, albeit usually only to the very last line, namely, "Man is but a knot of relations, relations alone matter to man."[5] But without exception, these commentators do so by way of giving to Saint Exupéry's words an approving but otherwise inconsequential Merleau-Pontian gloss. That is, they tacitly assume that over and above simply quoting from *Pilote de guerre*, Merleau-Ponty was expressing a philosophical agreement with or endorsement of Saint Exupéry's words taken in some more or less literal way. The underlying assumption is that, in philosophical terms, there is a "*continuity* between the phenomenological analysis of perception developed by Merleau-Ponty . . . and the lines quoted from Antoine de Saint Exupéry" (Noble 2011, 76, emphasis added). Monika Langer expressed the conventional wisdom in this way: "As an 'intersubjective field' we are, *as Saint-Exupéry noted*, 'but a network of relationships'" (1989, 147, emphasis added; see also Bannan 1967, 138; Steeves 2004, 158; Reynolds 2004, 24). The same assumption is standardly made in the literature on Saint Exupéry whenever Merleau-Ponty's allusion to him is discussed (Major 1968, 150, 243, 260f; DeRamus

1990, 134f; Devaux 1994, 81). The idea, as expressed by Colin Smith, is that at the end of *Phenomenology of Perception*, Merleau-Ponty "allows the author of *Pilote de guerre* to speak for him" (1980, 271).[6]

Yet, *qua* philosopher, Merleau-Ponty deliberately and conspicuously cut himself off here—the cited lines are preceded immediately by an unequivocal assertion that "it is at this point that we must fall silent [*c'est ici qu'il faut se taire*]."[7] Taken at his word, then, Merleau-Ponty was not even quoting Saint Exupéry, because *he* was no longer speaking at all.[8] *A fortiori*, he was not being spoken *for*. As Merleau-Ponty put it, with regard to Saint Exupéry, "it would be inappropriate for another *to speak in his name*" (PhP 520, emphasis added). We are to suppose, then, that Saint Exupéry is speaking for himself at the end of *Phenomenology of Perception*. Merleau-Ponty thus *deferred* to Saint Exupéry, ceding authorial voice to him *qua* "hero," that is, as someone who "lives to the limit [*jusqu'au bout*] his relation to men and the world" by enacting an affirmative response to the practical question: "Shall I give my freedom to save freedom? [*Donnerai-je ma liberté pour sauver la liberté?*]" (PhP 520). And, most importantly, Merleau-Ponty tied this deference directly to the *realization* of philosophy. Taking his cue from the young Marx (1975b, 181; cf. 187), albeit with a twist, he affirmed that philosophy "realizes itself by destroying itself as separate philosophy" [*se réalise en se détruisant comme philosophie séparée*] (PhP 520; cf. SNS 136, 235/79, 133; NI 99, 108, 123, 174),[9] with the implication that this destruction of philosophy's erstwhile separateness (as opposed to its destruction *simpliciter*, as Marx had seemed to imply) occurs somehow through the work of heroism.[10] Although the precise meaning of this dialectical claim is far from clear, what *is* clear is that on the final page of *Phenomenology of Perception*, Merleau-Ponty drew an unmistakable line between philosophy and non-philosophy that is meant to bear directly on nothing less than the success or failure of his philosophical project. Yet this seems to have passed under the radar of virtually all commentary. It is almost as if the book itself has not yet been read *jusqu'au bout*.

This point is neither trivial nor pedantic. The underlying concern may be initially motivated in this way: given that a fundamental leitmotif of Merleau-Ponty's thought is its opposition to "*la pensée de survol*"—literally, "fly-over thinking," but this phrase, which denotes the style of thought that takes itself as de-situated and thus as having an absolute perspective, is conventionally translated as "high-altitude thinking"[11]—given this leitmotif, is it not rather astonishing that *Phenomenology of Perception* concludes with the thoughts of an aerial reconnaissance pilot? Indeed, an aerial reconnaissance pilot who held that "flying and writing are the same thing," that they form a seamless "total experience" such that "the pilot and the writer converge in an equivalent act of awareness,"[12] and whose typical literary construction took the form: "*flying over* A, I was *thinking* of B" (Schiff 1995, x, emphasis added). *Qua* "hero," Saint Exupéry exactly paradigmatizes *la pensée de survol*. Surely, then, a complete understanding of *Phenomenology of Perception* demands a convincing explanation as to why it culminates with this turn to Saint Exupéry which is, at least *prime facie*, extremely incongruous.[13]

This work seeks to provide such an explanation. The "heroic" ending of *Phenomenology of Perception* is long overdue for serious critical scrutiny.[14] As we shall see, such scrutiny will reveal that there is in fact much more going on here than meets the eye. The deference to Saint Exupéry is a dense, liminal node into which are woven the main theoretical and practical postulates to which Merleau-Ponty's existential phenomenology was implicitly committed. In this way, the "hero" turns out to be nothing less than the methodological linchpin of this audacious project—for better or for worse, the key to its philosophical identity and distinctive standpoint within the traditions of phenomenology, Marxism, and post-Kantian transcendental thought in general.

■

With the Preface above having set out the specific methodological context within which an explanation for the ending of *Phenomenology of Perception* will be located (I will return to this in the Conclusion), the discussion will proceed as follows:

Chapter 1 does some of the groundwork by way of supplying what any serious reader of Merleau-Ponty needs to know about the person to whom Merleau-Ponty ceded authorial voice at the very end of his own *magnum opus*. Here, I marshal background material concerning Saint Exupéry's work and its reception, with a particular focus on *Pilote de guerre*. The aim is to render as manifest as possible the incongruousness of the passage with which *Phenomenology of Perception* culminates by showing that its literal meaning is unmistakably a matter of self-sacrificial disincarnation. In other words, the aim is to show that the passage in question is essentially, and not just circumstantially, an exemplary moment of *la pensée de survol*, and that as a result there is a major problem of interpretation in need of resolution.

Chapters 2 and 3 are based around the pair of references that Merleau-Ponty made to same part of *Pilote de guerre* in the first chapter of Part I of *Phenomenology of Perception*, "The Body as an Object and Mechanistic Physiology." The aim here is to show that Merleau-Ponty's notion of heroism reveals something crucial about the structure of human embodied existence or *être-au-monde*, to wit, that it forms an existential totality inclusive of the natural organism. Based upon his claims that *être-au-monde* involves a constitutive temporal duality between "habitual" and "actual" dimensions of embodiment, and that its historicity is emergent upon that duality but that it generates a single history, Merleau-Ponty uses the claim that heroic action involves the complete repression of "actual" embodiment to show the latent existence within the habitual dimension of an operative intentionality toward universal life, and that this intentionality represents an *a priori* condition of historical action.

Simply making these points might not require an entire chapter, let alone two. But truly to establish and appreciate them and their significance for Merleau-Ponty involves recognizing their underlying connection with the very important but largely overlooked impact that Georg Lukács' 1923 work, *History and Class Consciousness* [*Geschichte und Klassenbewußtsein*] had on Merleau-Ponty's thought. In the case at hand, this has to do with Lukács' claim regarding the methodological primacy of the category of totality. The bulk of Chapters 2 and 3 is thus actually devoted to this connection. After introducing the problem that the earlier references to Saint Exupéry pose, Chapter 2 lays out some contextual considerations concerning Lukács, along with some extended sociobiographical conjectures concerning the backstory of Merleau-Ponty's philosophical embrace of Marxism. The point of all this is to render more plausible the importance that my reading of Merleau-Ponty attaches to Lukács, and more generally, the relative priority of Marxism over phenomenology that I will claim obtains in Merleau-Ponty's postwar project, and how it forms the basis of his response to Fink. But in showing how Merleau-Ponty's Marxism originated in the context of left-wing Catholicism in the interwar period, it also serves to foreground the crucial theme of *incarnation* that remained fundamental in Merleau-Ponty's postwar work.

With this set out, Chapter 3 begins by considering Lukács' work directly. In then bringing this to bear upon Merleau-Ponty's discussion of embodiment, I claim that Merleau-Ponty's approach to embodiment in *Phenomenology of Perception* should be seen as situated within the framework of his interpretation of Marxism's conception of history. In other words, within the terms of Merleau-Ponty's postwar project, history has logical and phenomenological priority over embodiment. Such is how Merleau-Ponty could claim the habitual dimension of embodiment as the locus of historical apriority, and some preliminary consequences are drawn on this basis.

In order to develop further the suggestion that Merleau-Ponty's postwar project was, to a significant extent, an attempt to update and redeem a Lukácsian perspective, in Chapters 4 and 5, I consider in more detail what I term Merleau-Ponty's "incarnational Marxism" and show how his notion of heroism was related to this.

Chapter 4 charts a path through a cluster of related themes—sacrifice, death, politics, the proletariat, the tacit *cogito*, class consciousness, human productivity, and rationality—some of which are familiar, some not so familiar in Merleau-Ponty scholarship, but which, taken together, sketch out the militant sense of Merleau-Ponty's existential conception of Marxism, and of his rethinking of Lukács in particular. Discussion of these themes shows that they point back to a certain conception of the philosophy of history, and this partly anticipates the answer that will be given concerning the ending of *Phenomenology of Perception*.

But this conception of the philosophy of history ultimately hinges on Merleau-Ponty's notion of "heroism". Before getting to that answer, then, Chapter 5 will address this notion directly. This will be primarily by way of a close reading of "Man, the Hero"—a short but important essay with which Merleau-Ponty concluded the volume *Sense and Non-Sense*. This will show that Merleau-Ponty intended his idea of heroism to supply experiential evidence attesting to the latent presence of human universality. It is ultimately a mythic device intended to encourage the militant faith needed for the political project of a universal society, by showing that such a project is indeed possible, and that the transformative political praxis required need not imply agonistic sacrifice. The chapter concludes with some comparative considerations on Merleau-Ponty and Saint Exupéry intended as a way to ascertain just how the standpoint of the former does indeed differ from the *pensée de survol* associated with the latter.

In laying out the significance of Exupérian heroism for Merleau-Ponty's political thought, and clarifying the priority that the latter has with regard to his philosophical thought, these chapters provide the context for answering the question concerning the ending of *Phenomenology of Perception*. By way of conclusion, then, I will briefly recapitulate the relevant claims and draw them together in terms of the basic meaning of Exupérian heroism for Merleau-Ponty, the place and role of this notion within his postwar political thought, and finally, its significance for the methodological coherence of his reinterpretation of Husserlian phenomenology. This relates to the methodological problem posed by Fink (see Preface), with regard to which I draw out some further consequences. The principal claim that emerges is that the alternative conception of phenomenological methodology with which Merleau-Ponty responded to Fink was based on his incarnational conception of Marxism, and this in a way that made phenomenology out to be a project of militant *engagement* premised upon the dialectical sublimation of heroism. As will become apparent, this analysis is crucial for appreciating and understanding the ending—and thus quite possibly the whole—of *Phenomenology of Perception*.[15]

■

Two final points by way of wrapping up this Introduction.

First, I should perhaps underscore that this book is not itself an introduction to Merleau-Ponty's work, in particular, to *Phenomenology of Perception*. It could certainly be read profitably by anyone, irrespective of familiarity with the latter. But I do not spend much time recapitulating specific claims or rehearsing familiar themes, even very important ones. In part, this is because there are many fine books and articles available that do a fine job with those—at least within the relevant parameters of contemporary scholarship—and it is not my intention to produce superfluous commentary. But more importantly, it is because I am convinced that those parameters are unsatisfactory. My main priority in this book, then, is to motivate and articulate, at least in outline, a fundamentally new interpretive perspective on Merleau-Ponty's existential phenomenology. There is admittedly something polemical about my intentions in this work. But I believe that this is productive. For if I have done what I set out to do, then reading this book will not be an anodyne afternoon stroll along the predictable *grands boulevards* of Merleau-Ponty's thought, but rather a somewhat more intrepid and stimulating exploration of the unfamiliar back alleys from which his work derives much of its basic impulse, guiding orientation, and characteristic verve. So while it should be of interest to anyone who has an interest in Merleau-Ponty, the meaning and significance of the main claims that I shall make in this book will be felt much more keenly by those who are already familiar with Merleau-Ponty's work, and with the general contours of the secondary literature devoted to it.

Second, I should just like to point out that, as is conventional, gender-exclusive language in original texts—of which there is an abundance in the works under consideration—is reproduced in quotation. According to the sense, however, it is often also retained in discussion, in order to avoid conveying a misleading impression of inclusivity. There is not merely a matter of style, though, as there is an important philosophical motivation. For the broader context in which Merleau-Ponty's existential phenomenology took shape was formed by the discourse of renewed French humanism (see, e.g. Arbousse-Bastide 1930; George et al. 1946; cf. Kelly 2004, 128–38). And although Merleau-Ponty was, like so many others at the time, ostensibly committed to a universally inclusive humanism, it is patent that much of the relevant discursive context was compromised by implicit (and often explicit) masculinist and androcentric assumptions (among other forms of exclusion). The very fact that humanist discourse at the time was conceptually anchored on the idea of "Man" [*l'Homme*] makes this hardly surprising. Saint Exupéry is a case in point. No one seriously wonders about *his* feminist credentials. But the case of Merleau-Ponty is different. For it is a live and important question whether his work is similarly compromised by sexist ideology (e.g. Butler 1989; S. Sullivan 1997), or else whether it could actually serve as a valuable resource for feminist phenomenology (e.g. Bigwood 1991; Fielding 1996; Stoller 2000). I do not take up this question in this book, but I certainly hope that the discussion here, and the light that it throws on *Phenomenology of Perception*, is not without some relevance. In particular, I should just like to suggest that the methodological emphasis that my reading places on the significance of this text, and the resulting implication that a normative orientation to history is logically and phenomenologically primary within the Merleau-Pontian approach to embodiment, could be taken up in such a way as to show that both sides of the debate are right. Specifically, it could help to show that Merleau-Ponty's potential usefulness for feminist work—as well as, *mutatis mutandis*, for other forms of anti-oppression theory and practice—does not necessarily hinge on the absence of masculinist bias from his actual phenomenological descriptions. For it may not depend on those descriptions at all, but rather have mainly to do with a broader rethinking of phenomenology that would take it up—as I will describe Merleau-Ponty's existential project below—as a kind of "militant" philosophy.

1

Antoine de Saint Exupéry,
"Soliloquizing Angel"

It was claimed in the Introduction that even cursory scrutiny of the Exupérian ending of *Phenomenology of Perception* shows that it exhibits, at least *prima facie*, a surprising incongruity with the rest of that work, and that as such, it is overdue for critical analysis. Such analysis is the task of the book and the purpose of this first chapter is to do some of the initial groundwork for it by presenting a concise but critical introduction to Saint Exupéry as the figure who gets the final word in *Phenomenology of Perception*, yet whose presence within the parameters of Merleau-Ponty scholarship tends to be a matter of only vague familiarity. The intention is to examine Saint Exupéry's works and their reception, with a particular focus on *Pilote de guerre*, in a way that will lay the basis for a contextually accurate reading of the lines cited by Merleau-Ponty—surely something the hermeneutical importance of which every serious reader of *Phenomenology of Perception* should appreciate.[1] As we shall see, beyond simply affirming it, this reading will, in fact, amplify greatly the apparent incongruousness of the lines in question, thereby providing irresistibly compelling motivation for undertaking a fresh interpretive approach to Merleau-Ponty's text by way of its ending.[2]

Introduction

Antoine Jean-Baptiste Marie Roger Pierre de Saint Exupéry was born in 1900 in Lyon into an aristocracy in decline.[3] Not really knowing what to do with himself, he found meaning and fulfillment in the fledgling world of aviation.[4] Beginning in 1926, when he was hired on by the Société d'Aviation Latécoère, which later became the Compagnie Générale Aéropostale (usually known simply as Aéropostale, a forerunner of Air France), Saint Exupéry flew and helped expand the mail delivery lines along the northwest coast of Africa and in Argentina. And he wrote about his experience, doing so quite successfully. In fact, by the time of World War II, Saint Exupéry had already become a renowned pilot-writer on the basis of his novels *Courrier sud* (1929), *Vol de nuit* (1931), which won the Prix Fémina, and *Terre des hommes* (1939), winner of the Grand Prix du Roman de l'Académie Française. And, of course, he also wrote *Le petit prince*, a book which, since its original publication in 1943 (it did not appear in

France until 1946), has become one of the best-selling books of all time. Saint Exupéry died in 1944, failing to return from an aerial reconnaissance mission over southern France just weeks before the liberation of Paris.[5] He remains one of the most widely-read and translated authors in the French language, and until the conversion to the Euro in 2002, his likeness (along with that of the "little prince") appeared on France's 50-*franc* note.

The above paragraph probably contains about as much as—if not, indeed, actually a fair bit more than—the average contemporary reader of Merleau-Ponty knows about the man who gets the final word in *Phenomenology of Perception*. This chapter aims to redress this situation by providing background material concerning Saint Exupéry and his work that is crucial for understanding *Pilote de guerre* and hence for fully appreciating the significance of Merleau-Ponty's strategically located deference to Exupérian heroism.

The discussion will unfold as follows: I will first trace the development of Saint Exupéry's humanistic *Weltanschauung* as this culminates in *Pilote de guerre*, and situate this text in its historical context, in particular with regard to political debates concerning French opposition to German Occupation. I will then examine the main claims of *Pilote de guerre*, showing—and this is the most important thing—that it is based on religious invocations of self-sacrificial disincarnation, and discuss the death and immediate posthumous legacy of Saint Exupéry as factors of the context within which Merleau-Ponty's deference to him *qua* "hero" occurred. All of this will serve to confirm the unexpected fact that the ending of *Phenomenology of Perception* is wildly and disarmingly incongruous with respect to generally received views concerning the meaning of Merleau-Ponty's text, such that a significant question mark must be placed over these views until the ending can be properly understood and accounted for.

Toward a cosmic humanism

At a narrative level, Saint Exupéry's principal published works can be described as "heroic aviation stories." In contrast, however, to an earlier heroic literature based on the experience of World War I fighter aces—which, even though it typically presented a sanitized and chivalrous dimension of that conflict, was ineluctably constituted by division and enmity—Saint Exupéry's writing reflects the pioneering years of *commercial* flight. Its horizons are thus broader and its backdrop more universal as it vividly evokes the perilous human struggle against nature that this enterprise entailed. In this "golden age" of aviation, one literally flew "by the seat of one's pants."[6] Piloting was an undertaking still fraught with tremendous mortal risk, but one willingly engaged in by individuals such as Jean Mermoz and Henri Guillaumet, legendary men of the air whom Saint Exupéry knew personally and admired as heroes.[7] These were men who, over and above the adventurous derring-do and camaraderie that Saint Exupéry made central themes in his writing, felt themselves implicitly duty-bound to participate in the larger project of conquering and domesticating nature's wildest elements—mountains, deserts, oceans—that had previously separated peoples, with the aim of forging closer communicative bonds across the globe. In effect, in piloting, "Saint-Exupéry had discovered a last bastion of *noblesse oblige*" (Schiff 1994, 140).

Although pilots flew alone, this calling was anything but individualistic. It was certainly true for Saint Exupéry that, as André Gide wrote in his Preface to *Vol de nuit*, "man's happiness does not lie in freedom, but in the acceptance of a duty."[8] But for Saint Exupéry, a pilot's sense of duty included a pronounced submission to the discipline of the profession—the noble virtue of individual pilots only emerges from the context of aviation as a collective *métier*.[9] Fraternity and *esprit de corps* were in this way fundamental Exupérian themes, understood as involving the spiritual communion of those who challengingly transcend themselves through wholehearted participation in a common, existentially trying vocation. Saint Exupéry believed that human beings possess a natural propensity toward such comradeship, and that this is what ultimately gives meaning to human life. But he also held that the actualization of this requires a hierarchical and paternalistic structure to organize and uphold the collective project as the appropriate sort of *ordeal*, in the strict sense of the term.

This is how Aéropostale worked, and Saint Exupéry—nostalgic for authority, and increasingly critical of interwar French society—tended to see this organization as a paradigm for a renewed harmonization of individual fulfillment and collective needs in society as a whole. In the 1930s, he was increasingly concerned, as were many others as well, not just about the threats posed by fascism and communism, but also and especially about the spiritual vacuity and decadence of modern liberalism. In line with a wider conservative critique of culture at the time, Saint Exupéry deplored the growing massification and mechanization of humanity. In his preferred metaphors, the contemporary world was being reduced to a "termite mound" [*termitière*] or a society of "robots" (SV 174; PG 222, 232; EG 341, 377). As he expressed it in June 1943: "Robot-man, termite-man, man oscillating between assembly-line work and card games; emasculated of all his creative power, . . . spoon-fed a ready-made, standardized culture, as one feeds hay to cattle. That's what man is today" (EG 380). And in what must surely be the final thing he wrote (a letter dating from 30 or 31 July 1944), Saint Exupéry said: "If I'm shot down, I won't regret anything. The termite mound of the future appals me, and I hate their robot virtues" (EG 516).

In Saint Exupéry's view, the underlying problem with modern liberal democratic society was that its organization precluded "love," or more precisely, "genuine love" [*l'amour veritable*], understood in social-structural terms as a "network of bonds that fosters becoming" [*un réseau de liens qui fait devenir*] (PG 198). Saint Exupéry emphasized that such a network must be hierarchical. Human existence can enjoy a vibrant and vital meaningfulness only when interpersonal relationships are not directly horizontal or lateral, but are rather mediated by the vertical relationship that each individual has with a common transcendent goal. "We breathe freely only when bound to our brothers by a common and disinterested goal. Experience shows that love does not mean gazing at one another, but looking together in the same direction" (TH 198). Expressing a distressed but also fascinated concern about the rise of fascism in the late-1930s, Saint Exupéry put it thus: "pilots meet if they are struggling to deliver the same mail; the Nazis, if they are offering their lives to the same Hitler; the team of mountaineers, if they are aiming for the same summit. Men do not unite if they approach each other directly, but only by losing themselves in the same god."[10]

According to Saint Exupéry, then, what was lacking in France was any such "god" or "summit," there was no recognizable "common goal"—in a word, no "love," and thus no genuine becoming. By the time he published *Terre des hommes* in 1939, Saint Exupéry's writing had thus increasingly taken on the form and metaphorical style of a parable on the deeper meaning of human action. Pressing the question as to *why* Mermoz and Guillaumet, for example, (not to mention himself), would risk their lives to deliver a few sacks of other people's mail;[11] or why, to take another example from Saint Exupéry, a bookkeeper from Barcelona would become a Republican soldier willing to die in a civil war "that at bottom meant little to [him]"[12]—and asking this amid the growing spiritual decadence that he sensed within interwar French society, Saint Exupéry adopted an exalted tone of moral edification. Regarding the pilot increasingly as a special illustrative case,[13] he depicted variously engaged, seemingly selfless individuals as inspirational exemplars of self-overcoming.

> It must be understood that the gift of oneself, the risk of one's life, loyalty unto death—these are the actions that have greatly contributed to establishing the nobility of man. If you are searching for a model, you will find it in the pilot who gives his life for the mail, in the doctor who dies on the front line of an epidemic, or in the meharist who, at the head of his Moorish platoon, plunges into destitution and solitude. (SV 173)[14]

In consenting "to die for all men, to be part of something universal" (SV 141), such individuals "accept a truth which [they] could never translate into words, but whose self-evidence seized hold of [them]" (SV 138). What Saint Exupéry said of the Barcelonan bookkeeper-turned-soldier, prepared to engage in an absurd attack that would almost certainly cost him his life, applies to all: "owing to an ordeal . . . that stripped you of all that is not intrinsic, you discovered a mysterious character born of yourself. . . . A great breath [*souffle*] swept over you and delivered from its shackles the sleeping prince you sheltered—Man" (SV 141). The apparent selflessness of Saint Exupéry's exemplars thus, in reality, manifests a liberating metamorphosis into one's *true* self, whereby one incarnates "Man" [*l'Homme*], the "sovereign truth" [*vérité souveraine*] of human existence (SV 139). Thus, as Saint Exupéry said of Mermoz, "truth is the man that is born in him as he passes over the Andes" (SV 173).

Man is, in effect, Saint Exupéry's notion of human nature. This is not so much an objectively given fact, however, as a latent ideal that implies a moral task. Note that *Terre des hommes* ended on this enigmatic, conditional note: "Only Spirit [*l'Esprit*], *if* it breathe [*souffle*] upon the clay [i.e., "raw" humanity], can create Man" (TH 213, emphasis added).[15] As in the case of the pilot or the soldier, this "spiritual breath" would manifest itself in the form of an ordeal that eliminates from the lived experience of the individual that which is inessential and accidental *from the standpoint of the species*. For example, Saint Exupéry described the enlistment of the bookkeeper, upon hearing of the death of a friend on the Málaga front, as happening thus: "He was not a friend for whom you would have ever felt you had to lay down your life. Yet that bit of news swept over you, over your narrow little life, like a wind from the sea" (SV 137f). Man thus denotes human universality, posited as the as-yet-unrealized "common goal" of humanity, a goal which could—*if* Spirit "breathes" appropriately—unite a world divided, for example, along political, national, or religious lines. Man signifies the becoming of that specific organization of human coexistence which, transcending any opposition between individuality and totality, would optimize freedom and equality through the actualization of what we might call humanity's "natural fraternity." It must be emphasized, though, that this vision was deeply hierarchical—Saint Exupéry was not particularly concerned with democratic egalitarianism (Carnets, 67, 187, 228; PG 182, 241; cf. Thuillier 1957, 577ff). For him, neither equality nor democracy as generally understood in the modern context was a condition of fraternity. On the contrary, "[Saint Exupéry] thought that fraternity will follow from the establishment of a hierarchy between beings and will be its crowning achievement" (Ouellet 1971, 97).

Significantly, Saint Exupéry illustrated this sort of coexistence with anthropomorphizing "analogies" to the animal world. For example, in an extended simile, he pointed to the transformation of domesticated ducks when wild ones fly overhead:

> as if magnetized by the great triangular flight, . . . the call of the wild strikes in them some vestige of savagery. The ducks on the farm are thus transformed for an instant into migrant birds. In those hard little heads, until now filled with humble images of ponds, worms, and henhouses, there develops a sense for continental expanses and seascapes, the taste of the wind on the open sea. Tottering from right to left in its wire enclosure, the duck is gripped by a sudden mysterious passion, and by a far-reaching love whose object is unknown. (SV 138)[16]

Humans, too, have a *natural* tendency to a specific authentic existence. "There are two hundred million men in Europe whose existence has no meaning and who *yearn to be born into life*" (SV 177, emphasis added; cf. 179). "In a world become desert, we thirst for comradeship" (SV 178). But not unlike the ducks, the overcoming of our own domesticity typically requires some kind of instigating vision. The significance of pilots is that they provide a particularly apt image when they, too, literally rise above the vain mundanity and tedious mediocrity of ordinary everyday life. In this way, they were harbingers of a new humanistic creed.

Of course, the interspecific analogy breaks down when we contrast the respective metamorphoses. Humans are not ducks, and Man is not wild. What characterizes the specific "sovereign truth" of humanity is not a movement of reversion that in some sense recovers the primordial body, but an ecstatic, projective movement *out of* the body and into social relationships. This is illustrated in one of the most well-known passages from *Terre des hommes*. Here, Saint Exupéry recounted how Guillaumet, after crashing in the Andes, walked, *thinking only of others*, for five days out of the freezing mountains, uttering upon his return: "what I did, . . . no animal would ever have done" [*Ce que j'ai fait, . . . jamais aucune bête ne l'aurait fait*] (TH 52).[17] The idea is that any nonhuman animal would have welcomed the release of death before instrumentalizing its body in this way and to this extent for invisible symbolic ends.[18] Saint Exupéry presented Guillaumet's remark as "the noblest ever spoken," for it "situates and honors man" by re-establishing the "true hierarchies"—humanity's transcendence of animality through the subordination of corporeality to projects of meaning. This is the kernel of Exupérian humanism.

This view elicited a range of reactions from Merleau-Ponty's generation. Jean-Paul Sartre, for example, who was otherwise fairly positively inclined to Saint Exupéry on account of the quasi-Heideggerian descriptions he offered of his *métier* (Sartre 1984, 66, 107, 146f, 327f; cf. 1983, 326, 501, 503f), objected to it as a mawkish vestige of an outdated moralism.[19] Conversely, in a short but glowing review of *Terre des hommes* that acknowledged the centrality of that passage, Paul Nizan claimed that Saint Exupéry had "assessed with the greatest possible precision what is possible or impossible for man to be and to do."[20] Simone de Beauvoir had a more moderate view that struck a certain balance between these positions. She wrote that "although [Saint Exupéry] talks drivel [*déconne*] when he's thinking abstractly and in general," *Terre des hommes* "represents a radical change of scene, so that you feel strongly – so very, very strongly – the general possibility of another life for the human reality in general which each of us is. It's one of those rare books in a long while that has made me dream."[21]

This evocative quality stems from the central motif of Saint Exupéry's work—namely, that of *le survol*—and the growing recognition that flying provides a perspective that can reveal both the world and humanity in a new light. As he put it, the airplane is an instrument that "has disclosed for us the true face of the earth" (TH 63).[22] Freeing us from well-worn pathways of both movement and thought, it "has taught us to travel as the crow flies." Offering the vantage of "Spirit," it shows that "there is a truth that is higher than the pronouncements of intelligence [*l'intelligence*]" (PG 145). Whereas the latter takes an external, detached, analytical view of visible objects, the former takes a global, involved, and holistic view that focuses, not on objects as such, but on the invisible relations between them. "Spirit is not concerned with objects, but with the meaning that links them together" [*le sens qui les nous entre eux*] (PG 28). In this way, flying "plunges [one] directly into the heart of mystery" (TH 79), revealing *nature* as an indifferent cosmos that forms the backdrop for the "life of Spirit" (TH 61; cf. EG 377). "Only from the height of our rectilinear trajectories do we discover the essential foundation, the fundament of rock and sand and salt in which, here and there, like a bit of moss in the crevices of ruins, life has occasionally ventured to blossom" (TH 64). In this way, it becomes possible "to judge man in cosmic terms" (TH 65), that is, in terms of the coming of Man.

This perspective—which André Gascht (1947) aptly dubbed Saint Exupéry's "cosmic humanism"—came to the fore most clearly in *Pilote de guerre*, in the account Saint Exupéry gave in that text of the defeat of France in 1940 in the context of his military role as a reconnaissance pilot. This is the key text for our purposes. Before considering this work in textual terms, I will first situate it in its relevant historical context.

The historical context of *Pilote de guerre*

Following the French defeat and the signing of the Vichy armistice, Saint Exupéry wrote *Pilote de guerre* primarily as an intervention into the counterproductive and, to his mind, pointless sectarianism that bitterly divided the French opposition to

Nazism, both within France as well as abroad. By and large, the French were divided between, on the one hand, those factions who had sympathies or were apologetic for Pétain,[23] and, on the other hand, Resistance factions, which themselves were divided into pro- and anti-Gaullist camps. *Pilote de guerre* was an earnest call for unity that explicitly attempted to position itself above all political and ideological disputes. This is a standpoint to which he was first explicitly drawn while in Spain during the Civil War as a correspondent for *Paris-Soir*. The basic idea is this: "To understand mankind and its needs, to know its essential reality, we must never set one man's truth against another's. . . . What's the point of discussing ideologies? If they are all sound, they all cancel each other out, and such discussions lead us to despair of mankind's salvation— whereas everywhere about us men manifest the same needs" (TH 201f).

The same, that is, if seen from sufficiently high above, from the point of view of Spirit. Surveying in 1940 the *drôle de guerre* in this way, Saint Exupéry elaborated the idea of Man as the "common denominator" [*commune mesure*] of human reality, the universal human essence underlying the disorder that overwhelmed the perception of those caught up in the *débâcle* on the ground. According to Saint Exupéry's account of the defeat, *France had sacrificed itself* for the greater cause of realizing "the community of Man." "France played its part, which consisted in offering itself up to be crushed . . . and to have itself buried for a while in silence" [*la France a joué son rôle. Il consistait pour elle à se proposer à l'écrasement . . . et à se voir ensevelir pour un temps dans le silence*] (PG 140), and it should be judged by its willingness to sacrifice [*son consentement au sacrifice*] (PG 138). Saint Exupéry thus sought to establish the "transcendental image" of Man—the *truth* of the otherwise "phony" war—as a common goal and rallying point for those opposed to Nazism.[24]

Unsurprisingly, within the French exile community, who read the work first, in February 1942, and who took their political differences with the utmost seriousness, this standpoint did not win Saint Exupéry supporters on any side. With few exceptions (e.g. Maurois 1942), the work was simultaneously denounced from all directions: either for being defeatist, an apology for collaboration, or a treasonous call to arms. "Allying himself with no camp, [Saint Exupéry] was calumniated by all" (Schiff 1994, 350).

As an attempt to articulate the deeper meaning of the fall of France and of the seemingly futile deaths of its soldiers, Saint Exupéry also hoped that *Pilote de guerre*— translated as *Flight to Arras*—would boost the sagging prestige of France and help persuade America to look beyond the factional quarrels and to intervene in the war—if not on behalf of France, then at least on behalf of Man. In this regard, *Pilote de guerre* proved vastly more successful than it was among French émigrés. The reaction from American readers, even among those who had been dubious with respect to Saint Exupéry's earlier works,[25] was generally laudatory, and the book was regarded as "the single most redeeming piece of propaganda" on behalf of France (Schiff 1995, 363f). By early March, the anti-Vichy weekly *Pour la victoire* could state that "the American press was unanimous in greeting the emergence of the first great book of this war as an unquestionable masterpiece" (EG 232; cf. 229–33). "More than any other book at the time, this work by Saint-Exupéry created, in the American public, the desire to aid a country that had offered itself so fully to sacrifice" (Crane 1957, 118). In a comment that was endorsed by many others, Edward Weeks, editor of *The Atlantic Monthly*, declared that "this narrative [i.e., *Pilote de guerre*] and Churchill's speeches stand as the best answer the democracies have yet found to *Mein Kampf*" (cited in Cate 1970, 450; cf. EG 233; Schiff 1994, 363).

Finally, the reception of *Pilote de guerre* in France when it was published there in November 1942 was, aside from many reactionary detractors, certainly more favorable than it had been among the French exile community.[26] The first printing sold well, and there were numerous positive reviews (see EG 293–8, 312f). But owing to the hazards of speaking freely in Occupied France, this response was rather more muted than it had been in America. It was thus the hysterical furor that *Pilote de guerre* provoked among unabashed anti-Semitic collaborationists, and the campaign they orchestrated against it, that dominated the book's initial reception until its banning in early 1943 (see EG 298–312, 316–22). Ironically, perhaps, it was this more than anything that contributed to the book's popularity and reputation, for it served to mitigate certain lingering suspicions of Saint Exupéry's sympathies for collaboration.[27] Although it is difficult to trace the uptake of the book once it was driven underground and clandestine editions appeared (on which see Rude 1978; cf. Bounin 1999, 1320f), it is safe to say that it was, in fact, read (cf. EG 324), and that it resonated well, inasmuch as it was judged less as a failed political intervention than as a sincere expression of solidarity with those living under Nazi occupation and a moral call to arms in the name of their liberation.

Perhaps *le mot juste* from among the contemporary reviews of *Pilote de guerre* belonged to Irwin Edman when he judged that Saint Exupéry wrote like "a soliloquizing angel" (Edman 1942, 1). This rings no less true of the military call to arms against the Nazi Occupation that Saint Exupéry issued to all fighting-age Frenchmen abroad at the same time as *Pilote de guerre* appeared in France.[28] For he did this within a broader call for reconciliation and unity against the common enemy, reiterating the standpoint that had informed *Pilote de guerre*. "Our political discussions are the discussions of ghosts. . . . Men of France, let us be reconciled in order to serve. . . . It is time to unite, not to divide; to embrace, not to exclude. . . . Let us abandon all party spirit" (EG 265, 268).

This piece made Saint Exupéry the object of no small amount of ridicule and vilification—not least because in his call to "abandon all party spirit," he seemed content to send French men to war while delegating the "provisional organization of France" to Britain and America (EG 269). Perhaps the most devastating—and, for present purposes, the most pertinent—response was that by Jacques Maritain (1942), whom Saint Exupéry held in high esteem. Although not one easily given to polemic, Maritain engaged in it here, accusing Saint Exupéry's attempt to rise above politics of vagueness, irrealism, and equivocation, in particular with respect to the question of the armistice. Saint Exupéry's appeals to French unity, Maritain argued, cannot do away with the fact that some French people are partly responsible for the situation and need to be excluded from the movement for liberation. "The men who made the armistice did not have faith in the people of France, nor in the calling of France. Their resentment against the people and their political hatreds played an essential role in this event. Saint Exupéry would be aware of that if he did not close himself off in a biased way from all political considerations." Although Saint Exupéry did not want to speak about politics, "he broaches it despite himself, and this in a rather regrettable way."

According to Maritain, in the conflicts that divide the French, Saint Exupéry "sees only personal rivalries and ambitions," and not the political grounds for these conflicts. Although he does not want to set himself up as a judge, "despite himself, he cannot not judge, and he does not judge correctly" (EG 279f).

This is broadly applicable to *Pilote de guerre* itself. Although this work offered a grandiloquent moral vision of liberation, it was gravely compromised by being utterly detached from political reality. As we shall see, Saint Exupéry's moral arguments resorted to a religious discourse that "expressed the escape from history into the realm of eschatology" (John 1985, 103). In this way, the view of Man developed in *Pilote de guerre*, which makes this work "the highest expression of Exupérian humanism" (Ouellet 1971, 81), can indeed be fairly and accurately described—that is, with all due approbation but also, and especially, pejorativeness—as *la pensée de survol* of a "soliloquizing angel."

The claims of *Pilote de guerre*

Saint Exupéry's account of the situation in France was ultimately based on a sort of epiphany that he claimed he underwent during an extremely dangerous aerial reconnaissance sortie that he flew over Arras in May 1940, during which his aircraft came under heavy fire and was very nearly shot down.[29] Saint Exupéry's recounting of this episode is the centerpiece of *Pilote de guerre*, and it was from here that the sentences with which *Phenomenology of Perception* ends were drawn.

The overriding theme in Saint Exupéry's account of this experience is that it excluded any concern with his personal physical survival. On this basis, he proposed a more general claim to the effect that in those extraordinary situations when existence itself is at stake, "man ceases to be concerned with himself: what matters to him is only that of which he is a part. If he should die, he would not be severed from that, but would rather meld into it. He would not be losing himself, but finding himself" [*l'homme ne s'intéresse plus à soi. Seul s'impose à lui ce dont il est. Il ne se retranche pas, s'il meurt: il se confond. Il ne se perd pas: il se trouve*] (PG 169).

It is of the greatest significance to recognize that, according to Saint Exupéry's story, not only was it known that the odds of returning alive from this mission were extremely low, but it was also known that on account of the sorry state of the French forces at the time, there was no chance, even if he and his crew did manage to return alive, that any reconnaissance information could ever be put to use. In other words—and Merleau-Ponty also drew attention to this (SNS 328/185)—*the highly perilous mission was objectively useless*. Useless, that is, from the perspective of "intelligence." The point that Saint Exupéry went to great lengths to insist upon was that in willfully proceeding anyway, far from resigning themselves to a dismal fate, he and his crew had tacitly responded to a higher moral calling, one rooted in Spirit. According to Saint Exupéry's account, as with this particular flight, so too with the French war effort in general: "Spirit dominated Intelligence" [*l'Esprit . . . a dominé l'Intelligence*] (PG 139).

In Saint Exupéry's account of that flight, the theme of the existential primacy of meaning over life that had been brewing in his earlier works came to full fruition as the claim that bodies lack intrinsic worth, that one's body is nothing more than the dispensable instrument for one's acts of transcendence—and that the "essential act," historically neglected by humanism, is *sacrifice*: "a gift of oneself to the Being to which one will claim to belong" [*un don de soi-même à l'Être dont on prétendra se réclamer*] (PG 231). Note the future tense—as with Mermoz et al., what matters is what Saint Exupéry *becomes* through this ordeal. "What ultimately justifies his mission over Arras is not the War, nor Duty, nor Civilization, but rather the concrete Man that he becomes through this act" (Major 1968, 140).

More than just a riveting tale, Saint Exupéry's account of that near-fatal flight, presented as a *mise en abyme* for the larger national sacrifice, generated a didactic, sermonizing conclusion concerning the spiritual resurrection of France in terms of Man. As one commentator put it, "the experience of the flight to Arras taught the author of *Pilote du guerre* the mystery of the supreme sacrifice consummated by Jesus and the Christian martyrs: '"To bear the sins of men . . ." And each bears the sins of all men' [citing PG 212]. With this claim, the most radical of Exupérian ethics, we are urged to imitate Christ by expiating the lapse of humanity" (Wagner 1996, 123). *Pilote du guerre* thus culminated in a "Credo" that reads like a homily to self-sacrifice in the name of higher collective ends (PG 240ff). For instance:

> I shall fight for the primacy of Man over the individual, and of the Universal over the particular.
>
> I believe that the veneration [*culte*] of the Universal exalts and builds up [*noue*] the riches of particularity, and that it founds the only true order, which is that of life. . . .
>
> I believe that the primacy of Man founds the only Equality and the only Freedom that possess significance. . . . I shall fight anyone seeking to subject the freedom of Man to an individual or to a mass of individuals.
>
> I believe that what my civilization calls Charity is the sacrifice granted to Man to establish his dominion. Charity is the gift made to Man through the mediocrity of the individual. It founds Man. . . .
>
> I shall fight for Man. Against his enemies. But also against myself.

Although Saint Exupéry's tone in the conclusion is tediously sanctimonious, such that there is a strong temptation to simply dismiss this part of the book,[30] it is crucial to recognize that it is this alone that clinches the philosophical significance of the reconnaissance misadventure in terms of Saint Exupéry's account of Man. For, in these passages, Saint Exupéry establishes the specific nature of the secularization of the Christian tradition that his account of Man represents. Positing (a) traditional Christian values and (b) their vitiation by rational humanism, Saint Exupéry then proposed, as a kind of "negation of a negation," (c) the re-foundation of those values in a new, "cosmic humanism." "The profession of faith with which *Pilote de guerre* concludes is at once a vibrant tribute to Christianity for founding in God the values of equality, dignity, fraternity, hope, and charity; but it is also a farewell to Christianity and a call to a new religion [*religion*] of Man in which Man will henceforth be the 'common denominator' required to secure the universality of these values, which alone make life livable" (Devaux 1994, 78). In his own words, the religion of Man proposed by

Saint Exupéry seeks "to found human relations on the worship [*culte*] of Man beyond the individual, in order that the behavior of each with respect to himself and to others would no longer be blind conformism to the customs of the termite mound, but the free exercise of love" (PG 221f).

Saint Exupéry's main contention in *Pilote de guerre*—and this is why the narrative and the moral cannot be disunited—is that this loving religiosity cannot be based on a passive relation to Spirit, but only on human acts. "It is only through acts that we found within ourselves the Being to which we claim to belong" [*on ne fonde en soi l'Être dont on se réclame que par des actes*] (PG 230). Meaning is founded by active self-creation. According to Saint Exupéry, traditional rational humanism, based on the individualistic prejudices of intelligence, has failed to take action seriously (PG 231). In particular, it has neglected what he regarded as the essential act, namely, sacrifice, which he understood as a "gratuitous gift" (EG 209, 460), where "gratuitous" [*gratuit*] means that "the *useful* [utile] part is useless [*inutile*]" (Carnets 67). Yet, this is what is required for love, and for the founding of the new "Community of Man," which can only be the "sum of our gifts" (PG 239).[31]

Thus, "the fundamental discovery of *Pilote de guerre* could be defined as the passage from humanism as abstract and 'given' to a concrete and creative [because giv*ing*] humanism. The only Spirit who can create Man is man himself" (Major 1968, 140). The conclusion that turns *Pilote de guerre* into a "breviary of humanism" (Losic 1965, 77) expresses—*codifies*, in fact—this passage as the move from an attitude of passive spectation to one of creative activity in the context of a collective *métier*. Saint Exupéry called this "*participation*." This has an existential priority: "to know is not to demonstrate or explain, but to attain vision. To see, however, one must first of all participate" (PG 54). Saint Exupéry thus claimed that "the role of spectator or a witness has always disgusted me. What am I, if I do not participate? I have to participate in order to exist" [*le métier de témoin m'a toujours fait horreur. Que suis-je, si je ne participer pas? J'ai besoin, pour être, de participer*] (PG 183). It is only through effective creative action that *participates* in a larger social endeavor that abstract individuality can be overcome, and it is only in such overcoming that new bonds with others are effectively established. "It is in participation that man makes himself, that his whole being will shed its skin [*muer*] and acquire a new dimension" (Ouellet 1971, 41).

Participatory action is a matter of giving oneself; it is ultimately a process of self-sacrifice that is properly justifiable only in terms of the new humanity that comes into being through it. As Saint Exupéry put it: "the individual is only a path. What matters is Man, who takes that path" [*l'individu n'est qu'une route. L'Homme qui l'emprunte compte seul*] (PG 214). One must *become* Man, *see* as Man, as Saint Exupéry claimed happened to him during the flight over Arras, when Man "took the place" of his self-concerned individuality [*s'est installé à ma place*] (PG 217). Whence the high-altitude thoughts with which *Phenomenology of Perception* concludes.

Thus, to readers familiar with *Pilote de guerre*—and it is scarcely conceivable that anyone reading Merleau-Ponty's tome in postwar France would *not* have been familiar with it—the lines cited by Merleau-Ponty literally aver that the proper fulfillment of human life lies in a kind of self-sacrificial *ekstasis*, whereby corporeality is transmuted back into the intersubjective relationships wherein its subjectivity was originally constituted. Crucially, Saint Exupéry referred to this as "*exchange*." This notion was anticipated in *Terre des hommes*, but only elaborated in *Pilote de guerre*. For Saint Exupéry, *exchange* was effectively synonymous with *sacrifice* in the sense of creative participation (Losic 1965, 56; Major 1968, 143; Ouellet 1971, 30), and as such, it can be deemed with little controversy to be *the* central concept in Exupérian humanism (and it is also central to Merleau-Ponty's account of freedom, which will be discussed below). Key here is that the body is not the ultimate locus of personal existence, but rather a source of alienation, which is to be literally exchanged, up to and including the point of death, against projective meaningfulness. This is precisely what it means when we read at the end of *Phenomenology of Perception*, "you give yourself in exchange" [*tu t'échanges*] (PhP 520).

But as Saint Exupéry immediately added—although this fell to Merleau-Ponty's ellipsis—"you do not experience the feeling of loss in the exchange" [*tu n'éprouves pas le sentiment de perdre à l'échange*] (PG 168). In an important sense, then, this is not *really* sacrifice. As with the Maussian view of potlatch as ultimately not disinterested,[32] Exupérian exchange is a matter of restitutive equivalency. "*Rien ne se perd*" (SV 174). Although it *demands* nothing in return, sacrifice does not go uncompensated in the Exupérian economy. "From the moment one consents to sacrifice oneself for one's ideal, one's whole being enlarges to the dimensions of that ideal" (Ouellet 1971, 34). "What you give to the community founds the community—and the existence of a community enriches your own substance" (EG 209). And this holds true even of the ultimate sacrifice. "If one 'participates' in something wholeheartedly, and with the thought of getting nothing in return [*non-récompense*] – to save one's country, for example – exchange in death will be rewarded" (Losic 1965, 56f). For Saint Exupéry, "death, far from severing the knot [*nœud*] that ties the individual to the community of men, gains him a further bond. Through the gift of his life, supreme measure of his loyalty, [he] seals a pact with the living and the dead; and this bond, founded in blood, more tightly ensures their communion" (Ouellet 1971, 80f).

Thus, in the Exupérian world, self-sacrificial disincarnation leads to authentic liberation in spiritual communion. Nothing less nor different than this is expressed in the final words of *Phenomenology of Perception*—that is, the line about the "knot of relations"—that have so strongly endeared themselves to so many of Merleau-Ponty's latter-day readers. For as Saint Exupéry wrote in the immediately preceding line: "one's essence appears when the body comes undone" [*Quand le corps se défait, l'essentiel se montre*], that is, when that "knot of relations" [*nœud de relations*] is untied through the individual's death. And the line immediately following drives the point home unmistakably: "The body is an old crock that gets left behind" [*Le corps, vieux cheval, on l'abandonne*] (PG 171).

The death of Saint Exupéry

Perhaps the single most significant detail concerning Saint Exupéry's life actually concerns his death: the fact that Saint Exupéry—who, despite being not only one of France's best-known men of letters, but also too old and physically unfit to fly, had publicly insisted on being remobilized and finagled his way back into active military duty—famously disappeared while on a reconnaissance mission over southern France on the last day of July 1944. This was just a few weeks before the liberation of Paris, and not long before the completion of *Phenomenology of Perception* (Noble 2011, 73f). Although it was not immediately known precisely what happened to Saint Exupéry, such that for a short period of time the possibility was held open that he had survived and been taken prisoner, with the end of the German occupation, it grew increasingly apparent that he had perished, leaving behind that "old crock" that was his body. And although it was not until April 1948 that he was officially declared as having died for his country (Schiff 1994, 438), by the time *Phenomenology of Perception* was published in April 1945, it was generally taken for granted that its final words were those of a dead man, someone who had died *"une mort glorieuse"* (e.g. Morgan 1944; Cohen 1944; Barjon 1945; Gide 1945). This is directly tied to Merleau-Ponty's pronouncing Saint Exupéry a hero. In case there is any doubt as to what Merleau-Ponty intended the phrase "living one's life to the limit" to mean, it suffices to recall that in his contribution to the inaugural issue of *Les temps modernes*, "La Guerre a eu lieu," Merleau-Ponty had written, in no uncertain terms, that when it comes to heroism, "the man who is still able to speak does not know what he is talking about" (SNS 258/146).

The fact of Saint Exupéry's high-profile death—which quickly acquired a legendary, even quasi-hagiographic status—must be borne in mind throughout this discussion. This renown was reinforced by two posthumous publications. First, in December 1944, Saint Exupéry's *Lettre à un otage* ["Letter to a Hostage"] appeared in France. This short elegiac text—which was originally written in 1942 as a letter to (and as a preface to a book by) his close friend Léon Werth, a French Jew living under Nazi Occupation—was regarded by some at the time as "the most beautiful text since the Liberation" (Fouchet 1945, 4). And in hindsight, it is arguably "the most crystalline expression of Saint Exupéry's thinking" (Schiff 1994, 398). Here, Saint Exupéry pours out his distress over the peril faced by his friend—and, by extension, himself. For as he wrote in *Terre des hommes*, anticipating the lines of *Pilote de guerre* found at the end of *Phenomenology of Perception*, "there is only one veritable treasure—the treasure of human relations."[33] But Werth was just one of the millions of "hostages" trapped in Occupied France. An ode to friendship, Saint Exupéry's text is ineluctably an empathic and emphatic paean to France as the living force that sustained his being, and to which he would not hesitate to give his life. "One only dies for that by which one can live" [*On meurt pour cela seul dont on peut vivre*] (PG 236). For him, France was "neither an abstract goddess nor a historical concept, but rather a flesh [*chair*] on which I depended, a network [*réseau*] of bonds that governed me, a set of centres that founded the contours of my heart" (EG 334).

More generally, then, *Lettre à un otage* was about Man. Saint Exupéry offered two important illustrations of this. First, he described the "wordless contentment" that emerged one day in 1939 when he and Werth shared an impromptu Pernod with two bargemen—one German, the other Dutch—at a café in Fleurville overlooking the Saône. Saint Exupéry was struck by the spontaneous yet profound understanding, solidarity, and sense of human goodwill that this encounter seemed to epitomize. As

Saint Exupéry described it, Man is the "substance" of this natural concord—just as it had been earlier in Spain when, captured by Catalan anarchist militiamen, unable to speak their language, and unsure of his fate, Saint Exupéry broke the dehumanizing distance and tension through the "very discrete miracle" of smiling and bumming a cigarette. This is the second example. The idea is that by betokening a "spiritual certainty" among all those present, this gesture invoked the reciprocity of Man, utterly transforming the relationality of the situation. As Saint Exupéry touchingly (if somewhat mawkishly) put it: "We meet in the smile that is above language, class, and party politics" (EG 339f, 342). These two situations were essentially the same. In Fleurville, as in Spain, "our agreement was so complete, so solid and profound, and concerned with a creed which, although inarticulable, was so self-evident in its substance that we would have gladly agreed to . . . die behind machine guns in order to preserve the substance of that agreement" (EG 336).

By the time Saint Exupéry wrote *Lettre à un otage*, all this lay in tatters and under the boot of fascism. This anguished text thus expresses an unmistakable predisposition to sacrifice that buttressed the legend of Saint Exupéry's death.

The other posthumous publication that contributed to the Exupérian aura was, of course, *Le petit prince*, which was published by Gallimard in France in 1946 (it had been published in both French and English in 1943 by Reynal & Hitchcock in New York). This has become by far the best known of Saint Exupéry's works, despite being—or perhaps because it is—typically classified as a children's book (but cf. Rickman 1996). Sixty years ago, however, this story of a cherubic, cosmic urchin who descends to Earth but who ultimately returns to the heavens, leaving no trace, was read as having eerily and poignantly foreshadowed Saint Exupéry's own death. It stoked the mystique of saintly self-sacrifice, in the sense of life in *imitatio Christi*, which Saint Exupéry seemed to represent in the immediate postwar period.

But the hagiography was not to last. In 1948, to the vexation of most of those who were close to Saint Exupéry, Gallimard published *Citadelle*, a large, unfinished (possibly by design) manuscript that Saint Exupéry had been working on during the last decade of his life, and which presents, in its 219 chapters, the first-person ruminations of a desert chieftain passing down paternalistic wisdom to his son. This wide-ranging work is beyond present concerns. Suffice it to say that it is a didactic, turgid, repetitive, and disorganized tome that met with a decidedly cool if polite reception by critics at the time (e.g. Barjon 1948; Henriot 1948; Roy 1948). But this marked the beginning of the end of Saint Exupéry's apotheosis—his star would henceforth fade considerably. Although some would continue to indulge the legend and to regard him as "one of the universal geniuses of the age" (Maxwell Smith 1956, 4), and although even to this day, he continues strongly to inspire those who take him up in spiritual or religious terms (Weldon 2011; cf. Harris 1990), Saint Exupéry's status and reputation have suffered badly since the postwar period. Since the 1950s, there has thus tended to be "either an annexation of Saint-Exupéry," that is, the reduction of his work to some larger, more tractable movement or genre, "or else his total rejection, often motivated by the 'edifying author' interpretation with which he is saddled" (Major 1968, 256). Most efforts of "annexation" tend to follow Sartre's 1947 claim, made in "Qu'est-ce que la littérature?," that Saint Exupéry belongs "to our generation," and more specifically, that he was an important *"precursor"* of engaged existentialist literature (Sartre 1948, 326f n9, italics added; cf. 250f, 264).

As for the "total rejection" of Saint Exupéry, this is typically based on a developing image of him as an intellectual lightweight with an outmoded antidemocratic—if not fascistic (see Price 1957, 1960; Fife 1959)—message. Thus, for example, in the mid-1960s, Serge Losic commented that "in our youth we admired the heroism of Saint-Exupéry. Today we no longer believe in it: it over-idealized the man of action" (1965, 165). And around the same time, Jean-François Revel wrote: "Saint-Exupéry showed the French that a verbose piece of nonsense becomes profound philosophical truth if one takes it off the ground and raises it to an altitude of seven thousand feet. Stupidity in the cockpit takes on the allure of wisdom" (Revel 1965, 36f). Thus today, while the "broader reading public warmly but mistakenly regards him as a children's author," critics tend to make of Saint Exupéry "a footnote to existentialism, and a figure who is otherwise best passed over" (Harris 1999, 3).

Conclusion

Be that as it may, it is clearly imperative for those seriously interested in Merleau-Ponty to cease simply passing over Saint Exupéry's role in a *particular* "footnote to existentialism," namely, the final lines on the final page of *Phenomenology of Perception*. For in its phenomenological rehabilitation of corporeality as the central locus of existence, the thrust of Merleau-Ponty's work is powerfully opposed to Saint Exupéry's self-sacrificial disdain of embodiment. *Isn't it?* And yet it *is*—unmistakably—on a note of such "high-altitude" disincarnation that *Phenomenology of Perception* ends. Is there a reader of this book today who would not be taken wholly aback were it to conclude with the final line reunited with those immediately preceding and following it in Saint Exupéry's text (PG 171) as follows:

> Quand le corps se défait, l'essentiel se montre. L'homme n'est qu'un nœud de relations, les relations comptent seules pour l'homme.
> Le corps, vieux cheval, on l'abandonne.

> One's essence appears when the body comes undone. Man is but a knot of relations, relations alone matter to man.
> The body is an old crock that gets left behind.

In this light, and given how representative these lines are of the Exupérian *œuvre*, it is clear that the ending of *Phenomenology of Perception* can no longer be given a convenient and facile Merleau-Pontian gloss. Rather, it is patently the case that Saint Exupéry's being given the final word is nothing short of baffling. At least in *some* way, this is surely inconsistent with the main thrust of the work. So why does the book end this way? What is going on there? What was Merleau-Ponty thinking? So long as this situation remains unexplained, a very serious and potentially devastating philosophical question mark is left hanging over the work as a whole.

Embodiment and Incarnation

To reiterate the point with which the previous chapter concluded, it seems safe to say that virtually all readers of *Phenomenology of Perception* today would be confused, shocked, or even scandalized were the book actually to conclude as follows, with the final line re-embedded in its original context:

> Quand le corps se défait, l'essentiel se montre. L'homme n'est qu'un nœud de relations. Les relations comptent seules pour l'homme.
> Le corps, vieux cheval, on l'abandonne. (PG 171)

> One's essence appears when the body comes undone. Man is but a knot of relations, relations alone matter to man.
> The body is an old crock that gets left behind.

For the central thrust of Merleau-Ponty's phenomenology of perception, in its philosophical rehabilitation of corporeality as the locus of human existence, is powerfully opposed to the antipathetic disdain of embodiment that Saint Exupéry expressed unambiguously in these lines. Or at least that is how *Phenomenology of Perception* is overwhelmingly understood. Yet, it *is* on a note of such "high-altitude" disincarnation that it ends. That Saint Exupéry is given the final word—and that *that* is the word he gets—is, to say the least, quite puzzling. Why then does the book conclude in this way? Why is the final morsel of this otherwise delectable phenomenological feast so unpalatably bitter? For anyone with a modicum of familiarity with *Pilote de guerre*, the ending of *Phenomenology of Perception* is plainly inconsistent with the thrust of the work. Is it then merely, say, some sort of throwaway remark, the inconsistency of which is of no philosophical consequence? Or is there a deeper level at which some kind of consistency or coherence may be discerned? This is what we need to ascertain. For as long as the ending of *Phenomenology of Perception* remains unexplained, a serious and disconcerting philosophical question mark is left hanging over the work as a whole, as well as over standard interpretations of it.

Further remarks on the Exupérian ending

In fact, the more one probes this ending, the more one uncovers numerous unexpected and disquieting anomalies that add further emphasis to this question mark. These details can be boiled down to the following three observations.

First, according to his own account, Saint Exupéry was daydreaming or hallucinating during the death-defying episode in question. This may be fictionalized in this particular case, but he was, as a matter of fact, notorious for his absentmindedness while flying. Indeed, the whole of *Pilote de guerre* is written in an oneiric tone as established by its very opening line: "Sans doute je rêve" ["I must be dreaming"] (PG 9), and the text drifts regularly between dream and reality—in particular, between immediate actuality and the quasimythic irreality of Saint Exupéry's recollection of his childhood (see Ton-That 2000). The question at hand is thus not just why *Phenomenology of Perception* ends by deferring to a paradigmatic case of *la pensée de survol*. It is, moreover, the question as to why this philosophical work dealing with perception would conclude with a moment, not simply of nonperception, but one that would seem to lack reliable epistemic warrant of any kind.

Second, the episode from which the final lines of *Phenomenology of Perception* were drawn did not stem simply and directly from Saint Exupéry's own close encounter with death. Rather, it involved the recollection of the real death of his younger brother, François, as a result of heart failure caused by rheumatic fever nearly a quarter-century earlier, when Saint Exupéry's own life was under no threat whatsoever (PG 170f.).[1] It was his brother's words—"I can't help it, it's my body" [*Je ne peux pas m'en empêcher. C'est mon corps*]—and the pressing need he felt, shortly before dying, to bequeath to Antoine his modest worldly goods, in order to ensure a kind of vicarious survival of that which gave his life meaning, that first implanted in Saint Exupéry, albeit tacitly, the fundamental insight of Man concerning the priority of relations over the alien, contingent character of the body. This was later reinforced by Saint Exupéry's experience in Aéropostale, in particular by Guillaumet's walking ordeal in the Andes—an example that Saint Exupéry himself (along with his mechanic, André Prévot) emulated some years later in 1935 after crashing in the Libyan desert and having to walk for several days with minimal provisions before finally being rescued (an episode he described at length in *Terre des hommes*). Here, he claimed our striving toward others in this remarkable way as a "universal truth," and in the text, he gave Prévot the key line: "If I were alone in the world, I'd lie down right here" [*Si j'étais seul au monde . . . je me coucherais*] (TH 166).

Thus, even if we grant that for Saint Exupéry such thoughts were not fully driven home until his perilous flight over Arras in 1940, the ideas expressed in the lines drawn from *Pilote de guerre* at the end of *Phenomenology of Perception* do not exactly have the "heroic" pedigree that is implied by Merleau-Ponty's presentation of them.

Third, that fact may actually be felicitous, however. For whatever may have been the situation in 1944 (when he fatally disappeared), according to Merleau-Ponty's own express stipulation concerning heroism—namely, that "the man who is still able to speak does not know what he is talking about" (SNS 258/146)—Saint Exupéry could not possibly have been a "hero" over Arras in 1940. For it is *not* the case that he "entered history and melded with it" [*s'est joint et confondu à l'histoire*] at that moment (SNS 258/146), and he was certainly still able to speak—he was even able to write a book about his experience! There is obviously a paradox in any appeal to heroes, if it is effectively stipulated that they are dead. Merleau-Ponty was perhaps more circumspect at the end of the Preface to *Humanism and Terror*, written in 1947, where he said that he was writing "for friends whose names we would gladly inscribe here, *were it permissible to make witnesses of the dead*" [s'il était permis de prendre des morts pour témoins] (HT xlii/xlvi, emphasis added).

Taken along with the problematic nature of the passage itself, these anomalous details might seem to add up to a devastating objection to any construal of Merleau-Ponty's appeal to heroism as being philosophically significant in its own right. This would recommend reading the ending of *Phenomenology of Perception* as nothing more than a throwaway remark of some sort that may be freely glossed—or even disregarded altogether—without actually impacting the philosophical content of the work as a whole. And indeed, this is what we find in most scholarship devoted to Merleau-Ponty. As was pointed out in the Introduction, the passage in question is seldom addressed at all by commentators on *Phenomenology of Perception*, and whenever it *is* addressed, it is—without exception—either dismissed as extraneous rhetorical ornamentation, or else taken as a reiteration of something that Merleau-Ponty himself had, actually or effectively, already said.

Such readings might be understood in different ways, but none is plausible. It is worthwhile tarrying over this briefly. As noted earlier, for example, it is fundamentally unsound to offer an explanation of the ending of *Phenomenology of Perception* in terms of the sociopolitical context of the immediate postwar period (see Introduction, Note 4). To be sure, Saint Exupéry was being celebrated and eulogized in very positive terms at that time as a symbol of the Resistance and the defeat of fascism in France. And Merleau-Ponty's book—completed in August or September 1944, shortly after Saint Exupéry's death and in the immediate aftermath of liberation (cf. Noble 2011, 73ff)—was indelibly marked by these allegiances as well. But while Saint Exupéry may have been among the most famous heroes of the war, he was certainly not the only one. And he was by no means the most progressively-minded nor philosophically inspired person to die for France. Over and above implying that *qua* author, Merleau-Ponty was something of a conformist, then, a suggestion that seems disconfirmed on virtually every other page of the book, to attribute the ending of *Phenomenology of Perception* to the sociopolitical context is merely to rationalize it without offering any insight as to why the book ends on a "heroic" note at all, and why it was Saint Exupéry in particular to whom Merleau-Ponty turned.

Much the same could be said of claims to the effect that the ending of *Phenomenology of Perception* "betrays the displacement of [Merleau-Ponty's] philosophical concerns, and his impassioned interest in the political events of the day" (Saint Aubert 2004, 115). For aside from the most general level of allegiances that scarcely excluded anyone in France at the time, it is simply not the case that Saint Exupéry was in any way whatsoever reflective of Merleau-Ponty's political views—his political writings at the time never refer to him. And given the discussion above (Chapter 1), there are clearly very good reasons for this. So the main problems facing the contextual approach recur here. In general, it seems safe to say that with regard to understanding why *Phenomenology of Perception* ends with those lines from *Pilote de guerre*, any approach that focuses on who authored those lines while discounting or overlooking their textual content will always only amount at most to a rationalization rather than a genuine explanation. For the question at hand is not a matter of figuring out what conceivable sense at all there could possibly be in recognizing Saint Exupéry as a hero, but rather of ascertaining why Merleau-Ponty ended his book with a deference to a hero in the first place, and then why he chose *this* one, Saint Exupéry, for this purpose. Moreover, once the textual incongruity of the passage itself is also factored into the problem, then it becomes perfectly clear that these sorts of approach are woefully deficient.

Matters are no better, however, and probably worse, if we do focus on the textual content of the lines from *Pilote de guerre*. For given what we have seen, lest we willfully turn a blind eye to Saint Exupéry's book, we would have to say either that Merleau-Ponty did not notice the acute incongruity, a suggestion that seems unimaginably unlikely, or else that he made the choice despite that incongruity, and that he crafted the excerpt with some kind of deceitful or manipulative intent. But it is scarcely possible seriously to imagine him thinking that his ellipses would have fooled any sophisticated reader at the time. It is very likely that such readers would have been familiar with *Pilote de guerre*, and in any case, the bulk of the passage is enigmatic in a way that invites the reader to consult the original.[2] It is thus not insignificant that the textual incongruity of the cited passage was not called out by contemporary readers of Merleau-Ponty's book. But this can be accounted for satisfactorily by recognizing that those readers were preoccupied with trying to come to terms with the other 500-plus pages of groundbreaking philosophical investigation, combined with the fact that, at the time, a reference to Saint Exupéry was nothing particularly noteworthy (see above, Chapter 1, note 2). In that interpretive context, the ending could easily have been regarded as merely a rhetorical flourish or stylistic device. In other words, it could have been safely and innocently presumed that in textual terms, what the hero expresses at the end of *Phenomenology of Perception*, even if it clearly lacked philosophical rigor, was consistent with the basic claims of Merleau-Ponty's existential phenomenology. It is just that 65 years ago, readers were still in the process of figuring out what exactly those claims were.

Many readers today make the same presumption, that is, that the "heroic" ideas at the end of *Phenomenology of Perception* are a reflection, however enigmatic, of Merleau-Ponty's own thought. But given the current development of Merleau-Ponty scholarship, this can no longer be considered innocent. Knowing what we now know about *Phenomenology of Perception* and the basic claims of Merleau-Ponty's existential phenomenology, or at least given what we *think* we know about them, and given what we know about Saint Exupéry and *Pilote de guerre*, it quite simply will not do to deny that there is a major problem of interpretation here. As far as making out the end of *Phenomenology of Perception* to be merely a rhetorical device of some sort, then, this seems once again to engage in bad faith rationalization. For if Merleau-Ponty's interest was *merely* rhetorical, then why would he draw from a source so bizarrely at odds with his own position? Why would he risk such perverse misunderstanding for no compelling philosophical reason? This choice could only be seen as an alarming compositional blunder, inasmuch as it would obstruct seriously the uptake of the philosophical content of the book. Although Merleau-Ponty's ability to communicate clearly and effectively may have left some room for improvement, to suppose that at the very culmination of this major text, he committed such an outright authorial *faux pas* would raise difficult new questions while answering none. Such a claim would thus appear to be nothing more than a desperate attempt to avoid facing a very difficult hermeneutical problem.

In short, all of these ways in which the ending of *Phenomenology of Perception* may be discounted or disregarded are implausible. The common thread between them lies in regarding the ending as an extraneous element tacked onto an otherwise complete work, and rationalizing it or explaining it away on that basis. Refusing to consider the ending as an integral and irreducible part of what Merleau-Ponty was doing, they fail to provide any insight into it, and instead, simply tend to raise further questions and multiply problems.

At any rate, given the manifest textual incongruity of the lines drawn from *Pilote de guerre*, none of these stratagems is sufficiently plausible to justify refraining from investigating the possibility that those lines are, in fact, a necessary part of the phenomenological project undertaken in *Phenomenology of Perception*. Such is what I wish to do in this book. For while the textual content of those lines *is* inconsistent with the thrust of the work—I believe the passage is, in Merleau-Ponty's terms, a moment of *non-sense*—I would submit that there is nevertheless a deeper level at which it makes sense. Indeed, what I shall argue for in this book is that there is a deeper level at which the ending literally *makes sense*—that is, at which it contributes to producing or generating sense—and that this is how it should be accounted for. The fact that *Phenomenology of Perception* ends with those Exupérian thoughts has primarily to do, I will contend, not with what they *say*, but rather with what they *do*: as a subliminal experience of meaningful death, the invocation of heroism is intended to establish intuitively that the limits of what is humanly knowable coincide with the scope of existential phenomenology as conceived by Merleau-Ponty. In this way, the heroic ending is implicated performatively in the "realization" of the philosophical content of the work as a whole. Its significance is thus methodological, pertaining to Merleau-Ponty's main claims regarding what, following Husserl and Fink, he called the "phenomenology of phenomenology"— claims which were, as we shall see, bound up inextricably with Merleau-Ponty's simultaneous and concomitant attempt to come to terms with what he viewed as the central methodological problem facing Marxism. In a remarkable way, then, Merleau-Ponty's notion of "heroism" was the single stone with which, so to speak, he tried to kill two methodological birds at once.

So much by way of an anticipatory glimpse of what I shall argue for in this book, a view that will be more fully elaborated, naturally enough, in the Conclusion. It might just be added at this point, though, that even if what I will claim about the ending of *Phenomenology of Perception* is true, it would by no means follow immediately that it is philosophically unproblematic and defensible. Rather, it may emerge that it signals— and this in an unexpectedly conspicuous way—a fundamental methodological weakness in Merleau-Ponty's project of existential phenomenology, a weakness that could have important implications in terms of the epistemic status of the claims that Merleau-Ponty made in the context of this project. But regardless of how that further question plays out (it is beyond the scope of the present work), it is imperative for those interested in Merleau-Ponty's work to come to terms in the first place with the problem of Exupérian heroism.

•

This chapter will get this investigation underway by first considering a pair of earlier references to Saint Exupéry in *Phenomenology of Perception*. This will serve to further bolster the claim that the concluding reference to Saint Exupéry is not inconsequential by showing that there is, in fact, philosophically substantive content in Merleau-Ponty's interest in him. More importantly, though, my analysis of these earlier references—which will begin presently and resume in the latter part of Chapter 3—will also set the stage for the investigation of heroism by foregrounding the historical and political horizons of Merleau-Ponty's approach to embodiment. In particular, I will be claiming that these references to Saint Exupéry help to reveal a very important connection between Merleau-Ponty's thought in the postwar period and the Hegelian Marxism of György (Georg) Lukács. This claim may surprise many readers. But while the role of Lukács' work is largely unexplored in Merleau-Ponty scholarship, it is, I believe, of the first importance. Thus, after initiating an analysis of the early references to Saint Exupéry, the bulk of this chapter will be devoted to elaborating contextual considerations that serve to strengthen the plausibility of according a central significance to Lukácsian Marxism in Merleau-Ponty's thought. These considerations will pertain to the reception of Lukács' work in France, and to the "origins" or "sources" of Merleau-Ponty's attachment to Marxism. Concerning the latter especially, this sort of contextual work is unavoidably circumstantial and thus fraught with some risk. But it is very important inasmuch as it may be able to shed light on the underlying architectonic, so to speak, of Merleau-Ponty's existential phenomenology. Specifically, and what is important for my purposes, it can lend credence to the claim that Marxism has a certain theoretical priority over phenomenology in Merleau-Ponty's postwar project.

Many of the details of this discussion will recur later, but this general point provides the backdrop for the discussion in Chapter 3. There, my argument will rest upon certain philosophical connections that are demonstrable on the basis of textual evidence. In particular, in dealing with the earlier references to Saint Exupéry in *Phenomenology of Perception*, we will be brought to consider Lukács' claims regarding the methodological priority of the category of "totality" and the social mediation of nature in modern society, and how these are taken up by Merleau-Ponty in Gestalt-theoretic terms as the claim that human history forms an existential totality. It will consequently emerge that the holistic approach to embodiment and human *être-au-monde* that is central to Merleau-Ponty's existential phenomenology is to be understood as situated methodologically within the horizons of the meaning of human history as a whole. In other words, for Merleau-Ponty, *history has phenomenological priority over embodiment*. As we shall see, recognition of this priority is extremely important in terms of understanding Merleau-Ponty's project in the postwar period, including its appeal to Saint Exupéry and the heroism that he is taken to personify. But it is also a point that is generally not recognized—and often even unknowingly contradicted—in the literature.

Earlier references to Saint Exupéry (Part 1)

Readers of *Phenomenology of Perception* will recall that in a pair of linked footnotes found within the first chapter of Part I, "The Body as an Object and Mechanistic Physiology," Merleau-Ponty had already appealed to the same section (Chapter XXI) of *Pilote de guerre* to which he appealed at the very end of the book. And in this case, it was for a phenomenological illustration of a point that he was making about the structure of human embodiment, to wit, the possibility of a person's "human" situation fully incorporating her "biological" situation in moments of danger, that is, for her body to "enter into action unreservedly" [*se joigne sans réserve à l'action*]. The first reference reads as follows:

> Ainsi Saint Exupéry, au-dessus d'Arras, entouré de feu, ne sent plus comme distinct de lui-même ce corps qui tout à l'heure se dérobait: « C'est comme si ma vie m'était à chaque seconde donnée, comme si ma vie me devenait à chaque seconde plus sensible. Je vis. Je suis vivant. Je suis encore vivant. Je suis toujours vivant. Je ne suis plus qu'une source de vie. » (PhP 99 n1, citing PG 174)[3]

> Thus, Saint-Exupéry, over Arras, surrounded by [enemy] fire, no longer feels as something distinct from himself this body which, just moments before, was recoiling: "It is as if my life were given to me every second, as if with every second my life were becoming more palpable. I live. I am living. I am still living. I am always living. I am nothing but a source of life."

But Merleau-Ponty immediately added that this possibility is strictly *momentary*, occurring only in limit cases. Thus, the second reference—which consists in a citation that is actually drawn from a slightly earlier passage in *Pilote de guerre*—reads as follows:

> Mais certes au cours de ma vie, lorsque rien d'urgent ne me gouverne, lorsque ma signification n'est pas en jeu, je ne vois point de problèmes plus graves que ceux de mon corps. (PhP 100 n1, citing PG 169)[4]

> To be sure, though, in the course of my life, when not directed by anything urgent, when my meaning is not at stake, I see no problems more serious than those of my body.

Granting the appropriateness of these references to Saint Exupéry for Merleau-Ponty's discussion of embodiment—even granting for the sake of argument that, concerning embodied action, "what Saint-Exupéry is saying is *the same* as what Merleau-Ponty says" (C. Smith 1980, 269, emphasis added)—it is not clear why Merleau-Ponty would return at the very end of the book to a one-sided *disambiguation* of the point. That is, whereas in the discussion in Part I, the body's unqualified participation in action is minimized and exceptionalized on account of corporeal exigencies, the heroic ending of *Phenomenology of Perception* pertains to that unqualified participation taken in isolation. Of course, it might seem on the contrary to be perfectly clear why Merleau-Ponty would do this—the deference to Saint Exupéry *qua* hero at the end implies that he was dead, and death ensures unfailingly that the problems of one's body are indeed nullified. As I have argued, however, it is *not* clear why such a deference is needed at all. More particularly, though, it is also not clear why Merleau-Ponty made this point about embodiment in the first place, nor why it is something that becomes relevant again at the very end of the book. Why is it that at this preliminary stage of his phenomenological account of embodiment, where it would occur to no one to rationalize it as a piece of philosophically empty rhetoric or political homage,[5] Merleau-Ponty endorsed the implied distancing or even rupture between embodiment and life? It is, after all, to those moments at which the body is *least bodily*, or at least at which it is least *mine*, that the following statements apply: "I live. I am living. I am still living. I am always living. I am nothing but a source of life." It would be specious and arbitrary to dismiss this as insignificant simply on the basis of having similarly dismissed the ending of *Phenomenology of Perception*. Rather, we need first to understand these initial references, and then, on that basis, come to terms with the reference to Saint Exupéry with which Merleau-Ponty's book concludes.

In order to understand these earlier references to Saint Exupéry, it is necessary to reconstruct more fully the immediate context of Merleau-Ponty's discussion. The central notion under consideration here was that of the "habitual body," understood in conjunction with the idea of repression, which was a crucial conceptual element in Merleau-Ponty's understanding of the ambiguity of embodiment. And as we shall see, coming to terms with this will—somewhat surprisingly perhaps—involve us in an excursus on the work of Lukács, which will in turn motivate considerations on how Merleau-Ponty came to embrace Marxism philosophically in the first place. On this basis, which we will be in a better position to understand Merleau-Ponty's phenomenological approach to embodiment.

Embodiment and historicity

The point that Merleau-Ponty illustrated by way of reference to Saint Exupéry had to do with the distinction that he drew between what he termed "the habitual body" [*le corps habituel*] and "the 'actual' body" [*le corps actuel*] as two distinct "layers" [*couches*] of our embodied being (PhP 97). In brief, the habitual body is understood in terms of the persistence through "sedimentation" of the general form of past experiences, and thus as a kind of impersonal existence, while the "actual" body is understood in terms of spontaneous personal existence in the living present. He used this distinction—especially the concept of the habitual body—to formulate a framework for understanding cases of phantom limb syndrome and anosognosia without reducing them to either psychological or physiological factors. But as Merleau-Ponty emphasized, having a sedimented dimension of embodiment is not in itself pathological, but rather an essential feature of human existence in general. For it is in virtue of having a habitual body that a certain distance can be taken from the immediacy of one's "environing-world" [*milieu, Umwelt*], and it is only in virtue of this distance that, unlike animals, humans can gain awareness of a "world" [*monde, Welt*] properly speaking as the "common ground [*raison commune*] of all environing-worlds" (PhP 103), and then, on this basis, attain a critical distance from one's own immediate setting: "it is by renouncing a part of his spontaneity, and by engaging in the world through stable organs and pre-established circuits, that man can acquire the mental and practical space that will in principle liberate him from his environing-world and enable him to *see* it" (PhP 103). Somewhat paradoxically, then, the sort of "integration" that specifically characterizes human existence in contradistinction to animal life occurs precisely through a movement that begins by decentring and deactualizing that existence.

This movement is that of historicity, the active historical nature of human existence. For Merleau-Ponty, the distinction between the habitual and the "actual" body is essentially a *temporal* distinction, that is, between pastness and presence, and it is within the terms of this distinction that the dynamic of historicity emerges. The integration of human existence or *être-au-monde* thus occurs fundamentally through historical action that is ultimately based in a dialectic of embodiment, and which is oriented toward equilibrium understood in Gestalt-theoretic terms. This is a distinctive feature of Merleau-Ponty's existential phenomenology, and it is the reason why, for him, as we shall see, discussions of embodiment or corporeality at the level of individuals can lead with otherwise startling suddenness to discussions of history at the macroscopic level. This historical dialectic of embodiment is meant to provide a unified conception of human existence that would bridge the traditional divide between body and mind, or immanence and transcendence, thereby surpassing any one-sided attempt to understand human existence in either objective physiological or subjective psychological terms alone. For Merleau-Ponty, "man taken concretely is not a psyche joined to an organism, but this back-and-forth movement of existence [*va-et-vient de l'existence*] that sometimes allows itself corporeal being, while at other times it goes into personal acts" (PhP 104). And these poles of existence are not just connected but are interwoven—they *s'entrelacent*, as Merleau-Ponty put it—and they are thus deeply implicated mutually. Between the psychological and the physiological there are, Merleau-Ponty claimed, "relations of exchange" [*rapports d'échange*], such that "there is not a single movement in a living body that is completely accidental with regard to psychic intentions, nor a single psychic act that has not found at least its germ or its general outline [*son germe ou son dessin général*] in physiological dispositions" (PhP 104).

This general claim is, to say the least, quite audacious. It provides a good expression of the basic sense of Merleau-Ponty's conception of the irreducible ambiguity of human *être-au-monde*, and it is corroborated, at least partly, in and through the descriptive accounts of corporeality that are elaborated in the subsequent chapters of Part I. Yet, a moment of frank reflection would suffice to make it clear that description alone, however extensive and richly elaborated it may be, could never suffice to *prove* the full scope of the claim in any strict sense. It is thus worth noting what is at stake in it for Merleau-Ponty. On the one hand, there is the denial of any "free-floating" mental activity, that is, mental activity that would be autonomous of its corporeal situation. And on the other hand, there is the converse denial of any bodily movement that would be fully devoid of or detached from any psychological meaning. As discussed above in the Preface, the first denial is important for Merleau-Ponty inasmuch as he wanted to be able to claim his phenomenological descriptions as genuine *philosophical* contributions, and this requires establishing that they cannot be surpassed by a higher-level intellection capable of disambiguating them. Or, in other words, he needs to claim that philosophy itself is not a free-floating or disembodied mental activity. And as noted above, this is the task that Merleau-Ponty takes up explicitly in Part III of *Phenomenology of Perception*. The second denial is related closely to this first one, and can even be seen as providing its fundamental source of support. The denial that there is any human bodily movement or gesture that would be wholly independent of personal or existential meaning is important for Merleau-Ponty because of its relation to the claim that human existence as a whole, hence *inclusive of its natural organismic dimension*, falls within the movement of human history: "the organism and its monotonous dialectics are . . . *not* extraneous to history as though inassimilable to it" (PhP 104, emphasis added).

■

Here, we need to take a step back. A big step, in fact. For it seems likely that in making this last point, Merleau-Ponty had György (Georg) Lukács in mind, specifically certain points that Lukács made in his 1923 book, *History and Class Consciousness*. Before getting into that directly (in the first part of Chapter 3), though, it may be helpful to lay out some contextual considerations concerning Lukács, as well as the "origins" of Merleau-Ponty's philosophical attachment to Marxism.

Considerations on Lukács

A collection of essays written and revised between 1919 and 1923, *History and Class Consciousness*, is widely and duly regarded as being by far the most theoretically sophisticated contribution to the philosophical discourse of Marxism in the early part of the twentieth century, and as having inaugurated the philosophical tradition of "Western" Marxism (Arato and Breines 1979, 190–209; cf. Anderson 1976)—a label [*le marxisme « occidental »*] that Merleau-Ponty himself coined in *Adventures of the Dialectic* to designate theoretical developments which, emerging in western European contexts after 1917, were at variance with Marxist theory as officially promulgated by the USSR. As is well known, this work, *Adventures of the Dialectic*, was a trenchant examination of existing tendencies within Marxist philosophy that Merleau-Ponty wrote a decade or so after *Phenomenology of Perception*, and it includes an important chapter on Lukács (AD 43–80/30–58). *History and Class Consciousness* is thus often addressed (though rarely in any detail) in discussions of *Adventures of the Dialectic*. But it is seldom referred to in commentaries on Merleau-Ponty's earlier work, including *Phenomenology of Perception*, even those that do pay some attention to the political views he held at the time. As I will be arguing for a view of Lukács that would make *History and Class Consciousness* out to be an especially important source for Merleau-Ponty's existential phenomenology, a source on par with Husserl (cf. Miller 1979, 205f), it would be helpful, before getting into any substantive issues, first to make some comments pertaining to the reception of Lukács' text in France in order to contextualize what I take to be its general but undue neglect within Merleau-Ponty scholarship. These comments will lend some support to my argument, although this support will be limited and indirect. Before returning to Lukács and his connection with Merleau-Ponty's approach to embodiment (Chapter 3), then, it will also be helpful to elaborate some sociobiographical conjectures concerning the advent of Merleau-Ponty's attachment to Marxism. These remarks will lend further indirect support to my claims, but they will also do so in a way that casts instructive light on Merleau-Ponty's postwar thought in general.

History and Class Consciousness in France

As noted, Lukács, and *History and Class Consciousness* in particular, are seldom referred to in commentaries on Merleau-Ponty's existential phenomenology. There seem to be four main reasons for this.

The first and most direct reason is quite simply that Merleau-Ponty himself hardly seemed to talk about Lukács at the time—his only explicit written reference to him was in an article first published in 1946 (SNS 223/126). *Prima facie*, this suggests a strong presumption against the claim that *History and Class Consciousness* was a point of reference at all—let alone an especially important source—for Merleau-Ponty. To be sure, there is the countervailing fact that it was not in Merleau-Ponty's style always to devote explicit discussions to even his most important sources. But still, the absence of any published discussion is suspicious.[6]

The second and broadest reason is that *History and Class Consciousness* was not widely discussed at all in the 1930s and 1940s. This is due primarily to the fact that shortly after its publication, Lukács, along with some other communist intellectuals, were harshly denounced by Grigory Zinoviev and others at the Fifth Congress of the Communist International in June 1924.[7] This denunciation did not involve any sort of detailed philosophical critique, and it is highly unlikely that Zinoviev actually read *History and Class Consciousness*. Rather, fed by a series of critical reviews suggesting that Lukács' book amounted to a denial of objective scientific status of dialectical materialism and hence the assertion of some form of subjective idealism with ultraleftist implications, and fed as well by a growing mood of anti-intellectualism, especially with regard to new philosophical approaches to questions concerning revolution, Zinoviev's critique reflected the fact that the reception of Lukács' book collided directly with the USSR's need to consolidate and reinforce its ideological hegemony within the international Communist movement (see Arato and Breines 1979, 176–82, 186–9). Thus, despite some early positive accounts (Arato and Breines 1979, 182–6), this brusque official dismissal by and large held sway, and Lukács himself effectively capitulated, disavowing the work in order to accommodate himself, at least outwardly, to the new emerging Stalinist orthodoxy.[8]

History and Class Consciousness was thus absent from subsequent political and philosophical discussions occurring under the auspices of official Communism. So while it continued to breathe and have what Hans Mayer called an extensive "underground impact" (Mayer 1949, 219, cited in Arato and Breines 1979, 203) within certain circles of intellectual subculture in central Europe—and in Germany especially (Arato and Breines 1979, 200–9), where it was an important resource for much of the "critical theory" that emerged from the *Institut für Sozialforschung* in Frankfurt (Feenberg 1981)—it was firmly marginalized elsewhere until much later.

The third and fourth reasons follow from the second: *History and Class Consciousness* was not a point of reference for the political and philosophical debates that occurred within French Marxism during the interwar period, nor in the immediate postwar context. With regard to the former, for example, the work of the *Philosophies* group—"the first notable circle of French Marxist philosophers" (Jay 1984, 277) in the 1920s and 1930s, including Pierre Morhange, Henri Lefebvre, Georges Friedmann, Paul Nizan, Georges Politzer, and Norbert Guterman—was carried out without any apparent familiarity with Lukács (Burkhard 2000, 72). And this was the case despite sharing some common philosophical ground with Lukács.[9] Something similar may be true of others as well. The seeming exception that serves to corroborate the political and philosophical invisibility of Lukács in interwar France would lie in the fact that one of the earliest references to *History and Class Consciousness* by a French writer was in Raymond Aron's 1935 book on contemporary German *sociology* (Aron 1981, 64f).

As for the immediate postwar period, Lukács was largely absent here too. It is widely recognized that it was the work of Lucien Goldmann, who had studied with Lukács, that served as the main conduit whereby Lukács' thought was introduced into the French intellectual context (Axelos 1960; Furter 1961; Poster 1975, 47f; Gutting 2001, 235 n17), and that it was on this basis that *History and Class Consciousness* became "a most important influence on the direction of French Marxism after the Liberation" (Poster 1975, 44)—although until the publication of a French translation in 1960, even that was described as "a considerable *underground* influence" (Axelos 1960, 5, emphasis added). Yet this work by Goldmann dates from later in the 1940s (Goldmann 1948), *after* the immediate postwar period that concerns us here.

Taking these considerations into account, the picture that emerges is one of Merleau-Ponty as a pioneer with regard to the reception of Lukács in France. Jay's comment to the effect that Merleau-Ponty was "one of the first French thinkers to appreciate the significance of *History and Class Consciousness*" (1984, 367) is thus certainly true (cf. Schmidt 1985, 201 n196; Hughes 1968, 192), and in terms of those who took up this work positively (unlike, say, Aron), it may even be the case that he was *the* first to do so. But even if there were others—and there is absolutely no reason to exclude this possibility—the following conditional is clearly true: *if* Merleau-Ponty did draw upon *History and Class Consciousness* in working out his existential phenomenology, then his encounter and engagement with this text necessarily occurred prior to the formation of any significant context of political or philosophical discussion of Lukács' work in France (see Axelos 1960; Furter 1961). This point is relevant to the argument that I shall make about Lukács being an important point of reference for Merleau-Ponty's existential phenomenology, inasmuch as it would offer an explanation of sorts for the lack of explicit published discussion concerning Lukács on the part of Merleau-Ponty, and of other forms of contextual evidence that would support my claim—the relevant context simply did not exist yet, nor was it Merleau-Ponty's intention to try to create one.[10] The lack of such discussion in the immediate postwar period and earlier should thus not be taken as evidence of a lack of interest or familiarity. This does not, of course, contribute directly to showing that Lukács was an important source for Merleau-Ponty. But it does challenge some of the assumptions that support its denial.

Here, we should just add that by the mid-1950s, when Merleau-Ponty wrote and published *Adventures of the Dialectic*, such a context did indeed exist. The fact that, by far, Merleau-Ponty's most extended published discussion of Lukács was made on the pages of this critique of existing tendencies within Marxist philosophy thus has the consequence of closely associating Lukács with what is generally taken to be Merleau-Ponty's *rejection* of Marxism. Such a one-sided view is, I think, quite misleading, but it is perhaps also partly because of it that *History and Class Consciousness* is not recognized—even when the self-critical dimension of *Adventures of the Dialectic* itself *is* recognized—as having been a crucial inspiration for Merleau-Ponty's own Marxist politics in the immediate postwar period. That is, such a view has the effect of distorting the fact, if it is one, that Merleau-Ponty's earlier Marxism had drawn upon what was by all accounts the most theoretically sophisticated and innovative precursor of Marxist philosophy, as opposed to merely applying an existential sugarcoating to official Communist doctrine, say, or else flirting with a voguish but theoretically flimsy and eclectic radicalism. Recognition of this would make it more difficult to justify any offhand dismissal of Merleau-Ponty's Marxism as merely a short-lived misapplication of phenomenological ideas, or else (or perhaps also) as a matter of being swept up in the politics of the immediate postwar period in France.

This brings up the fundamental point, which concerns the relation between Marxism and phenomenology within Merleau-Ponty's thought. There is a common assumption among readers of Merleau-Ponty to the effect that his attachment to Marxism is to be understood as *theoretically secondary* to his commitment to phenomenology, as being derivative from or extraneously tacked onto it. It is only in virtue of such a view that many readers are able to subtract Merleau-Ponty's early Marxism out of their view of his work as a whole as an inessential—and, for most, regrettable—deviation (see above, Preface). The superficial plausibility of this subtractive move, however, would be upset if it could be shown that *History and Class Consciousness* was an important source for Merleau-Ponty's earlier postwar outlook. For Lukács was by no means *au courant* at the time, even if Marxism more generally was in vogue, and in terms of philosophical rigor and sophistication, Lukács' work is arguably on the same level of that of Husserl. This could lend indirect support to a view that sees Marxism and phenomenology as standing on a roughly equal footing in Merleau-Ponty's postwar thought, such that rather than a blithe dismissal, what would be required to subtract the former would be a more worked-out argument to the effect that within Merleau-Ponty's work, Marxism and phenomenology were "implicitly in conflict on a number of points" (Miller 1979, 205ff), that is, that their combination represents an incoherent and hence unworkable theoretical amalgam. Or, in other words, that Merleau-Ponty dabbled temporarily in Marxism against his better (read: phenomenological) judgment, that in doing so, he "betray[ed] his own best instincts" (Jay 1984, 371).

This claim is, I believe, fundamentally mistaken, and it is principally against it that my present argument is directed. For I want to claim that Merleau-Ponty did indeed draw upon Lukács' work, and I want to do this by identifying substantive points of connection on the basis of what textual evidence there is. But my interest is not primarily in claiming that Lukács was a source for Merleau-Ponty's *political* views, that is, his reinterpretation of Marxism. Given the low regard in which the latter is currently held by most Merleau-Ponty scholars, such a result would be of limited interest. Rather, I am primarily interested in claiming that Lukács was a *philosophical* source for Merleau-Ponty, that is, that *as a Marxist philosopher*, he was a source for Merleau-Ponty's *phenomenology*, that is, his reinterpretation of Husserl. Beyond simply denying the theoretical secondariness of Marxism within Merleau-Ponty's postwar thought by affirming that its status is comparable to that of phenomenology proper, I want to claim that these traditions are essentially interwoven in Merleau-Ponty's project of existential phenomenology and that in at least some respects, including methodologically, priority goes to certain ideas drawn from his view of Marxism. Contrary to the suggestion of a theoretical inconsistency, then, I submit that *it is only on the basis of certain ideas drawn from Lukácsian Marxism that Merleau-Ponty's reinterpretation of Husserlian phenomenology itself actually achieves methodological coherence*—that with regard to how the project of phenomenology could, contra Fink, be rendered viable on an existential and corporeal basis, basing it on certain Marxist ideas drawn from Lukács *was* Merleau-Ponty's "better judgment" at the time, that he *was* drawing on his "best instincts" in doing so.

Conjectures on the origins of Merleau-Ponty's Marxism

This goes against the grain of most current views of Merleau-Ponty's work. It may be helpful, then, to consider the "origins" of Merleau-Ponty's postwar thought, and how he first came to embrace the different traditions that are woven together therein. For the claims that I will be making would receive further indirect reinforcement if it could be shown that Merleau-Ponty developed a serious interest in Marxism, and in Lukács in particular, *before* making a decisive turn to phenomenology.[11] For this would make it plausible to suggest that his uptake of phenomenology occurred within the terms of a preexisting Marxist orientation. As with anything else concerning the earlier and largely undocumented part of Merleau-Ponty's intellectual life, however, such a suggestion would be very difficult to substantiate conclusively.[12] In particular, there would seem to be no way to identify when Merleau-Ponty first took up *History and Class Consciousness*, nor would it seem possible, even in principle, to pinpoint in any precise way when his "definitive" uptake of phenomenology occurred.

If, however, it is accepted that *The Structure of Behavior* predates that uptake—a claim that seems fairly uncontentious, and if we leave Lukács aside for now and just focus on Marxism in general, then it would suffice to show that that text, completed in 1938, reflects relevant Marxist commitments to a suitable degree.

Such a proposal may seem like a nonstarter, though, given that *The Structure of Behavior* does not mention Marx, and does not have any readily apparent political aspect at all. But the question is: does it have a Marxist *philosophical* aspect? Given its evident Hegelian character, such a claim may not be such a stretch. Consider, for example, Cooper's argument (1975) to the effect that *The Structure of Behavior* bears very strongly the influence of Alexandre Kojève's reading of Hegel (cf. Cooper

1976).[13] This conclusion is, I think, ultimately and quite seriously mistaken.[14] But it does emphasize the existential-Hegelian character of the book, and also raises the possibility of a Marxist inflection of that character, given that Kojève's reading of Hegel's *Phenomenology* did involve elements of a certain kind of Marxism (and Kojève may even have been familiar with Lukács' work). Thus, in pointing out that Merleau-Ponty started studying Marx "seriously" around 1934 or 1935, and that he was among a group organized by Marcel Moré to discuss Auguste Cornu's 1934 work *Karl Marx, l'homme et l'œuvre*, Geraets implicitly connected this to Kojève (1971, 25ff).

But there is something implausible about this connection. For even if Merleau-Ponty later stated that Kojève's lectures "created a deep impression" on him (1956, 436; cited in Rabil 1967, 77), and although there are some points of philosophical common ground,[15] it would be very hard to overlook how Merleau-Ponty disagreed utterly with Kojève on certain fundamental issues of substance, for example, whether history is a closed or open totality, something to be known absolutely or to be lived venturesomely. For contrary to Kojève's retrospective contemplation of history as a completed process, history for Merleau-Ponty was something to be engaged in and made:

> we are not spectators of a completed history, we are actors in an open history, our praxis maintains what is not to be known but rather to be done as an irreducible ingredient of the world, and that is why the world is not just to be contemplated but also transformed. What is for us unimaginable [*irreprésentable*] is a consciousness without a future and a history with an end. As long as there are men, therefore, the future will be open, and there will only be methodical conjectures but no absolute knowledge. (HT 99/92, translation modified)

This militantly engaged perspective contrasts sharply with Kojève, but it is certainly on the same wavelength as Lukács in *History and Class Consciousness* in terms of subordinating historical knowledge to historical praxis: "It is true that reality [*Wirklichkeit*] is the criterion for the correctness of thought. But reality is not, it becomes. . . . Only he who is called upon and willing to bring about the future [*nur wer die Zukunft herbeizuführen berufen und gewillt ist*] can see the concrete truth of the present" (HCC 223/204, translation modified). And for both Merleau-Ponty and Lukács, although for different reasons, there are thematic affinities with the young Marx's critique of Hegel from a revolutionary perspective.

But the view in question here from Merleau-Ponty stems from the postwar period— can something along these lines be found already in *The Structure of Behavior*, a text that was completed shortly after Merleau-Ponty's attendance at Kojève's lectures? In an underappreciated work, Douglas Low (1987) analyzed Merleau-Ponty's first book in a way that supplies an affirmative answer to this question. Specifically, his argument concerned *methodology*, and his central claim was that *The Structure of Behavior* exhibits an existential-dialectical *method* that is in significant conformity with the approach taken by Marx. What is key here is less the claim that Marx, whose dialectical credentials are beyond dispute, was a sort of proto-existentialist than the claim that Merleau-Ponty, circa 1938, was "a thoroughgoing dialectician" (Low 1987, 175). Low argued for this view on the basis of a close reading of *The Structure of Behavior*, a reading that serves to foreground three key features of Merleau-Ponty's Gestalt-theoretic notion of structure: the interconnectedness of all things, the interpenetration of subject and object, and the overall framework of a nonreductive hierarchy of mutually influencing forms of integration—the physical order, the order of life and that of consciousness (Low 1987, 162–75). Through comparison with representative texts from Marx, Low then claimed that "Marx's methodological approach parallels Merleau-Ponty's on a point-by-point basis" (Low 1987, 192), such that in *methodological* terms, there is a "striking similarity" between them (Low 1987, 191; cf. 175, 195).

We need not, for present purposes, rehearse the exegetical details of Low's claim. I should just like to say that his take on *The Structure of Behavior* is generally sound and, moreover, quite valuable in terms of understanding Merleau-Ponty. But it does have some limitations that are worth mentioning.

For instance, we should note that although Merleau-Ponty does not explore this explicitly in *The Structure of Behavior*, for which reason Low does not touch on it either, the dialectical methodological perspective under consideration here would lend itself readily to considerations of social and historical transformation. For, as Merleau-Ponty saw it, with a direct allusion to Hegel's philosophy of history, each "order" represents "the institution of a new dialectic" in such a way that "higher behavior retains the subordinated dialectics in the present depths of its existence, from that of the physical system and its topographical conditions to that of the organism and its 'milieu'" (SC 224/207f). Thus in the same way that animal life is conditioned by but irreducible to mere physical existence, the structure of human life likewise sublates the vital order of animal life dialectically—both human existence and animal life alike involve "a retaking and 'new structuration' [« *nouvelle structuration* »]" of the preceding level (SC 199/184), while in both cases, "all integration presuppose[es] the normal functioning of subordinated formations, which always demand their own due [*réclament toujours leur propre bien*]" (SC 227/210). This implies a point about historicity which, as such, can be taken as having significant political ramifications: "What defines man is not the capacity to create a second nature – economic, social, cultural – beyond biological nature; it is rather the capacity of going beyond created structures in order to create others" (SC 189/175).[16]

More importantly, though, Low's discussion of *The Structure of Behavior* tends to overlook what is actually most interesting. For in presenting Merleau-Ponty as attempting to avoid both materialist reductionism or critical idealism by claiming that "[d]ialectical structure does not occur only in nature or only in consciousness," but rather that "[i]t requires a synthesis of both, [a] synthesis which takes places in perception or lived, active experience" (Low 1987, 192), Low does not consider how this result presented Merleau-Ponty with a major new problem, to wit, how to understand perceptual consciousness, as well as its relation to intellectual consciousness. For in affirming that "the dialectic is found in the synthesis of the in-itself and the for-itself," and that this synthesis occurs in "lived perception" (Low 1987, 174), Merleau-Ponty may have definitively nullified the threat of materialist reduction. But he thereby admittedly came very close to some kind of idealism. This is the reason why *The Structure of Behavior* is in a certain way inconclusive, culminating as it does with a call to "to define transcendental philosophy anew" (SC 241/224). Low thus seems to read *The Structure of Behavior* partly through the lens of *Phenomenology of Perception*, in the sense that this problematic aspect of his understanding of "structure" is not seen as being particularly problematic at all.

Furthermore, though, Low does exactly the same thing with Marx, only in this case, the situation is slightly more complicated. For in claiming that Marx grounded his understanding of dialectic in "lived, active experience" and that he performed "the same synthesis between the in-itself and the for-itself that we find Merleau-Ponty performing" (Low 1987, 195), Low goes well beyond the textual evidence from Marx that he presents in his discussion. It is not that the point is incorrect. But here, too, the texts are clearly being read retrospectively, except that in this case, the relevant lens is not a subsequent text from Marx himself. What is it, then? Low himself tells us in an overview statement concerning his analysis of Marx: "with the help of *Lukács*, we will point up the dialectical character of Marx's method" (Low 1987, 161, italics added). And indeed, Low's account of the dialectical character of Marx's method, although relatively brief, relies heavily on points made in *History and Class Consciousness* (Low 1987, 189ff).

There is thus a plausible case to be made to the effect that *The Structure of Behavior* does indeed betray a philosophical orientation to Marxism, which would—on the assumption that that text does likewise—precede Merleau-Ponty's definitive turn to phenomenology. More specifically, given what we have just seen, it may even be plausibly suggested that this orientation is one that bears its affinities less with Marx himself directly than with Lukács, in particular, with regard to the pivotal point concerning the mediation of dialecticity in general by consciousness, that is, by the dialectical relation between subject and object. To be clear, this would not necessarily imply any sort of direct influence. There may well have been some, but I am not going to make an argument to that effect—pointing out the plausibility of the connection suffices for my purposes here.

But I also want to highlight a pair of important related points. First, Merleau-Ponty was clearly not fully content with the position elaborated in *The Structure of Behavior*, and he felt the need to develop it further in terms of a more worked-out account of perceptual consciousness—something he did, of course, in *Phenomenology of Perception*. If what I claimed above is true, then this suggests that the latter work stems as much (or more) from a desire to supply a corrective to Lukácsian Marxism as from simply advancing phenomenology for its own sake or for any other reason. Second, though, this working out, which certainly pertains to his definitive uptake of phenomenology, remained consistent with the overall dialectical framework presented in *The Structure of Behavior*. Given these points, it could be maintained with a high degree of plausibility that the underlying rationale behind Merleau-Ponty's reinterpretation of Husserlian phenomenology was to shore up a Lukácsian-Marxist philosophical framework with regard to its account of consciousness. I will return to this below.

■

Some readers may remain skeptical, and so we might still wonder about the origins of the Marxist perspective which, following Low, I have claimed exists in *The Structure of Behavior*. After all, it may remain somewhat implausible to claim that the material dealt with in that text would just by itself prompt a Marxist orientation—although there were certainly contributions being made to the field of psychology in France from theorists with distinctively Marxist outlooks (e.g. Politzer 1928).[17] Having claimed that Kojève cannot be considered a major positive influence on Merleau-Ponty in this regard, how might we make sense of the latter's having adopted a dialectical framework consistent with Marxism by 1938?

Usually when Merleau-Ponty's earlier intellectual development is considered, a prominent role is assigned to his Catholic religious outlook. This is entirely appropriate. However, it is also usually assumed that a sharp break separates his religious faith from his Marxism, that is, that they are basically incompatible, such that the demise of the former is a necessary condition of the advent of the latter. To be sure, there is a certain conceptual incompatibility. But concerning how Merleau-Ponty came to Marxism, the assumption in question is seriously misleading, and as such contributes to rendering falsely implausible the suggestion that Merleau-Ponty's attachment to Marxism dates from the mid-1930s, prior to his definitive uptake of phenomenology. For as a matter of fact, the context within which Merleau-Ponty initially developed a serious philosophical interest in Marxism was precisely a *religious* one—the Catholic "discovery" of the young Marx in the period of the Popular Front (1934–38). Approaching this within the broader context of intellectual *engagement* in interwar France, (a theme to which I shall return in the Conclusion), we will see how this interest on the part of Merleau-Ponty came to transform the Christian conception of "incarnation" and thus ultimately to eclipse his erstwhile religious faith from within. These considerations will complete the conjectural excursus on the backstory, so to speak, of Merleau-Ponty's postwar Marxism. This will lead us back in the next chapter to consider Lukács directly, which will then return us to the discussion with which the present chapter began, namely, the initial analysis of embodiment in *Phenomenology of Perception*, where Merleau-Ponty made the first references to Saint Exupéry.

Merleau-Ponty and *engagement*

Merleau-Ponty's intellectual development during the 1930s unfolded in a social context in which increasing economic and political crises, along with the lessons of the Dreyfus Affair,[18] made political abstention or complacency among French intellectuals, especially among Merleau-Ponty's generation, increasingly disrespectable. To be sure, in 1927, Julien Benda had written his notorious diatribe against the "treason" [*trahison*] committed by intellectuals [*clercs*] who involve themselves directly in partisan politics, rather than remaining independently committed to the values of truth, freedom, and justice considered in timeless universal terms. While not *per se* opposed to intellectuals publicly taking positions on political issues (he himself had been a "Dreyfusard"), Benda was concerned about the trend he perceived in the decades following the Dreyfus Affair in which intellectuals came to mistakenly "praise attachment to the particular and denounce the feeling of the universal" (Benda 1927, 97). For this resulted in the subordination of intellectual work to "political passions"—for example, those of nation, race, or class—and in Benda's view, this amounted to a betrayal on the part of intellectuals of their historical responsibility to give voice to universal values from a position of detached autonomy. (It is far from clear whether Benda himself truly lived up to this ideal, however, as the presentation of his argument was chequered by what would appear to be a rabid anti-Germanism.)

Although Benda's book provoked quite a stir, it did nothing whatsoever to alter the trend of which it was ostensibly so critical. On the contrary, in the following decade, the urgency with which intellectuals in France were faced with the question of political commitment intensified greatly—Benda himself even came to revise his considered view in a way that allowed, and even required, a certain measure of leftist partisanship (Benda 1937, 164). Specifically, during the Popular Front period and thereafter, French intellectuals were confronted with the question of *engagement*, which may be defined in this way: "the political or social action of an intellectual who has realized that abstention is a ruse, a commitment to the *status quo*, and who makes a conscious and willful choice to enter the arena, never abandoning his or her critical judgement" (Schalk 1979, 25). It is safe to say that Merleau-Ponty accepted this responsibility during the 1930s and it led, by way of his own involvement in Resistance-related activities during the war, to the existential Marxism that he espoused in the immediate postwar period.

But in considering this aspect of Merleau-Ponty's biography, it is very important to keep in mind that the development of his political thinking was connected inseparably to his early religious outlook. A believing Catholic until at least 1936,[19] he had been, as he later put it, "led 'to the Left' [« *à gauche* »] by the demands of his faith" (SNS 172).[20] Initially oriented toward social Catholicism and Christian democracy, from early on, his position was within earshot, so to speak, of Marxism.[21] It may therefore prove useful to approach Merleau-Ponty as having been, in a certain sense, pulled between the politics of two other men, both also trained as philosophers, but who, unlike Merleau-Ponty, had renounced their academic vocation: Paul Nizan and Emmanuel Mounier. It is worth considering briefly that and how it was from his position *as* a philosopher who chose to remain *intégré*—that is, within the system—that Merleau-Ponty worked out an independent position that transcended the tension between politics and religion.

Merleau-Ponty knew of Nizan from the École normale supérieure (ENS), although they were not particularly close (like Sartre, Nizan was a couple of years older). Like Merleau-Ponty, Nizan was once an observant Catholic. But he foreswore that early and joined the Parti communiste français (PCF) in 1928 (see Cohen-Solal 1980, 64–9; Scriven 1988, 10–25). He became a very dedicated and prolific member for over a decade, until dramatically quitting in 1939, following news of the Nazi-Soviet pact, which he considered a bitter betrayal. He was killed at Dunkirk in May 1940.

As noted above, as part of the *Philosophies* group, Nizan was involved in publishing some of Marx's early manuscripts in France. He was also a novelist (see Leiner 1970; Scriven 1988; Ishaghpour 1990), and a work from 1932 in particular, *Les chiens de garde*, a scathing critique of the academic philosophical establishment (especially Léon Brunschvicg) and a clarion call to philosophical activism (see Schalk 1973; cf. Maublanc 1935), posed for academic philosophers like Merleau-Ponty a compelling imperative to come to terms with the implicit political consequences of his chosen profession. This work was in part a direct retort to Benda (1927), and it attempted to put a very different spin on the idea of the "treason" of the intellectuals, in that for

Nizan, this would be committed when one tried to remain *au-dessus de la mêlée* by abstaining from progressive political commitment. Nizan thus represented something for Merleau-Ponty, the importance of which was greatly out of proportion to their actual personal relationship. For the two had similar bourgeois backgrounds, and so, the fact that Nizan himself openly committed a kind of "treason" in the sense of turning against his class and engaging himself uncompromisingly in the project of revolutionary working class politics was something by which Merleau-Ponty was philosophically but also personally fascinated. Not that he followed suit, of course. But the fact that Merleau-Ponty devoted a considerable portion of the Preface to *Signs* (Signs 32–47/23–35) to commenting critically on the Preface that Sartre had written for the republication of Nizan's 1931 novel *Aden Arabie* (Nizan 1960), along with the fact that he also responded to the critique to which those comments were subjected by Olivier Todd, Nizan's son-in-law (Todd 1961; Merleau-Ponty 1961), testifies to the deep and enduring significance of Nizan as a figure of political commitment in Merleau-Ponty's thought.

In contrast stood the left-wing Catholic personalism of Emmanuel Mounier. In 1932, Mounier founded the journal *Esprit* (the first issue appeared in October) which, as "a meeting ground for Catholic and non-Catholic 'revolutionary' intellectuals" (Curtis 1991, 166), contributed in an unsurpassed way to the conceptual formation of the term *engagement*, in particular by conferring upon it a nonconformist, *anti*-party connotation. Although both Nizan and Mounier spoke of radical commitment in opposition to the prevailing order, Mounier sought a third way, that is, to "take sides without being a party man" (Schalk 1979, 20). The difference was expressed in the distinction articulated by Paul-Louis Landsberg—whom Ricoeur once described as the most influential philosophical figure in the prewar development of *Esprit* (cited in Hellman 1981, 286f n44) —between *engagement* and what he called *embrigadement*, which denoted party-style activism (Landsberg 1937, 182). The personalist perspective of *Esprit*, in presenting a radicalized collective sense of *témoignage*—that is, bearing witness (for Christ), which originally implied *individual* acts of martyrdom—as the proper realization of *engagement*, was thus able to convey, at least for a few years, a viable *nonconformist* critique of established liberal democracy and of French (and European) bourgeois society in general (see Rauch 1971, 98–149).

Merleau-Ponty was interested in *Esprit* from the time of its first appearance, while he was teaching in Beauvais (Le Baut 2009, 136), and he accepted its orientation, although perhaps without ever finding it fully satisfactory (see above, note 20). But given his Catholic background, he certainly must have been closer to *it* than to any PCF activists like Nizan. The fresh contrast which personalism presented to the Christian establishment in France—and to the political scene in general—must not be underestimated. Hellman described it as "exhilarating" for those in a situation like that of Merleau-Ponty: "No longer need one feel oneself part of a rearguard for the retreating Christian Middle Ages; one was now in the vanguard of the second Renaissance." Importantly, especially for Merleau-Ponty, this meant that affiliation by no means entailed a "conversion" to Mounier's own views: "Even if one found some of Mounier's rhetoric unrealistic it was stimulating to work with some of France's brightest intellectuals at elaborating something new" (Hellman 1981, 86).

Merleau-Ponty most likely became more involved in the movement around *Esprit* during his research sojourn in Paris in 1933–34. In late 1933, "*Esprit* restated its determination to have an autonomous philosophical base," and by early 1934, "Mounier organized study groups with Landsberg . . . to define 'the personalist-communitarian philosophy of our movement'" (Hellman 1981, 80–1). In May 1934, when many "newcomers to *Esprit*" were divided into research groups on various political and scientific issues, the "philosophers group" was divided into subgroups to "'define means of spiritual efficacity', to study Marx [as was noted above] with the aid of Marcel Moré, and to study 'our metaphysics of the Person and the Community'" (Hellmann 1981, 81), that is, Scheler's notions of *Gesamtperson* and *Lebensgemeinschaft*. Although Merleau-Ponty taught in Chartres in 1934–35, where he was correspondent for *Esprit* and tried to establish a local "Amis d'*Esprit*" group, upon his return to Paris, he certainly participated in the groups organized around Moré (cf. Geraets 1971, 25), and he may have been connected to the "metaphysics" group as well. And in subsequent years, he also directed *Esprit*'s research group on psychology.

It is crucial to note—although Geraets did not emphasize this—that the role played by Marcel Moré in the development of Merleau-Ponty's early interest in Marx occurred *within* the context of his primarily religious affiliation with *Esprit*. It was initially in connection with Moré and articles that he wrote for *Esprit* (Moré 1934; 1936)—including a detailed exposition of Cornu's groundbreaking 1934 book on the young Marx (Moré 1935), a book which "occupied a central place in the reappraisal of Marxist philosophy which was beginning to emerge in the middle 1930s" (Kelly 1982, 29)—that Catholic intellectuals began to "discover" Marx (cf. Boivin 1936). It is crucial to emphasize that the personalist context with which Merleau-Ponty was closely affiliated was the original epicenter of this newfound Catholic concern with Marxism (Curtis 1991). This was the beginning of the Popular Front period, which among other things was marked by a strategic openness on the part of the PCF toward Catholics, including by 1936 the explicit policy of "*la main tendue*." Most believing Catholics rejected such overtures, perceiving Marxism—which was officially condemned in Pius XI's encyclicals *Quadragesimo Anno* (15 May 1931) and especially *Divini Redemptoris* (19 March 1937)—as "une doctrine diabolique" (Moré 1934, 470). And these Catholics tended to see the Popular Front itself as merely a Communist ploy. But given its success, and given the increasingly dynamic and influential presence of Communist ideas in French cultural and intellectual life (Curtis 2000, 78; cf. Kelly 1982, 47), a simple refusal would have been inadequate. Rather, what many Catholic intellectuals came to see as necessary to retain the hearts and minds of Catholic workers was a two-pronged reply, one that would show (i) that at the level of theoretical principles official Communist doctrine was a consistent and coherent system of atheistic materialism, for which reason it was, contrary to its own claims, fundamentally antihumanist, and as such fundamentally at odds with the worldview of Catholicism;—but also (ii) that Marxism, as a body of thought based on the work of Marx, could be given a very different philosophical interpretation, one that would portray it as having some profound affinities with Catholic thought.

In line with the papal view, this approach was anti-Communist. But it was pitched as a "*positive* anti-Communism" (Curtis 2000, 75f). This is what Mounier referred to as the "constructive critique of communism" that formed part of the mission of *Esprit* from its inception (Mounier 1937, 307), and which aimed "to take up Marxist analyses in order to separate the great work of lasting value from the one-sided philosophical biases" (*Esprit* 1935, 5). In other words, this was a polemically charged Catholic revision of Marxism that endorsed the most compelling aspects of its critique of capitalism and liberal democracy, but also contended that these claims could be maintained most securely and effectively by integrating them into a broadened Catholic perspective. And this was the sense of Moré's view that "accepting Marxism as a completed doctrine was just as untenable as rejecting it entirely" (Moré 1935, 19).

Both aspects of this two-pronged critique necessitated a greatly expanded and deepened knowledge of Marxism. Beginning with *Esprit*, it was thus the case that the level of discussion concerning Marxism within and across various Catholic milieux in France quickly rose considerably (Curtis 1991), and "an extensive literature of articles, pamphlets, and even books" on Communism was produced (Rémond 1960, 67).

Concerning the first point, the resulting discourse primarily took shape as a critique of anthropocentric humanism as the terms in which the PCF was then presenting its Marxism. The idea from the Catholic side was that such a view was inexorably shaped by Marxism's uncompromising commitment to materialism, and that as a result, it effectively nullified any serious concern with spirituality, thereby leading to a gravely impoverished conception of human life. Many Marxists *tried* to portray their theory as sensitive to the range and diversity of human experience, including spiritual richness. In his philosophical selections for the *Morceaux choisis* volume (Marx 1934), Nizan had included relevant passages from Marx's early work on alienation. And Lefebvre's work explicitly presented Marxism as devoted to the realization of the "total man" [*l'homme total*] through the overcoming of all forms of alienation (Lefebvre 1949, 147). But from the perspective of Catholic efforts to conceptualize a complete humanism— what Jacques Martitain called *un humanisme intégral* (1936), or what Gaston Fessard called *un humanisme réel* (1937, 128)—unconstrained by any materialist commitments, the humanism on offer from Marxism could not but appear to be shallow and crude. These efforts thus aimed to highlight a contradiction or inconsistency with the basic materialist presuppositions of Marxism (Maritain 1936, 97). The sort of complete humanistic view that Marxism ostensibly wanted to uphold—along with the "faith in man" that its revolutionary perspective implied (cf. Vignaux 1935; Daniélou 1938)—could only be conceived and maintained consistently and coherently within a Catholic Christian framework—duly updated, of course, through specific theoretical contributions from Marxism and other forms of modern thought.

Hence the second prong of the critique. Here, it was a matter of Catholic intellectuals trying "to assimilate elements of Marxism and to challenge Moscow's and the PCF's interpretation of the doctrine" (Curtis 1991, 166). Based heavily on the newly published *1844 Manuscripts* and *Theses on Feuerbach* (along with Cornu's work), the idea behind these efforts of revision was that Marx himself was, in fact, quite far from being the hardcore materialist as depicted in official doctrine, and that Marxism in general could be rethought accordingly. It was thus the case that despite some efforts on the side of the PCF, especially among those in the *Philosophies* group, discussion of the early philosophical work of Marx was overwhelmingly carried out in the milieux of the Catholic left as part of a strategy designed to pit Marx against received Marxism by assigning theoretical priority to the early work. This was intended to portray the received understanding of the doctrine as a one-sided deviation, and thereby to effect a "surpassing" [*dépassment*] of it in the name of a more authentic— because more *complete*—revolutionary humanism. Recognition of this fact is crucial for understanding the intellectual development of Merleau-Ponty.

The key to these attempts to surpass Marxism, in particular in the case of the personalist revision presented by Moré, lay in the Marxist problematic of alienation, or more specifically, what he called Marx's "*method* of alienation" (Moré 1935, 755, italics added), which is a "genuine method of knowledge" [*une véritable méthode de connaissance*] in virtue of stemming directly from revolutionary activity oriented toward the overcoming of human alienation (Moré 1935, 29). It was this method that enabled Marx "to cast unexpected light on the worst and most cruel drama of the modern world, that of the worker alienating his human substance in commodities," and Moré claimed that essentially the same approach could enable Christians "to understand all the humiliating and degrading aspects of the forms of labour in capitalist society" (Moré 1935, 756). The philosophical grounds for this method lay in the dialectical account of the relation between humans and nature that Marx sketched out in his early work. In Moré's gloss, this led to the following result:

> the identity of the I and the not-I, which is the crowning achievement of idealist philosophy, is replaced by a kind of synthesis between man and nature that obtains in practical activity.... There is no opposition between subject and object, between man and nature, but interpenetration: man is a product of nature just as nature is a product of man. (Moré 1935, 29, 53)

Moré endorsed this view, but he also claimed that it could support a broader approach than Marx actually developed. Specifically, he considered Marx's method to be "strangely deficient" in that it "considers man only from the angle of economic facts, refusing to see the fulgurations that illuminate his angelic and animal sides" (Moré 1935, 19). Related to this, he thought that Marx focused almost exclusively on "social man" to the exclusion of the "unique" individual and his relation to God (Moré 1935, 30). For Moré, it was primarily to redress such accidental shortcomings that Marxism had to be "completed, assimilated, and expanded" (Moré 1934, 568).

But Moré could consider this possible only because he discerned a more significant common ground. In line with Maritain's affirmation that Marx's problematic of alienation was "shaped by Judeo-Christian values" (Maritain 1936, 55 n3), Moré claimed that there is an important analogy between the Pauline view of the postlapsarian world and Marxism's dialectical understanding of history (Moré 1934, 464). In this way, Moré's critical understanding of Marxism read it into a broader theological discourse of "*incarnation*" (Curtis 1991, 168), in the sense of a *militant* orientation toward the worldly realization of spiritual values.[22] Such a discourse was in the ascendant in the interwar period. Seeking to "justify an attitude of incarnation among Christians in the modern world through an appeal to the Incarnation of Christ," this discourse was geared toward creating the social institutions of a *nouvelle chrétienté* (Besret 1964, 38–50)—a new Christian civilization which, in giving expression to the "totalistic" nature of faith (Congar 1935, 218), would be "the incarnation of a true [i.e., total] humanism" (Curtis 2000, 85). For people like Moré, then, "it was as a Christian 'heresy' that Marxism needed to be 'saved' from its own distortions. . . . It was a mode of thought which echoed imperfectly the incarnational themes which were central to the ideal of a *nouvelle chrétienté*" (Curtis 2000, 90; cf. 84). These "incarnational themes" were variously expressed, but they came to be articulated theologically in terms of the doctrine of the Mystical Body of Christ (e.g. Mersch 1936), that is, the originally Pauline conception of the unity of the Church and its members as one with the mystical body of Christ, that is, the body of Christ supernaturally construed in terms of the Christian community and its vocation as an organized and living whole. "All in all, the unity of the Church . . . is that of a very special reality composed of men united by a supernatural life proceeding from God and from Christ" (Congar 1937, 108).

Along these lines, perhaps the most striking—and most philosophically informed— contribution to the Catholic revision of Marxism came from Fessard, who posed the argument against the interpretation of Marxism as an atheistic and anthropocentric humanism in terms of a certain equivocation in Marx's conception of communism— whether it is to be understood teleologically as an end of history, the final overcoming of all alienation, or else as (merely) an open-ended movement of historical progress (cf. Marx 1934, 227f). Based on this equivocation, Fessard presented the Marxists with the following dilemma: either Marxism is atheistic and anthropocentric, in which case it is not oriented to "a real and true Transcendence" [*une Transcendance réelle et vértitable*] (Fessard 1937, 123; cf. 114). But in that case, it can only yield an account of historical progress that necessarily fails to overcome alienation fully (Fessard 1937, 119ff), and its humanistic pretensions are thus effectively voided by its foreclosing upon the existential and spiritual aspirations of humanity. In Fessard's view, these aspirations imply an ideal historical resolution, which in turn implies, beyond material immanence, an affirmation of real transcendence.

And Fessard thought that the considered view of the young Marx was in agreement: "despite its provocative appearances of atheism, Marx's humanism was secretly but truly open to the Infinite" (Fessard 1937, 118). For Fessard, then, "a Marxist capable of penetrating to the spiritual core of his doctrine as revealed in the young Marx would have to admit that his faith in Man . . . was close to the Christian's faith in God" (Curtis 1991, 77). On the other side of the dilemma, then, if Marxism does support a genuine humanism, if it is in fact "a 'total' philosophy" [*une philosophie « totale »*] (Fessard 1937, 124), then this could only be because, even if unbeknownst to itself, it retains a theocentric perspective. In other words, Marxism can draw revolutionary consequences from its critique of alienation only inasmuch as it affirms positively an ideal state of disalienation as a transcendent end of history. And according to Fessard, this affirmation can—indeed, can *only*—be seen as tantamount to the incarnational views alluded to above: "all the principles of the 'real humanism' for which Marx is currently celebrated have always belonged to the Christian consciousness that understands and lives its faith in the Mystical Body of Christ" (Fessard 1937, 128). This is the "profound truth" of Marxism that alone can give proper sense to its dialectical account of history by helping to reveal Marx himself as "an unconscious theorist and an unwitting builder of the Mystical Body of Christ" (Fessard 1937, 189).[23]

Just in terms of the general historical context, it is probable that Merleau-Ponty was familiar with Fessard's argument. But there was a more specific connection, in that both were regular attendees at Kojève's seminar on Hegel. In fact, it is entirely conceivable that Fessard—who was no less knowledgeable than Kojève about Hegel, and who attended largely in order to challenge Kojève's anthropocentric interpretation—interested Merleau-Ponty as much as, if not more than, Kojève himself. Not that Merleau-Ponty agreed with either. The key to this disagreement had to do with the idea of an end of history, an idea that both Kojève and Fessard endorsed, even while they disagreed between themselves as to whether it could be attained in the temporal world (Kojève) or else only in some transcendent sense (Fessard). As we have seen, Merleau-Ponty rejected that idea in no uncertain terms. But he also rejected the dilemma posed by Fessard. It was ultimately not without merit, however, for it did show very clearly that recognition of a profound affinity between Marxism and Christianity—which Merleau-Ponty accepted—was incompatible with a transcendent religious or theocentric interpretation, thereby strongly affirming that the philosophical task at hand was to show how a "total" humanism could be grounded satisfactorily in this-worldly immanence and in conjunction with a conception of historical progress as a kind of teleology without a telos. Despite itself, then, Fessard's argument served to confirm that no less than the attempt on the part of Marxism to found humanism on a strictly materialist basis, Christianity has its own self-defeating contradiction between incarnation and transcendence. Although it may acknowledge divine Incarnation in the human world, it also retains belief in a divine omnipotence residing outside of that world. As a result, "God is not completely with us. Behind the incarnate Spirit there remains that infinite gaze that strips us of all secrets, but also of our freedom, our desire, and our future, reducing us to *visible objects*" (SNS 314/177). Hence, "when it is true to the Incarnation Christianity can be revolutionary. But the religion of the Father is conservative" (SNS 315/177), in that its primary orientation to divine transcendence ultimately leaves it indifferent to this world. This is what accounts for the tendency toward political quiescence that had bothered Merleau-Ponty from the start. What Fessard inadvertently clarified, then, was that commitment to absolute transcendence is incompatible with *engagement*, and that transcendence must be reconceived accordingly, for example, in terms of historically situated humanity. As Merleau-Ponty later put it, "whatever is sound in my belief in the absolute is nothing but my experience of an agreement with myself and others" (SNS 166/95; HT 204f/187). To adapt a statement quoted above from Curtis (1991, 177), what Fessard's argument would have helped someone like Merleau-Ponty to see was that "a Christian capable of penetrating to the political core of his doctrine would have to admit that his faith in God . . . was close to – *or even essentially no different from* – the Marxist's faith in Man." It would follow that "Christians should live out the marriage of the Spirit and human history that started with the Incarnation" (SNS 314/177)—something done best, Merleau-Ponty thought, from a Marxist perspective.

■

Views like those of Moré and Fessard were not in line with Mounier's own perspective, which, less inclined to separate theory from practice, tended to draw a much sharper line between Marxism and Christianity—for example, in his claim that "Marxism is basically a negation of the spiritual as an autonomous, primary, and creative reality" (Mounier 1938, 52). More on that shortly. But let us first say a few more words about Moré's idea of "saving" Marxism by "completing, assimilating, and expanding" it, and how this relates to Merleau-Ponty.

In line with most revisionism of that time, Moré was mainly concerned about rethinking the relation between the economic "base" or "infrastructure" of capitalist society and its ideological "superstructure." The received Marxist idea concerning this relation founded the latter simplistically on the former, thus seeming to imply an objectionable materialist reductionism, one that would be especially anathema to anyone with serious spiritual concerns. This needed to be rethought, and Moré called for sustained theoretical work to be devoted to this problem on the basis of the latest developments in theory and science (Moré 1936, 566ff). This is the sort of research that was promoted more generally under the auspices of *Esprit*. What is significant for our purposes has to do with Merleau-Ponty's own role with regard to psychological research. To be sure, the research that went into *The Structure of Behavior* was not instigated or commissioned by *Esprit*. But there is no good reason to imagine that Merleau-Ponty's academic work during these years prior to 1938 would have been unaffected by his involvement in the personalist milieu. In fact, there are very good reasons to believe that the opposite is true. This would mean that we can regard the dialectical framework developed in *The Structure of Behavior* as an attempt to "complete, assimilate, and expand" the indications concerning the relation between humanity and nature that were sketched out in Marx's early philosophical work, and which, by and large, were positively endorsed by Moré and others at the time. What is of significance here is that in working this out in a philosophically rigorous way, and because in doing so, he was also "following out the Incarnation in all its consequences" (cf. SNS 313/176), Merleau-Ponty arrived at a position which, although it certainly effected a *dépassement* of the philosophical perspective of official Marxism, by no means pointed in the direction that Moré or Mounier or Fessard would have desired. For the claims laid out in that text did not at all affirm the basic presuppositions of Catholicism—for example, no less than any good PCF activist, Merleau-Ponty's work squarely denied that the spiritual is an "autonomous" or "primary" reality. But it did not do so by implying any sort of materialist reduction, for it accorded consciousness an irreducible role with a kind of *relative* autonomy. The dialectical framework presented in *The Structure of Behavior* thus outlined, as least in part, the philosophical basis of a revisioned Marxism which, though secular, laid out a potential common ground for materialism and spiritualism that supported a reciprocally informed conception of *engagement*. As noted above, this work did not represent a finished and final position. But it would be to phenomenology, not Catholic theology, that Merleau-Ponty ultimately turned in order to complete his own rethinking of Marxism, even though Catholic concerns were what originally brought him to consider it seriously. But the incarnational themes remained central.

These considerations clarify how it was that Merleau-Ponty's increasing association with Mounier and *Esprit* was simultaneous with a widening philosophical and political divergence. Recall that for Merleau-Ponty, as for so many others, "*Esprit* was simply the most lively vehicle for Christian thought in France" (Hellman 1981, 99), that is, his commitment to the organization *per se* was not particularly deep. Thus, even if he was far from embracing them, Merleau-Ponty was surely open to the several (quite harsh) critiques to which *Esprit* was subjected by its Marxist critics in the initial 1932–34 period (e.g. Nizan 1933a, 1933b; cf. Hellman 1981, 71–4), that is, during the formative years of its own critique of established Christian democracy. And when, in 1934, the perspective of the organization began to succumb to the tendency, against which Mounier had warned from the beginning, to construe *engagement* in an overly individualistic way that deemphasized its basis in collectively shared values (Schalk 1979, 20f), the difficulties faced by the effort to negotiate a "third way" between quiescent *témoignage* and uncritical *embrigadement* no doubt contributed to Merleau-Ponty's own heightening political consciousness. In the very effort to firm up the philosophical basis of *Esprit* beginning around 1934, a project to which he was surely drawn, Merleau-Ponty was thus out of sync with Mounier. For the motives of the latter ultimately lay in *clearly dissociating* the organization from Marxism, in order to stave off papal condemnation, rather than articulating a philosophically rigorous conception of *engagement* (cf. Hellman 1981, 78f). In other words, as the theoretical basis of *Esprit* matured, its radical edge dulled, such that while Mounier and the organization were growing more distant from Marxism, Merleau-Ponty was moving closer to it.

In this regard, it is noteworthy that Nizan was "an unusually sensitive critic of Catholicism," a Marxist who reproached it less as simply reactionary than as subject to an inherent dilemma whereby its politics would ultimately be torn between Catholicism and fascism (Hellman 1981, 73)—precisely the main axis of Merleau-Ponty's own disillusion. Beginning in 1934, under the auspices of the PCF's Popular Front strategy, Nizan publicly toned down his earlier critique of *Esprit* and was put "in charge of implementing a friendly approach toward the Catholics" (Cohen-Solal 1987, 111). More specifically, "Nizan was entrusted with the task of liaising with fellow-travelling intellectuals," a role which later included "the very specific task of entering into contact with the Catholic community within the framework of the PCF's 'outstretched hand' policy" (Scriven 1988, 83). No specific information is available as to how this affected Merleau-Ponty. However, given it as a contextual factor, and the fact that Merleau-Ponty was increasingly exposed to and had good relations with other Marxist activists, both in the PCF (e.g. François Cuzin) as well as in the Fourth International (e.g. David Rousset), it is safe to say that during the period of the Popular Front, his sympathy for the style of *engagement* and the "spiritual revolution" of *Esprit* began to be questioned by his deepening philosophical interest in political issues about which Mounier et al. tended to be reticent (Rauch 1972, 80ff; cf. Hellman 1981, 87).

Communist overtures to Catholics intensified in the run-up to the historic national election on 3 May 1936, but only fringe elements responded agreeably. Nevertheless, this was apparently enough to raise fears within *Esprit* that *it* would be censured by the nuncio, and once again, this motivated a sharper self-distinction from the nonbelieving left (Hellman 1981, 111f). But following the Popular Front victory, "there was a certain disparity between Mounier's public and his private reactions" (Hellman 1981, 112). Publicly, he warmly greeted the regime of Léon Blum, but privately, he was wholly committed to his own personalist movement. At the end of June, for example, a "well-publicized" debate concerning Christianity and communism, in which Mounier faced Nizan and André Malraux, presented an amicable discussion of common ground (Hellman 1981, 113f). Yet in his report for the same month to Cardinal Verdier, Mounier privately claimed that his was "almost alone among the . . . movements of the young to oppose communism on the metaphysical plane at the same time as competing with it . . . on the plane of technical research." And later that summer, Mounier composed a new *Personalist Manifesto* (Mounier 1938), which "articulated the basic doctrine of the personalist movement" as an alternative to capitalism and communism, and did so in more strongly anti-Marxist terms than had ever been previously used, suggesting that "nothing could be done with Marxists unless they abandoned several basic tenets of their ideology." Needless to say, "[t]he *Personalist Manifesto*'s Third Way did little to encourage co-operation with Blum's coalition, or with Marxism" (Hellman 1981, 116). Although there is no precise record, given his leftward development, it is reasonable to suppose that Merleau-Ponty felt alienated from these developments.

There is no question that Mounier recognized the importance of Marxism, and that he drew from it. In that same report to Verdier, Mounier stated that the goal was to "realize in the name of God and Christ the truth that the Communists are realizing in the name of an atheistic collectivity" (Rauch 1972, 180). Yet, although *Esprit* is often thought of as having had a sympathy, unusual among Catholics, for the Popular Front, "in fact this whole episode illustrated *Esprit*'s unwavering determination to create a 'new politics' on its own" (Hellman 1981, 117).

It was not for *that*, though, that Merleau-Ponty aligned himself with *Esprit*. Even as he was evolving along a different trajectory, Merleau-Ponty remained associated with *Esprit* because it offered a space of optimism and latitude for coming to nonconformist terms with the meaning of *engagement*, that is, a way in which one could *s'engage* in a collective project without having a Party line to toe as in the case, for example, of Nizan. In late 1936, however, Mounier became "determined to form a more broadly based, and more disciplined, movement." Membership requirements were made more stringent, activities became more regimented, and agreement with the tenets of the *Manifesto* became necessary—Mounier saw this time as "the end of our youthful years" (Hellman 1981, 126f). The *Esprit* congress held in the late-summer of 1937 at Jouy-en-Josas may have marked the last straw for Merleau-Ponty. At Jouy, the organization became tighter, less democratic, and "disciplinary standards" for its constituent groups were instituted. It is noteworthy that he was still at this point a co-director of the *Esprit* research group on psychology, since this was the main vector of his divergent intellectual trajectory. But he did not wish to be seen as collaborating with the organization (Geraets 1971, 26 n111). Some of same reasons that had turned him away from the Communist left now occasioned his exit from the personalist milieu. "Transformation of [*Esprit*] from a free and open laboratory of ideas into an organ of a disciplined, ideologically coherent movement soon brought the dissent of several important young intellectuals" (Hellman 1981, 129), and it would seem safe to conjecture that this included Merleau-Ponty.

At some point not long after this congress, Merleau-Ponty broke off contact with Mounier (Geraets 1971, 26; but cf. Le Baut 2009, 136ff), and it was "probably during the months that followed" that Merleau-Ponty "definitively renounced his religious beliefs" (Geraets 1971, 26). The latter point is hard to verify one way or the other. But in any case, consider the recollection of Jean Lacroix:

> Without a doubt it was in returning from Jouy-en-Josas . . . that I had the most intimate conversation with [Merleau-Ponty], the kind that happens between youths who just met and reveal themselves to each other less in what they are as in what they are tending to be. He told me about his doubts, his investigations. A sort of *atheistic humanism* was already coming through in his remarks, and one sensed that for him phenomenology was going to become the whole of philosophy.[24]

The final line of this statement presents a mixed message. As a recollection from a quarter-century later, it confidently reads back into the encounter in question what obviously became the case (i.e., Merleau-Ponty's turn to phenomenology). But it is clearly implied that that had not happened yet, while what was already present in Merleau-Ponty's thinking was what Lacroix called an "atheistic humanism"—this was "*already* coming through," while phenomenology was what "was *going to become* the whole of philosophy." And in this context, "atheistic humanism" would refer unambiguously to Marxism—in some sort of revisioned way, of course, but to Marxism nonetheless.

Recapitulation

Let me briefly recapitulate. I began by considering the references to Saint Exupéry that appear in Merleau-Ponty's initial discussion of embodiment in *Phenomenology of Perception*—and to those I shall return. But I noted that in that discussion Merleau-Ponty made a significant point about the organism in history—although its significance may not be apparent quite yet. In order to disclose that significance, it is necessary to consider the work of Lukács—and it is to this that we shall turn next. But because the main claim that I want to make is that Merleau-Ponty's phenomenological approach to embodiment in *Phenomenology of Perception* is to be understood within a methodological framework inspired by Lukácsian Marxism, and especially because this claim is quite unusual and may initially strike many readers as highly implausible, I offered (a) some contextual considerations that would account for the virtual absence of any explicit discussion of Lukács in Merleau-Ponty's work from the time, and (b) some extended sociobiographical conjectures that would locate the "origins" of Merleau-Ponty's Marxism in the Catholic discovery of Marx during the period of the Popular Front in France, set within the larger context of intellectual *engagement*. The point of these considerations is to set the stage for what now follows, by showing, contrary to standard assumptions, that it is *at least eminently plausible* that Merleau-Ponty's adoption of a recognizably Marxist philosophical outlook has temporal priority over his embrace of phenomenology—a fact, if it is one, that would lend considerable support, albeit indirect, to the claim that certain ideas based in what I shall call an "incarnational Marxism" also have a *logical* priority over the phenomenological approach to embodiment that is central to *Phenomenology of*

Perception. In other words, the foregoing considerations express in historical terms an analogous claim about the relative priority for Merleau-Ponty of Marxism and phenomenology. None of this can be demonstrated with absolute certainty, and the larger claims that I shall make do not strictly depend on this account being true. But the next chapter, and the remainder of the book, will benefit significantly from having it as a backdrop.

Totality and Embodiment

In the last chapter, we deviated from the discussion of Merleau-Ponty's account of embodiment in the chapter of *Phenomenology of Perception* entitled "The Body as an Object and Mechanistic Physiology" by noting that the significance of Merleau-Ponty's denial of any human bodily movement that would be wholly independent of personal or existential meaning lies in the fact that it derives from his claim that human existence as a whole, inclusive of its natural organismic dimension, falls within the overall movement of human history: "the organism and its monotonous dialectics are . . . *not* extraneous to history as though inassimilable to it" (PhP 104, emphasis added). And I suggested that in making *this* claim, Merleau-Ponty had certain ideas from Lukács in mind. We can now consider these ideas directly, and then return to the initial discussion.

Lukács on Totality

The main idea in question was made in the context of the opening essay in *History and Class Consciousness*, entitled "What is Orthodox Marxism?" The central thesis for which Lukács argued in this essay was that what is essentially distinctive about Marxism properly understood—and Marxism *properly* (as opposed to typically) understood is what he meant by *orthodox* Marxism—has to do fundamentally with its *method* as opposed to any substantive claims or doctrinal tenets. "Orthodox Marxism," he wrote, "does not imply the uncritical acceptance of the results of Marx's investigations. It is not the 'belief' in this or that thesis, nor the exegesis of a 'sacred' book. Rather, concerning Marxism, orthodoxy refers exclusively to *method*" (HCC 13/1). And for Lukács, what properly defines the method of Marxism is that it is based on and accords methodological primacy to a dialectical conception of "concrete totality" [*konkrete Totalität*] as "the true category of reality" [*die eigentliche Wirklichkeitskategorie*] (HCC 23/10). This method takes as its point of departure Marx's claim, made in *The Poverty of Philosophy* but reiterated elsewhere, that "the production relations of every society form a whole" (Marx 1976, 166; cf. HCC 22/9), and it reasons on this basis that it is only by construing all seemingly discrete facts of social life as moments of historical becoming, and integrating them dialectically into a totality, that "knowledge of the facts can become knowledge of *reality*" (HCC 21/8).

Such is the first aspect of the main idea in question. But there is more to it. For as Lukács also claimed, "only the dialectical conception of totality is able to comprehend *reality as a social process*" [Wirklichkeit als gesellschaftliches Geschehen] (HCC 27/13). A crucial aspect of Lukács' account of Marxist method concerns the scope of its concept of totality as encompassing human sociohistorical reality *but excluding nature*. Lukács made this point primarily as a critique of Friedrich Engels' efforts (in his popular 1878 work *Anti-Dühring*)[1] to articulate a dialectical account of nature which, following the model of Hegelian monism, would provide a materialist metaphysical grounding for Marxism's dialectical understanding of human history. As Lukács put it:

> This limitation of the method to sociohistorical reality is very important. The misunderstandings that arise from Engels' account of dialectics are based mainly on the fact that Engels, following Hegel's mistaken lead, extended the dialectical method to the knowledge of nature as well. However, the crucial determinants of dialectics – interaction of subject and object, unity of theory and practice, historical change in the reality underlying the categories as the basis of their change in thought, etc. – are absent from our knowledge of nature. (HCC 17 n1/24 n6, translation modified)

Without getting into an overly extended discussion of Lukács, we should note that what is at issue here is the *assimilability* of nature to Marxist historical analysis. In Lukács' view, the dominant theoretical tendency during the period of the Second International (roughly from the 1880s until World War I), strongly informed by Engels' philosophical contributions, sought to "naturalize" (or at least had the effect of "naturalizing") Marxism's account of human history by embedding it within an account of the objective dialectical laws of nature. The main problem with this tendency is that it occludes "the dialectical relation between subject and object in the historical process," with the result that the theory would amount to just another metaphysical interpretation of the world, whereas "for the dialectical method," in accordance with Marx's eleventh thesis on Feuerbach, "the central problem is *to change reality*" (HCC 15f/3). In opposition to that prevailing tendency, then, Lukács, deeply informed by the neo-Kantian distinction between *Natur-* and *Geisteswissenschaften*, affirmed the need to maintain a methodological duality vis-à-vis the natural and the sociohistorical.

This claim is elaborated in some of the other essays that comprise *History and Class Consciousness*, but not uniformly and consistently. For, at some points, Lukács claimed that the standard methods of natural science were all well and good within their proper domain, and that problems arise only when they are misapplied to human society and history (HCC 23/10), thus suggesting an ontological dualism. At other times, though, he implied that the standard methods of natural science are themselves actually skewed ideologically and are consequently unable to yield scientific truth even with regard to nature (HCC 226f/207). The precise status of Lukács' methodological separation of history from nature is thus not altogether clear. In fact, in a well-known remark, Lukács even seemed to go so far as to reduce the natural to the sociohistorical:

> Nature is a social category [*eine gesellschaftliche Kategorie*]. That is, whatever is held to be natural [*was ... als Natur gilt*] at any given stage of social development,

its relation to man and the form in which his confrontation [*Auseinandersetzung*] with it occurs, and thus what nature means in terms of form, content, range and objectivity, this is always socially conditioned. (HCC 240/234, translation modified)

This claim is certainly open to different interpretations, including those that would claim that it betrays, beyond ontological dualism, an underlying idealism. But in fairness to Lukács, he rejected both ontological dualism and any sort of idealism with regard to nature or our knowledge of it. His basic intention was simply to deny "that there is a socially unmediated, i.e., an immediate relationship of humans to nature in the present stage of social development" (TD 106), and to affirm conversely that our "metabolic interchange with nature"—which Lukács glossed regularly as an uninterrupted "exchange of matter between society and nature"—"[is] *mediated socially*" (TD 96), such that "[o]ur consciousness of nature, in other words, our knowledge of nature, is determined by our social being" (TD 100).

Lukács' considered view in *History and Class Consciousness* can thus be understood, first, as a claim to the effect that while nature undoubtedly does really exist in its own right, and that it may function according to objective dialectical laws, both of these claims are fully consistent with there being qualitatively distinct dialectical laws operating in the sociohistorical world, and with these laws being implicated in human knowledge of nature.

Self-evidently nature and its laws existed *before* society (that is to say before humans). Self-evidently the dialectic could not possibly be effective as an *objective principle of development* of society, if it were not already effective as a principle of development of nature before society, if it did not already *objectively exist*. From that, however, follows neither that social development could produce no new, equally objective forms of movement, dialectical moments, nor that the dialectical moments in the development of nature would be *knowable* without the mediation of these new social dialectical forms. (TD 102)

And it is crucial for Lukács to approach these issues—the epistemic status of nature and the dialectical character of society—within the dynamic perspective of "the present as becoming" [*die Gegenwart als Werden*] (HCC 223/204).

The dialectical conception of knowledge as a process does not only include the possibility that in the course of history we get to know new contents, new objects, that we have not known until now. It also means that new contents can emerge, which can be understood only with the aid of principles of knowledge that are just as newly available. (TD 102f)

This relates to Lukács' bold claim that "it is true that reality [*Wirklichkeit*] is the criterion for the correctness [*Richtigkeit*] of thought. But reality is not, it becomes—and not without the assistance of thought." (HCC 223/204). So while maintaining that all knowledge is conditioned by the historical development of society and its "metabolic interchange" with nature, he can nonetheless deny dualism and idealism by affirming an ontological discontinuity between nature and society and a corresponding epistemic distinction.

> The knowledge [of nature] achieved at any one time is relative only in as far as it can be modified, indeed can be proven false, through a higher development of the economic structure of society (and a corresponding expansion, greater intensity, etc., of the exchange of matter between society and nature). However – in as far as it pertains to the objective reality of social being and the nature mediated through this – it is objective truth, absolute truth, which only changes its position, its theoretical explanation, etc., because of the knowledge that "overcomes" it, and which is more comprehensive and more correct. (TD 105)

In sum, Lukács did not reject the idea that nature is dialectical. But given the active involvement of human subjectivity in the historical development of society, that is, the dialectical relation between subject and object in the historical process, he did want to insist that nature was not dialectical *in the same way* as human history, and that as a consequence, differentiated methodological approaches were required.

Now, it may seem that there is nothing particularly remarkable about these ideas. In a certain sense, this appearance is true, inasmuch as Lukács took himself (and we can take him in this way too) as aiming to recover methodological ideas that were already tacit or operative in Marx's own work, but which were in need of explicit reaffirmation and clarification in the face of the sort of objectively deterministic revisionism that, in his view, regrettably held sway within Marxist theory at the time. And indeed, it can be difficult to appreciate fully the sense and force of Lukács' claims outside of the theoretical and political context in which he made them, and without regard to their underlying rationale, which was (Zinoviev et al. notwithstanding) in effect to provide a theoretical understanding and philosophical justification for the Bolshevik-led revolution in Russia—that is, reconcile Marx and Lenin philosophically. For the Revolution of October 1917 was, as Antonio Gramsci had put it at the time, "a revolution against *Capital*" (Grasmci 1990, 34–7), in that it defied those who prognosticated on the basis of the objective laws of historical development as found, at least supposedly, in Marx's mature works (recall that the philosophical works of the young Marx had not yet been published). In order to integrate the Russian experience into a Marxist understanding of history, then, it was necessary to thematize the subjective (in addition to the objective) conditions of revolutionary change, and to this end, to conceptualize and articulate the irreducibly active and efficacious role that human consciousness—and, in particular, proletarian class consciousness as consciousness of the historical totality—can play in the historical process. This focus on the subjective conditions of revolution was in no way meant to accord them priority over the objective conditions, the primacy of which Lukács repeatedly affirmed in line with the materialism of classical Marxism. But whereas the latter tended to underrate consciousness by construing it in epiphenomenal terms, Lukács insisted on construing consciousness as involving an irreducible materiality of its own that can be decisive in certain objective historical circumstances.

Lukács and Merleau-Ponty

The foregoing remarks convey the fundamental sense of what Lukács undertook in *History and Class Consciousness*, and it is a view that shares important philosophical affinities with Merleau-Ponty. Consider the notion of totality. Jay's broad claims that "Merleau-Ponty's philosophy, indeed his entire outlook on the world, was deeply holistic from the beginning" (1984, 361), and more specifically, that "the concept of totality was at the center of his concerns" in the postwar period (1984, 367), are certainly accurate. As discussed above, the Gestalt-theoretic account of nature that Merleau-Ponty developed in *The Structure of Behavior* is consistent with a materialist approach that reserves a relative autonomy for consciousness, and which emphasizes the interaction of subject and object and the role of this interaction in creating new conditions of existence. All of this is shared with Lukács—indeed, Merleau-Ponty tended to blur any conceptual distinction between "structure" and "totality" (SNS 223/126)—and what is undertaken in *Phenomenology of Perception* is positioned within this framework.[2] (Recall that Fink had shown totality to be the key methodological issue facing phenomenology.) In this way, then, Merleau-Ponty was very much on the same page as Lukács in terms of trying to update Marxism with "a new conception of consciousness" that would be appropriate to this dialectical-holistic perspective (SNS 143/82).[3]

Given this perspective, however, along with his phenomenological tendencies and with the benefit of hindsight with regard to Lukács, Merleau-Ponty examined this problem more closely. For in claiming that "it is in *lived perception* that the dialectical synthesis of the subject and object takes place" (Low 1987, 174, italics added), he approached consciousness—and *a fortiori* proletarian class consciousness—as a matter of *perceptual consciousness* in its distinction from and relation to intellectual or reflective consciousness. This can be seen as the main way in which he tried to update and redeem the Lukácsian framework. More on that shortly.

Concerning that framework, though, what is most important is that Merleau-Ponty posited a methodological distinction between history and nature that followed Lukács' account. For he agreed with Lukács that, *pace* Engels, it would be idealistic to claim a direct connection between the dialecticity of the human historical world and any sort of dialectics in nature, maintaining to the contrary that inasmuch as "nature is nature, that is, exterior to us and to itself, then we can find in it neither the relations nor the quality that are necessary to sustain a dialectic" (SNS 224/126). In this way, he concurred with Lukács' dismissal of nature as not amenable to philosophical analysis except as socially mediated. "If [nature] is dialectical, then it is a matter of that nature that is perceived by man and which is inseparable from the human action that Marx talks about in the *Theses on Feuerbach* and *The German Ideology*. 'This activity, this perceptible and continuous action and work, this production are . . . the foundation of the entire perceptible world such as it currently exists'" (SNS 224/126, citing *L'idéologie allemande*, in Marx 1927–37, vol. 6 [1937], 163). In effect, this is the basis of Merleau-Ponty's claim that Marxism is "a philosophy of *history*" (SNS 130/231, italics added; cf. HT 165/153)—that is, it is a philosophy of the historically unfolding human world *in its dialectical distinction from nature as such*.[4]

Light can be cast on this by considering Merleau-Ponty's idea of a "logic of history," by which he meant the following: (a) that history is an integral whole, "a single drama" in which all events, however contingent, have a human significance; and (b) that the phases of this drama do not follow an arbitrary order, "but move toward a completion and conclusion" (SNS 212/121; cf. NI 15 [3]). In other words, that history is intelligible and has a direction—that "there is in the instant and in their succession a totality moving toward a privileged state which gives the meaning of the whole" (HT 166/153). Combined with the idea that the "privileged state" in question represents a genuine "reconciliation of man with man" in fully universal terms (HT 139/129f), this is, for Merleau-Ponty, the essential content of Marxism.

This conception of history corresponds to the need on the part of phenomenology to be able to come to terms with the outermost horizons of intentional experience. As discussed in the Preface, the most important methodological problem facing phenomenology stems from the fact that if all intentional experience is horizonal, in that objects of experience are necessarily conditioned by the backgrounds against which they appear, then the claims of phenomenology to achieve critical philosophical insight are fundamentally jeopardized by the possibility of a vicious regress. Fink, as we saw, offered a bold solution in the form of a "meontic philosophy of absolute spirit." Although this approach would redeem the philosophical pretensions of phenomenology in the strongest sense, it deviates sharply from some of the project's guiding ideas, and in these respects, it also tends to be highly dubious from an existential point of view. Merleau-Ponty's solution was rather different. The idea here was to show that the domain of phenomenology coincided with the human historical world as a well-defined totality, but also therefore to show that the horizons of this totality could be experienced as such—that there could in fact be certain experiences—specifically, self-experiences—characterized by *an indistinction between object and its external horizons*. For such an absolute experience of the concrete totality of history as such would be a necessary condition of the philosophical viability of an essentially incomplete (because situated) phenomenological reduction.

But how would this experience be possible? How could "totality" be anything more than empty rhetorical or polemical gesture? How would it be able to do real philosophical work? As Karl Jaspers asked in a critique of the notion of totality and the use to which it was put, especially by Marxists like Lukács: "In general, is man capable of grasping, knowing, wanting, or planning the whole? Is totality an object of thought and a goal of action for man? In my view, this is impossible" (EE 250). According to Jaspers, although this view was and is widely held, this impossibility would stem from the fact that, living in the world, we can only relate to "partial elements and aspects" which, as discussed above, are always conditioned by certain horizons. And Jaspers insisted that these horizons always retreat when approached, that there is always a more encompassing horizon. In principle, then, "no totality can ever be achieved" (EE 251)—"one never knows the whole because one is [always] *in* the whole" (EE 199).

This may certainly be true at the level of reflective or intellectual consciousness—Merleau-Ponty would agree that we do not have *this* kind of relation to totality. There is some ambiguity, however, as to Lukács' view of the matter. On the one hand, a key theoretical construct in *History and Class Consciousness* was the idea of "imputed" [*zugerechnet*] class consciousness, which applied primarily to Lukács' concern with the possibility of the proletariat attaining true knowledge of society as a totality.

> Relating consciousness to the whole of society discloses the thoughts, feelings, etc. that people in a determinate life-situation *would* have, *were they completely capable of grasping* that situation and the interests arising from it, both in relation to immediate action as well to the construction of society as a whole in accordance with those interests. (HCC 62/50, translation modified)

In other words, Lukács' notion of "imputed consciousness" is a counterfactual matter of the "thoughts and feelings" that would befit a certain objective situation, and as such it relies heavily on the Weberian idea of "objective possibility." To be sure, at least typically, there is a significant distance between the class consciousness imputed to the proletariat—which amounts to "a correct knowledge of the historical process"—and the actual or empirical consciousness of any individual proletarian. But given the unique social position of the proletariat, bridging this gap is a real possibility. "By 'imputed' class consciousness," Lukács wrote, "I mean the consciousness that corresponds to the objective economic position of the proletariat at any one time, and that can be attained by the proletariat" (TD 66).

Lukács thus affirmed that while the imputed class consciousness of the proletariat may have "no psychological reality" [*keine psychologische Wirklichkeit*] (HC, 88, cf. 86/75, cf. 73), it is no mere fiction. It takes *some* concrete form prior to its explicit realization. Thus, on the other hand, Lukács also approached proletarian class consciousness in terms of its latent or implicit existence, claiming that "the relation to totality does not need to become fully explicit, the full extent of its content does not need to be consciously integrated into the motives and objects of action. What ultimately matters is *the intention towards totality* [die Intention auf Totalität]" (HCC 217/198, italics added), or equivalently, what Lukács called the "intention toward what is right" [*Intention auf das Richtige*] (HCC 84/72), that is in some sense immanent within the life of the proletariat. Owing to the special (but not unique) relation that it has to the social standpoint of the proletariat, the category of totality operates and has effects prior to contributing to any specific cognitive achievements, and Lukács claimed that it does so by ensuring that even actions that seem to concern only particular objects nevertheless derive their objective sense from a practical, transformative intention with regard to society as a historical totality (HCC 192/175). The "intention towards totality" is thus in effect also the "intention towards the realization of the dialectical tendencies of [historical] development" [*Intention auf die Verwirklichung der dialektischen Tendenzen der Entwicklung*] (HCC 196/179). In short, in the case of the proletariat, the "intention towards totality" is involved in the overcoming of immediacy "regardless of whether it is already conscious or remains initially unconscious" (HCC 190/174), and proletarian class consciousness can be understood as "the *sense* [Sinn] . . . of the historical situation [*Lage*] of the class" (HCC 86/73, italics altered).

How this "sense" becomes conscious is, of course, the key question. But it is not answered simply by positing imputed class consciousness in an unconscious form—for example, in terms of the feelings and tendencies of "correct instincts" [*richtige*

Instinkten] (HCC 88/75). This just repackages the problem as to how the proletariat as a class existing *in*-itself becomes a class existing *for*-itself. Although in *History and Class Consciousness*, Lukács had much to say about this problem in terms of political organization, the philosophical basis of the advent of the self-consciousness with which he was concerned remained unclear.

While in general terms Merleau-Ponty followed Lukács' conception of totality, the main innovation that he introduced was to reconceive the latent intentionalities posited by Lukács—in particular, the "intention toward totality"—in prereflective terms. This is, at least to some extent, implicit in Lukács. But it is not worked out. Merleau-Ponty's contribution was thus to rethink explicitly the relationship between consciousness and the historical totality that was implied in Lukács' account on the basis of perceptual consciousness. Rather than simply claim with Lukács that "Marxist thought only raises to a higher level of thought the totality that we are forced to live with in daily life, whether we like it or not, and whether we are aware of it or not" (EE 252), Merleau-Ponty sought to show that history as a totality is something of which we are (or at least can be) aware at the prereflective level of lived perception—in other words, that *historical totality is a lived percept*. As he put it to Jaspers by way of defending the Lukácsian conception of totality against the worries alluded to above:

> a certain postulate of the rationality of history is something that we cannot avoid, for it belongs to [*se confond avec*] the necessities of our life. Anyone, from the moment he takes a political position, has a certain conception of the whole of historical life, and even if he does not formulate it in words, he nonetheless expresses it in action. (EE 253)

In other words, humans, at least in certain historical conjunctures, have an operative-intentional relation to the totality of history as the outermost horizons of experience. This is the "*perception of history*" (HT 105/98), or of its *logic*, that Merleau-Ponty saw as lying at the core of Marxism. I shall have more to say about this later. For now, we just need to note that *this* perception—which lies at the basis of the "operative knowledge" [*connaissance opérante*] of which Marxism supplies the "general formula" [*la formule générale*] (HT 100/94)—is primordial in Merleau-Ponty's phenomenology, in that all other perceptual experience is situated horizonally within it and has its epistemic status conditioned accordingly.

For this reason, Merleau-Ponty saw this "perception of history" as the basis for phenomenological truth. For it is the rationality and sense [*sens*] at the level of history as a whole that underwrites the rationality and sense that may be perceived at any subordinate level. As he put it, "where history has no structure and no dominant trends it is no longer possible to *say* anything, since there are no periods nor lasting constellations, and a thesis is only valid for a moment" (HT 156/144f). Whereas on the contrary, "the simple fact that someone perceives an historical situation as invested with a meaning that he believes to be true introduces a phenomenon of truth" (HT 102/95f)—that is, a presumptive rationality emerges in the course of historical development that "testifies to our rootedness in the truth" (HT 103/96). And this presumption is inescapable. Echoing the comments he made to Jaspers, Merleau-Ponty claimed that "the contingency of history is only a shadow at the margins of a view of the future from which we can no more abstain than we can from breathing" (HT 102/96). Thus, for Merleau-Ponty, the very experience of historical contingency is itself sufficient evidence of the historical logic outlined above, that is, of a "common history." In other words, the consciousness of historical contingency invalidates itself (cf. HT 206/188)—"we are condemned, whether we like it or not, to the philosophy of history" (SNS 297/167f).

It is thus the case for Merleau-Ponty that human *être-au-monde* is indistinguishable from "being-in-the-truth" [« *être-à-la-vérité* »] (PhP 452)—that is, that "we are in the truth" (PhP xi), that "we are *true* through and through" (PhP 520)—just in virtue of what we might call his *existential-communist* philosophy of history. But the latter is also a necessary condition. As Merleau-Ponty put it in a well-known passage:

> Marxism is not just any hypothesis that might be replaced tomorrow by some other. It is the simple statement of those conditions without which there would be neither any humanism, in the sense of a mutual relation between men, nor any rationality in history. In this sense Marxism is not a philosophy of history; it is *the* philosophy of history and to renounce it is to dig the grave of Reason in history. (HT 165/153)

The sense of this rather audacious claim is that "any philosophy of history will postulate something like what is called historical materialism," inasmuch as any philosophical position that takes history seriously as the locus of human existence could not fail to see it as a Gestalt totality that maintains the identity of subjective and objective factors, while still remaining oriented to truth in a universal sense.

Embodiment and repression

Although Merleau-Ponty's phenomenological approach to perception may correct for the problem of consciousness with regard to the Lukácsian notion of totality, there is another issue that must be addressed: if, following Lukács, Merleau-Ponty sees history as a totality to which nature as such is inassimilable, then what is to be said about human embodiment? The problem is not that the notion of concrete totality must be all-inclusive—Merleau-Ponty is in effect dealing with the human order in its dialectical distinction from the vital and physical orders as outlined in *The Structure of Behavior*. But if human beings are natural creatures as well as historical beings, then any sort of methodological duality would, so to speak, slice right through us.

It is because he claims that in lived perception, we experience history as such as a unity, and because he takes the fact of our naturalness to rule out methodological duality, that Merleau-Ponty affirms that "the organism and its monotonous dialectics are ... not extraneous to history as though inassimilable to it" (PhP 104). The significance of this claim lies initially in the fact that, as we have seen, for Merleau-Ponty, nature in general *is* extraneous and inassimilable to history. But there is something exceptional in the case of human embodiment understood in natural organismic—or biological or physiological—terms. Merleau-Ponty's accounting for this is based upon his notion of the habitual body in contradistinction to the "actual" body. Recall that, for Merleau-Ponty, there is an "inner necessity" for human existence "to provide itself with a habitual body" (PhP 103). For owing precisely to its impersonal (or prepersonal) character, the habitual body is an essential dimension of the historicity that enables a human being to transcend the immediate actuality of her environing world. It is only in virtue of having an impersonal corporeal anchorage that one can develop a genuinely personal existence in the world. A key point, however, is that this anchorage, and hence the historical assimilability of the organism, is achieved through the *repression* of the "actual" body. Repression [*refoulement*], which translates Freud's term *Verdrängung*, is thus a key concept in Merleau-Ponty's discussion of the habitual body. But there are some ambiguities that need to be sorted out.

To begin with, the main idea concerning Merleau-Ponty's view of repression in this context has to do, as just mentioned, with the repression, from the side of personal existence, of the "actual" body. In this sense, the "actual" body has a kind of "first-person existence"—a kind of corporeal *Jemeinigkeit*—and what transpires in its repression is its *impersonalization*, something that could be described equally as its *deactualization*. But this seems to represent the intertwining of two different processes that may be disentangled analytically.

First, it seems that in Merleau-Ponty's view, the habitual body effectively subsumes or incorporates within itself the "actual" body itself *qua* biological organism. The latter does have a certain independent being—it has, as we know, its own dialectic. But in the course of a human life in this or that historical context, the organism and its dialectical tendencies are sublimated and transfigured to such an extent that they typically comprise a virtually indistinct aspect of the habitual body as the impersonal dimension of human existence or *être-au-monde*—we might just call this the "habituated organism." The key idea behind this view was expressed most boldly in Merleau-Ponty's assertion that "man is an historical idea, not a natural species" (PhP 199).

This sublimation of the organism and its vital dialectic could be seen as a matter of what Merleau-Ponty—citing the work of Schilder (1923), as well as of Menninger-Lerchenthal (1934) and Lhermitte (1939)—referred to at one point as "organic repression" [« *refoulement organique* »] (PhP 92). The general thought behind this (originally Freudian) notion is that in addition to psychological mechanisms of repression pertaining to the level of representation, there also exist biological mechanisms pertaining to the level of bodily affect. Something along these lines is key to Merleau-Ponty's account of the specific pathologies that characterize cases of phantom limb syndrome and anosognosia. But still, Merleau-Ponty did not seem to place too much stock in this distinction between different modalities of repression. Repression is, he claimed, "a universal phenomenon," and "*all* repression is the passage from first-person existence to a sort of pedantic abstraction [*scolastique*] of this existence"—in this way, he described it as "the advent of the impersonal" (PhP 99, italics added).

Rather than in terms of "organic repression," then, we can get a better handle on the sublimation of the organism in terms of this idea of "the advent of the impersonal." What is supposed to occur in this sublimation is the absorption or transposition of the vital dialectical tendencies and exigencies of the biological organism as such into the historically specific operative intentionalities and affects of the subject "engaged in a certain physical and interhuman world" (PhP 97). There is a "natural movement" that becomes an interwoven part of the impersonal worldly inherence of individuals. If we construe biological embodiment in "first-person" terms of some kind, then it is in this sense that its sublimation can be seen as part of "the advent of the impersonal." Here it is important to keep in mind that "the impersonal" does not denote a general negation of "the personal," but rather a specific kind of anonymity that is the presupposed counterpart to "the personal" in the context of *être-au-monde*.

Second, the habitual body is also—and perhaps principally—the product of the repression of actual embodied *experience*. Although still perhaps within the ambit of "organic repression," this aspect tracks more closely the more common understanding of repression as a psychopathological condition, according to which, in Merleau-Ponty's gloss, "the subject commits to a certain path . . ., encounters on this path a barrier and, having the strength neither to surmount the obstacle nor to abandon the undertaking, he remains trapped in this attempt and endlessly uses his strength repeating it in his mind" (PhP 98). What is to be especially noted about this view of repression is that it is concerned directly with temporality and historicity: "the subject always remains open to the same impossible future, if not in his explicit thoughts, then at least in his actual [*effectif*] being. One present among all presents thus acquires an exceptional value, displacing the others and divesting them of their value as authentic presents. . . . Impersonal time continues to flow, but personal time is knotted up [*noué*]" (PhP 98).[5]

Viewed as "the advent of the impersonal" from this angle, the habitual body is the repository of the general form or structure of past experience. It is primarily in this way that, as a universal phenomenon, repression "clarifies our condition as incarnate beings by connecting it to the temporal structure of *être au monde*" (PhP 99). As noted above, though, an impersonal habitual body is an essential aspect of human existence. Thus, even if it is in some sense always a "pedantic abstraction," the repression involved in the formation of the habitual body is not *necessarily* pathological at all. On the contrary, it is, at least to a certain degree, a positively healthy mechanism that is indispensable for human self-realization—historicity requires repression. It becomes pathological only when it goes too far and becomes existentially preponderant, when the balance is skewed in the sense that what should provide anchorage for personal existence actually smothers it and arrests its development.

As a product of this dual form of repression—the sedimentation of the general form of experience, infused with and animated by sublimated biological tendencies, the habituated organism—which, in the discussion in question, Merleau-Ponty often refers to as "the physiological" or even simply as "the organism"—has an intentional orientation just as the personal or "psychical" dimension of existence does. This orientation is typically not the same at the two levels, and in terms of intentionality, the former has a prereflective character while the latter is reflective. Each thus has its own history or temporal rhythm that, in typical cases, does not overlap entirely with the other—Merleau-Ponty describes that of the habituated organism as "banal and cyclical," that is, "monotonous," while that of the psychical "may be open and singular" (PhP 103). But what is important is that the banality of the habituated organism is a source of meaning in history. Indeed, it is a very important source of historical meaning.

For this is the concrete locus of historical apriority. It is in virtue of literally embodying certain generic or stereotypical dispositions that "the subject of history does not create his role completely," but rather tends to act in certain predelineated ways (PhP 103). And in a characteristic move, Merleau-Ponty's discussion, which had been concerned with cases of phantom limb syndrome and anosognosia, makes sudden reference to Louis XVI and Nicholas II as subjects of history constrained *a priori* by the roles they embodied—strictly speaking, they are "repressed" in essentially the same way, in that their behavior likewise stemmed from their habituated organism understood as an "inborn complex" [*complexe inné*]. In this light, Merleau-Ponty affirms that "history is neither a perpetual novelty nor a perpetual repetition, but a *single* [unique] movement which creates stable forms and breaks them" (PhP 104). This is an elaboration of the fundamental perception of history, on account of which, as noted above, Merleau-Ponty is able to include the organism in history—as he put it immediately following this last point, "the organism and its monotonous dialectics are *therefore* not extraneous to history as though inassimilable to it" (PhP 104, italics added).

It is thus the univocal logic that Merleau-Ponty claimed is characteristic of human history perceived as a meaningful dialectical totality, in connection with the claim that the organismic and personal dimensions of human existence do not generate two distinct histories, that enables him to include the organism within the historical totality, and specifically as pertaining to the dimension of its apriority.

Two further consequences follow from this. First, it follows that human existence at the individual level, which unfolds within the Gestalt totality of history, is likewise to be considered an existential totality and to be approached holistically. As indicated earlier, the existential unity of human *être-au-monde* cannot be affirmed legitimately at the level of individual existence itself, and Merleau-Ponty's justification for it turns on the transcendental necessity of unity at a higher level. Analogously to how one first comes to see one's environing world as such from the higher standpoint of the world, individual human embodied existence can be glimpsed as a totality only from the perspective of the larger encompassing totality of human history. Second, it is on this basis alone that Merleau-Ponty could affirm the otherwise unprovable claim (noted earlier) that "there is not a single movement in a living body that is completely accidental with regard to psychic intentions, nor a single psychic act that has not found at least its germ or its general outline in physiological dispositions" (PhP 104). That is, it is only as a deduction from his transcendental claim that human *être-au-monde* is an existential totality—which itself is a deduction from his transcendental claims about history—that he can posit a quasi-isomorphism of this sort—the most important aspect of which is the implication that every bodily movement or gesture bears some connection to higher-order intentionalities, that any such movement or gesture has historical significance because it is enacted inescapably on the basis of the currently operative *a priori* structures of history.

•

The main consequence of the transcendental claims in question here is that Merleau-Ponty's phenomenological approach to embodiment must be situated within both the methodological as well as the normative horizons of the historical totality as he perceived it. Before bringing this to bear upon the discussion of Saint Exupéry, it may be helpful to emphasize clearly that, contrary to standard interpretations, Merleau-Ponty's approach to and account of history is *not* based upon an attempt, as Taylor Carman (for one) recently expressed it, "to *extend* some of the basic insights of his phenomenology [of perception] into the political sphere" (Carman 2008, 24; cf. Roland Caillois 1947; Miller 1979, 207f; Whiteside 1988, 155). Merleau-Ponty would fully agree that there is no legitimate Gestalt-theoretic basis for any such analogical move from body to world. But he would vigorously disagree with the claim that this is because "[t]here is no totalizing perspective for an entire society as there is for a single perceptual subject" (Carman 2008, 163). On the contrary, for Merleau-Ponty, it is *only* at the level of the historical world that we can begin with totality—and indeed, as he put it to Jaspers, this "belongs to the necessities of our life." It thus follows that *the order of logical priority is precisely the reverse from what is typically assumed.* That is, methodologically speaking, Merleau-Pontian phenomenology *begins* with a holistic view of the world in its historical becoming—what he once called "the Idea in the Hegelian sense" (PhP xiii)—which is *then* extended down to the level of perceptual experience. As noted, it is only because he is already working on the basis of the perceptual givenness of history as a totality that Merleau-Ponty can approach the phenomena of our embodied existence in holistic terms. This is a transcendental claim that derives from the deeper intuition regarding history. Absent the encompassing unity of its external historical horizon, there is simply no legitimate phenomenological justification for adopting a totalizing perspective on the perceptual subject. This is particularly crucial with regard to all the results that Merleau-Ponty draws from considerations of pathological phenomena—in particular, his important discussions of the case of "patient Schn." would have no definite philosophical import whatsoever without his philosophy of history. Approaching *être-au-monde* holistically may, of course, ultimately prove to be phenomenologically valid. But such validity would derive its epistemic status from the place of the phenomena within the horizons of the historical world as an open-ended process of becoming. It is for this reason that Merleau-Ponty's phenomenology of perception, including his approach to embodiment, cannot be properly understood in abstraction from his philosophy of history and the normative commitments underpinning it.

Earlier references to Saint Exupéry (Part 2)

Such is the context for Merleau-Ponty's initial references to Saint Exupéry. How does the foregoing discussion bear upon them?

Let us first recall the passage in question, which reads as follows, with the footnoted references inserted and italicized:

Just as we speak of a repression [*refoulement*] in the restricted sense when I maintain through time one of the momentary worlds through which I have passed and which I make into the form of my entire life, – in the same way we can say that my organism, as a pre-personal adherence to the general form of the world, as an anonymous and general existence, plays, beneath the level of my personal life, the role of an *inborn complex* [complexe inné]. It is not like an inert thing, [for] it too delineates [*ébauche*] the movement of existence. It can even happen in cases of danger that my human situation effaces [*efface*] my biological one, that my body enters into action unreservedly [*que mon corps se joigne sans réserve à l'action*].

> Thus, Saint-Exupéry, over Arras, surrounded by [enemy] fire, no longer feels as something distinct from himself this body which, just moments before, was recoiling: "It is as if my life were given to me every second, as if with every second my life were becoming more palpable. I live. I am living. I am still living. I am always living. I am nothing but a source of life."

But these moments can be no more than moments,

> "To be sure, though, in the course of my life, when not directed by anything urgent, when my meaning is not at stake, I see no problems more serious than those of my body."

and most of the time personal existence represses the organism without being able to disregard it nor to give itself up, – that is, without being able to reduce the organism to itself nor to reduce itself to the organism.

Merleau-Ponty's basic claims here seem to run like this: personal existence represses "actual" corporeality and embodied experience, thereby generating the habituated organism as an "inborn complex." Biological tendencies are sublimated and personal experience is sedimented in an anonymized and generalized form, with the result that human corporeal existence has a dual temporal structure and a corresponding intentional duality—for the organism *does* have an existential impetus of its own, something that is made visible in those limit cases, like that of Saint Exupéry, when "my body enters into action unreservedly." For Merleau-Ponty, repression along these lines is normal, but also normally incomplete, such that normal human corporeal existence is characterized by historical movement aimed at achieving an equilibrium at as high a level of integration as possible.

Normal existence would thus be delimited by two different limit cases: at one extreme, the reduction of the habituated organism to personal existence (bodily disregard), and at the other extreme, the reduction of personal existence to the habituated organism (self-renunciation). One of these limit cases is illustrated in the reference to Saint Exupéry—but which is it?

On the one hand, the idea of "effacing" my "biological situation" might suggest that what is involved is primarily a matter of bodily disregard—or more specifically, a matter of the complete instrumentalization of my body for the purposes of an action determined by my personal existence. In other words, it might seem that the illustration from Saint Exupéry is meant to describe how, in extreme situations of mortal danger, I can *use* my body in the service of my personal existential choices in ways that are both radically inhabitual as well as contrary to the vital tendencies of the organism as such. This would imply that what is going on with Saint Exupéry, at least in Merleau-Ponty's view, is a temporary moment of the complete repression—or perhaps more accurately, the complete suppression [*Unterdrückung*] (cf. Ayouch 2008, 341)—of the habituated organism. This would be a moment of complete bodily disregard that would correspond to a moment of the complete (and likewise temporary) *un*-repression of personal existence—an exceptional moment in which individual spontaneity triumphs over the exigencies of biology and the inauthenticity of habitual anonymity.

Although it may be initially tempting to adopt such a view, it is, I believe, mistaken. For on the other hand, and quite to the contrary, it would be much more plausible to claim that Merleau-Ponty's point was to illustrate the complete—though again, temporary—repression of "actual" corporeality as a way of bringing the habituated organism to phenomenological givenness and thereby showing that it has its own existential dynamic. For as he said, it is not inert, as "it too delineates the movement of existence"—and my "body entering into action unreservedly" was clearly meant to illustrate this. The action in question thus stems from the habituated organism— that is, *the body that "enters into action unreservedly" is the habituated organism*. The "effacement of my biological situation" thus refers to the complete repression of my "actual" body. It is, after all, to my *"human"* situation, not my "personal" one, that Merleau-Ponty attributes this "effacement"—and surely, he did not mean to imply that biological exigencies could be wholly suspended, even temporarily. *It is in complete repression that one coincides with one's embodiment in the way Merleau-Ponty describes of Saint Exupéry*—and the embodiment with which one coincides is the habituated organism. Contrary to the first view, the emphasis is clearly meant to be on the autonomous *activity*, not the passive instrumentalization, of the habituated organism. Entirely consistent with Saint Exupéry's view of the matter, it would seem that for Merleau-Ponty, existential abandon (the term is felicitous) in the face of mortal danger is *a personally selfless act*—or we should perhaps say that mortal danger exists only in the perception of an individual, while existential abandon in the face of it stems from the "anonymous and general" level of existence. It is a matter, to borrow Merleau-Ponty's phrase, of the dialectics of the habituated organism *"demanding their own due"* and directing the agency of my—or rather, *this*—body accordingly. And if so, then this would imply that the illustration from Saint Exupéry is primarily a matter of complete personal self-renunciation, the momentary reduction of "actual" corporeality and first-personal existence to the habituated organism—a moment of consummate repression whereby one comes to coincide temporarily with one's "inborn complex."

The second citation from Saint Exupéry might seem to offer better support for the view that I am rejecting, since it seems to imply that what characterizes the exceptional moment is the absence of the sort of bodily issues that typically predominate, suggesting that it is outside of those moments that the body exists in its own right, rather than, as I have claimed, that it is precisely in such moments that the body, as the habituated organism, manifests itself most clearly on its own terms.

Yet this contrasting view clearly equivocates with regard to the body in its "actual" and habitual dimensions. More importantly, such a reading of the second citation does not fit particularly well with Merleau-Ponty's main point, namely, that the "actual" body is normally (albeit incompletely) repressed. The exceptional moment that he described with the help of Saint Exupéry is supposed to illuminate this repression by showing what it leads to, namely, the anonymous habituated organism and its selfless tendency toward universal life. *That*, for Merleau-Ponty, is the organism on its own terms, *not* what the contrary reading of the second citation would suggest, to wit, that the organism *per se* is to be discerned in a bunch of bodily "problems"—it is highly implausible that that would be Merleau-Ponty's view here. That may well describe the typical experience of the organism, but that is because it situates it within human existence as a whole, which is to say, it situates the organism in its tension-filled relation with personal existence— that alone is the context in which the organism can be construed as raising problems, but that is clearly not where it exists on its own terms. In other words, although the second citation from Saint Exupéry might seem to describe the organism when it has returned to itself, at least for Merleau-Ponty in the discussion in question, it actually describes the organism in its typical state of significant but not total repression, as in his claim that "most of the time personal existence represses the organism without being able to disregard it," that is, it still raises problems vis-à-vis personal existence. But when it is wholly and problemlessly engaged in action, that can only be because all contrary personal or individual motives have been repressed.

In sum, although Merleau-Ponty's discussion contains numerous terminological ambiguities that will prevent any reading of it from being absolutely watertight, the soundest analysis of it shows that Merleau-Ponty meant for the references to Saint Exupéry to disclose the operative intentionality of the habituated organism on its own terms by glimpsing its activity in a moment of the total repression of "actual" corporeality and embodied experience. To be sure, in existential terms, this complete repression or de-actualization is abnormal, even pathological. But there is nothing at all unusual in Merleau-Ponty using pathological cases to arrive at phenomenological insights. It is just that the fact that this case *is* pathological, and is being dealt with as such, is not as obvious as it may be in other cases.

Consequences

What does all of this mean, then, given that the episode in question—Saint Exupéry's perilous flight over Arras—is the same as that which is invoked at the very end of *Phenomenology of Perception*? In other words, what is implied by the fact that, for Merleau-Ponty, "heroism" is a pathological matter of complete self-repression?

I shall develop this further in subsequent chapters. But what we have seen in this chapter strongly confirms the earlier claim that, taken literally, the invocation of Exupérian heroism at the end of *Phenomenology of Perception* represents a moment of radical disincarnation. And it also coheres strongly with Saint Exupéry's own account as far as rejecting any construal of the action in question in terms of individual agency. Merleau-Ponty is not interested in heroism *per se*, however, but in the fact that it is phenomenologically disclosive of something of the utmost importance for his view, namely, *the latent existence within habituated organismicity, at least in the current historical context, of an operative intentionality toward universal life, and the fact that this intentionality represents the historical apriority governing all action in that context.* In other words, with regard to heroism, it is the evidence afforded by actions that are effected in a pathological state of total repression, yet which nonetheless remain generative of historical sense and significance, that enabled Merleau-Ponty to claim that the logic of history forming the core of his understanding of Marxism was more than just some dogmatic partisan assumption.

In particular, this conception of heroism is what enabled Merleau-Ponty to say, in line with classical Marxism, that the historical movement toward a postcapitalist society is already immanent and underway (HT 135f/126), but that as a consequence—and here he deviated from classical Marxism on account of his conceiving the social in corporeal terms—revolutionary change is not to be pursued through historical action aimed at effecting a radical structural break with the present, but rather, through forms of action that are geared toward the concrete realization of the latent universal content of existing structures. In other words, it supports what we might call an "incarnational Marxism," in the sense that the fundamental structures of universal reconciliation are already embodied collectively and impersonally, and that the revolutionary task is therefore not to impose radically new social structures, but to realize those already tacitly embodied at the level of the habituated organism more fully at the level of "actual" embodied existence. As shall be discussed further in Chapters 4 and 5, Merleau-Ponty's notion of heroism, especially inasmuch as it involves total repression, was intended as part of an effort to rethink the Marxist category of the proletariat in existential terms. The central idea is that the lack of an existentially "healthy" equilibrium between "actual" and habitual corporeality—and hence the lack of freedom—within individual human existence is effectively identical with the lack of "harmony between the individual [in general] and history," which Merleau-Ponty regarded as an existential "postulate of human existence" in the sense of being a necessary condition of the realization of humanity.[6] Inasmuch as the latter can be viewed in terms of freedom construed socially, it follows that for Merleau-Ponty, there is a mutually implicatory relation between the realization of humanity and freedom at the individual level.

And broadly speaking, it is this political perspective that enabled Merleau-Ponty to complete and thus save phenomenology methodologically, that is, from the speculative construction of Fink. What is needed is a concrete apprehension of the outermost horizons of experience, and Merleau-Ponty supplied this with a prereflective existential interpretation of Lukács' idea of an "intention toward totality"—which, as he noted in reply to Jaspers, arises "the moment [one] takes a *political position*" (EE 252, italics added). This is fundamentally why, for Merleau-Ponty, phenomenology—and *a fortiori* his phenomenology of embodiment—is "profoundly and intrinsically political" (Coole 2007, 123). It is not from any philosophically arbitrary desire that it be so, any desire to "politicize" philosophy, or from any kind of extraneous connection at all. Rather, it stems from the fact that what phenomenology requires intrinsically to achieve methodological closure can only come from the practical realm of political engagement. This solution is, of course, not unique—different political perspectives on history *can* be adopted, and these would frame different interpretations of phenomenology. For his part, Merleau-Ponty believed that in existential and normative terms, the most defensible historical perspective was one broadly in line with classical Marxism—and as we have seen, this has significant implications for the methodological structure of his phenomenology, which in turn has ramifications with regard to his basic approach to embodiment. And this is how heroism fits in. By bringing to phenomenological givenness the latent tendency toward universal life in the contemporary world understood as a historical period of generalized repression and unfreedom, heroic action—or rather, the third-person experience of it—forms a connection between embodied inherence in that world and the concomitant possibilities of philosophy and revolutionary politics. I shall explore this in more detail in the next two chapters. What will be important to bear in mind, though, is that in providing indispensable experiential evidence that contributes crucially to justifying this overall perspective, and precisely because it does so, for Merleau-Ponty heroism itself necessarily remains *external* to the philosophical and political projects in question, in the sense that its involvement occurs indirectly through its dialectical sublimation.

Elements of an Incarnational Marxism

We have seen that, for Merleau-Ponty, the heroic action of Saint Exupéry referred to at the end of *Phenomenology of Perception* is a matter of total repression of his "actual" body, and that precisely for this reason, it discloses an operative intentionality toward universal life which, residing in the anonymity of the habituated organism, is a structure of historical apriority in the contemporary world. This was a key part of Merleau-Ponty's response to Fink as it enabled him to obviate the need for what the latter had termed "secondary enworlding," which was central to his proposal for a "constructive" phenomenology (see Preface). This will be further elaborated in the Conclusion.

To that end, however, we need first to relate the climax of *Phenomenology of Perception* to Merleau-Ponty's Marxism in more detail. We have already seen how, in general, Merleau-Ponty's thought, at least since *The Structure of Behavior*, was situated within a philosophical framework consistent with Marxism, and that in the postwar period, he specifically tried to take up and redeem Lukács' account of "orthodox Marxism." It is ultimately in terms of this redemption that Merleau-Ponty's notion of heroism needs to be located and understood—this is intertwined with his reinterpretation of phenomenology, but in methodological terms priority goes to the political dimension.

In order to address further the philosophical role and significance of Exupérian heroism in Merleau-Ponty's project, then, this chapter will explore certain themes in his thought, some of which have tended to receive short shrift in the literature, but all of which turn out to be quite relevant to the question at hand, inasmuch as they have to do with Merleau-Ponty's elaboration of what I earlier called an "incarnational Marxism," which provides the basic sense of his attempted redemption of Lukács. I will first consider the themes of sacrifice and death in Merleau-Ponty's thought, and then discuss how Merleau-Ponty understood his existential phenomenology as a project of political hermeneutics. I then consider this with respect to Merleau-Ponty's effort to rethink the Marxist category of the proletariat *qua* "universal class," and the idea of its world-historical revolutionary role, in existential terms. In particular, I examine Merleau-Ponty's account of the tacit *cogito* as the basic phenomenon of class consciousness. Finally, I draw these ideas together in terms of what Merleau-Ponty called "human productivity" and the conception of rationality that results from all of this. Although there are, to be sure, many points in this thematic survey that invite deeper analysis, it shall nonetheless emerge clearly that the cumulative import of these considerations pertains to Merleau-Ponty's attempt to reinterpret Marxism in a way that would be both militant and philosophically coherent. This reinterpretation has to do primarily with the philosophy of history, and it hinges on a certain conception of "heroism" that will be considered in more detail in Chapter 5.

Merleau-Ponty on sacrifice and death

Although the themes of sacrifice and death are not treated at length by Merleau-Ponty, and scarcely at all in the literature devoted to his work, in the context of his appeal to Exupérian heroism, they turn out to be quite significant. For Merleau-Ponty's views concerning sacrifice are strongly contrary to those stated by Saint Exupéry, and these are connected to an attitude vis-à-vis death that bears directly upon the political dimension of Merleau-Ponty's existential phenomenology.

Sacrifice

There are two texts prior to *Phenomenology of Perception* that need to be considered with respect to the theme of sacrifice. As we shall see, despite certain important differences, in each case, Merleau-Ponty makes a philosophical argument *against* the cogency of the notion of sacrifice, and this in a way that gestures toward his later construal of Marxism in incarnational terms.

First, there is Merleau-Ponty's review of Max Scheler's *Ressentiment* [1912], written a decade before *Phenomenology of Perception*.[1] Here, Merleau-Ponty expressed, in Christian terms, a defense of ascetic self-denial that was not altogether dissimilar from Exupérian heroism. Siding with Scheler's defense of Christianity—at least in its "true" form—against the Nietzschean accusation that its aspiration toward the "Kingdom of God" is based on a resentful "devaluation of the earth," Merleau-Ponty argued that the sacrifice of "natural movement" is not *opposed* to life, but rather signifies merely a certain "spontaneous indifference" to its own biological circumstances. Such spontaneity occurs immediately in non-human life: "in its naïve force, the life of plants and animals does not obsess over its vital welfare." With regard to humanity, then, what Christianity seeks, according to Merleau-Ponty, is to impart "a confidence and a spontaneity" that would be "supernatural" [*surnaturelles*], and "what [it] proscribes is precisely, and in the strongest sense of the word, a 'vital debility' [« *débilité vitale* »]" (CR 14/88, citing Scheler). Here, rather than as a system of self-preservation, Merleau-Ponty regarded life as a kind of self-overcoming, as "an expansion or a prodigality," indifference to the particular details of which can indeed have a "vital value" (CR 13/87f).

But this is equivocal—for "the assurance of the Christian is *only analogous* to the vital confidence of natural beings" (CR 16/89, emphasis added). It is thus not philosophically clear how Christianity can "back both horses" and simultaneously lay evaluative claim to both natural and supernatural life (CR 16/89). Merleau-Ponty's suggestion was that the separation of these can only be maintained on the problematic basis of unfounded philosophical prejudice—in Nietzsche's case, "biological monism." If, however, quoting Scheler, "'a logic of the heart reveals, beyond vital needs, an objective structure of spiritual and religious value, [then] Christianity can no longer be accused of depreciating terrestrial life through the sole fact that it aspires to something else: *transcendence can no longer be the sublimation of a vital weakening'* [la sublimation d'un affaiblissement vital]" (CR 23f/93f, emphasis added).

•

The second text to consider with regard to the theme of sacrifice is *The Structure of Behavior*, which, as noted earlier, Merleau-Ponty completed in 1938. Here, he no longer upheld a Christian perspective, and his thinking was disencumbered of certain unwarranted claims—in particular, the existence of "an objective structure of spiritual and religious value" and the metaphysical assurance that that would afford. Merleau-Ponty now linked such assurance with critical philosophy's misguided dream of achieving complete individual integration—the absolute self-consciousness of the pure subject whose history "is subordinated to its eternity" (SC 222/206), and for whom *death would be rendered meaningless* (SC 220/204). It is ultimately the impossibility of precisely this consummate individuation that Merleau-Ponty sought to demonstrate in *The Structure of Behavior*. He maintained instead that genuine lucidity can only come from facing up to our finite historical situation, not by projecting our preferred idealizations onto it. There is no absolute: "the contingency of the lived perpetually threatens the eternal significations in which it is believed to be completely expressed" (SC 240/223). *Death therefore has a meaning that is crucial to the meaningfulness of life.* Merleau-Ponty thus insisted on the need "to assure oneself that the experience of eternity is not the unconsciousness of death" (SC 240/223). This is no less important than the distinction, which he upheld more firmly than before, between "the love of life" [*l'amour de la vie*] and biological self-preservation (SC 240/224). In fact, following Goldstein, Merleau-Ponty held that human self-preservation is a "phenomenon of disease," that it is just a pathologically limited manner of self-actualization (SC 190n1/245n97; cf. Goldstein 1934, 162; 1995, 337). The real essence of human life is to project itself beyond situations—not just biological, but also humanly created ones (SC 189/175). It is fundamentally an *orientation to the possible* (SC 190/176). "The healthy man proposes to live, to attain certain objects in the world or beyond [*au delà*] the world, and not to preserve himself." This is not to set healthiness in opposition to self-preservation. It is merely to assert that the norms of healthiness are existential and thus ultimately independent of biological existence. Thus, as Merleau-Ponty noted, some suicides can be understood as manifesting the primacy of existential over biological norms by showing that "man is capable of situating his proper being, not in biological existence, *but at the level of properly human relations*" (SC 190 n1/246 n97, emphasis added). It is noteworthy in this regard that Merleau-Ponty drew close links between acts of suicide and acts of revolution: "both presuppose the capacity of rejecting the given milieu and of searching for equilibrium beyond any milieu" (SC 190/175, 245 n97).

Although the conclusion of *The Structure of Behavior* can be summed up in terms of the pithy methodological desideratum, expressed in the final paragraph, "to define transcendental philosophy anew in such a way as to integrate with it the very phenomenon of the real" (SC 241/224), what this portends is, in certain ways, more clearly revealed in the claim made in the penultimate paragraph to the effect that, given the fulfillment of that desideratum, "*the sacrifice of life will be philosophically impossible*; it will be a question only of 'staking' [« *mettre en jeu* »] one's life, which is a deeper way of living" [*une manière plus profonde de vivre*] (SC 240/224, emphasis added). The philosophical impossibility of sacrifice announced here would not render indefensible the self-denial of which Merleau-Ponty had earlier defended the vital possibility. Nor does it necessarily render revolutionary martyrdom indefensible. It just rules out understanding it as self-*sacrifice* on the grounds that there is no overarching, authoritative framework within which a sacrificial gesture involving one's biological being could be meaningfully made. It is the metaphysical impossibility of giving or exchanging one's life *for* some future state of affairs. For there is no eternal Absolute that could serve as the guarantor—the clearinghouse, as it were—of any such economy. This by no means rules out the possibility of giving one's life, nor of holding false beliefs concerning the possibility of doing so sacrificially.[2] But it does aim to render philosophically indefensible any attempt to disburden oneself of responsibility for one's life (and ultimately death), or to misunderstand the life (and/or death) of another, by trying to derive its meaning from the future. Meaning is immanent in the present. If life is, in fact, a matter of venturesome self-actualization in the absence of eternal truths, then recognition of the metaphysical impossibility of sacrificing it should encourage that non-biological "love of life" that can push the bounds of personal, communal, and historical integration. As we shall see, it was along these lines that Merleau-Ponty sought to interpret Saint Exupéry's glorification of self-sacrifice in immanent (and thus incarnational) terms.

The metaphysical impossibility of sacrifice claimed by Merleau-Ponty in *The Structure of Behavior* also has a specific philosophical significance, to wit, the methodological claim that transcendental insight concerning the *a priori* conditions of lived experience cannot be obtained from a standpoint that would be situated outside of or beyond human life, but can only be achieved from within. It must be the case, then, that transcendental philosophy is a function of human existence—this is in effect what Merleau-Ponty meant in saying that it would have to be "integrated with the very phenomenon of the real." But given the contingency and finitude of "the real," transcendental philosophy cannot be underwritten by any sort of metaphysical guarantee. Lest it illicitly take for granted what it seeks to achieve, transcendental philosophy cannot avoid hazarding commitment to some normative standpoint concerning the meaningfulness of reality, such that it too, like any act of genuine transcendence, will be a matter of "*staking one's life.*"

Merleau-Ponty thereby claimed that, from the perspective of transcendental philosophy, *engagement* is not simply something commendable or even imperative in a distinct ethical sense, but rather that it is *epistemically necessary*. This was closely in line with the personalist views of Landsberg:

At the same time as being a necessity of moral life, *engagement* for a historical cause that incarnates certain values is an *indispensable* means of knowledge itself. This kind of engagement alone makes a profound knowledge possible, . . . *knowledge of the historicity that we live*, . . . a genuine comprehension of history that happens solely in the act of solidarizing and identifying with a cause. (Landsberg 1937, 187)

For Landsberg as for Merleau-Ponty, just as *engagement* calls for a transcendental-philosophical justification, transcendental philosophy implies a stance of *engagement*. But whereas Landsberg drew a distinction between my experience of historical inherence and the choice or decision I make to align with one "cause" over others, Merleau-Ponty, aiming to work out the standpoint of philosophy and philosophical truth itself, inclined to Marxism in part as a way of providing a more univocal view of history that would integrate what Landsberg held distinct. Always averse to any sort of potentially arbitrary or irrational decisionism, Merleau-Ponty thus deviated from Landsberg's conception of *engagement* in that for him, it was not premised on the idea of realizing something in the future (Landsberg 1937, 1980)—an orientation that leaves open the possibility of sacrifice. Rather, working within the limits of immanence as described above, Merleau-Ponty's basic claim here is that the project of transcendental philosophy itself ultimately just *is* a kind of *engagement*.

Death

In "L'existentialisme chez Hegel" (SNS 109–121/63–70), a short but dense discussion that was ostensibly a critical review of a lecture given by Jean Hyppolite on Hegel's *Phenomenology of Spirit*,[3] Merleau-Ponty articulated a view concerning death that is of considerable significance for understanding his existential phenomenology.

In his lecture, Hyppolite had more or less concurred with the Kierkegaardian critique of Hegelianism in general as an abstract systematization of the world that excludes or suppresses existence. With respect to *Phenomenology of Spirit*, however, Hyppolite claimed that although it did ultimately subordinate individual existence to abstract universality, Hegel *had* actually dealt therein with real human existence, "the full scope of human experience" (Hyppolite 1971, 94). He described Hegel's account of the emergence of self-consciousness through the acquisition of an internalized awareness of the negativity of personal death as the irruption of a new modality of distinctly human being—namely, existence. "The taking consciousness of life is thus something other than life pure and simple, and human existence, like the knowledge of life, is a new way of being which we can well call existence" (Hyppolite 1971, 95).

Merleau-Ponty was by and large in agreement with Hyppolite, except in one important respect. Whereas Hyppolite limited the protoexistentialism of Hegel to certain parts of *Phenomenology of Spirit*, on the grounds that Hegel's account of "absolute knowledge" ultimately sewed up the dialectical movement of existence in such a way that the meaning of history would subsume that of individual death (thus legitimating sacrifice), Merleau-Ponty sought to separate the whole of *Phenomenology of Spirit* from Hegel's later "orthodox" idealism as his contribution to existential philosophy. That is, Merleau-Ponty offered a qualified defense of Hegelian absolute knowledge *circa* 1807 against the sort of Kierkegaardian critique of its systematization *circa* 1827—that is, when Hegel had written his *Encyclopedia* and *Philosophy of Right*—that Hyppolite allowed.

Thus, not unlike Hyppolite, Merleau-Ponty argued that Hegel's thought is existentialist "in the sense that it views man not as being from the start a consciousness in full possession of its own clear thoughts, but as a life which is given to itself [*donnée à elle-même*] and which tries to understand itself." But he adds, "*all* of *Phenomenology of Spirit* describes man's efforts to recover [*ressaisir*] himself" (SNS 113/65, emphasis added). Merleau-Ponty thus interpreted "absolute knowledge" as "the final stage of the evolution of spirit as phenomenon [*l'esprit-phénomène*] wherein consciousness at last becomes equal to its spontaneous life and regains its self-possession." Crucially, he suggested that this was not so much a philosophy as "a way of living [*une manière de vivre*]." Or, as he also put it, it was a "militant" philosophy (SNS 112/64; cf. 237/134). Concerning the theological trichotomy between "the Church triumphant," "the Church suffering," and "the Church militant" (see Chapter 2, note 22), Merleau-Ponty explicitly attributed the first view to the "orthodox" Hegel, and the third to the reading of Hegel that he himself was defending as his own view. It would seem that he implicitly meant to associate Hyppolite's position—presumably along with many other formulations of existentialism—with some sense of purgatorial suffering.

In contrast to both the undue pessimism of the purgatorial view and the undue optimism of the triumphant view, Merleau-Ponty construed the movement of human existence in "militant" terms as contingently directed toward a "genuine reconciliation between men" (SNS 112/65). He argued that Hegel's *Phenomenology of Spirit* offered a richer—because thoroughly intersubjective—view of human existence than that found in it by Hyppolite, and he thought that this was precisely in virtue of the link between absolute knowledge and death that Hyppolite found objectionable. Merleau-Ponty thus defended the "deathliness" of Hegelian absolute knowledge as a key facet of a living understanding of intersubjectivity. In his view, Hegel's main philosophical achievement as far as existentialism was concerned was to unmask the role played by the consciousness of death in realizing rationality and achieving mutual understanding.

The key point for Merleau-Ponty is that "consciousness of life is, in a radical sense, consciousness of death" (SNS 115/66). That is, the awareness we have of life is ultimately *rooted* in our awareness of death, which enjoys a certain priority. The gist of the argument that stands behind this claim is that consciousness, as a kind of nothingness [*néant*] or negation of being, represents a "rupture" with life, where the latter is understood as an anonymous *pre*conscious force that spontaneously expends itself in its action, and which is in itself devoid of self-awareness. And this rupture with life shares some of the essential features of death. This holds even if, in accordance with Merleau-Ponty's critique of Sartre, consciousness is understood nondichotomously as only obtaining in a "hollow" [*creux*] as opposed to a "hole" [*trou*] in being.[4] "Life is only thinkable as presented to a consciousness of life which denies it" (SNS 116/67).

This rupture cannot be *completely* like death, though. At least not normally. It is important to recognize that there are two senses of "life" here that Merleau-Ponty does not distinguish explicitly: on the one hand, there is the sense of life as an anonymous, spontaneous force subsisting below the level of consciousness. This sense has *universal* import, and I shall refer to it as *life-as-such*. It was with this that Merleau-Ponty was principally concerned—in particular, this is the object of what he calls "the love of life." On the other hand, there is the sense of life that refers to the *particular* manifestations of life-as-such—I will refer to these simply as *lives*. Lives are founded on and thus imply life-as-such, but the converse does not hold: life-as-such does not imply any *particular* lives.

To construe consciousness-of-life as ultimately rooted in consciousness-of-death is thus to say three things: first, that the proper object of consciousness-of-life is life-as-such; second, that as a universal awareness, this consciousness involves a virtually complete death-like rupture with particular lives, including one's own; and third, that this rupture is self-conscious, and hence consciousness of something essentially like death, because, following Hegel, the experience of death stands at the very origin of self-consciousness.

Merleau-Ponty thus effectively rendered death and life-as-such epistemically indistinguishable. Although there is a certain truth in the idea that death individualizes, it is evident that Merleau-Ponty was here distancing himself drastically from Heidegger's notion of *Sein-zum-Tod* (cf. Landsberg 1936, 41f). For Merleau-Ponty, what alone is thinkable is on the contrary that death *communalizes*. When we seek to think the totality of our existence in terms of death, as Heidegger, for example, asks us to do, what we are *really* doing is thinking it in terms of life taken universally. Hence Merleau-Ponty's assertion that "my consciousness of myself as death and nothingness is deceitful [*menteuse*] and contains an affirmation of my being and my life" (SNS 118/68). He turned to Beauvoir's *Pyrrhus et Cinéas* for a forthright statement concerning the alternative to Heidegger supposedly offered by French existentialism: "Death does not exist for me while I am alive" (SNS 121/70, citing Beauvoir 1947, 61). For Merleau-Ponty, this is supposed to mean that (normal) human existence is situated within the universality of life-as-such, and that it is consequently directed toward self-realization within historical horizons that transcend the life of the individual.

Such is the view that Merleau-Ponty wanted to defend against the deceitfulness shared by purgatorial and triumphant views of existence. Accordingly, he claimed that there are, broadly speaking, two ways of thinking about death (SNS 116f/67). The first way, which Merleau-Ponty rejected, resentfully sees death as just an incomprehensible and impenetrable end to existence. This view is thus "pathetic and complacent," and this is because it is deceived. Blind to the vital significance of death, it is blind to the vital significance of its own life. The underlying problem with this way of approaching death is that it is not self-consciously historical.

In contrast, the second way of thinking about death, which Merleau-Ponty accepts, *is* self-consciously historical. Specifically, it is *militant*. This means—and here Merleau-Ponty was contrasting himself to other readings of Hegel, notably that of Hyppolite, but Sartre's as well—that it recognizes both the abstractness of the universality of life, *and* that this abstractness is the reason for the above deception. "The abstract universal which starts out opposed to life must be made concrete." This approach—characterized by Merleau-Ponty as "dry and resolute" —thus "takes up [*assume*] death and turns it into a more acute awareness of life." It "interiorizes" or "transmutes"—that is, sublimates—death into (particular) lives. In this way, consciousness of death "goes beyond itself." The negativity of death is deployed in such a way as to promote the concrete realization of the underlying universality of human coexistence, the incarnation of life-as-such.

The point of this is most clearly seen in Merleau-Ponty's claim that "the only experience which brings me close to an authentic awareness of death is the experience of contact with another" (SNS 117/68). Here, Merleau-Ponty offers his interpretation of the struggle of consciousnesses as originally described by Hegel. Contrary to the views of Kojève and Sartre, for example, the idea is that scrutiny of the encounter and the ensuing conflict reveals that there must be an underlying common ground. "We cannot be aware of the conflict unless we are aware of our reciprocal relationship and our common humanity. We do not deny each other except by mutual recognition of our consciousness" (SNS 118/68; cf. PhP 408). The experience of objectification, of the death-like stripping away of all particularity, lays bare that "my consciousness of an other as an enemy comprises an affirmation of him as an equal," that is, as an equal participant in life-as-such. Just as I find consciousness-of-life in consciousness-of-death, so too do "I find myself in the other." Otherness is thinkable only on the basis of this sameness—recognition of which further revivifies my deathly self-awareness. "*If I am negation, then by following the implication of this universal negation to its ultimate conclusion, I will see its self-denial and its transformation into coexistence*" (SNS 118/68, italics added).

Thus, according to Merleau-Ponty, death is integral, not simply to historical life, but to historical progress. At root, this is because history is made through transcendence, the creative capacity of human existence to detach from the repetitiveness of life, to step beyond ourselves, *beyond our lives*, such as to alter the conditions of life—I shall further discuss this below in terms of "human productivity." Although necessarily underwritten by life-as-such, transcendence is a matter of the negativity of death, as understood by Merleau-Ponty. Death is a vital part of life-as-such, for it is precisely through it that life-as-such gains self-consciousness. The experience of vulnerability and dependence—whether in the face of death or in the face of the other—decenters my life, dislocates it temporally, drawing me out of myself in a way that elicits productive involvement. The power that is revealed in such an experience is one that "makes us wait with our own being somewhat in abeyance and in this way is a creative power which is not of ourselves but which invites and makes possible our own creative response" (Pax 1982, 198).

Such a temporal dislocation is central to Merleau-Ponty's reading of the interiorization of death by the Hegelian slave [*Knecht*]. Recall that in the story told by Hegel, what defines a slave is that he chooses life over death. What Merleau-Ponty emphasizes in his interpretation is that the life chosen is life-as-such. The slave "*consents* to live only for others," according to Merleau-Ponty, "but it is still he who *wants* to maintain his life at this price" (SNS 119/68f, emphasis added). The point in putting it this way is to insist that there is—or at least there was in the past—vital meaning and value even in servitude. To be sure, slavish living is unjust. But there is always something that exceeds it, and it is this that accounts for the "love of life" that puts the slave in contact with the "vital foundations" [*assises vitales*] of humanity, giving the slave "the most exact awareness of the human situation" (SNS 118f/68f). Familiarity with life-as-such is slavery's hidden strength. This is why it is the slave who makes history and why humanist egalitarianism will ultimately prevail: "it is he who will finally have the only possible mastery—not at the expense of others, but at the expense of nature" (SNS 119/69).

This is another way of expressing the historical process as the negation of the negation of abstract individuality that culminates in universal reconciliation. The lives of history's slaves attest to the following general point, which is the most important lesson that Merleau-Ponty draws from his reading of Hegel: "Death is the negation of all particular given being, and consciousness of death is synonymous with consciousness of the universal. . . . To be aware of death and to think or reason amount to the same thing, since one thinks only by taking leave of the particularities of life [*en quittant les particularités de la vie*] and thus by conceiving death" (SNS 115ff/67).

For Merleau-Ponty, this is tied to the realization of philosophy, inasmuch as it is a matter of bringing rationality into being—overcoming, that is, the mutual separation of particular consciousnesses in such a way that "perspectives meet up, perceptions confirm each other, [and] a meaning emerges" (PhP xv). In other words, overcoming what we might call the structural non-sense or even madness of a world of alienation by "taking leave" of *its* particularities, and instead bringing forth the underlying commonality and making *that* concrete. To realize philosophy is thus to redeem what Merleau-Ponty called "the promise of humanity" [*la promesse d'humanité*] through a process that grapples with death. "Learning the truth about death and struggle is the long maturation process by which history overcomes its contradictions and fulfils the promise of humanity—present in the consciousness of death and in the struggle with the other—in the living relationship among men" (SNS 119/69). And this is why, at the end of his discussion of Hegel and death, Merleau-Ponty suggested that existentialism might be *most completely* defined

> by the idea of a universality which men affirm or imply by the mere fact of their being and at the very moment of their opposition to each other, in the idea of a reason immanent in madness [*déraison*], of a freedom which becomes what it is by giving itself bonds [*liens*], and to which the least perception, the slightest movement of the heart, the smallest action, bear incontestable witness [*sont les témoignages incontestables*]. (SNS 121/70)

Key here is that understanding human existence in terms of these paradoxical views of universality, reason, and freedom, and in a way that implies the literal ubiquitousness of corroborating experiential evidence, is possible only in virtue of the idea of a militant intersubjective sublimation of death—as is encountered, for instance, at the very end of *Phenomenology of Perception*.

Thinking the political

Inasmuch as the foregoing view of death bears upon the realization of authentic intersubjectivity, it has consequences for the sort of *engagement* of which Merleau-Ponty intended his existential phenomenology to be a part. And as we shall see, it is ultimately in connection with his effort to rethink the Marxist understanding of revolution—against tendencies that would approach it, at least in effect, as some sort of mortal adventure—that the relevance of his view of heroism comes to light.

In "La Guerre a eu lieu," published in 1945, Merleau-Ponty argued that French philosophy, traditionally practiced from the isolated standpoint of the Cartesian "meditating ego" (a perspective that Merleau-Ponty tended to assimilate as much to Kantianism as to Cartesianism) (cf. SNS 257/145; cf. 180, 298/103, 168; NI 2 [23]), had received from the experience of the war an incontrovertible "wake-up call," so to speak, such that its principal task now was to come to terms with what had been "unthinkable" [*impensable*] from the traditional perspective—viz., *politics* (SNS 255/145). "Politics," he wrote, "is impossible from the perspective of consciousness" (SNS 256/145). This is because it has no grasp of the objective consequences of actions, nor of the concrete interconnectivity of the human world. As Merleau-Ponty put it, the abstract subjectivism of "this solitary Cartesian" means that "he does not see his shadow behind him projected onto history as onto a wall, that meaning, that shape which his actions assume on the outside, that Objective Spirit which *is* him" (SNS 257/146).[5]

The result of this was that in the interwar period, French philosophers (among others) tended to inhabit an idealized political reality, upholding universal humanistic values with an attitude of naïve pacifism. Phenomena that were inconsistent with this universalism—in particular, those based on ascriptions of nationality and "race"—were effectively dismissed as irrational and ultimately illusory. This is why, according to Merleau-Ponty, the real significance and portent of epochal events in the development of European fascism in the 1930s—such as the Anschluß, Guernica, and Kristallnacht—were lost on so many French intellectuals (cf. NI 22 [2], 27 [8], 32 [13]). And this was not a blameless ignorance. "No one's hands are clean" (SNS 259/147), he thought, because freedom is always ultimately complicit with worldly power.

For Merleau-Ponty, what the defeat of France in 1940 and the war as a whole taught was, above all else, *history* (SNS 265/150).[6] It was primarily in this way that his *examen de conscience* and its critique of Cartesian rationalism avoided both conclusions of a traditional religious nature, as well as the *ir*rational conclusions to which certain other, superficially similar analyses were led—for example, the reactionary perspective of Pierre Drieu la Rochelle: "France was destroyed by the rationalism to which its spirit had been reduced. Today, rationalism is dead. We can only rejoice in this collapse of rationalism" (1941, 171). For Merleau-Ponty did not reject the old values. The problem did not lie in those as such, but rather in the fact that they were not concrete. The lesson was that "values remain nominal and indeed have no value without an economic and political infrastructure that brings them into existence. . . . It is a question not of giving up our values of 1939, *but of realizing them* [les accomplir]" (SNS 268/152, emphasis added). To this end, philosophy needed to reorient itself so as to render human coexistence, in all its contingency and complexity, *thinkable* as a historically dynamic confluence of subjectivity and objectivity, of freedom and necessity. It needed to reorient itself to the living present. That is, it needed to form its ideas "in contact with the present" in order to be able to "accomodate all truths *and* to take a stand in reality" (SNS 273/154, emphasis added). The solution rested on a certain conception of totality—as discussed above, what was crucial in Merleau-Ponty's view was to grasp "the total intention" of society, "the Idea in the Hegelian sense" in which "everything signifies everything" (PhP xiii; SNS 268/152). As Merleau-Ponty put it—wrapping up "La Guerre a eu lieu" with a direct statement of the sort of gloss conventionally applied (or rather misapplied) by commentators to Saint Exupéry's words at the end of *Phenomenology of Perception*—"*there is nothing outside this unique fulguration of existence*" (SNS 269/152, italics added).[7]

It is interesting to note that Merleau-Ponty recognized that the totalistic character of his political outlook had certain superficial affinities with fascist thought.[8] This is evident from a short document entitled "*La Résistance: la France et le monde de demain*, par un philosophe" ["*The Resistance: France and the World of Tomorrow*, by a philosopher"].[9] Following discussions with Sartre and Jean-Toussaint Desanti, Merleau-Ponty drafted this document toward the end of 1941.[10] In it, he offered a fairly pessimistic description of the French Resistance at the time as suffering a profound spiritual crisis. Aside from its communist and conservative members, "the majority of patriots have an ideology that is confused, hesitant, purely negative, or else concerned solely with individual morality" (in Sartre 1970, 110), a situation that manifested itself in "a kind of laziness and fatalism" (cited in Michel 1962, 421). In this work, Merleau-Ponty attempted to account for this crisis in philosophical terms. He linked the infirmities of the French to their "analytical spirit," and contrasted this with the "synthetic thinking" that elsewhere gave rise to totalitarianism, in particular National Socialism. Merleau-Ponty cautiously commended this kind of thinking, "for it alone permits one to give an account of the diversity and the interaction of situations, whether particular or collective" (in Sartre 1970, 110). That is, it enables one to cease treating individuals in isolation, and instead, as organic parts of the whole. Merleau-Ponty thus thought that to be successful, *the defeat of fascist totalitarianism would also have to assimilate something of it*. Aspects of totalitarian ideology could be used in support of a genuine democracy. To some extent, according to Merleau-Ponty, the war had actually occasioned a spontaneous turn toward a more collectivistic outlook, but this was in deep conflict with the old individualistic ideals. This was the underlying reason for the hesitation: a straightforward communist solution was just as untenable as a simple return to *status quo ante*. The only solution could be a socialism that takes as its goal to overcome liberalism by concretizing its ideals. This is what Merleau-Ponty recommended as a viable strategy for securing French unity.

> Were a government in exile to take stock of the difficult situation in which we are struggling, and to choose for its slogan the realization of concrete freedom through the collectivization of the means of production, it would bring together around itself the majority of the French. It would give to the Resistance a positive faith; a France provided with such a message would regain a politics and a dignity; it would make a new place for itself in the world. (in Sartre 1970, 100f)

Although nuanced in important ways in light of the outcome of the war, this essentially remained Merleau-Ponty's position *circa* 1945. The key idea concerns the material conditions of liberal values. It is from this standpoint that he issued his critique of the impassive idealism and apolitical neutrality of prewar thinking. Although it is unclear to what extent he meant it to apply to himself as well, this critique clearly had a special pertinence to the particular social sector to which he himself had belonged, to wit, progressively-minded but largely contemplative intellectuals, especially *normaliens*. There were exceptions to this, of course: Nizan is a case in point—there is no sense whatsoever in which Communist activists like him were guilty of the leisurely philosophical illusions later censured by Merleau-Ponty.

Nevertheless, they may have been guilty of *other* theoretical errors, and Merleau-Ponty's analysis did have something to say about Marxism as well. For at least in its official forms, Marxist theory was at a deeper level surprisingly similar to the detached Cartesianism that it claimed to repudiate in practice. For it, too, ultimately made politics—and the war in particular, which it saw as ultimately only an internecine conflict between capitalist factions—into a matter of mere appearance, in this case, of the class struggle: "what remained real beneath that appearance was the common fate of proletariats of all nations and the profound solidarity of all forms of capitalism through the internal contradictions of the regime" (SNS 261/148). So whereas the naïve Cartesian humanist thought that there were only "men" and thus could not understand anti-Semitism, for example, because there is no such thing as a "Jew," the Marxist thought that there were only "classes"—"no proletarian in uniform can feel *anything but* proletarian" (SNS 262/148)—and thus reduced anti-Semitism to a moronic "capitalistic episode," a social contradiction that was in truth but a node on the path to a classless society. But Merleau-Ponty insisted that historical truth cannot be understood to lie *behind* the phenomena of events. "There are not two histories, one true and the other empirical; there is only one, in which everything that happens plays a part, *if only one knows how to interpret it*" (SNS 263/149, emphasis added).

Merleau-Ponty believed that existentialism, understood as a holistic, pheno-menological Marxism, offered the hermeneutical framework that progressive left-wing politics in general required. It was primarily for this reason that Merleau-Ponty was, as Whiteside aptly put it, an "*indefatigable proponent*" of existentialism in the postwar period (Whiteside 1988, 36, italics added). That is, he actively strove to promote his project as a political-philosophical common ground, especially for Marxism and social Catholicism. In his own work, and in his representations of the work of others,[11] Merleau-Ponty aimed to portray his existentialism as an approach uniquely suited to theorize political phenomena adequately, that is, to render them "thinkable" in all their concrete complexity, and to do so in an ideologically (but not normatively) neutral way.

The proletariat question

The themes of sacrifice, death, and politics come together in the problem that lay at the heart of Merleau-Ponty's political thinking, to wit, the status of the proletariat *qua* universal class of history. Merleau-Ponty wanted to save the latter notion, that is, universal class, from Hegel but also from Marx by approaching it otherwise than by way of the contrast between its being-*in*-itself and being-*for*-itself—a dualistic approach that was still present even in Lukács' work. In particular, his aim was to conceptualize class anew in terms of intercorporeal coexistence, rather than in terms of objective economic structure, in order to be able to approach the political problem of proletarian class consciousness in terms of "*the social*," that is, that "dimension of existence . . . with which we are in contact by the mere fact of existing, and which we carry about inseparably with us prior to any objectification" (PhP 415).

Following Marx, Merleau-Ponty regarded Hegel's account of history and the liberation it realizes as incomplete, inasmuch as it merely ushered in a higher stage of exploitation, one in which "slaves" are so dehumanized, so de-particularized, as to be effectively reduced to life-as-such. Merleau-Ponty thus took up Marx's account of the proletariat as the class whose historical task is to do away with servitude once and for all. Although he had some misgivings, Merleau-Ponty recognized as the core of Marxism a theory of the proletariat as the latent existence of universal concrete intersubjectivity. "In the name of the proletariat, Marx describes a situation such that those in it, and they alone, have the *full experience* of the freedom and universality which Marx considered the defining characteristics of man" (HT 122/113). In other words, "the proletariat as Marx conceived it embodied simultaneously the experience of individuality and universality" (HT 155/144). Proletarians thus embody the truth of the species, and Merleau-Ponty makes this out to be a matter of their lived experience. "The very exercise of life" in their objective situation leads them "to the point of detachment and freedom at which it is possible to be conscious of dependency" (HT 123f/115), that is, the interpersonal dependency to which rational idealism is blind. Hence the "inseparability of objective necessity and *the spontaneous movement of the masses*" (HT 17/15). As the "moving force" [*moteur*] of history, workers have "instincts" for it (HT 121/113), such that their collective praxis transforms the world "as a spontaneous development in their own lives" (HT 39/36). For the proletarian, "individuality or self-consciousness and consciousness are absolutely identical" (HT 124/115). In short, the working class is universality incarnate:

> the condition of the proletarian is such that he can detach himself from particularities not just in thought and through a process of abstraction, but in reality and through the very movement of his life. He alone *is* the universality that he thinks, he alone realizes the self-consciousness that philosophers have sketched out in reflection. (HT 124f/116)

All of this is very much in line with Lukács' understanding of the proletariat as the "subject-object of history." But whereas Lukács had emphasized more directly the political consequences of this conception, Merleau-Ponty was primarily concerned with using it to show that the philosophical standpoint that he wished to endorse was possible—or rather, that it was "possible" precisely because it was *already actual* (cf. PhP xv). Although nowadays, few philosophers take the idea of the proletariat very seriously, what is significant, as we shall see, is that this idea is implicated directly at the very heart of Merleau-Ponty's philosophical work (which *is* taken very seriously).

But given Merleau-Ponty's view of death, the classical conception of the proletariat did raise a serious problem. For unlike the Hegelian "slave," who chooses a life of subservience, the revolutionary task of the proletariat is to reject servitude altogether. An honorable idea, to be sure. *But this task is, by definition, to be performed from the standpoint of absolute knowledge.* And what the task involves is precisely overcoming that standpoint—overcoming, that is, the *manière de vivre* definitive of the proletariat. This is meant to imply what Lukács called its "self-abolition" [*Selbstaufhebung*] *qua* exploited class (HCC 82, 84/70, 71; cf. AD 65/47, where Merleau-Ponty cites HCC 93/80). But since that way of living, thus conceived, includes all living particularity, the revolutionary moment would thus imply, as Merleau-Ponty's then-close colleague Trân Dúc Tháo later put it, "an ultimate form of *sacrifice*" (1951, 318; cf. 1949, 321f, 327).

As we have seen, for Merleau-Ponty, this was metaphysically indefensible. He thus thought that the formulations of classical Marxism concerning the proletariat had to be rethought. But this was not because the objective composition of the proletariat— that is, its being-in-itself—had changed since Marx's time through some degree of bourgeoisification of the working class and proletarianization of the *petit bourgeoisie*, such that the "intellectual needs" of the "objectively revolutionary class" could no longer be satisfied by Marxism in its orthodox form. Such was Trân's view (Trân 1946, 173; 1949, 328f). But while there may have been some truth to this, it did not challenge the sacrificial view of revolutionary change. Trân expressed this in the following illuminating way: "if, in accordance with Heidegger's magnificent line, 'Dasein [*la réalité humaine*] chooses its heroes' [*das Dasein wählt sich seinen Helden*], its choice is the act of a real [*effective*] freedom only if it bears precisely upon the destiny prefigured in its objective situation, if its project is not just any project, but *the very project of its own dereliction*" (Trân 1946, 173, citing SZ 385; cf. Trân 1949, 320).

For Merleau-Ponty, the basic problem with Marxist theory as it stood at the time was that it was fundamentally *morbid*. This is *not* because it thematized death, but rather because it did so *in the wrong way*. Although Merleau-Ponty thought that Marx had correctly denied the possibility of thinking the future (HT 136f; EP 41/50f), this denial was effectively lost on Marxism such as it actually existed. Its overly futural orientation was thus a kind of "triumphant" thinking that invoked an "experience of eternity" that led to a certain "unconsciousness of death" in the present (cf. SC 240/223). Its call for revolution thus worked at cross-purposes, inasmuch as the life of the new humanity for which it militated could not be brought into vital connection with the lives of those who would comprise the collective agency of its realization. There was a profound split between end and means (and hence between theory and practice) in that the communist ideal implied an impossible hiatus from life's "vital foundations." The problem for Merleau-Ponty was how to tell the Marxist story of humanity "smashing the given structures of society and acceding through praxis to [what Marx, in the third volume of *Capital*, called] 'the reign of freedom'" (SNS 226/128), and to do so in terms of living experience, *but without invoking any philosophically indefensible sacrificial imperative*. In a nutshell, this is the idea of an *incarnational* Marxism—that the structures of human universality that represent the ideals of communism already exist in latent form, and that revolution is thus not a matter of inventing them, but of realizing them—a process that can be described as "working out the consequences of the Incarnation" through forms of praxis that are ultimately based not upon autonomous decisions and detachment but passive prepersonal inherence and the historical necessity of those structures themselves. As Merleau-Ponty put it, being a Marxist in this way "is indeed to reach the universal, but without ceasing to be what we are" (SNS 265/150).

The tacit *cogito*

In line with the thrust of "Western Marxism," as well as with the Catholic interest in Marx in France in the 1930s, Merleau-Ponty held that the classical formulations of Marxism were due for a theoretical overhaul in the light of twentieth-century conditions. The point of this overhaul would be to express the fact that with respect to the realization of universal proletarian class consciousness, "ideological" issues are no less politically real than economic issues. Merleau-Ponty rejected the idea—and claimed that most Marxists did likewise—of any simplistic materialist construal of consciousness in epiphenomenal terms (SNS 135/78). Marxist analysis is credible only when it does not "suppress the subjective factors of history in favour of objective ones, but rather tie[s] them together" (SNS 263/149). No account of class consciousness as the coming to awareness of an intersubjective situation can do away with individual consciousness, which is to say, Marxism cannot avoid giving an account of the *cogito*. "Every man, even a Marxist, is obliged to agree with Descartes that if we know some external reality, then it is only on condition of grasping within ourselves this process of knowing, that no in-itself would be accessible to us if it were not at the same time for-us, and that the meaning we find in it ultimately depends on our assent" (SNS 138/79).

Clearly, though, agreement with this claim—which, in any case, may go well beyond what can be legitimately attributed to Descartes—is consistent with divergent interpretations of the *cogito*. In particular, it is consistent with the rejection of the traditional Cartesian interpretation. In Merleau-Ponty's view, this interpretation is "false" because it one-sidedly emphasizes the autonomy of consciousness; "it removes itself and shatters our inherence in the world" (SNS 235/133). It sets up the *cogito* as a merely contemplative escape, and thus remains a conceptual expression of "that phase of history where man's essence and existence are still separated" (SNS 136/78). What was required is "a new conception of consciousness," one that would "found both its autonomy *and its dependence*" (SNS 143/82, emphasis added). To attain this would require surpassing the Cartesian *cogito* in a way metonymical to the dialectical realization of philosophy as a whole through the destruction of its *separateness*. "The only way to do away with [the Cartesian *cogito*] is to *realize* it, that is, to show that it is *eminently contained in interpersonal relations*" (SNS 235f/133, emphasis added).

Merleau-Ponty thought that Marxism, in its discovery of "social existence as the most 'interior' dimension of our life" (SNS 142f/82), implicitly contained an account of the *cogito* that satisfied this desideratum, that is, an account of "the process of knowing" that situates it squarely in the context of intersubjective relations. But it had yet to furnish this with a sound theoretical formulation. This is, I would argue, the principal theoretical task that Merleau-Ponty's account of the *cogito* (PhP 423–68) in terms of the "tacit *cogito*," or the "true [*véritable*] *cogito*," was designed to fulfill. The point was to specify the site of contact between thought and being that would be the *conditio sine qua non* of human existence and coexistence.

A complete review of Merleau-Ponty's discussion of the *cogito* is unnecessary here, and would take the present analysis far afield. I shall therefore just focus on those aspects that are directly relevant to the purposes of this chapter.

Noting the paradoxical nature of interpersonal relations, that is, the dialectical mixture of autonomy and dependence that they exhibit, Merleau-Ponty expressed their possibility in terms of situated corporeality: they are possible only because Ego and Other are "defined by their situation and are not freed from all inherence." That is, they are only possible

> provided that at the very moment when I experience [*éprouve*] my existence, *even at the extreme limit of reflection*, I lack the absolute density which would place me outside time, and that I discover within myself a kind of internal weakness standing in the way of my being totally individualized, which exposes me to the gaze of others as a man among men. (PhP vii, emphasis added)

As Merleau-Ponty pointed out, this is at odds with the traditional understanding of the *cogito*, which identified egoic existence with self-awareness, thus occluding being-for-others. The "true *cogito*" is the result of a "radical reflection" that *is* able to account for being-for-others. It does this by discovering in me "not only my presence to myself, *but also the possibility of an 'outside spectator'* [« *spectateur étranger* »]" (PhP vii, emphasis added). Radically pursued, reflection attains "an affirmation of myself by myself [*une épreuve de moi par moi*]" that reveals me in a social and historical situation (PhP 462; cf. vii). "The certitude I have of myself here is a real [*véritable*] perception: I grasp myself . . . as a particular thought, as a thought engaged with certain objects, as a thought in act [*une pensée en acte*]" (PrP 61/22). Rather than identifying my existence with my thoughts thereof, radical reflection "recognizes my thought itself as an inalienable fact, and eliminates any kind of idealism in discovering me as 'being toward the world' [« *être au monde* »]" (PhP viii).

By focusing on "the presence of oneself to oneself" (PhP 462) in this way, this approach to the self-experience of the thinking subject follows an alternative path that is supposed to cut between, on the one hand, the wholly constitut*ed* private psyche of objectivism, and, on the other hand, subjectivism's wholly constitut*ing* universal thinker. This is the sense in which Merleau-Ponty claimed that "the tacit *cogito* . . . is anterior to all philosophy" (PhP 462). It is also the case, however, that, paradoxically, "the tacit *cogito* is a *cogito* only when it has found expression for itself" (PhP 463). It is a matter of reflection "recapturing itself" and acquiring an "awareness of its own dependence on an unreflective life which is its initial, constant, and final situation" (PhP ix). This unreflective life is life-as-such, and so, in a manner of speaking, the true *cogito* concerns *its* self-experience—an experience that comes to "know itself [*se connaît*]," that is, to gain self-consciousness, only by becoming *my* thought, a shift that occurs "only in those extreme situations in which it is threatened" (PhP 462).

Given what we have seen of Merleau-Ponty's view of death and its connection to alterity, it not surprising that the examples he gives of such threatening situations are "the dread of death or of another's gaze upon me" (PhP 462). Merleau-Ponty argued that there is a fundamental link between "the reflective recapture [*reprise*] of the unreflective," that is, the openness of my reflection to life-as-such as the unreflective basis of my existence, and "the tension of my experience towards another" (PhP 413). Both involve the same apparent paradox. In each case, "it is a matter of knowing how I can break outside myself [*faire une pointe hors de moi-même*] and have a lived experience of the unreflective as such [*vivre l'irréfléchi comme tel*]" (PhP 413). The underlying idea that serves to resolve the seeming paradoxicality is that because life-as-such is universal, the experience of self-givenness can be achieved—in fact, can *only* be achieved—within the intersubjective dynamics of social and historical situations.

This is why for Merleau-Ponty, the archetypical instance of the tacit *cogito* lies in the "tacit commitment" with which one comports oneself un-self-consciously with respect to the sociohistorical background of a given situation, and which can—in the event that that background becomes foregrounded, that is, focal—be transformed into a more explicit and possibly collective self-consciousness. As Merleau-Ponty expressed it: "during periods of calm, nation and class are there as stimuli to which I respond only absent-mindedly or confusedly; they are merely latent. A revolutionary situation, or one of national danger, transforms those preconscious relationships with class and nation, which were merely lived, into the definite taking of a stand." Just as with Saint Exupéry's Barcelonan bookkeeper-turned-soldier, "*the tacit commitment becomes explicit*" (PhP 417, emphasis altered).

It is in this context that Merleau-Ponty presented the clearest phenomenological formulation of the problem that gives the tacit *cogito* its meaning, to wit, "how the presence to myself (*Urpräsenz*) which defines me and which conditions every alien presence, is at the same time de-presentation (*Entgegenwärtigung*) and throws me outside myself" (PhP 417, italics removed). As to the significance of this problem, Merleau-Ponty was clear: "this double sense of the *cogito* is the basic fact of metaphysics" (SNS 164/93). This is why, as he put it—with clear import for the question concerning the deference to Saint Exupéry at the end of *Phenomenology of Perception*—"philosophy does not culminate in a return to the self" (PhP vi). And what is crucial is that for Merleau-Ponty, this double sense of the *cogito*—which Merleau-Ponty related to the "double anonymity" of our *être-au-monde*—is best captured through a Marxist-inspired approach to historicity.

In general, Merleau-Ponty's account of the tacit *cogito* would thus provide the outstanding theoretical grounds for the analysis of "the moment when the subjective and objective conditions of history become interwoven, the mode in which class exists before becoming aware of itself—in short, the status of the social and the phenomenon of coexistence" (SNS 140/81). Specifically, this would enable a viable approach to the intersubjective nature of class consciousness as "a fact-value" [*fait-valeur*] or "incarnated value" [*valeur incarnée*] (SNS 140/80), by approaching it in the context of "absolute history"—that milieu wherein "man no longer appears as a product of his environment nor an absolute legislator but [rather] emerges as a product-producer, the locus where necessity can turn into concrete liberty" (SNS 226, 237/128, 134).

In this way, the tacit *cogito* is the fulcrum of history, and *a fortiori* of the realization of philosophy. For both philosophy as well as for Marxism, inasmuch as they accept the need to apprehend "the process of knowing," the upshot is clear: "we must not only adopt a reflective attitude, in an irrefutable *cogito*, but also reflect on this reflection, understand the natural situation which it is conscious of succeeding and which is therefore part of its definition." We must "not merely practise philosophy, but also become aware [*nous rendre compte*] of the transformation which it brings with it in the spectacle of the world and in our existence. *Only on this condition can philosophical knowledge cease to be a specialization or a technique* [i.e., cease to be 'separate'] *and become absolute knowledge*" (PhP 75, emphasis added), that is, "integrated with the very phenomenon of the real."

Class consciousness

This account of the "tacit *cogito*" relates directly to the Marxist—and especially Lukácsian—problematic of proletarian class consciousness. Readers of *Phenomenology of Perception* know that Merleau-Ponty included a somewhat lengthy discussion of this problematic (PhP 505–12) in the middle of the final chapter of the book (PhP 496–520)—the chapter devoted, at least nominally, to freedom.[12] But what is the point of this discussion? Is it, for instance, an illustrative reiteration of the conceptual analysis of freedom as *situated* freedom that is developed in the preceding parts of the chapter as a critique of the Sartrean idea of *absolute* freedom? After all, the segue with which Merleau-Ponty launched into the discussion of class consciousness stated that "we would arrive at *the same result* by considering our relations with history" (PhP 505, italics added). One may thus be tempted to regard this discussion as an incidental supplement to the main argument, an example that may be illuminating and perhaps even have some corroborative value, but one the specific content of which is *inessential* to the philosophical thrust of the work. Indeed, something along these lines is probably the standard wisdom in contemporary philosophical scholarship on Merleau-Ponty (inasmuch as it considers the question at all), which—as discussed earlier—discounts all allusions to Merleau-Ponty's Marxism in a similar way.

But this view is unsatisfactory. Here, it must be noted that Merleau-Ponty's statement about reaching "the same result" can easily mislead. For while it is certainly true that the discussion of class consciousness supports the account of situated freedom that Merleau-Ponty had outlined *contra* Sartre in the initial part of the chapter, it is also the case that this discussion goes *well beyond* that result. And it is on this basis alone that Merleau-Ponty was able to claim that our *être-au-monde* is the "concrete bearer" of a "double anonymity," the fact that our existence unfolds between impersonal poles of generality and idiosyncrasy—which is, as he immediately added, the transcendental condition of there being "situations, a meaning [*sens*] of history, and a historical truth—three ways of saying the same thing" (PhP 512). Moreover, it is from here that he was able to go on to claim that "I am an intersubjective field" and pose the question: "From *this* point of view, then, what becomes of the freedom we discussed at the outset?" (PhP, 515, italics added). After a brief critique of the idea of freedom as absolute choice, which does not repeat what had been developed earlier, Merleau-Ponty finally asks: "What then is freedom?" (PhP 517), and takes this up in the final few pages that follow.

A straightforward reading would thus show that the discussion of class consciousness lies at the very heart of the chapter on freedom (corollary to which it could be claimed that, if anything, it is the *beginning* of the chapter, i.e., the part explicitly focused on Sartre, that is inessential to the chapter as a whole). For it is with regard to class consciousness that the philosophical heavy-lifting, so to speak, in Merleau-Ponty's argument is accomplished. Again, that this is lost on most readers nowadays can be attributed in large part to the widely-held assumption that, however strong his proclivities may have been, for Merleau-Ponty, Marxism is *theoretically secondary* to phenomenology. As discussed in the Preface, I believe that this assumption is false, and that on the contrary, Marxism and phenomenology are equally important and essentially interdependent aspects of Merleau-Ponty's postwar thought, but also that, in certain respects, Marxism has priority. The interdependence of Marxism and phenomenology has primarily to do with method, and it manifests itself at numerous places within Merleau-Ponty's work. But it is the discussion of class consciousness in *Phenomenology of Perception* that provides perhaps the most insightful glimpse into the methodological ground of Merleau-Ponty's existential phenomenology.

The methodological significance of freedom

I suggested that the final chapter of *Phenomenology of Perception* is "at least nominally" about freedom. It *is* about freedom, but this qualification is appropriate because the point of this chapter has not been well understood. (One will search the literature on Merleau-Ponty in vain for a compelling account of the philosophical *raison d'être* of the "freedom" chapter.) In particular, it is not simply about freedom *per se*, as if the point were to give a phenomenological account of freedom as just another—even if the most important—in a motley list of topics that Merleau-Ponty wished to address. Nor is it the case, as suggested above, that Merleau-Ponty was principally concerned with the view of freedom that Sartre had presented in *Being and Nothingness*, and which was being widely discussed in France at the time. To be sure, that was a concern. But we miss the true rationale for the chapter if we fail to locate it within a broader frame of reference. We thus need to ask why *Phenomenology of Perception* ends with a discussion of freedom at all.

We need to approach the chapter on freedom as belonging to the Third Part of the book which, in structural terms, was methodological, offering a meta-level "phenomenology of phenomenology," that is, a transcendental account of the pheno-menological reduction (see above, Preface). The point of the last part of *Pheno-menology of Perception* (which also includes the chapters on the *cogito* and temporality) is thus to offer a methodological validation of the approach taken in the preceding (two) parts of the book. It is crucial to recognize the location of the chapter on freedom as the culmination of this metalevel exercise, and the implication that this discussion represents the highest expression of Merleau-Ponty's understanding of the phenomenological reduction—in other words, the deepest justification of the pretensions of *Phenomenology of Perception* to convey genuine philosophical truth.

Rather than the Sartrean account of radical freedom, then, the primary point of reference here is *Husserl's* idea of the "perfect freedom" [*vollkommenen Freiheit*] that stands behind the performance of the reduction, a view initially stated in the first book of *Ideas* (Husserl 1982, 58), and his subsequent recognition of the inadequacy of this idea. Merleau-Ponty picks up on this in his treatment of freedom, and in characteristic fashion, he writes as if he were elaborating what was implicit in Husserl's own thought.

Notably, the only philosophical reference that Merleau-Ponty makes in the final part of the chapter is indeed to Husserl, where he attributes to him an idea of "conditioned freedom" [*liberté condtionnée*] (PhP 518). More notable, in fact, is that this reference to Husserl is made indirectly by way of Fink—Merleau-Ponty cited Fink's use of the expression "*bedingte Freiheit*" (Fink 1930, 285). This is significant because, as we know, a principal motivation behind Merleau-Ponty's attempt to work out a "phenomenology of phenomenology" was to respond to the claims that Fink himself had made in his *Sixth Cartesian Meditation*. This work was instrumental for Merleau-Ponty in terms of grasping the fundamental methodological question that phenomenology must be able to answer: if all human experience—including "phenomenologically reduced" experience—has horizons that condition it, then how can phenomenology ever attain *true* philosophical insight? Is the project not doomed to uncritical dogmatism or else vicious regress?

As discussed in the Preface, Fink's response to this problem was premised on the possibility of an ideal reduction as Husserl had originally conceived it. However, recognizing that this involved an extramundaneness (or freedom from horizons) that is, in fact, not humanly possible, Fink developed a highly speculative interpretation of phenomenological methodology which, among other things, construed the active subject of the reduction in suprahuman terms—the "non-participating transcendental onlooker."

For his part, Merleau-Ponty premised his response on the idea that phenomenology *is* indeed a human activity, and that the outermost horizons of human experience are those of the totality of history. Owing to what he took to be the metaphysical fact of our corporeal situatedness, Merleau-Ponty agreed with Fink's claim that an ideal (or complete) reduction was not a human possibility—hence his well-known remark about its necessary "incompleteness." So whereas Fink assumed that a complete reduction was possible in nonhuman terms and speculated about what must be the case if that were so, the question for Merleau-Ponty is whether human situatedness nonetheless affords sufficient freedom for the phenomenological reduction—or, more to the point, *whether a phenomenological reduction that is necessarily "incomplete" can nonetheless provide an adequate methodological basis for genuine philosophical results.*

On the face of it, the answer would be *no*. If there are only situated perspectives, then there can be no *bona fide* truth. Something needs to be added to the picture. As we saw above, Merleau-Ponty approached this problem by considering whether, after all, there might not be certain experiences characterized by *an indistinction between object and its historical horizons*—in particular, whether self-experience could have this property. If so, then this would be an experience of "absolute knowing," which is the formal condition that would need to be met in order to uphold the philosophical credentials of a situated reduction.

This is why Merleau-Ponty was drawn to the Lukácsian conception of the proletariat as the "identical subject-object" of history, in the sense that it represented the effective convergence of self-knowledge and knowledge of the historical totality. That is, Merleau-Ponty was drawn to this conception because of his need to identify an experiential moment in which human activity would be indistinct from its historical horizons, something which could only be the case if that activity were a matter of actively *generating* those horizons—in other words, a participatory experience of making history.

Where Merleau-Ponty deviated from Lukács, however, albeit in an attempt to redeem his account, was in making an explicit attempt to construe class consciousness as primarily a matter of perception and feeling rather than of cognition or explicit awareness. Employing what he called "a genuinely existential method" [*une méthode vraiment existentielle*] (PhP 506), Merleau-Ponty thus regarded class consciousness as emerging from class belonging understood in terms of a pre-reflective existential project—a "mode of communication" with the social world that motivates my basic political orientation and explicit judgments about class. In the case of the proletariat, "*j'existe ouvrier*," in the sense of existing a certain repressed style of *être-au-monde* "within [the] institutional framework" of capitalist society (PhP 506)—which is to say, in the sense of repressedly embodying these institutions as pre-reflective operative intentionalities, carrying them in my habitual body and living them accordingly as a kind of "obsessive presence" [*présence obsédante*] (PhP 509f)—the "inborn complex" of the proletarian situation.

Merleau-Ponty offered a description of the molecular emergence of proletarian class consciousness using the figures of a factory worker [*ouvrier*], day-laborer [*journalier*], and a tenant farmer [*tenancier*]. Although quite different, all do comparable work in similarly alienating conditions—they "coexist in the same situation" and thus *feel* alike, not through any explicit comparison, but on the basis of their "tasks and gestures" (PhP 507). This common feeling does not imply any explicitly chosen judgment or objective awareness of the alienating conditions, but in each case, there is a *tacit* normative claim to the effect that this life is "difficult and constraining" (PhP 507)—that there is some degree of dehumanization and that consequently "things must change" [« *il faut que ça change* »] (PhP 508). The initial situation of the proletariat can be described as a "multiple solipsism" [*solipsisme à plusieurs*], in that mutual detachment is partly constitutive of (but not unique to) proletarian existence, and Merleau-Ponty sketched out the passage to class consciousness that represents the overcoming of this separation. The main point that he wanted to make was that this passage was not primarily a theoretical or cognitive achievement, but rather was a matter of *altered historical perception*. For example, in the case of the day-laborer vis-à-vis factory workers, if class consciousness does emerge, then this is not due to a decision on his part to adopt a revolutionary perspective, but rather because "he perceived concretely the *synchronicity* [synchronisme] between his life and that of the workers, and their common destiny" (PhP 507, italics added). This perception of historical synchronicity with some groups—and by implication, historical *a*synchronicity with others—motivates a perceptual "regrouping" [*regroupement*] or *Umgestaltung* that polarizes the perception of social space in a way that brings to appearance "a region of the exploited" (PhP 508). This is how, for example, the farmer can feel himself [*se sent*] to be on the same side as the others, even though superficially, he may have nothing in common with them. For Merleau-Ponty, this is how the proletariat as such comes into being [*se réalise*], and this means that a revolutionary situation is one in which different exploited groups *feel* themselves moving toward a common "crossroads," that is, when the objective unity of the exploited "is finally lived in the perception of a common obstacle to the existence of each" (PhP 508). Thus, for Merleau-Ponty, "the revolutionary project is not the result of a deliberate judgment, or the explicit positing of a goal" (PhP 508f). While in many cases it does come to take such form, Merleau-Ponty viewed this as just the completion or fruition of the deeper existential project that provides the fundamental orientation for my existence, and which "merges [*se confond*] with my way of giving form to the world [*mettre en forme le monde*] and coexisting with others" (PhP 511). This existential project is anchored on the "tacit commitment"—« *il faut que ça change* »—discussed above. Usually lived pre-reflectively, in "extreme situations," this commitment can be transformed into a "conscious taking of a stand." What happens in the advent of a revolutionary outlook, that is, an outlook in which historical horizons are engaged transformatively, is—as we saw above—that "*this* tacit commitment becomes explicit" (cf. PhP 417).

Thus it is that, in the case of proletarian class consciousness, "the horizon of a particular life and revolutionary goals *coincide*" (PhP 510, italics added). In the case of the proletariat, then, Merleau-Ponty identified prereflective class existence with the object of the "tacit *cogito*" understood as *immediate historically situated self-awareness*, and he similarly took class consciousness *per se* to represent the coming to expression of the "tacit *cogito*." What we have here, in other words, is the sort of experiential indistinction between self and outer horizons that Merleau-Ponty needed—and in this case, that of the proletariat, what results is not just some arbitrary perspective, but one with universal import.

This is what is crucial. It is not simply that the discussion of class consciousness does the substantial work enabling Merleau-Ponty's rejection of unconditioned freedom. More importantly, it shows that and how the "incomplete" phenomenological reduction can be a philosophically viable method. For it shows the possibility of gaining universally valid insight without detaching from one's particular historical standpoint. What we need to appreciate, in other words, is that Merleau-Ponty's initial analysis of freedom (i.e., the critical discussion of Sartre) that supports the claim about its situatedness is wholly inadequate with regard to the rationale of the chapter, which has to do with warranting the claim that we are sufficiently free to perform the phenomenological reduction successfully—how it could be that situated freedom suffices for philosophy. For, indeed, far from showing that such is the case, simply affirming the situatedness of human freedom actually points in the opposite direction, that is, it would lend credence to the claim that the reduction is, in fact, *not* philosophically viable, that its necessary incompleteness is a devastating defect. What Merleau-Ponty needs is to show how our being corporeally situated is nonetheless consistent with the possibility of a universal view, a view that would not be compromised by the particularities of life. And this is precisely what he took the historical situation and transformative praxis of the proletariat to represent, the actuality of a (collective) form of human embodied subjectivity that is at once empirically concrete and yet also capable of underwriting the tasks of transcendental phenomenology. This is because the vital structures that necessarily remain horizonal to—and therefore ineluctably presupposed by—phenomenological experience, are one and the same as the structures of historical apriority that are effectively thematized in the class consciousness of the proletariat, and which, through the revolutionary praxis of the latter, are incorporated into the historical truth which phenomenology aspires to articulate.

This is the methodological key to Merleau-Ponty's view of the realization of philosophy, and it was on this basis that he was able to obviate the need for what Fink had called the "secondary enworlding" of phenomenology. I shall return to that in the Conclusion. For now, we need to consider in more general terms what it is that makes the historical situation of the proletariat so philosophically significant for Merleau-Ponty. For while a class of people being in that situation may be essential for the realization of philosophy, it is certainly not essential for *them* to be in it, and them alone, and so, there must be some human feature that becomes particularly salient in that situation.

Human productivity

The key idea here for Merleau-Ponty is what he called "human productivity" [*la productivité humaine*] (SNS 229/129). This idea can be seen as an elaboration of the notion of "transcendence" as a response to the need to spell out and elucidate the creative capacity—ostensibly distinctive to human existence, if not the very principle of anthropogenesis—in virtue of which human beings are able to overcome the monotonous rhythms of their "natural" being: how one can, as Merleau-Ponty put it, *faire une pointe hors de soi-même* and in this way "draw life"—*life-as-such*—"away from its spontaneous direction [*sens spontané*]" (PhP 519).

We should be wary of Merleau-Ponty's use of the term "spontaneity" and its various cognates, however, at least as he applies these to vital phenomena. For they tend to be infected with the same ambiguity found in his usage of the notion of life, namely, that between the generality of life-as-such and the particularity of lived lives. For the sake of clarity, we should reserve the term "spontaneity" for the sense of passive momentum that pertains to life-as-such, that is, to that which underlies the human body as a "*natural self*, a current of given existence" (PhP 199). As for the sense of spontaneity that pertains solely to individual particularity, Merleau-Ponty gave a clear expression of this when he described it—in a way reminiscent of Sartrean *mauvaise foi*—as "a sort of *escape* [échappement]," but one that involves "a process of mystification" or "equivocation" (PhP 199, 201). For short of death, it is not *really* an escape, remaining rooted in life-as-such. Inasmuch as someone presumes to escape the latter, to repress her "actual" body, she is engaged in a kind of self-deceiving "metaphysical hypocrisy" that works through "the medium of generality," that is, the generality of the habituated organism. But just like repression, as discussed above, this sort of "hypocrisy" is "part of the human condition"—it is even, or perhaps especially, to be found "in the 'sincere' or 'authentic' man whenever he claims to be something unreservedly [*sans réserves*]" (PhP 190).

Merleau-Ponty's idea of productivity is related very closely to that of freedom, and may be understood as the generative quality of historicity.[13] For while historicity may be an essential feature of human *être-au-monde*, its effective quality can vary considerably. That is, the dialectical relation between the habitual and "actual" dimensions of embodiment can unfold more or less dynamically depending on the nature and degree of repression. At its core, the idea of productivity points to a normative balance or harmonization between the two respective forms of activity: on the one hand, the spontaneous vital force that propels life, albeit blindly, that is, as a matter of subjective passivity; and on the other hand, the active decisiveness of individual "escape," the nihilating power of consciousness whereby "we tear ourselves away from ourselves" (PhP 489). It is important for Merleau-Ponty that both aspects are required—in particular, lacking substantial effectivity of its own, conscious decision in isolation can only manifest itself negatively by turning that positive vital force against itself sacrificially. Both aspects belong to the "human condition," and the idea of productivity is meant to encompass them in a way that captures the meaning of "the living subject" [*le sujet vivant*] in terms of (a) the transcendence and (b) the decentered relations to alterity that are implicit in the notion of historical development (cf. PhP 200). In this way, it is meant as a *generalization* of the concept of human production that would be able to provide the philosophical ground for Marx's theory of the self-realization of humanity. It would do so by showing that "the living subject," as "the real [*réel*] subject of history" (PhP 200)—that is, "the vehicle [*porteur*] of history and the motor [*moteur*] of the dialectic" (SNS 228/129, italics removed)—is "man *as* productivity" [*l'homme* en tant que *productivité*] (PhP 200, emphasis added). This makes it clear that the historical subject cannot be understood in individual terms, but rather that it is "man engaged in a certain way of appropriating nature in which the mode of his relationship with others takes shape." In other words, "it is *concrete human intersubjectivity*, the successive and simultaneous community of existences in the process of self-realization, each created by and creating the other" (SNS 228/129, emphasis added).

Although this intersubjectivity is understood to be concrete, in that it is understood on a corporeal basis, it is not taken in *material* terms in any reductive sense. As discussed above, Merleau-Ponty was quite dubious with respect to the materialist basis of historical materialism, in particular with respect to nature. It is important to recognize that Merleau-Ponty thought that the basic reason for the morbidity of Marxist theory was that what he later called Marx's "ground-breaking intuition" [*intuition si neuve*] (EP 43/53) had never been given a proper theoretical formulation, and this because it had never been placed on a proper philosophical foundation. According to Merleau-Ponty, this intuition amounts to Marx's discovery of "a historical rationality immanent in the life of men," immanent in interhuman praxis, in "the meaning [*sens*] which works itself out spontaneously in the inter-twining [*entre-croisement*] of those activities by which man organizes his relations with nature and with other men" (EP 41/50). Or more simply, Merleau-Ponty described "the principal thought" [*la pensée principale*] of Marxism as the claim that "there is an incarnation of ideas and values" (SNS 190/108). The problem was that this "put into question the usual categories of philosophy" without furnishing the "intellectual reform" that the transcendence of these categories required (EP 43/53). Merleau-Ponty intended his rethinking of Marxism based on the idea of human productivity to furnish the outstanding philosophical foundation of historical materialism and thereby to supply precisely the "intellectual reform" needed to redeem Marx's "ground-breaking intuition."

As discussed above (Chapter 3), Merleau-Ponty followed Lukács in conceiving the historical totality as exclusive of nature as such. Concerning materialism as traditionally and "crudely" understood, then, Merleau-Ponty was blunt: "there is no question of any pure [*nue*] matter, exterior to man and in terms of which his behavior could be explained" (SNS 231/130). In fact, Merleau-Ponty argued—as did Sartre in "Matérialisme et révolution" (1946), although to different effect—that the idea of a dialectical materialism is ultimately self-contradictory, inasmuch as matter is self-coincident, hence inert, and thus incapable of carrying "the principle of productivity and novelty [*nouveauté*]" as exhibited in human history. But he also maintained that Marx had already recognized that it would be "the height of subjectivism" to locate the dialectic of praxis in *things* considered materialistically. According to Merleau-Ponty, what Marx did was to "shift it into men" (EP 42/52) through the proto-phenomenological "expedient" of "human matter" or "human objects" (EP 44/54; SNS 232/131). Merleau-Ponty's solution to the problem of materialism was to suggest that Marx had really only seriously considered matter within "the system of human coexistence" (SNS 229/129), where it becomes dialectically animated by "human productivity," and that "all the ideological formations of a given society are synonymous with or complementary to a certain type of praxis" (SNS 231/130). "When Marx speaks of *human* objects, he means that . . . significance adheres to the object as it presents itself in our experience. . . . The spirit of a society is realized, transmitted, and perceived through the cultural objects which it bestows upon itself and in the midst of which it lives" (SNS 232/131).

It is for this reason that Merleau-Ponty could say, citing Marx by way of defending Lukács, that the milieu of history is neither natural nor supernatural, but rather "transnatural" [*transnaturel*], where this means that within this environment, "man's *natural* behavior has become *human* . . . human being has become his *natural* being, [and] his *human nature* has become his nature." In short, that "history is the genuine natural history of man" (SNS 230/130). And this makes it clear how the idea of human productivity was intended to show that the theoretical development required by Marxism calls for a philosophical union with Husserl's phenomenology of the *Lebenswelt*. For this, Merleau-Ponty suggested, had contributed more than anything to "describing consciousness incarnate in an environment of human objects and in a linguistic tradition" (SNS 239/135).

∎

Given the general sense and significance of Merleau-Ponty's idea of human productivity, what exactly does it mean?

Human productivity is that whereby existential transcendence is achieved through praxis. It is a matter of a dialectical relation—internal to the context of intersubjective involvement in the world—whereby a certain harmonization of the impulses of vital inherence with the intentions of symbolic thought is achieved. The former represent the indeclinable bases of the living subject, the structures of the habituated organism that comprise the historical apriority of a given context, but they are typically dissembled by the latter. For most humans throughout history, this may actually have been existentially favorable. But in the contemporary world, in Merleau-Ponty's view, transcendence no longer requires alienating repression, and the time is ripe finally to overcome it. The salience of Merleau-Ponty's notion of productivity thus shows itself most clearly in the sense of *therapeutic* transformation at the individual as well as at the social level.

Human productivity is thus not a matter of achieving an exact synchronization between vital spontaneity and the negativity of consciousness—in general, that would imply the death of historicity and the end of history. The harmonization in question may have an intentional orientation toward such an impossible coincidence, but it is primarily a dialectical coordination geared for vital flourishing and personal integration. It is the means of individual and collective self-realization that proceeds by taking up a meaning offered by the world and re-projecting it symbolically through a "series of shifts [*glissements*]" (PhP 519). Through interaction and dialogue, the otherwise blind evolution of vital spontaneity can be reoriented consciously and deliberately. At the social level, this is history in the making, and Merleau-Ponty was content to leave the mechanics of such moments of genuinely engaged participation in the realm of mystery. With an immoderate rhetorical flourish even by his own standards, Merleau-Ponty described such moments in fulgurant terms: "sometimes there is that blaze of fire, that flash of lightening, that moment of victory, . . . that *gloria* that eclipses everything else" (SNS 330/186; cf. SNS 171/98).

Nonetheless, some substantive points can still be made about human productivity. The first relates to death. I argued above that transcendence depends upon "the negativity of death." In this way, death is an aspect of life-as-such. This can be related to self-realization as a transformative matter of self-overcoming, that is, an overcoming of one's given or previously realized empirical self. The suspension of or detachment from the latter that self-realization implies could be described as a quasi-suicide or self-sacrifice—for example, what Emile Bernard called "Cézanne's suicide" (SNS 21/12). This is merely *quasi*, though, in that one remains vitally rooted in life-as-such.[14] This would express the gist of the incarnational alternative that Merleau-Ponty would propose to the mistaken understanding of revolution in terms of the "self-annihilation" of the proletariat. Given how Merleau-Ponty linked death with the universal in thought, the idea is that inasmuch as the process of self-realization is taken as a matter of coinciding with or reappropriating vital spontaneity, this can only occur through the death-*like* denial of personal particularity.

More specifically, for Merleau-Ponty, this is a matter of "*exchange.*" We saw in Chapter 1 that this notion was central to Saint Exupéry's thinking, where it was effectively synonymous with self-sacrifice. It thus represented an alternative to the modern ideal of individual autonomy, which Saint Exupéry regarded as just an expression of flight from the world and from the possibility of authenticity (Geneste 1968). For Saint Exupéry, "true freedom" is a fundamental mode of becoming that "is found only in the creative process" (EG 182)—it obtains only in and through participation with the world and with others. Saint Exupéry thus proposed "a freedom that resides in acts rather than in rights or in ideas, and which is realized in concrete relationships rather than in escapism or detachment from bonds [*liens*]" (Major 1968, 167). Through these bonds, necessity is viewed positively with regard to self-realization, and there is a richer sense of self-conscious, self-assured autonomy that Saint Exupéry valorized. "If I look for the example of a genuine freedom," he once wrote, "I will find it only in a monastery, where men have a choice between different impulses in the richness of their interior life" (EG 182). This is a telling example, in that Saint Exupéry's cosmic worldview—especially in *Pilote de guerre*—amounts to a secularized Christianity, with Man substituting for God—recall that "that the primacy of Man founds the only meaningful Equality and Freedom" (PG 241). And indeed, *it is only in an eschatological context of this kind that freedom as the metabolic condition of human growth and creative self-realization could possibly take the form of self-sacrificial exchange.*

The Exupérian notion of freedom has much in common with Merleau-Ponty's view. Here, too, for example, freedom and necessity are two sides of a single coin—recall Merleau-Ponty defining existentialism partly in terms of a freedom "which becomes what it is by giving itself bonds [*liens*]" (SNS 121/70). In both views, one can detect palpable misgivings with respect to the liberal idea of "negative" freedom, understood in terms of deracination and alienability. Both opposed this as a kind of inauthentic escapism, and did so in terms of a notion of freedom as "exchange." In particular, Merleau-Ponty's portrayal of freedom can be seen as based upon a sharp critique of the Sartrean view, and Saint Exupéry's account can likewise be approached as offering "a conception of freedom exactly opposite to that of Sartre" (Simon 1950, 150f; Ouellet 1971, 106f; but cf. Major 1968, 169 n108).

But Merleau-Ponty's view of freedom as exchange is ultimately quite different from that of Saint Exupéry. In particular, it denies sacrifice by denying the sort of eschatology that sacrifice implies. So from Merleau-Ponty's view, while Saint Exupéry may have moralized *ad nauseam* about creating bonds, his position failed to articulate any means of achieving them. Turned away from the living present, he "[can]not offer us so much as a single example of a pilot successfully reintegrated into one of those villages over which he flies so patronizingly" (Harris 1999, 33). It remains a dream, and unfulfilled aspiration to immanence. Occurring solely as a one-way relation between the individual and the whole, exchange in the Exupérian scheme fails to be historically creative, at least in a politically progressive sense.

Matters are otherwise with Merleau-Ponty (and with his *interpretation* of Saint Exupéry), for whom exchange occurs fundamentally within the structure of embodiment: "there is an exchange between generalized and individual existence *in which each receives and gives*" (PhP 513, italics added; cf. 501, 517). The idea is that concrete freedom as an event of human productivity occurs when a meaning [*sens*] that was adumbrated in the realm of anonymous intersubjective generality [*l'On*], "and which was nothing but an insubstantial possibility threatened by the contingency of history, is taken up by an individual" (PhP 513). There is a reciprocal exchange of real significance and concrete actuality that occurs through an appropriative "shift" [*glissement*] (as opposed to an outright negation or rupture) made in the living present. Consider, for example, Merleau-Ponty's claim that "the act of the artist or philosopher is free. . . . Their freedom resides in the power of equivocation . . . or in the process of escape. . . . It consists in taking up a factual situation by giving it a figurative meaning [*sens figuré*] beyond its real meaning [*sens propre*]" (PhP 201). In art as in philosophy—and Merleau-Ponty said something similar about revolutionary politics—it is a matter of *seeing differently* by effecting a perceptual Gestalt-switch. In each case, this implies "the power to suspend vital communication" with the world, "or at least to limit it" (PhP 279). It is in conjunction with the universal, and hence with some degree of self-denial, that such "shifts" can transcend the given. This does not involve an eclectic mixture of determinism and radical choice, but rather a motivated reconfiguration of tacit and focal existential commitments.

However, as a kind of equivocating escape from the reality of alienating repression, such a "shift" can be realized concretely only on condition that the new structure of commitment is "worked out in interhuman relations" (PhP 509). As Merleau-Ponty put it, "it is not enough for a painter like Cézanne, an artist, or a philosopher, to create and express an idea; they must also awaken the experiences which will make their idea take root in the consciousness of others. A successful work has the strange power to teach its own lesson [*s'enseigner elle-même*]" (SNS 33/19). Ideally, then, the self-denial of freedom as exchange will prove contagious. For thereby death would be, in a certain sense, overcome by being transmuted into intersubjectivity, or communalized. "I thus live not for death but forever [*à jamais*], and in the same way, not for myself alone but with others" (SNS 121/70).

The commitments relevant to freedom are therefore not arbitrary. Contrary to the Sartrean view of freedom as an essentially centrifugal process of signification, Merleau-Ponty argued that freedom concretely understood is rooted in a pregiven field of intersubjective meaning. This results in a view of freedom that emphasizes centripetal appropriation over centrifugal nihilation—it is primarily a matter of taking up the "autochthonous meaning [*sens*] of the world" and making agentive decisions on that basis (PhP 503). It is a question for Merleau-Ponty of according proper weight to the historical situation of the world as a field of possibilities for meaningful action. Freedom needs to be enabled by existing structures, in the sense of truly *having something to do*—in general, it obtains when we take up "open situations calling for a certain completion" (PhP 500; cf. SNS 294/166). This does not necessarily diminish the sense of autonomous commitment in freedom. Rather, the idea is that we are always already committed, albeit in an ambiguous and prereflective way, to a more basic project concerning the world and our *être-au-monde*. This is the "tacit commitment" discussed above. To take up the "autochthonous meaning of the world" is thus to take up "a *spontaneous* meaning [*sens*] of my life" (PhP 511, emphasis added). "It is I who give a direction [*sens*] and a future to my life," it is just that this does not originate with me as a thinking subject. Rather, that direction and future "spring from my present and past, and in particular from my present and past mode of coexistence" (PhP 510). It is a matter of the existential style of my life, that is, its orientation as an existential project toward a certain "determinate-indeterminate" goal that *is* mine, *but not mine alone* (PhP 509). In this way, productivity through freedom as exchange is ultimately an expression of the dialectical reciprocity within the synergic system of self–others–world.

Rationality

This operation of human productivity represents the advent of rationality which is, in a word, the solution to "the human problem," the problem of "establishing human relations among men" (HT xi/xv). Rationality is the "marvel [*prodige*] of the connection of experiences" (PhP xvi). "To say that there exists rationality is to say that perspectives intersect, perceptions confirm each other, a meaning [*sens*] emerges" (PhP xv). As witness to the primordial emergence of *sens* from *non-sens*, perceptual consciousness amounts to the "consciousness of rationality" itself. This awareness is lost when the achievement of rationality is taken for granted, as it is by objective thinking. Merleau-Ponty wanted us to rediscover it "by making it appear against the background of inhuman [*inhumaine*] nature" (PrP 67f/25).

This is a Gestalt-switch that is exactly analogous to—or rather, that is the general form of—that which Merleau-Ponty performed with respect to violence and political order in *Humanism and Terror*. There, he tried to show that instead of judging violence as aberrational against the background of political order, a better grip on matters is attained if one approaches political order in general as emerging from a background of violence. By establishing that all political order originates in violence, Merleau-Ponty was concerned in particular with restructuring the moral optics of liberalism, in order to make it at least possible to perceive violence as progressive with respect to advancing the cause of human reconciliation. Merleau-Ponty thought that Marxist political analysis of the present "deciphers events, discovers in them a common meaning and thereby grasps a leading thread which, without dispensing us from fresh analysis at every stage, allows us to orient ourselves toward events" (HT 105/98). He was prepared to defend a "perception of history" supportive of judgments calling for violence to realize the human universality that liberalism takes for granted (cf. HT 38 n1/35 n11). This would be legitimate and defensible, he thought, to the extent that it could be reasonably expected to help "bring reason out of madness [*déraison*]" (HT 105/98), that is, help to realize a world of non-violence and thereby solve the human problem.

The key point, though, is that the human problem is not a "geometrical" problem in the sense that the solution is simply a determinate unknown that is related to the givens of the problem according to a rule of deduction or subsumption (HT 203/186). This is what Merleau-Ponty meant when he emphasized that "rationality is not a *problem*" (PhP xv). Because we are not spectators of a closed history, judgments concerning the future historical development of rationality as the solution to the current state of the human problem cannot be what Kant called "determining" [*bestimmend*] judgments, which work through the subsumption of particulars under a fully adequate universal concept. Rather, they must be what Kant described, in his *Critique of the Power of Judgment*, as "reflecting" [*reflectierend*] judgments, that is, judgments that work without an adequate concept, yet which are no less valid (KU 5:179).

Merleau-Ponty did not develop the application of this distinction very explicitly. However, he did suggest that Kant's account of aesthetic reflecting judgment in the third *Critique* has epistemological priority over theoretical reason. He argued that if there can be an awareness of "a harmony between the sensible and the concept, between myself and others, which is itself without any concept," and if the subject of this awareness is not a universal thinker but an embodied perceiver, then "the hidden art of the imagination must condition categorial activity. It is no longer merely aesthetic judgment, but knowledge as well which rests upon this art, an art which forms the basis of the unity of consciousness and of consciousnesses" (PhP xii). Merleau-Ponty was making the same general point when he claimed that "the understanding ... needs to be redefined, since the general connective function ultimately attributed to it by Kantianism [i.e., in the first *Critique*] is now spread over the whole intentional life and no longer suffices to distinguish it" (PhP 65).

Merleau-Ponty approached this "art" hidden in the human soul in terms of "operative intentionality" [*fungierende Intentionalität*], in order to take it up as the basis for an expanded phenomenological reinterpretation of the transcendental aesthetic—"the Logos of the aesthetic world" (PhP xii–xiii, 491). Like any art, however, this too is "aware of itself [*se connaît*] only in its results." As it is with Cézanne's painting, for example, "'conception' cannot precede 'execution.'" There is no conceptual way to determine in advance whether one will hit upon sense, whether one is in fact attuned to the sense of history, or else is just caught up in a subjective dream: "only the work itself, completed and understood, is proof that there was *something* rather than *nothing* to be said" (SNS 32/19).

The upshot is that the establishment of rationality through praxis occurs "through an initiative which has no guarantee in being, and whose justification rests entirely on the actual power that it gives us for taking responsibility for our history" (PhP xv). For Merleau-Ponty, militant philosophy involves a perception of history that launches us into uncharted territory, into the "unfinished world of the revolutionary" (HT 104/97), or of phenomenology itself (cf. PhP xvi). As noted above, in *Phenomenology of Perception* Merleau-Ponty put this quite dramatically: "we take our fate in our hands, we become responsible for our history through reflection, as well as through a decision whereby we commit our lives, and in both cases what is involved is a violent act that proves itself in practice" (PhP xvi).

This "violence" is presumptive, in the sense that our perceptual grip on things is always an imposition that claims more than it knows. But Merleau-Ponty was not just speaking metaphorically about the violence we do to errors, say, by correcting them. The issue is that, according to his account, to perceive is to be committed to a certain perceptual background, that is, a view of the totality of history, and thus to be committed, even if only tacitly, to the future realization of a certain world as a system of rationality and truth. "To perceive is to engage all at once *a whole future of experiences* in a present that never strictly guarantees it" (PhP 343f, italics added). But on account of the "permanent givens" [*données permanentes*] (PrP 68/25; cf. HT 203f/186, 110/102) of the human problem, this is a site of conflict and contestation. That we coexist against a backdrop of nature, and that the future is open beyond any conceptual determination, all of this is conditioned by the subjectivity of perception. "This is the price of there being things and 'others' for us, not through an illusion, but through a violent act which is perception itself" (PhP 415).

There are two important illustrations of the sort of militant praxis that Merleau-Ponty had in mind here. The first concerns Lenin and Trotsky as leaders of the Russian Revolution, an event that was still a major point of historical reference for Merleau-Ponty. What is at issue here is political judgment in the absence of objective criteria. Although his discussion of them was fairly selective, Merleau-Ponty saw Trotsky and Lenin as gifted readers of historical situations. Contrary to portrayals of Marxism as a kind of science that issues solely in determining judgments, Merleau-Ponty cited

Lenin to the effect that one must "put one's own mind to work to find one's bearing in each particular case" (SNS 293/165). It is a matter of reading history, trying to decipher its tendencies, and ultimately all that one has "to guide him is *his own* view of events" (SNS 293f/166). Likewise with regard to Trotsky's analysis of the Russian Revolution, which he thought was based upon an apprehension of the "total intention" of society, Merleau-Ponty affirmed that "the greatest objectivity is often the subjectivity of he who lived it" (NI 18 [6]); cf. Whiteside 1988, 122). In both cases, rather than attempting to deduce concrete political judgments from the outlines of Marxist theory, a perception is attained of the "lines of force and vectors" in the present that takes into account the complex "subjective" dimensions of the situation. "The problem is to recognize the proletarian spirit *in each of its momentary guises*" (SNS 291/164). This can be done well or poorly, and Merleau-Ponty commented that there is something "sublime" about those who do indeed gain profound historical insight into the milieu they inhabit (HT 85/80). This is viewed in hindsight, of course, and it appears that way only to the extent that the perception in question was borne out by later events. For Merleau-Ponty, historical judgments admit of no other proof. A good appraisal of concrete political situations "requires a certain Marxist flair or a Marxist perception of the local and world situation which is on the level of talent or genius" (SNS 293/165). Merleau-Ponty was under no illusions about the potential dangerousness of this. But he accepted the general idea that "the ways of history are [ultimately] unfathomable" (SNS 290/164). Lacking a demonstrable rational structure, all historical action is adventurous, and one cannot avoid using a certain degree of cunning [*ruser*] (SNS 294f/166). But Merleau-Ponty did not see any justification for giving up the attempt to understand history. He thus looked to what he called Lenin's "Marxist 'perception' of situations," articulated in numerous practically oriented writings, as implicitly containing "a theory of contingency in history" that could be extended "onto the theoretical plane" (SNS 217 n1/123 n1).

The second illustration of militant praxis comes from Ludwig Binswanger. It is highly instructive to read *Phenomenology of Perception* in the light of Binswanger's 1935 article "Über Psychotherapie." Based around a case of an ostensibly successful cure of an aphonic hysteric, this article presents an account of existential psychotherapy that emphasizes not only the importance of the "inner life history" of the patient, but also and especially, the uniqueness and *artistic creativity* of the therapeutic intervention itself, and the necessity of deep existential bonds between patient and therapist, in order for the treatment to succeed. In this regard, Merleau-Ponty endorsed Binswanger's principal claim, expressing it as follows:

> in psychological treatment of any kind, the coming to awareness would remain purely cognitive, the patient would not accept the meaning of his disturbances as revealed to him without the personal relationship formed with the doctor, or without the confidence and friendship felt toward him, *and the change of existence resulting from this friendship.* (PhP 190, italics added)

Here, we find a particularly important inspiration for Merleau-Ponty's claim that philosophy and even politics are "like art." In a way that suggests its own sort of Leninist practice, Binswanger described his therapeutic intervention not as a theoretically derived procedure, but as an "artful response" based on an impulsive, confident daring [*Wagemut*] (ÜP 209). He presented psychotherapy as a kind of art that doctors performed according to their particular styles. He saw psychotherapeutic cure as coming about through the establishment of an original existential relationship between the doctor and patient, a relationship involving "an original communicative novelty, a new linking of destiny—and this not only with regard to the patient-doctor relationship, but also and above all with regard to the purely human relationship in the sense of a genuine 'with-another' [*Miteinander*]" (ÜP 215).

According to Binswanger, successful therapy is a matter of establishing new intersubjective bonds that overcome the patient's "detachment from life," thus freeing her from captivation in and by her subjective realm. In this sense, the therapist is a link between individual idiosyncrasy (non-sense) and the shared intelligibility of the public world (sense). His task is thus to foster the "genuine communication" that will free the patient

> from blind isolation, from the *idios cosmos*, as Heraclitus says, thus from mere life in his body, his dreams, his private inclinations, his pride and his exuberance, and to illuminate and liberate him for the ability to participate in the *koinos cosmos*, in the life of genuine fellowship [*Koinonia*] or community. (ÜP 215f; cf. TE 114f)

Binswanger's account of the therapeutic encounter is significant for several reasons. The first has to do with the way in which, after taking it up earlier—Merleau-Ponty referred to Binswanger's article six times in the chapter "Le corps comme être sexué"— and endorsing its principal claim, Merleau-Ponty implicitly (but unmistakably) alluded to it at the end of *Phenomenology of Perception* in claiming that analysis succeeds by "binding the subject to his doctor through new existential relationships," so that the complex can be dissolved, not by "a freedom without instruments," but rather by "*a new pulsation of time* with its own supports and motives" (PhP 519, emphasis added). The effectiveness of this depends on the strength of the new existential commitment, and Merleau-Ponty added—with class consciousness clearly in mind—that "the same applies in all cases of coming to awareness" [*il en est de même dans toutes les prises de conscience*] (PhP 519). Merleau-Ponty thus saw Binswanger's account of the therapeutic encounter as providing important clues regarding the mechanics, so to speak, of the advent of explicit class consciousness construed as a matter of overcoming quasitherapeutically a repressed form of existence.

Binswanger's account shed light on this from a different angle as well. He noted that the patient manifested various symptoms, and that his treatment included a variety of techniques. In particular, when the patient was suffering a violent attack of hiccoughing, Binswanger reported the following intervention: "I remember now how the idea, or if you will, the inspiration suddenly came to me, to quietly approach the patient lying in bed, to lay the fingers of my right hand across her throat, and to compress her trachea so firmly that she had difficulty breathing and tried to resist the grasp, and as the pressure decreased for a moment, a strong act of swallowing occurred" (ÜP 209f). Other such interventions were performed, although not all were mentioned in Binswanger's article (see Lanzoni 2004). Nonetheless, this treatment figured relatively prominently in the account, as Binswanger used the contrast precisely as a way to emphasize the importance of strong existential bonds.[15] This was significant for Merleau-Ponty, in that it showed a very concrete enactment of reflecting judgment, while providing an example, however dubious and disconcerting, of emancipation through violence.

In this way, Binswanger's account sheds light on Merleau-Ponty's understanding of the "realization of philosophy." This is supposed to occur dialectically through its destruction insofar as it is "separate." At root, this separateness has to do with the mutual isolation of discrete theatres, so to speak, of subjective experience—in this regard, the philosopher, the proletarian, and the psychopathological patient are essentially in the same position of silent isolation. Significantly, Merleau-Ponty interpreted the loss of speech in Binswanger's patient as a "refusal of coexistence," a withdrawal from the lived situation, such that the task was to have her regain her voice (PhP 187)—for Merleau-Ponty, the philosopher is likewise the one "who wakes up and speaks" (EP 51/63). What Binswanger helps us to see is that, for Merleau-Ponty, the realization of philosophy, and the realization of revolutionary class consciousness that it presupposes, are matters of integrating, respectively, the philosopher's and the proletarian's silent "*idios cosmos*" into the concrete intersubjective horizons of discursive experience—that it is a matter of moving from the *non-sens* of a "multiple solipsism" to a self-consciously historical intersubjective community.

Binswanger is significant here because existential encounter in the psychotherapeutic context engages with the problem of alterity in the most general way, and this because it engages with the problem of mutual senselessness *in its most acute form*. It thus shows most clearly the intersubjective character of human productivity at work in the emergence of *sens* through the exploration of the irrational and its integration into "expanded reason [*raison élargie*]" (SNS 109/63; cf. PrP 77/30). It thus represents, in germinal form, the philosophical militancy advanced by Merleau-Ponty. The shared and mutually transformative understanding that results through such an encounter—whether in the clinical, quotidian, political, or philosophical context—prefigures the objectivity and truth of which authentic intersubjectivity would be the living embodiment.

In this way, Binswanger's therapeutic encounter paradigmatized the molecular structure of achieved universality over and against the structural madness of a world of alienation. At the heart of this conception lies the idea of "a new pulsation of time." This refers to Merleau-Ponty's claim that it is precisely in the context of productive existential exchange, and in conjunction with the human communion that emerges, that human embodied existence "secretes" [*sécrète*] time (PhP 277).[16] That is, it refers to Merleau-Ponty's claim that it is in this context that existence "becomes the location in nature where, for the first time, events, instead of pushing one another into being, project around the present a double horizon of past and future and receive a historical orientation" (PhP 277). It is by being polarized and oriented in this way that, for Merleau-Ponty, "*we are the upsurge* [surgissement] *of time*" (PhP 489, italics added)—hence the "synchrony" characteristic of class consciousness.

This "proto-temporalization," like historicity, belongs to the core meaning of human productivity as the ecstatically transgressive overcoming of nature that effectively defines anthropogenesis. But as noted earlier, this can be compromised and degraded.

This points back to the dual temporal structure of embodiment, which quite literally for Merleau-Ponty is the locus of both freedom and servitude. In situations of alienating repression, there is a pathological dislocation and imbalance in which the habituated organism holds sway as an "inborn complex"—for instance, the way the proletariat lives class as an "obsessive presence." In such ways as this, the body *is* problematic—for it is the locus of unfreedom in that it de-dialecticizes the historicity of individuals, thereby effectively removing them from the world and powerfully isolating them. It is certainly not natural, nor historically typical, for humans to have what we might call "bodies of freedom." This can only be an historical achievement. And Merleau-Ponty did think that it was on the agenda. For he followed Marx and Lukács in holding that the abject de-humanization of the proletariat would, or at least could, be overturned dialectically through a kind of "return of the repressed." In other words, he did believe that as an "inborn complex," the habituated organismicity of the contemporary proletariat was implicitly a matter of universality and thus a force for historical progress—if only the appropriate subjective consciousness would take hold.

What Merleau-Ponty took Binswanger's account to show is that the cure for repression in general lies in regaining an "existentially healthy" form of historical being through the dissolution of those impersonal sedimentations which, in disrupting historicity, govern the style of our (alienated) behavior. This would serve to reinsert the patient (or the proletarian or the philosopher) within a shared history or temporal synchrony, thereby overcoming intersubjective separation while enhancing the scope of effective action, increasing "*tolerance* of the corporeal and institutional givens" of life (PhP 518), and enabling a surer grip on one's own life-history (cf. TE 118). That this occurs through "a new pulsation of time" means that it is based upon the projection of a shifted perception of one's historical being, and a joint existential commitment to the temporalization that that perception implies. This is ultimately the sense in which, for Merleau-Ponty, "true philosophy is a matter of learning to see the world anew" (PhP xvi; cf. NI 139 [62])—it is a matter of a Gestalt-switch that refocuses our perception of the world by setting it out against the background of "nature" in such a way that it comes to appearance as the totality of history involving a "contingent logic" of universality. This is a *better*, because more complete way of seeing. "Whether it is a matter of things or of historical situations, philosophy has no other function than to teach us again to see them *well*" (PhP 520, italics added).

This perceptual normativity accrues directly from the militantly engaged character of Merleau-Ponty's standpoint vis-à-vis the as-yet unrealized universality of life-as-such. Indeed, his postwar project is normatively charged through and through. But he did not see this as unproblematic—there are issues of justification that need to be addressed. It was not despite but rather because he held that, as with life in general, doing philosophy inevitably implies political commitment of some kind, whether this is embraced self-consciously or not, that Merleau-Ponty was keenly mindful of the need for justification. In other words, notwithstanding his sometimes fiery rhetoric regarding *engagement*, he was particularly concerned to make his decision as *un*-"decisionistic" as possible, that is, as broadly appealing as possible. And for him, this meant relying on the *perception* of the meaning and direction of history as the progressive realization of rationality. There is, of course, a certain circularity here, in that any perception will always retain a degree of decision. But Merleau-Ponty wished his perception of history to be as unambiguous as possible—he thus wanted this perception *to impose itself* as forcefully as possible. So while much of what he wanted to say was redolent of Lukács' work in *History and Class Consciousness*, there was a crucial difference, in that the latter was developed in the immediate post-1917 context when class struggle was manifest and revolutionary change was a palpable part of social reality. Merleau-Ponty was acutely aware that his time was different, at least on the surface. Nothing fundamental had been altered, but finding compelling phenomenological evidence attesting to the veracity of the Marxist conception of history was not so straightforward. In the next chapter, we will consider Merleau-Ponty's conception of heroism in some detail, and see how it was meant to play an evidentiary role of precisely this sort. This will then bring us to the Conclusion where, drawing upon the overall discussion, I will relate Merleau-Ponty's reinterpretation of Marxism to his reinterpretation of phenomenology in order to lay out a methodological explanation as to why *Phenomenology of Perception* concludes on a note of deference to Saint Exupéry *qua* "hero."

Contemporary Heroism

Phenomenology of Perception is not unique among Merleau-Ponty's works in terms of ending with heroism. It is also the case that Merleau-Ponty crowned *Sense and Non-Sense*—a collection of articles from 1945 to 1947, published in 1948—with "Man, the Hero" ["Le Héros, l'Homme"], a short essay which took up this theme explicitly (SNS 323–31/182–7). Although this piece has an obvious potential to shed light on the ending of *Phenomenology of Perception*, it has received negligible scholarly attention. Of course, this is presumably because, as discussed above, no one has seriously thought that this ending was in need of any critical illumination. As in the case of *Phenomenology of Perception*, then, the invocation of heroism at the end of *Sense and Non-Sense* is typically ignored or glossed over. Even the relatively detailed treatment (nearly two paragraphs) recently given to it by Bernard Flynn (2007, 136f) still skirts the basic question as to the philosophical significance of heroism for Merleau-Ponty in the first place.

The first part of this chapter undertakes a close examination of "Man, the Hero" as a source of insight into Merleau-Ponty's thought in the immediate postwar period, and particularly, into his deference to heroism at the end of *Phenomenology of Perception*. The discussion is framed by the original intentions behind the essay, which had to do with Merleau-Ponty's efforts to rethink Marxist praxis on the basis of an existential attitude vis-à-vis post-Hegelian philosophy of history. Unpacking the implicit contrasts that Merleau-Ponty drew with respect to other positions—including those of Kojève, Aron, Caillois, and Bataille—I analyze his rejection of traditional understandings of heroism, and then examine his account of what he called "the contemporary hero" [*le héros contemporain, le héros des contemporains*], which is the term he uses to denote his own view. What emerges is that Merleau-Ponty intended this sense of "heroism" to supply experiential evidence attesting to the latent presence of human universality. It is ultimately a mythic device intended to encourage the militant faith needed for the political project of a universal society, by showing that such a project is indeed possible, and that the transformative political praxis required need not imply agonistic sacrifice.

In the light of negative responses to "Man, the Hero," in the second part of this chapter, I discuss some comparative considerations between Merleau-Ponty and Saint Exupéry as a way of ascertaining what difference there is, if any, between the standpoint of *engagement* of the former and the sort of *pensée de survol* associated with the latter.

The existential attitude

"Le Héros, l'Homme" was originally published under the title "Le Culte du héros" ["Hero Worship"] in the pro-PCF (Communist Party of France) weekly *action* [*sic*] in February 1946.[1] Aside from a few words quoted in the frosty and dismissive editorial preface, signed by Francis Ponge,[2] that accompanied its publication in *action*,[3] no documentary evidence is available to explain exactly why Merleau-Ponty submitted this piece to this particular publication.

However, it is reasonable to say that this submission was linked to Merleau-Ponty's active efforts to publicly promote the political credentials of existentialism. For *action* was not a dogmatic organ of PCF policy—on the contrary, it was "*l'enfant terrible*" of the Party (Desanti 1997, 260; cf. Leduc 2006, 85–114). In particular, following the end of the European war, *action* was (along with *Les temps modernes*) an important forum for debate between Marxism and existentialism.[4] Of special interest to Merleau-Ponty with regard to his existentialist proselytizing were relatively open-minded intellectuals within the PCF. Among these, Merleau-Ponty's "privileged interlocutor" was Pierre Hervé, a leading figure in the party who was at the time "at the very centre of a liberalizing movement within the party" (Whiteside 1988, 211),[5] a movement that aimed, as did Merleau-Ponty, for a broad unification of the Left in France, including left-wing Catholicism (see Poster 1975, 110f). Most importantly, Hervé was on the executive committee of *action* (along with Maurice Kriegel-Valrimont, Victor Leduc, Pierre Courtade, Alfred Malleret-Joinville, and Marcel Degliame-Fouché). Thus, in the context of his active promotion of existentialism, the key reason why Merleau-Ponty sent his essay on heroism to *action* was because it formed a moment in his ongoing political dialogue with the milieu of Marxist thinkers and activists who, centered around Hervé, were relatively open to existentialism.

Broadly following the main claims of Lukács' "What is Orthodox Marxism?," the general idea that Merleau-Ponty aimed to establish in this dialogue was that as a practical project of proletarian self-emancipation, Marxism was less a body of truth than a *method* for interpreting political phenomena, and that with respect to subjectivity and consciousness, what its advancement required could be supplied by existential phenomenology. "A living Marxism should 'save' and integrate existentialist research instead," as was its tendency, "of stifling it" (SNS 143/82). If Marxism is still true, he wrote, "then we will rediscover it on the path of present-day truth [*la vérité actuelle*] and in the analysis of our time" (SNS 303/171). For Merleau-Ponty, it was always a matter of being attuned to historical actuality—"our time" [*notre temps*], and he believed that in the postwar context, existential analysis had a better grip on this than Marxist theory. Concerning the former, he wrote that "we don't have the feeling of doing sectarian work, but of taking up research at the point where it was *carried* [portée] *by our time*" (NI 63 [153], italics added).

Existential research and analysis as such, however, are not what the essay on heroism offered. Rather, as Merleau-Ponty stated in the cover letter that he sent to *action*, its task was more specific: to define "the existential attitude (as a general phenomenon of our time, and not as a school of thought)," and to do so "positively and on the basis of examples" (quoted in the editorial preface, see note 3). The aim of the essay was to offer this "existential attitude" as a heuristic principle of orientation in the neo-Marxist political hermeneutics called for by the postwar situation.

Heroism and history

Merleau-Ponty defined the "existential attitude" by personifying it in what he called "the contemporary hero." Because he did so by way of a critique of what I will call *traditional* and *ideological* views of heroism, I will first examine Merleau-Ponty's treatment of these before turning in the next section to the account of "contemporary heroism" itself.

Traditional heroism

Merleau-Ponty claimed that "hero worship" has "always existed," but identified Hegel as the key turning point in its history. Previously, the idea of the hero was essentially that of an "agent of a Providence," paradigmatically the (Christian) saint. Here heroic action is understood as self-sacrifice in the name of certain transcendent, other-worldly goals. This changed when Hegel brought heroism down to Earth by conceiving it in terms of "the individuals of world history."[6] In this view, heroes are particular concrete individuals who gain an awareness that their social world "has no future," and who take it upon themselves to intervene, in effect, on behalf of historical progress. They were "the new race [*la race nouvelle*] that already existed within the old."[7] World-historical individuals are the state-founding agents of the *Weltgeist*, inchoately grasping the needs of History and acting accordingly. "They have a presentiment of the future, but of course they have no science of it. . . . They forsake happiness and by their action and their example create a new law [*droit*] and a morality [*morale*] in which their time will later recognize its truth" (SNS 324/183).

The Hegelian hero is thus an historical individual who, based on a vague sense of universal history, acts *against her own time*. Retrospectively, such action could be seen as a matter of historical wisdom. But *only* retrospectively. Such heroes are in general *not* heroes for their contemporaries. For the latter come too soon to benefit from the world-historical actions in question. Hegelian heroism consists in "carrying out and winning for others . . . what will *afterwards* seem the only possible future and the very meaning of history" (SNS 324f/183, italics added).

In contrast to this Hegelian view, which dialectically embeds the hero in the unfolding of universal history, Merleau-Ponty also extracts a view of heroism from Nietzsche's account of the *Übermensch*. The idea here is of being situated outside of both providence and historical reason—there is no meaning or logic in history, no nonarbitrary substantive goals to aspire toward. This Nietzschean idea of heroism thus involves a rejection of *any* overarching framework as a condition of historical action. So whereas the Hegelian hero sacrifices happiness and personal well-being for the sake of achieving historical order, the Nietzschean hero "is beyond everything that *has been or is to be done*; he is interested only in power itself" (SNS 325/183).

That is, this figure is situated beyond history, and is thus concerned solely with the assertion of pure power *against others*. There can be no constructive exercise of power here, for there is nothing to do: there are no historical tasks to fulfill, and there is no dialectical framework within which the exercise of power could be sublimated as sacrifice and deployed in a transformative way. Conquest alone remains meaningful, and in particular, the conquest of death, "the most powerful opponent of all." The Nietzschean hero is thus ultimately caught up in the impossible quest for "a life which truly integrates death into itself and whose free recognition by others is definitely assured" (SNS 326/184).

Merleau-Ponty reverted to Hegelian terminology in this reading of Nietzsche. As he described it, the Nietzschean hero, seeking unreciprocated recognition, finds himself precisely in the existential impasse of the Hegelian "master." The contrast is thus posed in an unexpectedly simple way: the Nietzschean hero is the Hegelian "master" [*Herr*], while the Hegelian hero is the Hegelian "slave" [*Knecht*], that is, the one who has "chosen life and who works to transform the world in such a way that in the end there is no longer a place for the master" (SNS 326/184; cf. SNS 118f/68f).

There is clearly little exegetical rigor in these interpretations of Hegel and Nietzsche. Although they might prove defensible, were they to be developed more carefully, that was not Merleau-Ponty's purpose. Rather, as was his wont, he was primarily interested in outlining certain philosophical tropes that would serve his own argumentative purposes. It is in simultaneous contrast to both the so-called Hegelian and Nietzschean figures of heroism that he presented his own account of "the contemporary hero."

But we would overlook the significance of what Merleau-Ponty was doing if we fail to recognize that these tropes *do* represent opposed orientations with respect to Hegelian philosophy of history among which Merleau-Ponty found himself at the time compelled to stake out an interstitial position. "There are," as he said elsewhere, "several Hegels," and "interpreting Hegel means taking a stand on all the philosophical, political, and religious problems of our century" (SNS 110/63f).

First, the view he attributes to Hegel himself is the "triumphant" view that maintains that there can no longer be heroes because all of the tasks of universal history have been fulfilled (cf. Hegel 1967, 245). This "Hegel" is more accurately associated with Alexandre Kojève, whose lectures on Hegel in the 1930s Merleau-Ponty had attended (see Chapter 2, notes 13–15). According to this interpretation (Kojève 1947), the "end of History" had been attained—that is, human consciousness had become the Concept, thus concluding the movement by which it had sought to overcome the opposition between thought and being. We need not enter into the details of this view here. It suffices to point out that the linchpin of Kojève's view is his assertion of the possibility of what he termed the "Sage," someone who is "*fully* and *perfectly self-conscious*" (Kojève 1947, 271; see Preface, note 41). This is crucial because it is only on the basis of the total historical knowledge thereby implied that one could legitimately claim of historical heroes, not only that they did, in fact, attain a partial glimpse of the universal truth, and thus did, in fact, engage in genuine heroic activity, but also that as a whole, they have been rendered obsolete—that is, that History, the domain of the hero, had ended.

However, in *The Structure of Behavior*, completed in 1938, Merleau-Ponty had demonstrated that Kojève's Sage is not humanly possible, by showing that the integration constitutive of acquired self-consciousness "is never absolute and it always fails." In fact, the impossibility of "complete integration"—that is, Sagely wisdom—is precisely what Merleau-Ponty aimed to substantiate in that work, by showing that "all integration presupposes the normal functioning of the subordinated forms, *which always demand their own due*" (SC 227/210, emphasis added; see Chapter 2).

Second, with regard to Merleau-Ponty's trope of Nietzschean heroism, one might be tempted to think of Georges Bataille, with whom Merleau-Ponty was likewise personally acquainted. Bataille was a major proponent of Nietzschean ideas in France. Yet, this was primarily because he accepted Kojève's thesis that human society was entering a terminal stage of universal homogeneity in which human negativity had nothing to do. In his terms, this gave rise to the problem of "unemployed negativity" [*la négativité sans emploi*], and in particular, to the problem of securing recognition for it as such.[8]

For Bataille, however, the end of History was rolled together with the death of God in a way that at once opened up and radically undermined the possibility for genuine subjectivity. This yielded the paradoxical or "impossible" situation of "sovereignty" that was central to Bataille's thinking. In this sense, he was not so much a follower of Nietzsche as someone who aspired to *imitate* Nietzsche. He took up Nietzsche as a sacred "hero" of nonconformism, but this precisely in his tragic, mad solitude—it was a matter, so to speak, of an *imitatio anti-Christi*. This is why, in his works from the war years, including *Le coupable*, Bataille stated that his aim is "to invent a new way to crucify myself" [*un nouveau moyen de me crucifier*] (Bataille 1973, 257). He made of his existence a "combat" [*bataille*] that incarnated sacrifice by trying to mimic the sacrifice of God.

This effort on the part of Bataille was the result of his having accepted—and having tried to live out the consequences of—the basic premises of *both* the Hegelian and Nietzschean tropes of heroism. This made Bataille himself the focal point of their underlying conflict. Thus, while his uptake of Nietzsche was infused with the themes of war and violence, it was primarily directed inward in a self-destructive way that does not conform to the model of self-assertive mastery sketched by Merleau-Ponty. So although Bataille was one of Merleau-Ponty's more or less covert interlocutors (he will resurface below), he does not, as we might be tempted to think, represent the trope of Nietzschean heroism.

To capture the contrast that Merleau-Ponty wanted to establish with Kojève, our attention should rather turn to Raymond Aron, someone who was sharply critical of Kojève. Aiming to directly refute him (among others), Aron wrote in 1938 that "the traditional philosophy of history is completed in Hegel's system. *Modern philosophy of history begins with the rejection of Hegelianism*" (Aron 1969, 15, emphasis added). He went on to develop a decidedly skeptical position concerning the limits of historical objectivity, which regarded historiography as inescapably based on subjective *mises en perspective*. To be sure, this view shares a certain measure of common ground with Merleau-Ponty's own disagreement with Kojève. But Merleau-Ponty thought that Aron went too far in the direction of perspectivism.[9] *At least in theory.* Although he does not name him directly, Merleau-Ponty was undoubtedly referring to Aron when he wrote the following:

> It has not been sufficiently noted that, after demonstrating the irrationality of history, the skeptic will abruptly abandon his methodological scruples when it comes to drawing practical conclusions. . . . A skeptical politics is obliged to treat, at least implicitly, certain facts as more important than others and to that extent it harbors an embarrassing [*honteuse*] philosophy of history—one which is lived rather than thought, but which is no less effective. (SNS 297/168)

In case there is any doubt, we can consider Merleau-Ponty's response to Jaspers in Geneva in 1946 alluded to earlier (see Chapter 3). Immediately after defending the Lukácsian conception of totality against Jaspers' concerns by claiming that "anyone, from the moment he takes a political position, has a certain conception of the whole of historical life, and even if he does not formulate it in words, he nonetheless expresses it in action" (EE 253), Merleau-Ponty referred explicitly to Aron:

> I see, for example, in France, that a theorist like Raymond Aron, who has defended this idea that history is not amenable to objective interpretation, is nonetheless brought, when he personally takes a stand, to implicate therein an entire conception of the future. (EE 253)

Merleau-Ponty was alluding to the increasingly Gaullist and pro-imperialist political views that Aron defended after the war (Aron 1946; cf. Whiteside 1986, 147f). Merleau-Ponty reasoned that Aron's practical pragmatism stemmed from the fact that his theoretical skepticism was based on an at least tacit acceptance of Kojève's overly strong criteria concerning what would count as historical objectivity (cf. NI 347f [103f]). Correctly rejecting the possibility of this sort of absolute knowledge, he thus wrongly rejected historical objectivity as such, leaving his practical assessments with no principled basis beyond sociological facts. Hence Merleau-Ponty's claim that "historical skepticism is always conservative, although it cannot, in all strictness, exclude anything from its expectations—not even a revolutionary phase of history. Under the pretext of objectivity it freezes the future and eliminates change and the will of men from history" (SNS 298/168).

Although Merleau-Ponty contrasts the Hegelian and Nietzschean tropes of heroism, we can see that because they are rooted in the same absolute view of historical objectivity—the one accepting it, the other rejecting it—the conceptions of subjectivity they respectively embody actually share a fundamental infirmity: each is oblivious to concrete historical praxis. What Merleau-Ponty noted of Aron's skeptical position applies equally well to Kojève's posthistorical view: he sees "neither true subjectivity, which is never without motives, nor true objectivity, which is never without evaluation, nor the junction of the one with the other in Praxis" (NI 348 [104]). There is in neither case any recognition of historical tasks to be performed, either on the grounds that they have all been accomplished (Kojève), or else because there never were any to begin with (Aron). For what goes unperceived in both cases is the present's being oriented toward and predelineating a future that is "*à faire*," to be made. Both Kojève and

Aron consequently exhibit a conservative acquiescence in events that is antithetical to historical subjectivity and agency concretely understood. This is why neither offers a suitable framework for a neo-Marxist hermeneutics—in this regard, Merleau-Ponty was actually closer to Fessard![10]

What is lacking in the positions of both Kojève and Aron (and *this* would apply as well to Fessard), according to Merleau-Ponty, is *living contact with the present* as the germinal origins of the future. "Our only recourse lies in a reading of the present which is as full and as faithful as possible, which does not prejudge its meaning, which even recognizes chaos and non-sense where they exist, but which does not refuse to discern a direction and an idea where they manifest themselves [in the present]" (SNS 299/169). This "reading of the present" is the central plank of Merleau-Ponty's proposed political hermeneutics. As we have seen, his was not so much a philosophy of history, but a *perception* of historical phenomena that calls philosophies of history into question (NI 352, 350 [107, 105]). The reform of Marxism that Merleau-Ponty had in mind would thus extract it from all such frameworks. The course he tried to steer between Kojève and Aron, between abstractly one-sided views of history in either objective or subjective terms, was intended in part against the background of long-standing disputes within Marxism between evolutionism and voluntarism, between falling back on the inexorable movement of history, or else making it out to be simply a matter of decision and will.

Although Merleau-Ponty associated his approach with Marx, he did so only inasmuch as Marx could be read in conformity with Merleau-Ponty's own (idiosyncratic) reading of Hegel's *Phenomenology of Spirit*. "There can be no definitive understanding of the whole import of Marxist politics without going back to Hegel's description of the fundamental relations between men" (HT 110/101f). This reading rejected the gnosiological understanding of absolute knowledge that forms the reference point for both Kojève and Aron. Merleau-Ponty's account of the "contemporary hero" will aim to bring about an *Aufhebung* of the Hegelian and Nietzschean tropes in order to account at once for what is held artificially separate in this distinction, namely, objective historical progress as an agentive possibility *and* the subjective motivation to pursue it. It is thus meant to flesh out an alternative view of absolute knowledge, understood as a "way of living" [*manière de vivre*] wherein "consciousness at last becomes equal to its spontaneous life and regains its self-possession" (SNS 112/64).

As traditionally understood, such would not be a moment of knowledge at all. But that is the case only inasmuch as the tradition fails to recognize knowledge as a normative practice of embodied perception. *And this includes historical knowledge.* Merleau-Ponty thus made historical objectivity relative to practical participation in the project of realizing human universality. Such participation consequently possesses a certain epistemic privilege. As noted in the previous chapter, citing the perspicacity of Trotsky's analysis of the Russian Revolution, for example, Merleau-Ponty affirmed that "the greatest objectivity is often the subjectivity of he who lived it" (NI 18 [6]); cf. Whiteside 1988, 122). The point is not that all lived experience carries equal epistemological weight. It is rather that, even if it cannot be captured discursively, the object of individual lived experience *can* be the "*the* total intention" of society, "*the* Idea in the Hegelian sense" (PhP xiii, emphases added).

Merleau-Ponty's broader point was that this possibility could underwrite a common framework within which all those engaged in history as the process of fulfilling "the promise of humanity"—Marxists and militant Christians in particular—could be reconciled. The idea is that substantive ideological disagreement is superficial and that it stems from a prior epistemological agreement—exemplified by Kojève and Aron—concerning objectivity which stipulates what would count as substantive agreement in a way that actually renders it impossible. In occluding the living present, this common theoretical prejudice prevents people from seeing that what motivates genuine historical *engagement* is ultimately *not* a matter of ideological profession.

Ideological heroism

Concerning historical action, Merleau-Ponty was gripped by the phenomenon of uncompromising engagement, especially on the part of Communists (like Nizan), where there was little or no expectation that the goals pursued would be realized during the agent's own lifetime. Let's call this "ideological heroism." In contrast to the traditional Hegelian hero, whose vision of human universality is inchoate and whose projects contribute to it only inadvertently, the ideological hero clearly imagines the universal and sees that there is an unfulfilled historical objectivity, on behalf of which she acts self-consciously. But Merleau-Ponty did *not* think that this offered a viable model for political agency. In "Man, the Hero," where he hinges his discussion on selected literary examples of communist political action, his strategy is to parlay a critique of the *roman à thèse* as a "self-defeating genre" (Tane 1998, 11) into a broader critique of political ideology as a motivating force. The problem with the *roman à thèse* is that its political didacticism necessarily involves a closed teleology—heroes are modeled on pregiven prototypes, with the result either that the political message is delivered ventriloquially or else that it is actually overshadowed by characters' subjective deviations from orthodoxy (Tane 1998, 453). Either way, ideologically motivated heroic action remains an abstract idea that is not brought into *living* connection with particular individuals.

For instance, Merleau-Ponty considers Hemingway's Robert Jordan (*For Whom the Bell Tolls*), the idealistic American college professor who volunteers to fight for the Loyalist cause against the fascists in Spain, and who ultimately gives his life in doing so. Unlike Hemingway's earlier protagonists, who tended to be detached and individualistic, Jordan is strongly socially-oriented and concerned with communion and fraternity (Smetana 1965, 124ff). Nonetheless, as Merleau-Ponty notes, in risking his life for the "interests of humanity" (Hemingway 1940, 11), "Jordan cannot manage to make the society of the future the sole motive for his sacrifice." Rather, such sacrifice is tied to the living present such that "the society of the future" "is desirable to [Jordan] only as the probable guarantee, for himself and for others, of the freedom he is exercising at that very moment" (SNS 327/184).

Turning to Malraux's Kyo Gisors (*La condition humaine*), a leader of a failed socialist insurrection in Shanghai, Merleau-Ponty notes that here the same question is confronted "at the *very core of Marxism.*" The problem is that with respect to political action, in principle there cannot be any *a priori* determination of when to cede to the objective momentum of history and when to subjectively "force its hand," as it were. Either way, it seems to be an inescapably subjective decision. Merleau-Ponty draws the same conclusion concerning the "paradoxes of liberty" from Roger Vailland's 1945 work *Drôle de jeu* (cf. Lloyd 2003, 165f). The idea is that communist discipline results from a free choice to limit free choice for the sake of effective collective action, but that this basic choice itself cannot be objectively determined.

Merleau-Ponty wanted to show that this basic "choice" should not be understood as an intellectual decision, but rather in terms of *existential style*. Merleau-Ponty used the example of Hemingway's Jordan to illustrate this. Wounded behind enemy lines, and having urged his comrades to go on, Jordan remains with them in spirit, prepared until the very end to do what he could to protect them. As he says, "*there is something to do yet*" (Hemingway 1940, 470, italics added). But does Jordan truly believe the ideological rationale he gives himself for his actions, and is this what actually motivates him? Is it the case that "right up to the end [*jusqu'au bout*], he will satisfy the highest demand: 'uphold through action the honor of being a man, and do something *useful* for the others'" (Smetana 1965, 126, citing Astre 1959, 153, italics added)? Is heroism a matter of *service* to the "interests of humanity"?

Merleau-Ponty answers firmly in the negative. According to his interpretation of Hemingway's Jordan, "the man who is still living has no other resource – *but this is sovereign* – than to keep on acting like a living man [*un homme vivant*]" (SNS 329/186, emphasis added). In continuing to act, in particular, by not taking his own life, Jordan was just living out his existential style—*just being himself*. He was wounded, but alive, and so, however short it might be, there was still a future to be made to which he would belong. In Merleau-Ponty's view, this evinces *sovereignty*, not service. This is why it is not the society of the future that is the key to understanding Jordan, but rather "the freedom he is exercising at that very moment." And this is why it is immaterial whether he was actually able to do anything useful for the others.

Thus, for Merleau-Ponty, heroic action is not a self-sacrificial matter of one's reflective ideological commitments tragically piloting one's body into a lethal situation. That is to say, in the terms drawn from Part I of *Phenomenology of Perception*, it is not a matter of a temporal dislocation in which the "actual" body fatally detaches itself from the habituated organism. For Merleau-Ponty, to say that heroic action is a matter of existential style is to affirm that *the locus of heroic action is the habituated organism*. Hence, inasmuch as ideology informs heroism, it does so only as a kind of corporeal sedimentation. But again, this does not mean that heroic action is a matter of sedimented ideological commitment fatally compromising the "actual" body. Rather, Merleau-Ponty's view is that heroic action precisely instances the coincidence—or the *contemporaneousness*—of the "actual" body and the habituated organism. This is the condition of absolute knowledge, "the point at which consciousness finally becomes equal to its spontaneous life and regains its self-possession" (SNS 64/112).

To clarify this, Merleau-Ponty turns to Saint Exupéry, who, significantly, was a real person, not a fictional character (even if his stories are highly stylized).

The contemporary hero

The idea behind the contemporary hero is that *"our time,"* as Merleau-Ponty very frequently put it, appears as a time neither of faith nor of reason, but rather of a world out of joint. Events exhibit no clear overarching pattern, and in particular, the schemata of Marxism are unable to account for them (SNS 288/162f; cf. 216f/123). It is thus a time when "duties and tasks are unclear," for there are no absolute reference points for historical action. Not even utility. Merleau-Ponty seizes on the fact that the flight described in *Pilote de guerre* was, as Saint Exupéry's account of it likewise emphasized, *objectively useless*. As noted above (Chapter 1), not only was the mission extremely perilous, but it was understood that due to the state of the French forces at the time, no reconnaissance information could be put to use anyway. "What sense did it make" to fly that mission? "How is [Saint Exupéry] to serve if service is useless?" (SNS 328/185).

The answer, of course, is that he was not *serving* anything. Not unlike Jordan, Saint Exupéry was "sovereign" *because* his action was useless, *because it made no sense*, that is, because it was not intelligible according to existing parameters of rationality.[11] But Merleau-Ponty added that this was not a demonstration of a morbid fascination with death or a cavalier contempt for it in the manner, for example, of Montherlant's *Service inutile* (1935). "It is not death that I love, said Saint-Exupéry, but life" (SNS 330/186).[12] Merleau-Ponty thus interpreted Saint Exupéry's action in 1940 in this way (SNS 328/185):

> Saint-Exupéry throws himself into his mission because it is an intimate part of himself, the consequences of his thoughts, wishes and decisions, because he would be nothing if he were to back out. He recovers his own being to the extent to which he runs into danger. Over Arras, in the fire of anti-aircraft guns, when every second of continuing life is as miraculous as birth, he feels invulnerable because he is *in* things at last; he has left his inner nothingness behind, and death, if it comes, will reach him right in the thick of the world.

And without question, Merleau-Ponty meant to imply that what was true of Saint Exupéry's flight in 1940 also applied to his final flight in 1944. Incarnating pure human productivity and eschewing all circumstantial compromise, Saint-Exupéry melded with the world, thereby achieving the organically complete agentive integrity characteristic of absolute knowledge.

For Merleau-Ponty, heroes are those who "really were outwardly what they inwardly wished to be" and thus "became one with history at the moment when it claimed their lives" (SNS 258/146). Equivalently, the hero is someone who "lives to the limit [*jusqu'au bout*] his relation to men and the world" by enacting an affirmative response to the question: "Shall I give my freedom to save freedom?" (PhP 520). Subjectively, the hero is fully invested in the realization of freedom, *understood in universal terms*. Owing to her tacit acceptance that true freedom knows no singularity, the hero gives the *appearance* of a wholehearted readiness for personal sacrifice. This just means that heroic living embodies an uncompromising commitment to life considered universally—the hero is an individual who lives out her own vital particularity *as* human universality. The hero is thus an exemplary *vivant*, or living person (SNS 328f/185f; cf. HT xli/xlv), whose thinking and acting are fully saturated with that "love of life" that is irreducible to biological existence. This fulfills Merleau-Ponty's claim that "man is capable of situating his proper being, not in biological existence, but at the level of properly human relations" (SC 190 n1/246 n97). It would kill us, but we *can* do it.

In a paradoxical way, then, the hero is *pathologically alive*. Merleau-Ponty endorsed Hegel's idea that human beings are "sick animals" (SNS 116/67). That is, *normal* human existence is constitutively "sick" on account of the schizoidal duality of being-in-itself and being-for-itself to which anthropogenetic reflective self-consciousness leads. Through his complete internalization of the negativity of death, the hero effectively *heals* this split by achieving a self-coincidence that amounts to a condition of pathological health. Subjectively, this parallels the Marxist account of the proletarian that Merleau-Ponty presented in *Humanism and Terror*. The contemporary hero is likewise a de-humanized—which is to say, de-particularized—agent of the species, *but without the objective social conditions*.

The case of Saint Exupéry thus addressed the motivational problem of how human universality can be concretely realized *without sacrifice*. This is because, as Merleau-Ponty put it, his self-giving resulted, not from pursuing this or that ideological goal, but rather from living out the "loyalty to the *natural* movement that throws us toward things and toward others" (SNS 330/186, emphasis added), something Merleau-Ponty implied is equivalent in the hero's case to remaining "poised in the direction of his *chosen* ends" (SNS 330/185, emphasis added).

What were those ends? Simply to leave "his inner nothingness behind" and to "recover his own being." Whatever his real military contribution may have been, what *he* was doing was living out his subjectivity, "recovering his being" by personally incorporating the centrifugal thrust of natural spontaneity. Attaining the condition of sovereignty, the hero becomes a kind of *natural purposiveness*, a living embodiment of humanity's being its own highest end.

Unlike the Hegelian hero, who, in working *against* her time, suffered a pronounced dislocation between habituated organism and "actual" body, the contemporary hero simply *lives her time*—this is the deeper sense of her "contemporaneity." The heroic achievement is to subjectively exist one's own corporeality as a prototype of one's sociohistorical milieu. For Merleau-Ponty, this means that the hero lives out explicitly the universality that world-historical heroism in the Hegelian sense realized only to the point of latency. He thus argued that it is "by living my time," "by plunging into [*en m'enfonçant*] the present and the world . . . that I am able to understand other times" (PhP 520)—that is, accede to the universal.

Merleau-Ponty held that the disordered and contingent appearance of "our time" harbored a "logic of history" that could be taken up and realized. As we saw earlier, by a "logic of history," Merleau-Ponty meant (a) that history is an integral whole, "a single drama" in which all events have a human significance; and (b) that the phases of this drama do not follow an arbitrary order, "but move toward a completion and conclusion" (SNS 212/121). The distinctive feature of a Marxist view, according to Merleau-Ponty, is that it makes the completion of history dependent upon contingent acts of revolutionary agency—it "admit[s] that history is both logical and contingent, that nothing is absolutely fortuitous but also that nothing is absolutely necessary" (SNS 211f/120). In other words, for Marxism, the logic of history is just one possibility among others (SNS 213/121). But this would seem to reduce it, when the class struggle wanes, as in "our time," to the conjured product of revolutionary ideology. In a disordered world, can there be any evidential basis for upholding the Marxist hypothesis?

For Merleau-Ponty, the hero provides such evidence. Although the hero incarnates a historical period that is, to all appearances, one of disorder, the hero himself, his *manière de vivre*, is not at all disordered. "Today's hero is not skeptical, dilettantish, or decadent." Rather, "it is simply the case that he has experienced chance, disorder, and failure. . . . He [thus] has a better experience than anyone has ever had of the contingency of the future and the freedom of man" (SNS 330/186). The hero thus surpasses the theoretical failure of abstract discourses of history. Committed to universality and accepting that freedom knows no singularity, the practical lesson that he draws from this experience is to detach from freedom in its given forms and to ground his commitment within a deeper, transhistorical level of being. The hero thus withdraws to the sovereignty of "absolute knowledge"—a move which, through a transgression of existing rationality, places the hero in the extrahistorical realm of *non-sense*. While this makes of the contemporary hero, not unlike the Hegelian hero, a "junction of madness [*déraison*] and reason [*raison*]" (SNS 324f/183; cf. 9/4), it is precisely in virtue of this departure from history that the hero is able to play an evidentiary role with respect to its logic.

By incarnating human productivity, and despite being paradoxically lethal, heroic self-realization evidences history's being a dramatic, teleological whole driven by contingent human agency. It thus presents a *mise en abyme* of the possible self-realization of humanity. If we accept the account of Saint Exupéry's death that Merleau-Ponty offers, then we have grounds for positing a natural spontaneity that is in harmony with our aspirations to the realization of concrete universal reconciliation. This rationalizes the need Merleau-Ponty felt to rank this possibility as more than just one among many. The heroic spectacle legitimizes the privileging of fulgurant moments of transgressive communication by seeing them as based in and expressive of "that very movement which unites us with others, our present with our past, and by means of which we make everything have meaning" (SNS 330/186). This movement is what Merleau-Ponty later described as the "spontaneity which gathers together the plurality of monads, the past and the present, nature and culture into a single whole," and which thus "accomplishes what appeared to be impossible when we observed only the separate elements" (Pros. 47f/10). To be clear, being a matter of extrahistorical non-sense, the action of the contemporary hero does not itself accomplish such results. It doesn't accomplish *anything*. Rather, its significance lies solely in its bringing to phenomenological self-givenness the natural teleological purposiveness that (*possibly*) stands behind those achievements. In this way, the contemporary hero motivates and rationally substantiates the militant faith of a neo-Marxist historical praxis.

This militant faith is what Merleau-Ponty meant by "the existential attitude." To renew Marxism, which, he thought, is weakest "when faced with concrete events taken moment by moment" (SNS 217/123), Merleau-Ponty wanted to trace the molecular emergence of transformative political consciousness from the "living present" up. This presupposes the heroic manifestation of humanity's intrinsic purposiveness. The evidentiary value of heroism is thus perceptual, not theoretical. By providing an appropriate new perceptual background, it supports a Gestalt shift that discloses historical significance in the seemingly insignificant phenomena of everyday life. It is what enables us to see, in other words, that even "the least perception, the slightest movement of the heart, the smallest action, bear incontestable witness" to human universality (cf. SNS 121/70).

Saint Exupéry and Schn.

It would be appropriate at this point briefly to relate Merleau-Ponty's view of the contemporary hero to his existential interpretation of Adhémar Gelb and Kurt Goldstein's analyses of their patient "Schn." (Johann Schneider). As is well known, Schn. suffered a serious occipital injury during World War I that resulted in his being diagnosed by Gelb and Goldstein with a manifold of psychosomatic disorders, central to which, however, was apperceptive visual agnosia.[13] And this case played a major role in Merleau-Ponty's phenomenological account of embodiment.

Merleau-Ponty portrayed Schn. as having lost the ability to use his body freely to project around himself a situation into which he could proceed. While his intellectual capacities were sound, he had lost the power of imagination, and so, he lived in a world without possibility—he was tied to actuality and all but totally absorbed in the present. His experience appears to him as self-evident and self-sufficient. Unable to project himself into imaginary situations, Schn. lacks "living thought" (PhP 149). He is incapable of any act of authentic expression (including political opinion)—he cannot create an "opening" in being because his own being is so thoroughly closed. Based on his inability to put himself into a situation, he lacks freedom (PhP 158). This is primarily because he lacks the power of apprehending simultaneous wholes and of cognitively shifting from wholes to parts—that is, as Merleau-Ponty put it, what Schn. cannot do is *survoler* the objects of his experience (PhP 147, 157f). In an important sense, Schn.'s core problem is a total *lack* of "high-altitude thinking."

According to Merleau-Ponty, we could say that Schn. was a model of immanence, in that his habituated organism had virtually collapsed onto his "actual" body, such that his subjective existence was entirely inscribed by his objective being. He thus has a kind of agentive integrity. But it is inverted in such a way as to imprison him in the actuality of a drastically contracted lived world. Merleau-Ponty portrayed Schn. as a kind of "perfect" Cartesian—what we would all be like were Cartesian principles true. As living negative proof that the capacity to project and competently communicate meaning is not just an intellectual exercise, but rather depends upon corporeal processes of signification and intentionality, Schn. offers powerful evidence to refute the Cartesian dualist account of human existence, and all forms of objective thinking that are based upon that.

The subjective transcendence of Merleau-Ponty's hero and the universal scope of his world stand at the opposite end of the existential spectrum from the objective immanence of Gelb and Goldstein's patient. Virtually, the one is all "actual," the other all habitual. Saint Exupéry and Schn. thus provide Merleau-Ponty with the limiting cases of human *être-au-monde*. In them, we have the two extremes of dualistic existential style—deanimated body and disembodied spirit—two pathological poles of uncommunicative, disengaged, and ahistorical solitude between which unfolds that "third kind of existence," which characterizes the intercorporeal coexistence of the overwhelming majority of human beings. This may have been what Merleau-Ponty had in mind in saying that "to be completely a man, it is necessary to be a little more and a little less than man" (EP 51/63f).

Merleau-Ponty's myth of man

Without question, Merleau-Ponty's is an unusual conception of heroism, one that verges on antiheroism. Indeed, he began "Man, the Hero" by echoing Marcel's distrust of heroism. And he is absolutely clear that heroism does not offer a viable model for historical agency. His intervention is intended effectively to *dissolve* the discourse of heroism by rendering what is crucial to it a quotidian phenomenon, and raising its exceptionality to the level of humanist myth. He thus concluded "Man, the Hero" by identifying the contemporary hero with "man" *qua* universality incarnate. But he did so by way of contrast with two other mythic figures: "the contemporary hero is not Lucifer; he is not even Prometheus; he is man" (SNS 331/187). Untangling the meaning of this dual contrast that is found at the very end of *Sense and Non-Sense* will shed further light on Merleau-Ponty's humanist myth.

Prometheus and Lucifer have, at least in modernity, often been seen as closely allied, the latter (often as Satan) being portrayed as a kind of Christianized version of the former. This is prevalent in Romantic literature, but it is also the case in German Idealism (von Balthasar 1947). The general sense shared by these Promethean and Luciferian figures is that of a spirit who liberates humanity from ignorance, one that seeks to enlighten humanity against the wishes of the prevailing powers to maintain humanity in a state of servile enthrallment.

But Merleau-Ponty evidently discerned a noteworthy difference between Lucifer and Prometheus, one that was relevant to his account of heroism. Although he offered few clues as to what exactly he had in mind, a sound account can be pieced together.

Lucifer

Although the theme surfaces in other relevant ways,[14] concerning Lucifer, I submit that we are dealing with an allusion to Roger Caillois. For Caillois was *the* proponent of Luciferian thinking at the time, and he also had an important and closely related interest in Saint Exupéry.

We might approach this first by stepping back to consider Caillois' views on "militant" thinking, in particular, as expressed in a short essay entitled "Pour une orthodoxie militante: les tâches immédiates de la pensée moderne" ["For a Militant Orthodoxy: The Immediate Tasks of Modern Thought"] (Caillois 1936).[15] This essay is useful to consider for how it can help to contextualize Caillois' view on Lucifer, and thereby to cast contrastive light on Merleau-Ponty's own position vis-à-vis Saint Exupéry.

In the piece in question, Caillois sketched out a vision of a radicalized rationalism as a kind of nonconformist intellectual reform that would yield a "a scientific heterodox 'orthodoxy'" (ES 130). This was to be a rigorous yet imaginative science which, as a contemporary counterpart to myth, would integrate lucidity and affect so as to compel intellect and emotion equally, and in this way contribute to revivifying society against its decadent decline and the threat of fascism. It was thus by no means anti-Enlightenment. The point was to recover the radical challenge to social order enunciated by nineteenth-century *maudit* poets like Baudelaire and Balzac—but with a twist. For now the problem was the oppressiveness of social *disorder*. This is why Caillois called for a *militant orthodoxy*. On the one hand, this was militant: the proposed intellectual reform had a fundamentally "activist" character, in the sense of being radically opposed to determinism—it aimed to *produce* phenomena, not predict them. Caillois sought "a form of revolutionary thought that would not be restricted to the intellectual sphere, but would open out onto real life,"[16] "a mode of thought that would impress itself upon the real and trigger a whole series of phenomena in the real" (cited in ES 131).

On the other hand, though, this was to be an orthodoxy. For "the adversary must be defeated with its own weapons: through a more rigorous coherence and a tighter systematization – through a construction that both implicates and explicates it, rather than itself being reduced and decomposed by it" (MH 215). This implied an endlessly open-ended process of integration and generalization (MH 215f). The authority of this approach would derive, not only from "the solidity of its principles [and] the rigor of their application," but also from "*the appeal of its demands*" (MH 217). A militantly orthodox system of knowledge would, at once and in a reciprocal way, be "immune to all methodological criticism" and appear to human sensitivity "*directly in the form of an imperative attraction that is capable of mobilizing it instantly*" (MH 220). For Caillois, militant systematicity would ultimately rest on a myth of organic human unity. That is, militant orthodoxy is premised on "the *presumption that there exists an ideal unitary undertaking*, that would take as its task to set *the whole of man's being* to work, in such a way as to make its different functions converge in a continuous process of living creation" (MH 221). The aim and orientation of the project is to verify this myth in the sense of *making* it true. There is thus a dialectical logic in Caillois' notion of militant orthodoxy that would account for its difference from both archaic myth and modern science.

Caillois presented Lucifer as a mythic prototype of this sort of militant knowing, "the incarnation of a new epistemological spirit," the figure of an "aggressive" and "conquering" vision of knowledge (Massonet 1998, 74). As the "demon or angel of lucidity," Caillois "viewed Lucifer as the truly effective rebel" (ES 166, 144). In this way, Lucifer superseded nineteenth-century Romantic Satanism—here, Caillois made an important distinction. For Satanism was ultimately ineffectual with respect to dealing with the sources of the alienation to which it was opposed. "Satanic rebels emanating from Romanticism foresee no recourse other than ongoing profanation or an inevitable identification with other marginal or disenfranchised groups" (Richman 2003, 36). In contrast, the figure of Lucifer represented a more transgressive, albeit elitist, individualism which, based on scientific and Nietzschean self-mastery, is able to maintain the critical demands of Romantic Satanism, but with an intensified lucidity and practical consequence.

> Calculating and conquering, [Lucifer] did not believe that revolt was sufficient in and of itself, nor that bursts of instinct always led to victory. His lucidity, which he viewed as his primary and most powerful weapon, gave him a coolly detached and sometimes cynical indifference, which made him an accurate accountant of reality. (Caillois (1937), cited in ES 171)

In this way, "Lucifer is entirely focused on what is possible and undertakes it without delay. He is Satan in action; an intelligent Satan; and, in a certain sense, a courageous Satan" (Caillois (1937), cited in ES 171).

This movement from the Satanic to the Luciferian "supposes a certain education of our sense of rebellion, that would take it from riotousness to a broadly imperialist attitude and would persuade it to subordinate its impulsive, unruly reactions to the necessity for discipline, calculation, and patience" (cited in Hollier 1988, 36). Caillois asserted that "the Luciferian spirit" corresponds "to the moment in which rebellion turns into a will for power and, losing none of its passionate and subversive character, attributes to intelligence, to the cynical and lucid vision of reality, a role of prime importance for the realization of its plans. It is the passage from *agitation to action*" (MH 199).

Key to this "passage" is the move from empty profanation to founding acts of sacralization. The latter were a preoccupation of much post-Durkheimian sociology in France, in particular for Caillois, whose main concern was with the oppressiveness and alienation wrought by social disorder. Thus, notwithstanding the Nietzschean themes, Caillois' Luciferian hero also bears similarities to Hegelian world-historical individuals. In each case, it is a matter of establishing order in the world. A crucial difference from the Hegelian view, however, is that what Caillois describes is ultimately arbitrary— there is no sense in which the civilization to which Luciferian praxis leads is in any way part of a larger rational scheme. That is, it cannot be justified transcendentally. At any rate, such is how Caillois saw Exupérian heroism. As a literary man of action, Saint Exupéry represented the post-Satanic, mythic hero who "conquers and brings order to a domain of nascent and still ailing civilization" [*conquiert* [*et*] *aménage un domaine de civilisation naissante, encore chétive*] (Roger Caillois 1953, xii). As Saint Exupéry himself stated of Aéropostale: "I do not admire men for serving the postal line, but I uphold the myth of the postal line because it forms such men" (Carnets, 69). In this way, "Saint-Exupéry, as writer and aviator, best conveyed Caillois' new cult of individual heroism" (Frank 2003, 37; cf. Roger Caillois 1946; 1947).

Merleau-Ponty clearly saw Exupérian heroism otherwise. Although in specific contexts he could valorize the Luciferian traits of cool aplomb, cerebral lucidity, and calculated practical intervention, what interested Merleau-Ponty in Saint Exupéry was the complete *absence* of these traits. Specifically, the fact that Saint Exupéry was so *un*-Luciferian that with an absolutely naïve idiosyncrasy he directly manifested the universality in terms of which political situations can be perceived as such in the first place. This is the sense in which Merleau-Ponty placed the heroic act outside politics and history. To be sure, Merleau-Ponty shared with Caillois a militant concern for bringing order out of disorder, and their projects are both normatively driven, practical, creative undertakings that ultimately rest on humanistic myth. But in Merleau-Ponty's view, politics and history cannot be objectively manipulated from above. Rather, they concern intersubjective phenomena of human relationality and communication, to which historical productivity is internal. There is no disjunction between ends and means—sociality is not separate from its founding moments. In this way, Merleau-Ponty took more seriously Caillois' own militant postulate of "an ideal *unitary* undertaking, that would take as its task to set the *whole* of man's being to work, in such a way as to make its different functions converge in a *continuous process of living creation*" (MH 221, italics altered).

Prometheus

Caillois' "La naissance de Lucifer" was published alongside Bataille's "Van Gogh Prométhée" (1937; cf. 1930), and the contrast between Lucifer and Satan in terms of a constructiveness that goes beyond disruptive insubordination—a view to which Merleau-Ponty was sympathetic—reflects important disagreements between Caillois and Bataille. Because of the importance of the issue of sacrifice, consideration of Bataille's view of Van Gogh will, oddly enough, help shed light on Merleau-Ponty's view of Prometheus—and hence on his view of "man."

Bataille related contemporary cases of self-mutilation, in particular that of Van Gogh, to human-divine relationships in archaic religion, which he took to be mediated by sacrificial mutilation. Such acts, he thought, represented "the desire to resemble perfectly an ideal term, generally characterized in mythology as a solar god who tears and rips out his own organs" (Bataille 1985, 66). Citing the work of Mauss and Hubert (1964), Bataille noted that unlike many acts of sacrifice performed by humans, which make use of animal avatars, "the god who sacrifices himself gives himself irrevocably. . . . The god, who is at the same time the sacrifier [*sic*], is one with the victim and sometimes even with the sacrificer. All the differing elements that enter into ordinary sacrifice here enter into each other and become mixed together" (Bataille 1985, 69f).

Bataille argued, however, that Mauss and Hubert wrongly assumed that this was "only possible for mythical, that is ideal, beings." In his view, in cases of human self-mutilation there remain vestiges of this divine phenomenon. "There is . . . no reason to separate Van Gogh's ear . . . from Prometheus' famous liver" (Bataille 1985, 70). "If one accepts the interpretation that identifies the purveying eagle [*aetos Prometheus*] with the god who stole fire from the wheel of the sun, then the tearing out of the liver presents a theme in conformity with the various legends of the 'sacrifice of the god'" (Bataille 1985, 70). For Bataille, Prometheus and the eagle form a single system of self-mutilation, and in this way manifest the deepest significance of the spirit of sacrifice, to wit, "throwing oneself or something of oneself *out of oneself.*" This is not fundamentally a matter of expiation or propitiation, but simply of the "radical *alteration*" of the person—self-mutilation epitomizes personal transformation that disrupts the social context. The claim is that this has "the power to liberate heterogeneous elements and to break the habitual homogeneity of the individual" (Bataille 1985, 70).

Thus, for Bataille, Van Gogh is an instance of the sovereign Promethean gesture of self-transcendence, the unity of sacrificer and sacrificed. His self-mutilation is interpreted by Bataille as an expression of the sacrificial impulse at the root of human religiosity in general, the aim of which is to overcome individuality by mimicking divine self-immolation. In particular, it exemplifies the "absolute dismemberment"—*déchirement absolu, absolute Zerrissenheit*—around which Bataille's reading of Hegel pivots: "Spirit attains its truth only by finding itself in absolute dismemberment" (see Bataille 1955).

Bataille thus rejected the Durkheimian view of sacrificial ritual as primarily reasonable and useful with respect to social order and unity, emphasizing instead its irrational, purposeless, and unassimilably destructive qualities. Whereas for Durkheim, sacrifice forged bonds of social integration, for Bataille, it was primarily a matter of disintegration through insubordination, refusal, revolt. It was a subversive, self-divinizing act whereby a disenchanted individual *amputated* himself from the established social order and its values (cf. Bataille 1970, 275f).

However, Bataille *did* think that sacrifice thus understood could also have a communally unifying function. Through this violent rupture of her empirical wholeness, the self-mutilator can also experience an ecstatic union with the whole. She can, that is, "come to embody and reflect the larger community, just as Durkheim's person does when [she] engages in sacrificial ritual" (Stoekl 1992, 51f). For Bataille, sacrifice can generate an affective power that achieves a sort of interpenetration between self and other, such that "the different separate beings *communicate*, come to life by losing themselves in *communication* with one another" (Bataille 1973, 263; cf. 37).

Notwithstanding such gestures, Bataille's account of sacrifice remained, for Caillois, precisely the kind of Romantic Satanism which he thought should be superseded by the Luciferian spirit (see Frank 2003, 27, 31, 167). Fundamentally, this was because Bataille had an overly deathly view of the sacred, to which Lucifer offered a more vivacious alternative. Caillois' position "does not call for crime, transgression, or sacrifice; as the basis of sacred community, he highlights not death but a *reason to live*" (Frank 2003, 27). In this way, "the cerebral Luciferian self-mastery" championed by Caillois offered a radical antithesis to the "ecstatic self-sacrifice of Van Gogh's life and work" that Bataille held up as a paradigm of Promethean self-overcoming (Frank 2003, 168).

Bataille's view of self-mutilation clearly shows the link between Prometheanism and self-sacrifice. As from the latter, Merleau-Ponty also always disinclined from the Promethean myth,[17] and thus, he did not accept Bataille's view, the upshot of which would be to analogize the proletariat and Van Gogh in terms of the need for self-directed violence. Yet it remains the case that Bataille's account of communication does have affinities with Merleau-Ponty's own view. It is just that whereas Bataille invoked death *simpliciter*, Merleau-Ponty spoke of vital universality. This put Merleau-Ponty closer to Caillois, who also sought a more affirmative approach. But Merleau-Ponty rejected the arbitrariness of the Luciferian solution. For Merleau-Ponty, Caillois was not so fundamentally different from Bataille—he just deployed impersonally at the level of historical apriority the arbitrary violence that the latter directed internally against the habituated organism of the individual.

For Merleau-Ponty, what Caillois and Bataille had in common—and what distinguished them from the historical apraxia (so to speak) shared by Kojève and Aron—is a genuine orientation toward transformative action. But in their respective admixtures of Hegelian and Nietzschean ideas, what they powerfully illustrate are *the impasses to which historical agency is led in the absence of an alternative philosophical interpretation of absolute knowledge*. Merleau-Ponty's construal of absolute knowledge as a possible "way of living" is his crucial (albeit mythic) gambit. For it supports his postulates of latent human universality and purposiveness. Whereas both Caillois and Bataille invoke a violent rupture, the one directing it outward, the other inward, Merleau-Ponty's founding gesture is one of *perceptual* violence (cf. PhP xvi, 415). It amounts to the motivated decision to see heroism as an extrahistorical manifestation of human productivity, and to make this the background of historical perception, against which vital communication *can* become the means and end of historical agency.

Marxism

Bataille was neither a principal interlocutor of Merleau-Ponty, nor a key player in the political debates in which Merleau-Ponty was engaged. But he did give the clearest expression of the existential implications of the valorization of the Promethean myth. The significance of this lies in the fact that Merleau-Ponty's reference to Prometheus was surely also—and, indeed, primarily—an allusion to classical Marxism. It is well-known that Marx himself admired Aeschylus' *Prometheus Bound*, and that he regarded Prometheus as a revolutionary figure of Greek mythology, appealing to him as a symbol of human divinity and self-emancipation: "Prometheus is the most eminent saint and martyr in the philosophical calendar" (Marx 1975a, 31). And this sentiment was reflected by many Marxists in the postwar French context, including Hervé (1948, 37).

It is often raised as a criticism of Marxism that it indulges in an overly strong motif of Promethean self-divinization in ways which could, in principle, be avoided (e.g. Kolakowski 1978, 412ff). As Wessell argued, however, beyond being *a* "mythopoetic symbol in Marx's thinking," the "salvational archetype" of Prometheus actually provides *the* "mythico-ontological root metaphor" for historical materialism. "The 'myth' of the fall, suffering, and ultimate self-redemption of Prometheus constitutes the dramatic model underlying and informing Marx's Marxism" (Wessell 1984, 62ff; cf. 22, 38f, 189). That is, this myth plays a crucial transcendental role by structuring the antepredicative background of Marxism's historical perception. In particular, owing to its dual role in the soteriological myth as Prometheus both bound and unbound, the proletariat in this view comes to embody "an absolute agonal tension"—the "ontological form of the proletariat is *to be* a self-abolishing tension" (Wessell 1984, 187).

For Merleau-Ponty, such sacrificial implications represented the main problem with classical Marxism—not that it was based on myth, but that it was based on the *wrong* myth. Promethean assumptions are what stand behind the problem discussed earlier, that of seeing the revolutionary moment as the *self-annihilation* of the proletariat. It was precisely to avoid this sort of lethal rupture that Merleau-Ponty sought to ground a commitment to Marxism in the incarnational myth attested to by the universal purposiveness evinced by the contemporary hero. Presupposing the agonistic drama of the proletariat would not only lead to distorted practical strategies, but it would also impose an ideological structure that conceals rather than reveals genuine political phenomena—most crucially, those of the possible emergence of genuine agencies of universality, and other concrete manifestations of the proletariat.

For Merleau-Ponty, the aim of a neo-Marxist hermeneutics would be to "decipher facts, discover in them a common meaning, and thereby grasp a leading thread which, without obviating the need to analyze each period on its own terms, allows us to discern an orientation of events." Far from any utopianism or dogmatic philosophy of history, it would aim "to provide a *perception of history* which would continuously bring to appearance the lines of force and vectors of the present" (HT 104f/98). Merleau-Ponty's incarnational humanist myth was meant to provide the transcendental horizons for this perception. What is needed is to learn to see the world anew. Generalizing from production to productivity, Merleau-Ponty thus sought to reform Marxism by reconfiguring the perceptual field as the human world *that is to be made*, that is in the process of being made, knowing full well that this means taking a new perceptual background on faith. "To perceive is to engage in a single stroke a whole future of experiences in a present that never strictly guarantees it—it is to believe in a world" (PhP 343f). The singular human world as an unfinished historical project is the object of this militant *Weltglaube*—faith in the possibility of the complete realization of which is no arbitrary dream to the exact extent to which Exupérian heroism is accepted as a limit form of *être-au-monde* that evinces the living presence of a universal purposiveness.

Response to Merleau-Ponty's "Hero"

Merleau-Ponty's essay on heroism, "Man, the Hero," and particularly, the central significance he accorded in that essay to Saint Exupéry in preference to recognizably communist heroes, met with a hostile reaction from the readership of *action* (Blanc-Dufour et al. 1946).[18] Indeed, this reaction was all but prefigured in the editorial preface that preceded the essay itself (see note 3). It is difficult to know the extent to which (if at all) this surprised Merleau-Ponty. In any event, his attempt to define "the existential attitude" specifically failed to draw Hervé any closer to existentialism. A fortnight later, Hervé responded quite harshly to the claims Merleau-Ponty had made in "Pour la vérité" (SNS 271–303/153–71), originally published in the previous issue of *Les temps modernes* (January 1946), to the effect that classical Marxism—and in particular, the politics of *action*—"no longer has a grip on the facts" (SNS 299/169). Significantly, in a way reminiscent of Maritain's criticism of Saint Exupéry, Hervé accused Merleau-Ponty of being disengaged and noncommittal, a "solitary spectator" [*spectateur solitaire*] hovering indecisively "above the fray" [*au-dessus de la mêlée*] (Hervé 1946, 3).

And Hervé did not do so without grounds. Consider how Merleau-Ponty expressed his approach to political phenomena at the time: "It is up to us to *observe* the world during these years when it begins to breathe again. . . . *If* the class struggle once again becomes the motivating force of history and, definitely, *if* the alternative of socialism or chaos becomes clearer, then it is up to us to choose a proletarian socialism" (SNS 218/124, emphasis added). And even more tellingly, Merleau-Ponty admitted that "to speak of humanism without being on the side of 'humanist socialism' in the Anglo-American way, to 'understand' the Communists without being a Communist, is to set oneself very high [*se placer bien haut*], at any rate, above the fray [*au-dessus de la mêlée*]" (HT 203/185f).

Is this not plainly inconsistent with the stance of militant *engagement* to which Merleau-Ponty was ostensibly committed? Does *Phenomenology of Perception* end on a note of Exupérian high-altitude thinking because such *was* in fact Merleau-Ponty's own true standpoint? It can certainly appear that way. Thus, expressing what many Communist critics thought of Merleau-Ponty's "policy of waiting [*politique d'attente*], without illusion" (SNS 303/171), or *attentisme*, Hervé argued that "the attitude of a solitary, spectative consciousness that would consist in placing itself outside the struggle [*se mettre hors du jeu*], in order to avoid any concession to tactics, is a pathetic utopia." Contrary to Merleau-Ponty's own express aim, Hervé regarded his position as "less a matter of political thinking than of a fascination exerted by the gestures and language of a bygone era" (Hervé 1946, 3).

In theoretical terms, then, Hervé's criticism effectively placed Merleau-Ponty in the same boat as Saint Exupéry. Politically and philosophically, this is a damning indictment—but is it sound? In order to assess it, let us briefly take stock of the relation between Merleau-Ponty and Saint Exupéry in terms of some of the key points of convergence and divergence between them. As we shall see, although the latter plays an important role in Merleau-Ponty's existential phenomenology, it is not the case that this is based in any substantive concordance.

Saint Exupéry and Merleau-Ponty

Saint Exupéry was at best a philosophical dilettante. As Beauvoir put it, he "talks drivel when he's thinking abstractly and in general" (Beauvoir 1992, 175). Even Colin Smith, who dedicated the final chapter of his 1964 book on contemporary French philosophy to him, admitted that Saint Exupéry's reputation was not based on the philosophical value of his work, and that in this regard, he did have "a tendency to say things of incredible inanity" (C. Smith 1964, 243). Nonetheless, there are some significant common themes that join the *Weltanschauungen* of Saint Exupéry and Merleau-Ponty (although many of these themes are by no means unique to either of them). It is against this background that their differences can be most clearly understood.

An inventory of the key commonalities between Saint Exupéry and Merleau-Ponty would include the following considerations:

1. Saint Exupéry and Merleau-Ponty were both critical of the cultural condition of capitalist society in the interwar period, in particular of secular humanism as an outgrowth of abstract rationalism and liberal individualism. Although Merleau-Ponty did not directly resort to the more disparaging metaphors—"termites," "cattle," "robots" —through which Saint Exupéry expressed himself, he did speak in like terms of a degenerate form of human animality that would signify the (not irrevocable) loss of the living capacity of historical agency. This would be a pathological reversion to an ahistorical unconsciousness of death consequent to the stabilization—through the imposition of tyrannical oppression or traumatic repression—of the restless negativity, the *Unruhe*, definitive of human existence (SNS 114/66).[19] To the extent that he thought people needed to be reawakened to their own historicity, and to perceive the world accordingly, Merleau-Ponty's view tended in the same direction as that of Saint Exupéry.

In the context of Cartesianism, animals and robots are not so far apart. Specifically, it was to the general the idea of mechanism—the hegemony of the "machine-man" and the alienated and alienating "machine-society" based upon it (see Harrington 1996, xvi–xvii, 19ff)—that Saint Exupéry and Merleau-Ponty were opposed.[20] Against this, they both envisioned an organically holistic sort of sociality as a way to recover universality and therewith intersubjective relations that would be more "authentic."[21] Although Saint Exupéry tended to put this in terms of "love," whereas Merleau-Ponty preferred idioms such as that of "communication" and "reconciliation," their views do not differ fundamentally. At root, both are concerned with the realization of human bonds [*liens*] between persons. As Barral put it in a discussion of Merleau-Ponty, "[l]ove is the growth of two consciousnesses building together a new reality, a new world" (1993, 165).[22]

2. Saint Exupéry and Merleau-Ponty both advocated a new humanism that aimed to spiritualize—or *re-enchant*—human coexistence on the basis of a post-Christian myth of "man" (or "Man"). Although both purported to go beyond Christianity, in each case, the project was informed in a profound way by the Christian idea of the God-man, the Word become Flesh. Prioritizing active engagement, both held that universality was to be attained through humanity's self-creation or autonomous self-realization. And, construing it against the backdrop of nature's cosmic indifference, both saw this self-realization as a matter of self-*overcoming* that entailed a certain staking of one's life, a mortal suspension of the particularities of one's given empirical individuality. Although this is more spectacular in the case of Saint Exupéry, in each case, there is a crucial, if paradoxical, *dis*engagement implied at the heart of this sort of self-transformative engagement. Exupérian aerial takeoff [*envol*] is in this way nontrivially analogous to the general idea of a phenomenological reduction, "the universal meditation which cuts the philosopher off from his nation, his friendships, his prejudices, his empirical being, in short, from the world, and which seems to leave him in complete isolation" (PhP 414). Either way, such separation and departure from the *sens* of rational intellect is to be redeemed through reintegration into the context of an "expanded reason" (SNS

109/63; cf. PhP xiii).[23] As one of the first reviewers of *Terre des hommes* disapprovingly recognized from a reactionary perspective: "this World of Men is a World of the Hero, but of the Hero alone; despite the common dangers and the camaraderie, it is a World of Solitude" (Brasillach 1971, 67f, italics removed; cf. EG 585).[24] However, he also noted that "this solitude has a slightly barbaric greatness [*a sa grandeur un peu barbare*] that a healthy [*saine*] philosophy will endeavor to preserve intact [*ne pas mutiler*] and to incorporate into a vaster and purer reason" (Brasillach 1971, 67f). (Needless to say, Brasillach did not think that *Pilote de guerre* moved in this direction!)

3. Saint Exupéry and Merleau-Ponty both linked this expanded reason with a new vision, a new way of seeing the world—"a mode of perception that is at once more intimate and broader" than analytical understanding, a new "attitude of consciousness that reaches beings in their existential and affective context" (Major 1968, 63, 90). The high-altitude view of the Exupérian pilot is analogous to that of the Merleau-Pontian phenomenologist, and this precisely in terms of the practice of *survoler*. For Merleau-Ponty, to perceive is fundamentally to perform a Gestalt operation of picking out a figure against a given background. Inasmuch as perceptual acuity is a function of the breadth and inclusiveness of the relevant background, this operation implies a certain distance and leeway, which can be described as the power to *survoler* lacked by Schn. Humanity mechanically reduced to a "machine for swinging a sledgehammer or a pickaxe" (TH 211), as Saint Exupéry put it, is in a certain way epitomized by the pathological Schn. Or at least this is the case in Merleau-Ponty's portrayal of Schn., where the patient's symptoms not only corroborate the mechanistic threat posited by the spiritual-holistic critique,[25] "but also the presumption that holistic insight into the essence of experience is itself the highest mental faculty of man" (Goldenberg 2003, 298). On this basis, both Saint Exupéry and Merleau-Ponty keenly claimed to discern the germs of universality in the smallest concrete phenomena—in "the least perception, the slightest movement of the heart, the smallest action" [*la moindre perception, le moindre mouvement du cœur, la moindre action*] (SNS 121/70) or "the simplest dialogue" (HT 206/189). Like Saint Exupéry's smiling over a bummed cigarette with Spanish anarchists, the riverside drink, or the mere act of flying, such an awareness embraces the human world in its contrast with nature—it "contains indivisibly all the order and disorder of the world" (HT 206/189). "In a completely explicated human perception we would find all the originalities of human life" (PrP 99/40).

4. Saint Exupéry and Merleau-Ponty were both anti-ideologues, and were reticent about taking sides in ideological disputes, which they tended to regard as superficial—*Humanism and Terror* met a similar fate as *Pilote de guerre*, at least among French émigrés, in that it was denounced from all sides (Campbell 1947, 49ff; Cooper 1979, 77ff; Poster 1975, 157). Both strove to surmount ideological disagreement, and the phenomena of "multiple solipsism" in general, through the disclosure, in the present, of a common universal terrain and a commitment to its realization. The self-decentering occasioned by mortal risk that we saw emphasized by Merleau-Ponty is also for Saint Exupéry a key means of this disclosure. "We make our way for years side by side, each enclosed in his own silence, or else exchanging words that convey nothing. But at the moment of danger, then we stand shoulder to shoulder. We discover that we belong to

the same community. We are broadened by the discovery of other consciousnesses. We look at each other and smile" (TH 42; cf. PhP 417). However syrupy this may seem in the context of Saint Exupéry's prose, it is precisely in the self-evidence betokened by such a "smile" that Merleau-Ponty located the fulgurant "glory" of successful dialogue and communication, that which can be taken as an indication of "the community of fate [*la communauté du sort*] among men," and of the "agreement" [*accord*] and commonality that is more essential than even biology (SNS 171/98).

Ultimately, what the respective projects of both Saint Exupéry and Merleau-Ponty aimed to do was to participate in giving meaning and direction—*sens*—to human life by disclosing its transcendental, universal basis. For both, there is a certain "love of life" which alone can lead to a genuine "life of love".

•

These convergences, however, by no means exhaust the relationship between Saint Exupéry and Merleau-Ponty. If we examine the nature and practical consequences of their respective humanisms more closely, then we discover the following countervailing considerations:

1. While Saint Exupéry and Merleau-Ponty can be seen as agreeing that modern, rational humanism was problematic, and that this was tied to its vitiation of Christian themes of egalitarian community and, more generally, its state of spiritual disenchantment, their views of this situation differed significantly. We can pose this in terms of the modern ideals of equality, freedom, and fraternity. At least as they are conventionally understood, Saint Exupéry regarded these ideals as fundamentally incompossible. "These words [*liberté, egalité, fraternité*] once comprised a fertile seed. The tree grew, but it died. . . . We need a new seed" (EG 184). He saw freedom in its modern guise of individual autonomy as the negation of communitarian equality, and posed the fraternity symbolized in Man as the negation of that negation. Taking Aéropostale as an organizational paradigm for the communal reconciliation of personal fulfillment with societal needs, Saint Exupéry effectively promoted a conservative reprise of the organically hierarchical social order of pastoral France as a way to recast freedom and equality. "I believe," he said in the Credo of *Pilote de guerre*, "that the primacy of Man founds the only meaningful Equality and Freedom" (PG 241). This view implies a secularization of traditional religious community that re-situates it cosmically, thereby refounding it on its own dynamic activity. But this is hierarchical and thus historically retrograde in the sense that it views modern individual autonomy as a deviant development in need of retraction. "By assigning to each a well-defined place in the order of human relations, the hierarchy confers on the individual a unique and irreplaceable character that attributes an inestimable value to him" (Ouellet 1971, 97). Even if it is entirely this-worldly, the Exupérian social ideal remains, if not an expression of antimodern reaction, then at the very least an exceedingly illiberal attitude.

Merleau-Ponty, on the other hand, regarded the apparent incompossibility of the ideals of equality, freedom, and fraternity as an indication that at the social level, they remained abstract. The task was to make them concrete by "realizing" them, in particular, by further developing, not sacrificing, freedom. In this sense, Merleau-Ponty did not think that modernity was fully unfolded, or at any rate that its anomies were irredeemable. Focusing on the intersubjective dynamics of historical becoming, he held that the ostensible ideals of modern society, as lived out in interpersonal relations, were not only *not* fundamentally incompatible, but that they themselves portended the positive supersession of their apparent incompossibility. Merleau-Ponty resisted the essentialization and historical stasis (or even *un*becoming) entailed by the encapsulation of the truth of humanity as "Man." Whereas Saint Exupéry in effect hypostatized the latter as a truth transcendent to human lived reality—"the Man of my civilization is not defined on the basis of men. Rather, it is men that are defined through it" (PG 219)—Merleau-Ponty let human existence speak for itself. This was a leitmotif of his phenomenology that he drew from Husserl: "it is a matter of leading experience that is still silent to the pure expression of its own meaning."[26] For Merleau-Ponty, the fulguration of evidentiary "glory" is not simply a prefigurative glimpse of the achieved universality of natural fraternity. More importantly, it is an indication of human productivity in action—it is the effervescence, not of the transcendence of contradictions, but of the creative confluence of them *as* contradictions. The difference between Exupérian "Man" and Merleau-Pontian "man" is thus the difference between a "top-down" approach to the phenomena of human coexistence, and one that proceeds "from below"' (*von unten*, as Husserl would say). The latter is, at least in theory, more amenable to concrete political analysis—in particular, to the task of discriminating between the phenomena of the genuinely progressive movement of history and those of chaos and repression. It can have this epistemic advantage because, as an implementation of Lukácsian totality, its *survolant* perspective remains anchored to the standpoint of the proletariat.

2. Notwithstanding the fact that both Saint Exupéry and Merleau-Ponty strove to surmount ideological disagreement, there is the patent difference that Saint Exupéry did so by effectively eschewing altogether that which Merleau-Ponty explicitly sought to cultivate, namely, political thinking. Saint Exupéry aspired to have "no political agenda whatsoever" (Schiff 1994, 350). Although in the mid-1930s he travelled as a correspondent for *Paris-Soir* in the USSR (see SV 35–79), before going to Spain, he resisted taking sides on the basic political questions of the day.[27] He "neither advocated nor denounced" (Schiff 1994, 230), upholding instead the sovereignty of Man through an equivocal mixture of aristocratic individualism and nostalgia for authority. This had certain affinities with reactionary antimodernism. In fact, rather than for de Gaulle, Saint Exupéry's stated neutrality during the war did harbor much greater sympathies for Pétain, whom he did not publicly criticize and whom he tended to defend from disparagement. But as suggested by Maritain's critique, even the neutrality of *Pilote de guerre* could not be easily justified politically. Given the conditions of occupation in terms of despoliation and persecution at the time of publication, "it hardly helps to be told that 'le culte de l'Universel exalte et noue les richesses particulières' . . . or that the 'primacy of Man' is the only proper foundation for liberty and equality. . . . Confronted with the cruel realities of 1942, these vague gestures in the direction of spirituality strike one as the last remnants of an archaic and discredited rhetoric" (John 1985, 103f, citing PG 241).

The apolitical "neutrality" of Saint Exupéry's thought expresses his view that within the context of modernism, all sides are in the wrong. "Saint-Exupéry rejects fascism and communism, he rebuffs capitalism and socialism equally. He withdraws from or is frightened by the modern world, its termite mounds, its crowds, its mass production. . . . He dreads democracy, unable to find in it the source of legitimate power" (d'Astier de la Vigerie 1971, 109). What ultimately underwrote his attempt to rise above political divisions was his antipathy to what he constructed as a vaguely defined, indiscriminate totalitarianism. "*I hate this age*, where, under a universal totalitarianism, people become docile, polite, and placid cattle" (SV 229, emphasis added). Saint-Exupéry turned to Man because, in short, he had "no faith in man" (d'Astier de la Vigerie 1971, 109).

However vaguely defined that view might be, though, it clearly placed Saint Exupéry quite far from Merleau-Ponty. For as we saw above, at around the same time as Saint Exupéry was composing *Pilote de guerre*, Merleau-Ponty argued that certain aspects of totalitarian thinking had to be appropriated for victory, both in the war and more generally for democracy. His thought at the time was quite thoroughly imbued with holism, and so his embrace of Marxism was antipodal to Saint Exupéry's blunt rejection of it: "what I hate about Marxism is the totalitarianism to which it leads" (EG 380; cf. SV 229).[28]

This statement may, however, be something of an exaggeration. For in another posthumously published text (which, appearing in 1981, was not something to which Merleau-Ponty could have had access), Saint Exupéry tempered his opposition to Marxism somewhat. He did so by distinguishing between the method of Marxism and its specific empirical claims, and by noting that the former can retain its value even if the latter are mistaken or outdated. "The only mistake of the Marxists is to rely on a fixed bible of truths set forth by Marx, the currency of which, like that of all truths, is obviously momentary – instead of nourishing it by recreating these truths in accordance with the evolution of this society using the method which itself can always remain valid" (MAM 12). Such sentiments nearly paraphrase Lukács! What Saint Exupéry objected to in general was any sort of social science that claimed strong predictive power (cf. Carnets 173f). In Saint Exupéry's view, as carried out by most if not all of those who professed it, Marxism seemed to be especially guilty of this sort of sophism, in that it painted a very specific picture of the future. Against this, Saint Exupéry argued that "I can claim only one thing, and that is to think the world of today. . . . It is absolutely vain to claim that [social-scientific thinking] enables one to think the world of tomorrow" (MAM 19f). In methodological terms, "Marxism itself is opposed to finalism" (Carnets 174), and so, in Saint Exupéry's estimation, "Marxism as it is understood by the Marxists is profoundly anti-Marxist" (MAM 20).

As far as it goes, this is surprisingly consistent with Merleau-Ponty's own view, which as we have seen also emphasized the unthinkability of the future as a key tenet of Marx's thought (EP 41/50f). "One can only validly think what one has in some way lived, the rest being nothing but imagination" (HT 136/127). Any pretension to being able to think the future would subvert Marx's central intuition that "historical meaning is immanent in the interhuman event, and is no less fragile" (EP 42/51). Marxism properly dwells in the present, without reliance upon representations of a transcendent future. For "to live and die for a future projected by the will, rather than live and act in the present, is precisely what Marxists have always considered utopianism" (HT 85f/80).

But the import of this particular concurrence does not go very far. It certainly did not alter Saint Exupéry's basic criticism of Marxism, a view which constituted, for him, sufficient grounds to reject it, namely, that Marxism crudely reduced human beings to producers and consumers. More importantly, though, there is at best only a verbal agreement between Saint Exupéry and Merleau-Ponty concerning the need to focus attention on the present. The reason why Saint Exupéry thought that Marxism effected that illicit reduction, why he found it "absolutely impossible to understand what the historical mission of the proletariat could mean" (MAM 18; cf. Carnets, 73, 103, 173ff), and more generally, why the present as he saw it was populated by cattle, termites, robots, etc. is that he did not have a view of the present in its historical depth—he did not see what Merleau-Ponty called the "living present" (PhP 384, 495).[29] It is true to say that "there is in Saint-Exupéry an unshakeable refusal to go beyond immediate existence" (Major 1968, 222). But Saint Exupéry uncritically accepted as given the fragmentation that characterized the surface of modern social phenomena, and contrasted this with the ideal of Man. Even granting that he could see bonds of love when they emerged against this backdrop, he was blind to their emergence itself. That is, his purview occluded the ambiguous "lines of force and vectors" (HT 104f/98) which in the present make it such that the future, while nowise determined, "is not any empty zone in which we can construct unmotivated projects," but rather that "it is sketched [*il se dessine*] before us like the end of the day underway—*and this outline* [dessin] *is ourselves*" (HT 102/95, emphasis added). For Merleau-Ponty, the sense in which the proletariat could be said to have an historical mission is that universal human recognition is delineated by its spontaneous intercorporeal existence in the given historical constellation of forces and vectors, such that the realization of that recognition is achieved through the "prolongation and fulfillment" of that existence (HT 120, 125f/111, 116f).

3. In this way, the Marxism proposed by Merleau-Ponty aimed to offer a "perception of history" through which an individual could relearn to see the world in a truer way in terms of its historical emergence (HT 117/98). It was thus that Merleau-Ponty sought to help "give" meaning (*sens*) to human life. As at the level of intentional consciousness, it is not a simple matter of *Sinn-Gebung*. *Sens* is already there—indeed, Merleau-Ponty emphasizes that "we are present [*assistons*] at every moment" at its emergence (PhP xvi)—it is just matter of rendering it visible and bringing it to expression. The fundamental problem of modern capitalist society was systemic bodily repression that resulted in a reified misperception of the world—a structurally endemic case of "apperceptive historical agnosia," if I may put it that way—the remedy for which lay in a new transcendental aesthetic that would reaffirm the full dimensionality of the field of human historical experience in its totality.

Whereas Merleau-Ponty wanted in this way to be something of a therapist who might help others to see and grasp actual historical meaning, Saint Exupéry set himself up as more of an inspiring preacher, a *giver* of meaning to those without. As Jean-Louis Major contrasted Saint Exupéry to Merleau-Ponty, "it is less a matter of describing perception than of proposing a more human mode of knowledge—his [Saint Exupéry's] intention is consequently of the ethical order" (Major 1968, 71 n23). However, inasmuch as Merleau-Ponty did not simply describe perception, and since it is hardly the case that his position was devoid of ethical significance, it would be more accurate to say that Saint Exupéry's position was *strictly* ethical, that is, a utopian moralism. Which is to say that in an important sense, his account lacks motivation, and that its prescriptions are, at root, arbitrary. In the context of senseless disorder, this can be a matter of the *instauration* of an ethical order, the heroic imposition of normative bearings for action where there are none—a kind of foundational *Sinn-Gebung*. As we saw above, such was Caillois' view, although he was not alone in regarding Saint Exupéry along the Luciferian lines of "a creator, a builder, a maker of laws" [*un réalisateur, un bâtisseur, un faiseur des lois*] (Simon 1950, 129). There is an element of secular messianism in such heroism—precisely what Merleau-Ponty sought to avoid in arguing that it was not for the introduction of *new* values that social transformation was necessary. As he put it, it was just that the consequences of messianic incarnation still needed to be fully worked out (cf. SNS 313/176), and that the completion of that incarnational project is the historical mission of the proletariat. In contrast, instaurational acts of signification are nowise predelineated, and there can be no discursive account of their historical genesis, thus no rational justification. This is the sense in which "[t]he work of Saint-Exupéry is not an argument. It is an example. It is made up of events which are recounted to inspire, not to persuade" (Knight 1957, 181). This would be a kind of pure action outside of truth. "Yesterday's truth is dead, and that of tomorrow has yet to be built" [*La vérité d'hier est morte, celle de demain est encore à bâtir*] (EG 341). The problem is that this implies sacrificial rupture inexorably.

For Merleau-Ponty, however, even this position of sovereignty is regulated by the primordial truth of the world and of our "participation" in it. "'Being-in-the-truth' [« *être-à-la-vérité* »] is indistinguishable from *être-au-monde*" (PhP 452). Provided we are situated within the world in its historical totality, "we are in the truth" (PhP xi), "we are *true* through and through [*de part en part*]" (PhP 520). Through exploration of the "living present," we can discover the irrepressible core of history's existential meaning, the existential project of which we are a part. And this—contrary to the eternalness of Exupérian Man and to Saint Exupéry's hatred of "this age"—can "make us love our time" (HT 206/189).

Strategic detachment

In turning back to consider Merleau-Ponty's dialogue with Hervé, we should note that an important extension of what Merleau-Ponty meant by "exchange" was his idealization of a Marxist political party. According to this view, the Party is the site of intersubjective exchange in the form of "a vital communication between individual judgment and historical reality" (SNS 320/180). Its democratic-centralist organization would serve the epistemic function of generating optimal historical perceptions of the present and the soundest political judgments of the reflecting kind. That is, its intersubjective structure would compensate for the absence of absolute criteria, and would allow individuals to participate collectively in history on the larger stage. In this way, the Party could be seen as playing a therapeutic role. Not that Merleau-Ponty saw the PCF as instantiating this ideal.

Commenting on Hervé in *Humanism and Terror*, Merleau-Ponty argued that his Communist interlocutor was incapable of maintaining the dialectical tension between the party and the class it claimed to represent, and that, granting priority to the former, he effectively assumed "the standpoint of a God who comprehends Universal History" (HT 155/143f). This is precisely one of the forms of *non*-political thinking that Merleau-Ponty sought to overcome, for it is ultimately inconsistent with what it means to be a living human being. As Merleau-Ponty insisted, a key tenet of Marxism is that history is always open and that we cannot think the future. To pretend to do so would subvert Marx's central intuition concerning historical meaning, and thus deny "the human meaning and *raison d'être* of communism," which is for humanity democratically "to take their history into their own hands" (HT 158/147).

This is why Merleau-Ponty took up the young Marx's claim against Hegel about the realization [*Verwirklichung*] of philosophy involving its dialectical transcendence [*Aufhebung*] along with that of the proletariat (Marx 1975b, 187), and why he interpreted this in terms of its ceasing to be "separate" (rather than being done away with altogether). As Merleau-Ponty put it: if, unlike Hervé, for example, the philosopher "forsakes the illusion of contemplating the totality of *completed* [italics added] history and feels caught up in it like all other men and confronted by a future *to be made*, then philosophy realizes itself by doing away with itself as separate philosophy." (Although it might appear that Merleau-Ponty is here stating a sufficient condition of the realization of philosophy, it should actually be seen as a necessary condition.) "This concrete thinking, which Marx calls 'critique' to distinguish it from speculative philosophy, is what others"—namely, Merleau-Ponty—"propound under the name existential philosophy" (SNS 236f/133). Although Marx had centered this "critique" on the proletariat understood in terms of a certain relation to the means of production, Merleau-Ponty saw that this view needed to be contemporized by means of existential phenomenology. But he aimed to do this, if not on the same grounds, then certainly in the same spirit—the idea is that rationality is no longer taken as deriving from "the concept," but rather from "the heart of interhuman praxis" (EP 42/51).

It is thus ironic that Hervé accused Merleau-Ponty of being enthralled by "the gestures and language of a bygone era" (Hervé 1946, 3), for example, the notion of "*patrie*," or Stendhal's idea of "sincerity" (cf. SNS 271/153). For it was precisely Merleau-Ponty's point that contemporary debates were "still using the political vocabulary of the nineteenth century" (SNS 284/160), in particular, that Marxists still tended to deny the apparent inactuality of the proletariat *qua* universal class and instead accept uncritically the classical conception of it as an article of faith. Hence, *they* were the utopians, even by their own standards. For "to live and die for a future projected by desire rather than live and act in the present is precisely what Marxists have always considered utopianism" (HT 85f/80). Not that Merleau-Ponty preferred some sort of acquiescent Hegelianism. But true to the idea of Lukács, he did think that one could follow the "orthodox" spirit of Marx without any specific doctrinal commitment.

Perhaps Hervé failed to see that Merleau-Ponty had not invoked the idea of Stendhalian "sincerity" in order to resuscitate and endorse it. Rather, it was to cast into relief the fact that such a standpoint was, as a matter of fact, no longer a real possibility, and that Marxists themselves could not surreptitiously avail themselves of anything analogous. Merleau-Ponty's point was that "we are *all* knaves [*coquins*] in Stendhal's sense" (SNS 273/154, italics added). By this, he meant that "in the absence of a political thinking that would be capable both of taking in all truths and of taking a stand in the real," all political forces in France at the time were playing a "double game" that would run afoul of nineteenth-century republican sincerity. But his argument was that the ubiquitous political duplicity and "knavery" was grounded in the "vital situation" of the world (SNS 287/162). *Our time* was "an ambiguous moment in history" (SNS 285/160), and this was *not* a salutary ambiguity. For it implied that "we are *not* in the truth" (cf. PhP xi), thereby portending the unavoidability of playing a double game. In such conditions, could there be an alternative? Merleau-Ponty thought so, and this is why he placed himself *au-dessus de la mêlée*. "In reality, it is simply *a refusal to commit oneself* [s'engager] *within confusion and outside of the truth*" (HT 203/185f, italics added). In these conditions, he thought that the role of intellectuals like himself was

> to clarify the ideological situation, to underline, beyond the paradoxes and contingencies of contemporary history, the true terms of the human problem, to recall Marxists to their humanist inspiration, to remind the democracies of their fundamental hypocrisy, and to keep intact against propaganda the chances that history may still have of becoming clear once again. (HT 196/179)

> We must preserve liberty while waiting for a fresh historical impulse which may allow us to engage it in a popular movement without ambiguity. (HT xix/xxiii)

The philosophical task in this situation was "to define a practical attitude of comprehension," a "political consciousness" that would be commensurate with the central intuition of Marxism (HT 159f/148). For Merleau-Ponty, this was precisely the "existential attitude" he sought to define in his essay on heroism. Although his original intervention concerning heroism in *action* may not have had the immediate political effects he wanted, it is clear, given the pride of place that he later accorded it in *Sense and Non-Sense* (at a time when Saint Exupéry's reputation was starting to decline),[30] this response did not diminish Merleau-Ponty's own estimation of the views he expressed therein concerning the "practical attitude of comprehension" that he made central to his existential-phenomenological project.

■

We are potentially offered an intriguing elaboration of this "attitude" from an unexpected source, namely, English poet Stephen Spender. Merleau-Ponty and Spender became friends at (if not before) the first *Rencontres Internationales* in Geneva in September 1946, largely on the basis of their broadly congruent political sympathies.[31] They surely met again over the years,[32] but there is little record of their relationship. Interestingly, however, "One More New Botched Beginning," one of Spender's most important poems (Leeming 1999, 210), which recalls the memory of various friends, includes a touching recollection of Merleau-Ponty in its opening stanza.[33]

The source of the elaboration of Merleau-Ponty's position *au-dessus de la mêlée* comes from a piece of prose by Spender that appeared in translation in *Les temps modernes* in October 1946 (Spender 1946b).[34] As the managing and political editor of *Les temps modernes*, Merleau-Ponty may have arranged for this piece at the *Rencontres Internationales*, or possibly during an earlier visit by Spender to France (cf. Spender 1946a). Given what we have seen regarding the controversy, both philosophical and political, over Merleau-Ponty's use of Saint Exupéry's *Pilote de guerre*, one cannot fail to be struck by the extraordinary pertinence of this work by Spender, beginning with its title: "Pensées dans un avion au-dessus de l'Europe" ["Thoughts in an Airplane over Europe"]. It seems scarcely conceivable that there was not some sort of deliberate effort on the part of Merleau-Ponty to have Spender's piece make a critical, nondogmatic leftist contribution to debates concerning "high-altitude" political thinking. There is no basis on which to claim that Merleau-Ponty endorsed everything that Spender had to say. But the main lines of his reasoning do have clear counterparts in Merleau-Ponty's own work, and so, Spender's essay may be cautiously read as an elaboration of certain basic elements of Merleau-Ponty's own thought, at least by way of expressing a divergence from Saint Exupéry.

Flying over France, Spender's basic observation concerning contemporary society echoed Merleau-Ponty's claim about the situation of the world itself being one of duplicity: "whatever you do is wrong . . . because you are either involved in the systems of the modern societies, or you are not involved in them" (Spender 1946b, 66). Inside or outside, one cannot do right. "Whatever you do, it is impossible for you, in the age in which you live, to be either right or wrong. Nevertheless, you must now choose. It is no longer possible to evade choice" (Spender 1946b, 76). What to do? What can one do? The response Spender gave is meant to be connected with an aerial perspective. "You can enlarge your consciousness to include humanity. . . . The world, aware of itself as a single vibrating existence in which every part acts on every other part at the same moment, is unable to integrate such an awareness into the idea of a single personality." How to achieve such an integration? "By enlarging your personality [in such a way as] to understand the nature of all the different parts. By creating within yourself the personality of this divided humanity. By humanizing this inhuman humanity" (Spender 1946b, 77).

However vague this perspective may have been, it did express Merleau-Ponty's idea of "accepting all truths *and* taking a stand in reality." What Spender was calling for was the recognition of all political realities without overlooking the concrete effects. That is, the gaining of as complete a view as possible of the present situation. What is needed is "an internationalism of those who care for civilization, who believe in charity and have a passion for humanity" (Spender 1946c, 998).

There are certainly shades of Saint Exupéry in this, at least inasmuch as it may be "the distinctive trait of humanism to encompass all things from a certain altitude that enlarges the field of its vision and expands its outlook" (Gascht 1947, 39). But there is a critical difference. As Spender described it, the shadow of the airplane he was in, which was separate throughout the flight, "merged into the substance of the airplane" upon landing (Spender 1946b, 78). More than anything else, this is the crucial moment that is missing from Saint Exupéry, who always held that "landing is disappointing" [*l'atterrissage est décevant*] (SV 21). At least from a Merleau-Pontian perspective, the view offered by Spender is that of the place of philosophy in historical praxis—an initial moment of detachment in which the philosopher withdraws ascensionally in order to gain a view of the totality, followed by a moment in which this separation is overcome through the philosopher's successful descent and re-integration. As Merleau-Ponty himself later observed, "at the conclusion of a reflection which at first isolates him, the philosopher, in order to experience more fully the ties of truth which bind him to the world and history, finds neither the depth of himself nor absolute knowledge, but a renewed image of the world and of himself placed within it among others" (EP 51/63).

Merleau-Ponty's Marxist commitment to the category of totality clearly implies *some* positive sense of "*la pensée de survol.*"[35] The idea is that precisely in order to offer, instead of a "speculative solution," a "more acute consciousness of on-going experience" (NI 9 [21]), philosophy must premise itself on an apprehension of the movement of history as a whole as the touchstone of truth. Interestingly, inasmuch as it is geared to the proletariat, this perspective goes further—or, if you prefer, *higher*—than Saint Exupéry, and yet, it is in virtue of this that Merleau-Ponty could—at least in principle—reintegrate on the ground. It is on this basis that we might say of Saint Exupéry that he did not truly perceive, that his perception was repressed, and hence why he expressed such abhorrence at the world around him. His cosmic humanism was not based on perceptual contact with the living present, and therefore remained a solitary dream—recall how *Pilote de guerre* opens: "*Sans doute je rêve.*" Lacking any perceptual grip on the world, Saint Exupéry's experience was devoid of living meaning. Over Arras, he may have achieved "absolute contact" with himself as he dreamt of his childhood home and the security offered by his governess. But the epistemic significance of his experience of human relationality was not *for him*. Rather, as in Hegel's *Phenomenology of Spirit*, it is *for us* [für uns]. Not that this implies a cognitive achievement on our part. As in Hegel's work,[36] the climax of *Phenomenology of Perception* takes the form of an image that serves to secure the *standpoint* of cognition—in this case, that of a virtually "complete" phenomenological reduction, the complete repressive coincidence of self with habituated organism, and yet this in a way that *merges with history*. This is what is crucial. For if transcendental philosophy is to be realized as Merleau-Ponty intended—namely, integrated with "the very phenomenon of the real" (SC 241/224)—and if the phenomenon of the real is historical, then it must be the case that the productivity operatively presupposed by transcendental philosophy belongs essentially to historical truth. In other words, if truth is historical and (*contra* Hegel) absolute self-consciousness impossible, then the realization of philosophy will occur, if at all, through the practical generation of rationality. The core meaning of "proletariat" for Merleau-Ponty is the collective embodiment of this generative agency, which in this way is rationality incarnate. The question of the realization of philosophy is thus tied to the existence of the proletariat so understood, something which Merleau-Ponty did not take for granted. In the postwar context, then, he held that "the question of our time is precisely to know [*savoir*] if the world [of tomorrow] will be rational" (NI 31 [13]). Marxism collapses without belief in a rational future. Strictly speaking, however, we could never have *knowledge* of this. But a basic goal of Merleau-Ponty's project was to respond affirmatively, yet without simply begging the question, by disclosing compelling perceptual self-evidence of the rationality of human history—this is precisely what the sublimative spectacle of the hero is meant to provide. Epistemically, the decisive experience that results necessarily remains at the level of myth, but it provides the basis for the sort of rational faith in its own realizability that philosophy requires.

Conclusion: Heroic Sublimation

The aim of this book has been to problematize the Exupérian ending of *Phenomenology of Perception* and to provide at least the outlines of a compelling answer to the question as to why this work concludes with lines drawn from *Pilote de guerre* that express in an unmistakable way Saint Exupéry's self-sacrificial disdain of corporeality. The key elements of this answer have already been discussed in the preceding chapters. In these final pages, I will briefly recapitulate the relevant claims and draw them together in terms of the basic meaning for Merleau-Ponty of "the contemporary hero," the place and role of this notion within his postwar political thought, and finally, its methodological significance for his reinterpretation of Husserlian phenomenology.

Who or what is "the contemporary hero?" As he made clear in his essay in *action*, Merleau-Ponty's hero is, in a word, "man," and more specifically, "man as [*en tant que*] productivity" (cf. PhP 200). As a mythic expression of human universality, the notion of the contemporary hero can thus be seen as a militant incarnational reinterpretation of "Man" as understood and promoted by others (including Saint Exupéry) as a transcendent ideal, *for the sake of which*, in their view, heroic deeds are sacrificially enacted. The difference is crucial. That Merleau-Ponty's hero *is* "man" means that the existence of the individual in question is de-particularized in such a way as to embody this universality subjectively. The hero thus instantiates the claim that "man is capable of situating his proper being, not in biological existence, but at the level of properly human relations" (SC 190 n1/246 n97). More specifically, the de-particularization of the heroic individual is a matter of corporeal de-actualization—the contemporary hero *is* the habituated organism, his "actual" existence is folded into this entirely. This is the sense in which the individual who becomes "man" is wholly repressed. He is thus someone who is neither running ahead of nor lagging behind her historical time, but who is rather exactly synchronous with it, *jusqu'au bout*. He subjectively embodies human universality by existing unfalteringly the natural purposiveness "that throws us toward things and toward others" (SNS 330/186). In other words, the contemporary hero is someone who, through acts of sovereign uselessness, that is, acts that are their own ends, fully and consummately *lives her time*. It is for this reason that he "melds with history" at the moment of death (SNS 258/146), which carries the implication that the hero's death is fully internalized in an authentic way—that heroic existence "transforms the fatality of death into freedom" such that death becomes a kind of existential fulfillment (cf. Landsberg 1936, 40f).

To a certain extent, this is not altogether dissimilar to the views of Saint Exupéry (cf. L. Sullivan 1980, 80ff). But the crucial difference lies in Merleau-Ponty's incarnational approach—his conviction that the present stage of history already incarnates human universality, and that consequently, repression can overcome itself dialectically through the concrete realization of what is implicit in the *status quo*, rather than any sort of discontinuous rupture with it. In Merleau-Ponty's view, such an approach to existential issues differs fundamentally from any that would be considered "heroic" in the more standard sense, that is, any sense in which heroism is seen as involving self-sacrifice. Thus Merleau-Ponty's interpretation of Saint Exupéry diverged quite sharply from typical views at the time, and quite possibly from Saint Exupéry's own self-understanding, by implying that the idea of sovereign uselessness—exhibited over Arras circa 1940—applied to Saint Exupéry's final flight in 1944 as well. It was on this condition alone that Merleau-Ponty could use the case of Saint Exupéry to show that human existence can *be* universal, that one can become "man" through the (existentially pathological) denial of personal particularity in a way that is not ultimately a form of *self*-denial.

　　How does the contemporary hero relate to Merleau-Ponty's postwar political thought? The notion of contemporary heroism as an interpretation of the death of Saint Exupéry is firstly an element of Merleau-Ponty's political thought. Its role there is to provide evidence of the existence of the proletariat—not in the sense of the working class understood in terms of social-structural relation to the means of production within capitalism, but in the sense that truly matters historically, namely, the existence of the proletariat *qua* universal class, the incarnation of human universality (however that may play out in sociological terms). In other words, the contemporary hero is meant to play an evidentiary role with regard to the basic premise of an incarnational Marxism. This premise may have been self-evident at other times, but not for Merleau-Ponty in immediate postwar France. And so, just as he could not credibly affirm the existence of the proletariat on the basis of any biased ideological assumptions, Merleau-Ponty could not use the example of any avowed Marxist who gave her or his life in the fight against fascism. That would not prove anything. Merleau-Ponty *had* to use a non-Marxist. Indeed, that Saint Exupéry had tried to eschew politics, and even that the political views that he nevertheless held were quasi-reactionary, actually served Merleau-Ponty's purposes very well, in that his interpretation of Saint Exupéry presented his actions and behavior as instantiating something altogether contrary, namely, that notwithstanding such superficial differences, there is a deeper natural purposiveness in human existence, an objective teleological thrust in virtue of which fascism could be defeated and a common world could be realized through nonsacrificial historical action.

　　Before considering this further, it is important to reemphasize Merleau-Ponty's long-standing repudiation of sacrifice, and that, given the emphasis he placed on the embodied nature of human coexistence, actualizing the consequences of what is already "incarnate" is the only manner of radical social transformation that he could sanction. Contrary to what a cursory reading of his interest in heroism might suggest, then, Merleau-Ponty did not celebrate or venerate it in any way. Although he did not disparage individuals who perished through what was deemed to be heroic action, he had no grounds for esteeming heroism as a political virtue, let alone a political tactic or strategy. Indeed, the opposite is the case. For if not just a matter of tragic circumstances, then heroic death is based either in political injudiciousness or else the existential pathology of contemporary heroism. So while the latter may have been very phenomenologically useful for his purposes, to say that Merleau-Ponty esteemed it as an actual form of human behavior would be like saying he esteemed "patient Schn.," or that he celebrated severe cases of agnosia.

In providing evidence of the existence of the proletariat *qua* universal class, the larger point of Merleau-Ponty's notion of the contemporary hero was to offer unequivocal evidence of the universal sense of human history, and of how revolutionary change is not a utopian dream but rather a concrete project grounded in the living present. The idea is that accepting Merleau-Ponty's interpretation of Saint Exupéry's death, as opposed to seeing it in sacrificial or even aleatory terms, would motivate an embrace of the "existential attitude" and the implied manner of comporting oneself vis-à-vis the horizons of the historical totality, or of operationalizing, so to speak, the methodological primacy of totality in a prereflective way. But this entailment is not straightforward, because this evidence is not simply given unequivocally. As the universal limit case of human existence, the fatal disincarnation of the contemporary hero could be seen as tantamount to a virtually complete phenomenological reduction. That is, it could be seen as a moment of "absolute knowing" in the sense of attaining "the point at which consciousness finally becomes equal to its spontaneous life and regains its self-possession" (SNS 112/64). This is how Merleau-Ponty would have us see Saint Exupéry's death. But as it is not a living possibility, heroic experience is not directly communicable (although with Saint Exupéry, Merleau-Ponty could avail himself of the account of the *near*-death experience that transpired over Arras). We the living, of course, can never experience absolute knowing. But nor can we ever simply experience another's experiencing of absolute knowing. What we can experience is just the radically individuated *appearance* of death. But as with anything else, the experience of death is not univocal. It therefore remains theoretically undecidable whether the individual in question, in fact, attained the perfect existential self-coincidence characteristic of contemporary heroism. This can only be settled on practical grounds. Merleau-Ponty thus called for a certain practical faith in the possibility that someone might indeed privately enjoy a final moment of "sovereign" absolute self-possession. This affirmation—which, it must be emphasized, is entirely *for us*—is essential to the "existential attitude." For it is what ultimately serves to merge object and horizons in the perception of the architectonic structure of history as an open-ended totality with a contingently realizable logic. For Merleau-Ponty, *engagement* on the basis of this perception of history is indispensable to the revolutionary perspective of Marxism in terms of its dialectical unity of theory and practice, and its overall existential coherence.

We saw above that Merleau-Ponty was attracted, at least in a general philosophical way, to Kant's third *Critique*. Much could be said about this. But in particular, we can now see that he sought to reform Marxism partly on the basis of an idea drawn from that work, to wit, that the power of judgment is able to provide palpable experiences of purposiveness that can serve to confirm the reality of the abstract ideas of practical reason:

> the power of judgment provides the mediating concept between the concepts of
> nature and the concept of freedom, which makes possible the transition from

the purely theoretical to the purely practical, from lawfulness in accordance with the former to the final end in accordance with the latter, in the concept of a *purposiveness* of nature; for thereby is the possibility of the final end, which can become actual only in nature and in accord with its laws, cognized. (KU 5: 195f)

In this way, Merleau-Ponty's contemporary hero was meant to furnish sensory or intuitional evidence attesting to the genuine possibility of a solution to the human problem. In *our time*, as Merleau-Ponty understood this, that is, a period when the logic of history is difficult to discern, such evidence is particularly important. Through the interpretation of the pathological one-sidedness of the contemporary hero as an instantiation of a natural purposiveness that is fully congruent with the *sens* of history, we are able to "cognize"—Merleau-Ponty would prefer to say "*see*"—that the realization of universal human reconciliation is fully consistent with the dialectics of the natural world. In other words, if we believe Merleau-Ponty's account of Saint Exupéry— particularly the insinuation that the latter's aim, *even on 31 July 1944*, was to "recover his own being" and to "leave his inner nothingness behind," and (most crucially) *that he succeeded*—then the spectacle of heroic death motivates the specific kind of "rational faith" (cf. Kant 1998, 10) that properly orients Marxism heuristically, namely, belief in the latent incarnation of human universality and the possibility of its realization through historical praxis—that is, the myth of "man." One thus comes to adopt the "existential attitude" vis-à-vis history through the sublimation of the disincarnation of the contemporary hero. Merleau-Ponty's interpretation of Saint Exupéry is thus the linchpin of his defense of Marxism as the political theory of the self-emancipation of the proletariat, and of his effort to sharpen the capacity of Marxism to perceive political phenomena, inasmuch as it is what justifies treating history as a totality based on the idea that human intercorporeal praxis incarnates the communication and confluence of freedom and necessity.

Here, I should reiterate that my aim in this work is simply to get clear about what is going on in Merleau-Ponty's project of existential phenomenology, and not to assess its strengths and weaknesses. To anyone with a serious interest in Marxism, however, it is all but self-evident that many features of Merleau-Ponty's embrace of Marxism in the immediate postwar period appear unduly simplistic and disconcertingly naïve. But we need to be careful. For one could easily mistake the myth of "man" that is operative in Merleau-Ponty's thought, and which serves to support the possibility of a certain formal conception of the proletariat, for some kind of dogmatic affirmation of the category of the proletariat as found in classical Marxist theory—that is, "the myth of the proletariat." This is a line of critique that can be found in the work of liberal critics of Marxism in France from Raymond Aron (1955) to Tony Judt (1992), and no doubt something like this can be applied legitimately to many French intellectuals. But it seems quite *in*applicable to Merleau-Ponty, whose main preoccupation was with the horizons of political theory *qua* theory, the ineluctability of *engagement*, and the resulting imperatives of normative justification. In other words, Merleau-Ponty was lucidly aware of his appeal to myth and the reliance of his position on a certain kind of faith—there was no mindless dogmatism or willful self-deception.

Given well-motivated views concerning the limits of theoretical cognition, myth and faith are in and of themselves not necessarily objectionable. One can certainly disagree with Merleau-Ponty's militant incarnational orientation, but it would be inadequate to do so simply by pointing out that it involves myth and faith, for example, without also engaging with the distinct issue as to whether or not all political positions involve, knowingly or not, analogous epistemic soft spots. For if that is the case, then it would not be a dispute over the use of myth and faith as such, but over *which* myth and *which* faith, and the nature of the reliance upon them. Much more would need to be said about this. But granting what I just suggested, it would follow, I believe, that while many aspects of it may be dated and problematic, and notwithstanding his own subsequent gestures of self-criticism, a strong case can be made to the effect that the basic sense of Merleau-Ponty's postwar political project merits renewed attention (cf. Coole 2003).

What is the significance of the contemporary hero for Merleau-Ponty's reinterpretation of Husserlian phenomenology? As suggested in the Preface, and throughout the discussion, the philosophical significance of Merleau-Ponty's use of Saint Exupéry is fundamentally methodological. There is a close derivative link with the foregoing discussion of the role of Saint Exupéry in Merleau-Ponty's political thought, the central claim of which is that a methodological commitment to totality implies certain practical postulates that are only consistent with an incarnational formulation of Marxism. In turning to Merleau-Ponty's reinterpretation of Husserlian phenomenology, the basic idea, as intimated above in the Introduction, is that the contemporary hero plays a role with regard to "the realization of philosophy." More specifically, the Exupérian ending of *Phenomenology of Perception* plays an evidentiary role with regard to the historically transformative praxis that is, in an ultimate sense, the agency of philosophy's realization. This ending thus shows that Merleau-Ponty deployed his Marxist philosophy of history and its concomitant incarnational conception of the proletariat to shore up transcendental phenomenology methodologically.

It is crucial to approach this in terms of the internal critique of phenomenological methodology and the resulting account of "constructive" phenomenology that Fink presented in his *Sixth Cartesian Meditation* (as discussed above in the Preface), and Merleau-Ponty's existential response to this. The central point concerns Fink's claims concerning what he termed "enworlding" [*Verweltlichung*]. This has a "primary" or "proper" sense that refers to the emergence of the objective world, and which is the object of transcendental phenomenological investigation. But Fink also claimed a "secondary" or "non-proper" sense of enworlding, which refers to the concrete realization of transcendental phenomenology itself. Crucially, in Fink's account, these two forms of enworlding are sharply *separate*. And this is because, in taking for granted the possibility of a complete phenomenological reduction, Fink construed the active subject of phenomenologizing *per se* in suprahuman terms, that is, the wholly detached "non-participating onlooker" [*unbeteiligte Zuschauer*], thereby introducing the distinct problem of how to bring transcendental insights *back into* the empirical world. In contrast to this, Merleau-Ponty, basing himself on the claim that transcendental subjectivity *is* intersubjectivity, insisted on seeing transcendental phenomenology as a human practice that never really leaves the empirical world. From this perspective,

Merleau-Ponty simply dismissed Fink's problem of secondary enworlding. This is why he repeatedly claimed that philosophy "realizes itself by destroying itself as *separate* philosophy" (PhP 520, emphasis added), with the implication that the realization of philosophy implies its integration with reality, or the realization of the world, through transformative historical praxis.

Broadly taken, this may be an appealing view. But as discussed earlier, it is not clear just how it could work methodologically. This is what Merleau-Ponty tried to clarify in the "phenomenology of phenomenology" that comprises Part III of *Phenomenology of Perception*. In general terms, this metalevel undertaking was intended to substantiate the claim that phenomenology offers a coherent and exhaustive program of *bona fide* philosophical investigation. And it was intended to do this by showing, as Merleau-Ponty put it, that "if we rediscover time beneath the subject, and if we relate to the paradox of time those of the body, of the world, of the thing, and of the other, then we will understand that *beyond these there is nothing to understand*" (PhP 419, italics added). It was meant to establish, in other words, that the nexus of concrete intercorporeal praxis is itself the absolute (HT 20/18; cf. Zahavi 2002, 24), and that "*there is nothing outside this unique fulguration of existence*" (SNS 269/152, italics added). These claims were made in defense of phenomenology as an "intuitive science," the concrete intentional explications of which can in fact yield what Husserl deemed an "*ultimate* understanding of the world," that is, an understanding behind which "there is nothing more that can be sensefully inquired for, *nothing more to understand*" (FTL 242, italics added).

Merleau-Ponty thus wanted to redeem phenomenology as a complete philosophy by showing that the transcendental phenomenal field is coextensive with the totality of meaningful reality. The chief methodological task is to articulate the corresponding conception of the phenomenological reduction—its "performance structure," to borrow Fink's term. Having rejected the human possibility of the *unbeteiligte Zuschauer* on which Fink's account of the performance structure of the reduction was centered, the problem for Merleau-Ponty is clear: how to redeem phenomenology as a *complete* philosophy while also admitting that the phenomenological reduction is necessarily *incomplete*?

Recall that the grounds for claiming the impossibility of a complete reduction have to do with the fact that phenomenology itself, like any other human practice, relies inescapably upon certain productive capacities from which it cannot fully detach. Phenomenology thus inevitably presupposes certain operative intentionalities that reside in the habituated organism, making it impossible for it to thematize them exhaustively. The kind of complete detachment from the habituated organism that a complete reduction would require is not even a momentary existential possibility—as a life without life-as-such, it implies an absolutely individuated or "de-habituated" existence that not even "patient Schn." comes close to instantiating. But Merleau-Ponty needs to be able somehow to include those intentionalities within the purview of phenomenology in order to prosecute successfully his existential alternative to Fink's speculative interpretation.

The key here is that those operative intentionalities residing in the habituated organism are, for Merleau-Ponty, the *a priori* dimensions of history. In a move that is frankly somewhat breathtaking, then, he was able to include them within the purview of phenomenology through the apprehension of history as a totality. This is why Merleau-Ponty's claim that "the organism is not extraneous to history" is so vitally important, and why it needed to be carefully unpacked. For as discussed earlier, it shows that Merleau-Ponty's phenomenological approach to embodiment is premised methodologically upon a prior perception of history—specifically, Merleau-Ponty's incarnational Marxist understanding of history which, as just discussed, draws its intuitional warrant from the spectacle of contemporary heroic death. And we can now see very clearly why that must be the case. For otherwise, phenomenology would be methodologically incomplete and consequently, for all intents and purposes, a philosophical charade.

It may strike some readers as dubious to claim that Merleau-Ponty's rich phenomenological account of embodiment could possibly be logically posterior to—or even have anything whatsoever to do with—any such considerations regarding history as a whole. But is it really all that strange? Indeed, concerning embodiment, could phenomenological claims with *bona fide* philosophical import actually be arrived at in any other way? This is just a suggestion, but the idea would be that if one accepts a generalized view of embodied cognition, say, then one's own claims, which are likewise embodied, will necessarily fall short of philosophical truth, unless one historicizes corporeality in a way that inscribes some sort of normative teleological impetus within it. In other words, if primacy is accorded to corporeality in a consistent and thoroughgoing way, then philosophy is fundamentally jeopardized in the absence of some account of a larger purposiveness that can plausibly underwrite the possibility of intersubjective truth. Of course, one is free to reject a radical focus on corporeality and/or a serious concern for philosophical truth. But if one does wish to retain both, as Merleau-Ponty did, then it is not at all odd to claim that phenomenology requires some sort of methodological supplementation drawn from the philosophy of history. This is basically Merleau-Ponty's point about Marxism being "*the* philosophy of history" in the sense of doing nothing more than stipulating the transcendental conditions of historical rationality which, given a scrupulous recognition of the embodiedness of human existence, is arguably a condition of philosophy itself.

The supplementation that Merleau-Ponty relies upon is the historical mission of the proletariat. As we saw earlier, *ex hypothesi* proletarians are in a position to achieve what is in effect a standpoint of universal philosophical insight. For this reason, what Fink had distinguished as primary and secondary enworlding are concretely unified within the class-conscious historical praxis of the proletariat. Merleau-Ponty thought that philosophy just needed to recognize this and accept it as the concrete basis of historical truth. And it needed to accept that, even if truth is historical, it still has universal import, and so on its own, the corporeally situated freedom of human *être-au-monde* is insufficient to carry out the tasks of philosophy. In other words, the realization of philosophy is possible only on condition of its being underwritten and carried by the historical praxis of the proletariat. For this alone obviates the need, the impossibility of which would otherwise undermine the pretensions of philosophy, to thematize *directly* the full operative content of the habituated organism.

This is why Merleau-Ponty's phenomenology of phenomenology culminates with a discussion of freedom. For therein lies the crux of Merleau-Ponty's position: a denial that we are sufficiently free to perform the transcendental reduction as Husserl had originally conceived it, coupled with an argument to the effect that transcendental phenomenology in its full scope is nevertheless still a human possibility in virtue of the *necessity* embodied (literally) in the historical praxis of the proletariat. *Only on this condition is situated freedom sufficient for doing philosophy.* The upshot for phenomenology is that the reduction cannot be seen simply as an act of freedom, a kind of heroic detachment, but rather must be understood in incarnational terms as a matter of "living my time . . . by plunging into the present and the world" (PhP 520), and thus—in direct contrast to Fink, including with regard to his view of the passivity of the *Zuschauer*—as a matter of intensified participation in the ongoing generative process of history.

As in the political context, the manner of demonstration at the climax of *Phenomenology of Perception* is not straightforward. For Merleau-Ponty did not set up Saint Exupéry as a positive exemplar of anything. Just as it is not a viable political strategy, contemporary heroism does not instantiate an epistemic ideal, nor make any cognitive contribution. In particular, as noted above, it does not achieve absolute knowing in any communicable sense, but rather presents *for us* the phenomenon of absolute knowing, as it were, that betokens the uncognizable outer limit of cognition. This is the fundamental way in which philosophy places "our relationship with the world . . . once more before our eyes and presents it for our affirmation [*constatation*]" (PhP xiii). And Merleau-Ponty wanted to sublimate this liminal experience into the structure of phenomenological reason. That is, he wanted his readers' encounter with the mortal failure of Saint Exupéry—whom they *did* overwhelmingly regard as a hero of some kind—to be transmuted dialectically into the uptake of the militant faith of his incarnational Marxism—in effect, a kind of sacrifice of sacrifice. And Merleau-Ponty wanted this to occur, not simply for any directly political ends, *but precisely in order to convey accurately his methodological reinterpretation of phenomenology*. In attesting to the logic of history, the spectacle of the contemporary hero is what provides intuitional grounds for affirming the theoretically undecidable claim that the productivity presupposed by phenomenology is a naturally purposive spontaneity that coheres fully with the project's universal philosophical aspirations, and this by dovetailing with the historical mission of the proletariat. By way of analogy with the political context, it thus motivates a "rational faith" in the latent incarnation of human universality by which phenomenology needs to orient itself at the limits of "regressive" (in the sense of *Rückfragen*) intentional analysis.

Concerning the lines from *Pilote de guerre* that are cited at the end of *Phenomenology of Perception*, then, it is clear that Merleau-Ponty had no truck with their actual textual content. Strictly speaking, in the context of Merleau-Ponty's work, these lines are non-sense, and they do not properly *say* anything. But Merleau-Ponty did want them to *do* something. That is, he wanted the apogogic invocation of the disincarnate "nœud de relations" as intended by Saint Exupéry (cf. Milligan 1955, 251) to prompt on the part of his readers the practical adoption of a transformed existential stance and a correspondingly new way of seeing the world in terms of the coextensivity of meaningful reality with the nexus of concrete intercorporeal involvement. It is in this way that non-sense could, despite itself, contribute to *making* sense. Here too, one must be careful. For contrary to what is typically assumed, this perception is *not* informed in any way by Saint Exupéry's claim that "man is but a knot of relations," but rather is based upon the dialectical sublimation of the radical disincarnation that is expressed therein. The resulting incarnational view may still be mythic in epistemic terms (cf. Eliade 1947, 29–32), but it is based upon a myth with an entirely different content and motivational structure in virtue of the fact that it concerns the possibility of progressive historical agency rather than any sort of transcendent ideal.

The fact that Merleau-Ponty's militant position does not dispense with myth and practical faith is what decisively distinguishes it from Fink's triumphant view, which is oriented to the absolute as an attainable object of theoretical knowledge. In a certain way, then, Fink and Merleau-Ponty can be taken as representing two basic forms of post-Husserlian phenomenology. The main issue concerns how phenomenology is to provide its own foundation (in the sense of Husserl's maxim of "*die Rückbeziehung der Phänomenologie auf sich selbst*"), and in particular, how it is to deal with the *limits* of intuitional givenness, the outer horizons of experience which are themselves not given to intuition. Broadly speaking, there are two ways to address this: either reject the primacy of intuition by subordinating evidence to a principle of metaphysical speculation; or else uphold the primacy of intuition by phenomenalizing the limits of intuitional givenness noncognitively. What is at stake is the methodological status of Husserl's "principle of all principles" (see Preface, note 30). Fink pursued the first alternative, which rejects this principle, while Merleau-Ponty took up the second, which defends it. Merleau-Ponty's own "phenomenology of phenomenology" culminated in the spectacle of heroic death—which metaphorizes the existential failure of a complete reduction—because this serves to substantiate his deflationary argument against Fink to the effect that meaningful reality is coextensive with human intercorporeality, and thus that the methodological resources adequate to the complete realization (or enworlding) of transcendental phenomenology do not exceed human capacities. It is just that these capacities are now taken to include the historical agency of the proletariat—which is to be included within the performance structure of the reduction accordingly.

It is instructive to consider the contrast between Fink and Merleau-Ponty as reflecting two fundamentally different ways in which phenomenology can relate to Kant's "Copernican Revolution." On the one hand, Fink tried to surpass this (see also Fink 1976a). As we saw, whereas for Kant, there can be no canon of pure theoretical reason, for Fink, the canon of phenomenological reason is expressly conceived for the theoretical task of distinguishing appearance-truth from genuine transcendental truth. As "absolute science" phenomenology would leave transcendental illusion behind. In particular, any positive regulative function that it might have had would be superseded, as there would no longer be a meaningful distinction between subjective and objective, hence no conflation. Likewise, Fink did not recognize the primacy of practical reason, nor the need for faith, regarding these as expressions of the limited and dogmatic nature of critical philosophy. Ultimately, through the breakthrough to the phenomenological onlooker, he aimed to go beyond the sort of ectypal knowledge to which Kant limited human knowledge, to a kind of archetypal theoretical knowing that would be akin to the intellectual intuition that Kant had, of course, strictly ruled out.

On the other hand, Merleau-Ponty tended more toward completing than surpassing Kant. Regarding Fink's proposal of a constructive phenomenology as still transcendentally naïve (see Preface), Merleau-Ponty reinterpreted phenomenology on a practical basis in a way that placed limits on theoretical claims. So whereas Fink confronted Kant on the terrain of the first *Critique*, Merleau-Ponty, as we have seen, turned to the third. Although he did not elaborate the implications of this in any detail, his idea of method clearly involved granting reflecting judgment epistemic priority over theoretical understanding (PhP 65; cf. Coole 1984). This is exemplified with perfect clarity in the case of judging Saint Exupéry to instantiate contemporary heroism. Agreeing with Kant that philosophical inquiry is not entirely oriented by principles that are constitutive of objects, Merleau-Ponty thus likewise retained a positive role for transcendental illusion. Whereas Fink did not see how any sort of subjective principle could have objective validity, Merleau-Ponty, in contrast, agreed with Kant that it is essential to reason to take certain subjective ideas that do not and, indeed, could not arise from experience and to include them in the field of investigation (Grier 2001, 278). Like Kant's claims concerning the systematic unity of reason, Merleau-Ponty's claims regarding historical totality provide a regulative vision for doing philosophy. And as in Kant's case, the epistemic status of this vision is ultimately borne by transcendental illusion, namely, that of heroic absolute knowing. Concerning this, Merleau-Ponty's position is consistent with Kant's assertion that "this illusion (which we can, after all, prevent from deceiving us) is indispensably necessary [if] we want to direct the understanding beyond every given experience . . . and hence also to direct it to its greatest possible and utmost expansion" (KrV A645/B673).

Recognition of this sort of affinity with Kant goes against the grain of prevailing wisdom concerning Merleau-Ponty, where it is typically assumed that his radicalization of Husserl's own radicalization of Kant must have placed him at a further remove from Kant. But when Fink's methodological contribution is taken into account, it becomes clear that in order to redeem transcendental phenomenology on an intuitional basis, it was, in part, back to Kant that Merleau-Ponty turned. But still, this should not be overstated. These points of affinity with Kant are in effect assimilated elements of the militant incarnational perspective of Merleau-Ponty's (Lukácsian) Marxism. Broadly speaking, the idea is that it is within the terms of Marxism understood in this way that Kant's "Copernican Revolution" can be best completed. Likewise for transcendental phenomenology. Merleau-Ponty's reinterpretation of Husserl's project ultimately works by relying on intuitional experience beyond theoretical knowledge, and thus by embracing a kind of faith, rather than, as with Fink, postulating theoretical experience beyond what can be experienced intuitionally. It thus "provides its own foundation," not through theoretical speculation, but through practical participation in a historical project of intersubjective self-realization wherein the world is not something to be known, but something to be made. As discussed above, Merleau-Ponty was of the view that this participation presupposes the "existential attitude," and that in turn this presupposes the sublimative recognition of Exupérian heroism. This is what is supposed to *happen* at the end of *Phenomenology of Perception*, and that is why it ends in the way that it does.

Notes

Preface

1 For instance, Matthews (2002, 2006); Priest (2003); Carman and Hansen (2004); Toadvine (2006); Hass (2008); Carman (2008); Marshall (2008); Diprose and Reynolds (2008); Romdenh-Romluc (2010).

2 For instance, Hass and Olkowski (2001); Toadvine and Embree (2002); Baldwin (2007); Semonovitch and DeRoo (2010); Flynn et al. (2010).

3 For instance, Davis (2001); Steeves (2004); Gordon and Tamari (2004); Olkowski and Weiss (2006); Hatley et al. (2006); Coole (2007); Cataldi and Hamrick (2007); Dillard-Wright (2009); Johnson (2009); Toadvine (2009); Park and Kopf (2010); Kaushik (2011).

4 For instance, Low (2002); Carbone (2004); Barbaras (2004); Besmer (2008); Hamrick and Van der Veken (2011).

5 Maurice Merleau-Ponty, *Phénoménologie de la perception* (Paris: Gallimard 1945). The original English translation was by Colin Smith (London: Routledge & Kegan Paul 1962), which was reset with new pagination and published in the Routledge Classics series (London: Routledge 2002). The new (and much improved) English translation is by Don Landes (London; New York: Routledge, 2012). Given this plurality of English editions, and the ready availability of page concordances between them and the French original, page references will be made only to the latter, hereafter cited as PhP. All translations will be my own, although I have consulted those of both Smith and Landes.

6 The situation is similar in French-language scholarship, with the possible exception of Saint Aubert (2004), the first volume of a trilogy of works on Merleau-Ponty which make use of extensive unpublished materials.

7 But cf. Spiegelberg (1973, 1974), for example, on the question of the necessity of the reduction in general, and Dillon's claim (1988, 120) that Merleau-Ponty in particular "was not committed to the methodology of the reduction."

8 There is a considerable literature on Husserl and the reduction. Regarding some of the basic issues, see Boehm (1965) and Kern (1977). For an excellent recent discussion of Husserl's view of the reduction, see Luft (2004). See also Husserl (2002), which presents previously unpublished material on the reduction. For a brief overview of the reduction in some post-Husserlian contexts, see Taminiaux (2004).

9 Over the years, several commentators have made specific contributions toward an understanding of Merleau-Ponty's methodology, in particular with regard to the phenomenological reduction, but there is no clear picture or substantive consensus. See, for example, Murphy (1966); Herbenick (1973); Devettere (1973); Bender (1983); Sheets-Johnstone (1999): 273–319; Heinämaa (1999, 2002); Seebohm (2002); Depraz (2002); Smith (2005).

10 Here, *étonnement* is Merleau-Ponty's rendering of Fink's term *Verwunderung*. Merleau-Ponty was citing Fink's 1933 *Kant-Studien* article, but the pagination in his reference is incorrect. He cited pp. 331ff of the original article (pp. 96ff. in Fink (1966)), whereas the point in question was made on p. 350 (pp. 115f in Fink (1966)). The allusion that Merleau-Ponty made to this idea of wonder later in *Phenomenology of Perception* (PhP 341f) does provide the correct page reference.

11 But note that in Fink (1966d), this idea is developed in terms of "astonishment" [*das Staunen*] (Fink 1966d, 182–5).

12 See Plato, *Theaetetus* 155d. Cf. Aristotle, *Metaphysics*, A2 982b 12ff.

13 See, for example, Husserl (1970, 285). As Spiegelberg (1982, 81) put it: "Phenomenology in general may be characterized as a philosophy which has learned to wonder again and to respect wonders for what they are in themselves." And Welton (2000, 13): "What gives rise to phenomenological analysis is an unsettling wonder in the presence of things, which themselves come to us through certain modes or manners that are not themselves objects." Of course, Husserl regarded "the pure ego and pure subjectivity" as "the wonder of wonders" (1980, 71, 75; see Melle 1992). For a more general discussion of wonder and phenomenology, see Barnacle (2001), and for a more critical discussion, see Kingwell (2000).

14 Concerning the problem of the beginning of phenomenology, see Lenkowski (1978); on the natural attitude, see Luft (1998).

15 Merleau-Ponty suggested that from this stems "Husserl's entire misunderstanding with his interpreters, with the existential 'dissidents', and ultimately with himself" (PhP viii).

16 Statements to this effect are very common.

17 But cf. Madison's claim (1981, 194)—made with reference to a working note from February 1959 in which Merleau-Ponty wrote that "the incompleteness of the reduction . . . is not an obstacle to the reduction, it is the reduction itself" (VI 232/178)—that "[i]t is precisely by thinking the impossibility of a total reduction that phenomenology thinks a 'Being in transcendence not reduced to the 'perspectives' of 'consciousness''" (citing VI 292/243).

18 With regard to Fink, Bruzina (2002) is an exception; but cf. Smyth (2011). With regard to Saint Exupéry, see Smyth (2010).

19 See the Introduction below, and the end of Chapter 1.

20 Reference will also be made to Fink's 1933 *Kant-Studien* article, "Die phänomenologische Philosophie Husserls in der gegenwärtigen Kritik," which was based on the *Sixth Cartesian Meditation* and which Merleau-Ponty had certainly read, but in which Fink had tempered the force of the internal critique of phenomenology that the *Sixth Cartesian Meditation* had implied.

21 For a detailed history of the document, see Bruzina (1995, vii–xxxv).

22 Bruzina (1995, lxxxiii n121; see also lxxviii n74). Note that the copy lent to Berger did not include the final section 12, "'Phenomenology' as Transcendental Idealism" (Bruzina 1995, xxi).

23 Bruzina (1995, xxxiv; cf. lxxxiv n125), citing a letter from Fink to Gerhart Husserl (25 October 1946).

24 Bruzina (1995, xxxiv), citing a letter from Fink to Van Breda (26 November 1946).

25 In a letter to Merleau-Ponty (17 December 1945), Van Breda wrote that the *Sixth Cartesian Meditation* "is basically a critique of the very bases of Husserl's thought," and in another letter of the same date to the publisher Aubier, Van Breda wrote that "Fink did not like to have his draft widely known, because his critique is basically quite severe" (cited in Bruzina 1995, lxxxiii n119).

26 Fink's text was first mentioned in Berger (1941, 115n1; cf. 106). Concerning Merleau-Ponty's reading of the *Sixth Cartesian Meditation*, see his letter (1 October 1942) to Hermann Van Breda, cited in Van Breda (1962, 421f).

27 See Van Breda's letter to Merleau-Ponty (17 December 1945) where he suggested that *Phenomenology of Perception* "is too strongly under the influence of the 'Sixth Meditation'" (cited in Bruzina 1995: lxxxiii).

28 Kersten (1995) expressed a similar idea, but misread Merleau-Ponty as having aimed at the same goal as the *Sixth Cartesian Meditation*, which may be related to his apparent unawareness (1995, 49) that Berger's copy of Fink's text excluded section 12 (cf. Bruzina 1995, xxi). Kersten's account is alluded to positively in Crowell (2001, 263). A similar but more accurate view was expressed (but not developed) in Waldenfels (1997, 71ff).

29 We must also set aside for present purposes the question as to whether and to what extent this text accurately reflected Fink's own views. On that, see Bruzina (2004), which relies in part on the valuable material now available in Fink (2006, 2008).

30 As Husserl expressed it, this principle states "that every originary presentive intuition is a legitimizing source of cognition, that everything originarily ... offered to us in 'intuition' is to be accepted simply as what it is presented as being, but only within the limits in which it is presented there. . . . Every statement which does no more than confer expression on such [originary] data by simple explication and by means of significations precisely conforming to them is ... called upon to serve as a foundation" (1982, §24).

31 Note that Merleau-Ponty did not strongly emphasize that the idea of constructive phenomenology came from Fink, referring it in the text to "Husserl's final works," while mentioning in the footnote that it was "composed [*rédigée*] by Eugen Fink" (PhP i).

32 As we shall see, since it thus transcends the categories of ontology, Fink refers to this account as "*meontic.*" See Bruzina (1995, lv–lvii; 2004, 366f).

33 Although at one point Fink suggests that the onlooker "produces itself" (SCM 43/39), thereby emphasizing the onlooker's radical difference from both the human and transcendental-constituting subjects, his considered view is that it is merely the "*functional exponent*" [funktionelle Exponent] of transcendental life (SCM 44/40; cf. 65, 73/58, 65).

34 But cf. SCM 37–41/34–7, as well as Fink (1966a, 45f), where Fink gives indications to the contrary; see also Merleau-Ponty's positive reference to the latter text (SC 222 n2/248 n40).

35 Even though, for Kant, it represents the determination of the formal conditions of a complete system of pure reason, and as such is prefigured throughout the work as the real conclusion (see Grondin 1990).

36 Kant: "By canon I mean the sum of *a priori* principles governing the correct use of certain cognitive powers as such" (KrV A796/B824).

37 Although Fink largely avoids this more provocative terminology in the *Sixth Cartesian Meditation*, it does express the salient idea more clearly (see SCM 147/134; cf. 111/101).

38 See Husserl's discussion of the "transcendental illusion" of solipsism, which expresses the need to press ahead with the "systematic unfolding of the constitutive problematic" (1969, §96.b, 241f).

39 As Fink put it: the onlooker "becomes *passively* participant in world-constitution insofar as ... it is encompassed by the self-enworlding of the constituting I" (SCM 119/108). Transcendental life turns in upon itself and the constitutive

activities of primary enworlding "sweep the [onlooker] along" [*reissen . . . mit*] into the world (SCM 119/109)—the onlooker is "carried off [*fortgetragen*] by it and made mundane" (SCM 119/108; cf. 125/114).

40 "The concept of 'intellectual intuition' and above all that of (Hegel's) 'speculative knowledge' is a genuine presentiment of the productivity of phenomenologizing 'theoretical experience'" (SCM 86/77).

41 Or equivalently, the impossibility of Fink's onlooker—which Merleau-Ponty had already effectively dismissed in *The Structure of Behavior* by demonstrating—*contra* Kojève's claim about the "Sage"—the impossibility of "complete integration" (SC 227/210). Cf. Kojève (1947, 271): "the Sage is the man who is capable of answering in a *comprehensible* or satisfactory manner *all* questions that can be asked him concerning his actions, and of answering in such a way that the *whole* of his answers forms a *coherent* discourse. Or else, what amounts to the same thing: the Sage is the *fully* and *perfectly self-conscious* man."

42 Marx (1975b, 187, translation modified): "Philosophy cannot realize itself without the transcendence [*Aufhebung*] of the proletariat, and the proletariat cannot transcend itself without the realization [*Verwirklichung*] of philosophy" [*Die Philosophie kann sich nicht verwirklichen ohne die Aufhebung des Proletariats, das Proletariat kann sich nicht aufheben ohne die Verwirklichung der Philosophie*].

43 Cf. SNS 236f/133, where Merleau-Ponty wrote slightly differently that philosophy "*se réalise en se supprimant* [by abolishing itself] *comme philosophie séparée*." See also SNS 136, 235/79, 133; NI 99, 108, 123, 174.

44 As he also insisted upon attributing it to Husserl (PhP xiii, 415; SNS 237/134; 1960, 97; 1964d, 107; 1973, 45). On this, see Zahavi (2002, 23–8).

45 A claim he also made explicitly (HT 20/18). See Zahavi (2002, 24), where a 1927 research manuscript of Husserl's is cited to the effect that "the absolute reveals itself as the intersubjective relation between subjects."

46 It is "by living my time [*mon temps*]," "by plunging into [*m'enfonçant*] the present and the world . . . that I am able to understand other times"—that is, approach the universal (PhP 520).

47 Recall Merleau-Ponty's claim that "the experience of absurdity and that of absolute self-evidence are mutually implicatory, and even indistinguishable" (PhP 342).

48 This view also contradicts Aron Gurwitsch's claim (1957, 142) that "Merleau-Ponty did not develop a phenomenology of perception that would be considered transcendental in the full sense of the term [because] the existential framework of his investigations prevented him from radically pushing the phenomenological reduction to its limit [*jusqu'au bout*]."

49 See above. Cf. also Fink's later comment about phenomenology's "methodische 'Schizophrenie'" (1976, 192).

50 "The revolutionary movement, like the work of the artist, is an intention which itself *creates its instruments and its means of expression*" (PhP 508, emphasis added; cf. PhP 519). Cf. SNS 109/63.

51 "[O]nly the work itself, completed and understood, is proof that there was *something* rather than *nothing* to be said" (SNS 32/19; cf. PhP 491). Similarly, a revolutionary project "ceases to be the abstract decision of a thinker and becomes an historical reality only if it is worked out [*s'il s'élabore*] in interhuman relations, and in the relations of man with his work [*métier*]" (PhP 509).

52 Merleau-Ponty was presumably citing Fink (SCM 43/39): "In der universalen Epoché, in der Ausschaltung aller Glaubenssetzungen, produziert sich der phänomenologische Zuschauer selbst."

53 Cf. SC 240/224, where Merleau-Ponty hinted that an appropriately redefined transcendental philosophy would involve "'staking' [« *mettre en jeu* »] one's life."
54 Robert Campbell once quoted Merleau-Ponty, albeit without reference, as saying that philosophy "is not content to be subjected to its historical surroundings, but is inserted in them, riveted, committed, *militant*" (1966, 274).

Introduction

1 Saint Exupéry wrote *Pilote de guerre* while living in "exile" in New York City, following the defeat of France in 1940, and that is where it was first published. Parts of the English translation first appeared in three instalments in *The Atlantic Monthly* at the beginning of 1942 (January, pp. 1–20; February, pp. 184–205; and March, pp. 313–33), and the book was published simultaneously (20 February 1942) in French (Saint Exupéry 1942a) and English, under the title *Flight to Arras* (Saint Exupéry 1942b). Although substantially the same, there are numerous minor differences between these texts, including the organization and division of chapters. Gallimard published *Pilote de guerre* in the Occupied Zone later that year (27 November 1942), after submitting it to the Propagandastaffel, which passed it after censoring one line about Hitler (cf. Assouline 1988, 270f). This line, which would have appeared on page 32, appeared on page 34 of the Éditions de la Maison Française edition (Saint Exupéry 1942a) in the following passage:

> Ils sont tous des imbeciles. Celui qui ne sait pas trouver mes gants. {Hitler qui a déclenché cette guerre démente.} Et l'autre, de l'État-Major, avec son idée fixe de mission à basse altitude.

> They are all idiots. The one who doesn't know where my gloves are. {Hitler, who unleashed this mad war.} And that fellow on the General Staff, and his obsession with low-altitude sorties.

This line remained absent from subsequent printings of the Gallimard edition—it was only reintroduced to the text of *Pilote de guerre* in the most recent edition of Saint Exupéry's complete works (1999, 125).

Concerning the 1942 Gallimard edition, the limited print run of 2100 copies sold well, but the book was subsequently (11 February 1943) banned and recalled at the instigation of French anti-Semites, notably Pierre-Antoine Cousteau and others associated with the collaborationist journal *Je suis partout* (Ragache and Ragache 1988, 241ff; Bounin 1999, 1305). They were offended by Saint Exupéry's having extolled the bravery of a Jewish comrade named Jean Israël. The head of the Propagandastaffel, Gerhard Heller, was reprimanded for this oversight (EG 299f; cf. Heller 1981, 134). Gallimard was also not permitted to reprint Saint Exupéry's earlier works. Clandestine versions of *Pilote de guerre* subsequently appeared, first in Lyon in December 1943 (Imprimerie Nouvelle Lyonnaise) and subsequently in Lille in 1944 (S.I.L.I.C.) (see Rude 1978; Bounin 1999, 1320f). Owing to the scarcity of paper, these clandestine editions reproduced the book with about half as many pages (the Lille edition was about eight pages longer than the one produced in Lyon), and both, but especially the Lille one, contained errors and minor omissions. The Gallimard edition was first republished in 1947.

2 There are some minor textual discrepancies between Merleau-Ponty's citation and
   the Gallimard edition of Saint Exupéry's text, where they appear as follows:

> Ton fils est pris dans l'incendie? Tu le sauveras!. . . . Tu vendrais, s'il est un
> obstacle, ton épaule pour le luxe d'un coup d'épaule! Tu loges dans ton acte
> même. Ton acte, c'est toi. . . . Tu t'échanges. . . . Ta signification se montre
> éblouissante. C'est ton devoir, c'est ta haine, c'est ton amour, c'est ta fidélité,
> c'est ton invention. . . . L'homme n'est qu'un nœud de relations. Les relations
> comptent seules pour l'homme.

It is unlikely that these differences were intentional, but nor is it the case that
Merleau-Ponty was working with a clandestine edition that contained typographical
inaccuracies. (Note that Merleau-Ponty did not list *Pilote de guerre* in the
bibliography of *Phenomenology of Perception*.) Consider the page references that
Merleau-Ponty gave. He cited pages 171 and 174, whereas in the Gallimard edition,
the lines appear on pages 168f and 171 (it is the final line that comes from a different
paragraph), while in the Éditions de la Maison Française edition, they are on pages
173f and 176. However, Merleau-Ponty had earlier referred (PhP 99 n) to a passage
on page 174 of *Pilote de guerre* that is, in fact, on page 174 in the Gallimard edition;
likewise for page 169 (see PhP 100 n). (The passages in question are on pages 180
and 174, respectively, in the Maison Française edition.) The pagination is thus
tightly correlated to the Gallimard edition, whereas, as noted above, the clandestine
editions differed considerably with respect to pagination. In all probability, then,
Merleau-Ponty was using the banned 1942 Gallimard edition, and the textual
differences simply stem from citational nonchalance, and the page references are
just an error.

3 But see Smyth (2010, 2011). Another exception to this tendency is Dorfman (2007),
   on which I shall comment below (see note 14).

4 Plausible-sounding explanations that might be given for this neglect could be based
   on the idea that the citation falls outside of the philosophical content of the book
   proper. It might thus be seen, for example, as merely a reflection of the immediate
   postwar context. Albeit in passing and in a work on Sartre, Hollier made this
   claim quite crudely in saying that the ending of *Phenomenology of Perception* was
   "imposed by the postwar agenda" (1986, 19). And while it goes against the grain of
   his discussion otherwise, Dorfman said as much in claiming that Merleau-Ponty's
   view of Saint Exupéry "is certainly to be explained by the context of the immediate
   post-war period and the influence of Sartre" (2007, 151 n3), although this allusion
   to Sartre is puzzling. However, neglect of the reference to Saint Exupéry could
   also be viewed more tactfully as simply reflecting Merleau-Ponty's own political
   outlook. Saint Aubert expressed such a view in claiming that "the very last page
   [of *Phenomenology of Perception*] . . . betrays the displacement of the author's
   philosophical concerns, and his impassioned interest in the political events of
   the day" (2004, 115). But while this view would attribute to Merleau-Ponty the
   agency with regard to the composition of his own book that is effectively denied
   by any sort of "contextual explanation," it does remain fully consistent with a sharp
   bifurcation of Merleau-Ponty's thought into mutually exclusive philosophical
   and political compartments, as if his political interests were in no way implicated
   within the reinterpretation of phenomenology that he presents in *Phenomenology
   of Perception*—as if, in other words, the liminal frontier between philosophy and
   politics were only reached on the final page. As we shall see, however, such a view is

fundamentally mistaken, as aspects of Merleau-Ponty's "political" thought are woven into his philosophical work at pivotal points.

5 Cooper (1979, 20) referred to the entire citation, but still gave it an uncritical Merleau-Pontian reading. Dorfman (2007) considered the whole citation as well, but focused his analysis on Saint Exupéry's term "invention" (see below, note 14). Some commentators have alluded to Saint Exupéry without actually making reference to the ending of *Phenomenology of Perception* at all. For example, while making indirect reference to Saint Exupéry, Laurie Spurling noted Merleau-Ponty's many "almost mystical" statements about human existence (1977, 133). And Gary Madison pointed out some similarities between *Phenomenology of Perception* and Saint Exupéry's *Terre des hommes* (1981, 52, 316 n21).

6 Such a reading might appeal to the Preface of *Phenomenology of Perception*, where Merleau-Ponty clearly alludes to Saint Exupéry in saying, in his own words, that "we are this knot of relations" [*nous sommes ce nœud de relations*] (PhP xvi). However, because Merleau-Ponty was predicating it of the plural "we," *this* "knot of relations" refers to a reality very different from that invoked at the end of the book, which declares that the *individual* human being is a matter of pure relationality ("man is *but* a knot of relations"). This is linked to the usual—though erroneous—translation of Saint Exupéry's use of the term "nœud" as "network" (cf. Langer 1989, 147)—a translation which *does* work for Merleau-Ponty's use of the term in the Preface. For the latter takes the term "man" as the collective noun "humanity" and thus imparts a much more unproblematic intersubjective meaning to the Exupérian lines than they actually support. In other contexts, Saint Exupéry does refer to humanity as a network [*réseau*], but in the passage in question, "man" refers unambiguously to the human individual. Lewis Galantière, who produced the original English translation of *Pilote de guerre* (under the title *Flight to Arras*) in close consultation with Saint Exupéry, rendered the locution "nœud de relations" adjunctively as "a knot, a web, a mesh"—and this not *of* but "*into which* relationships are tied" (Saint Exupéry 1942b, 183, emphasis added).

7 See Froman (2005) for a critical discussion of this silence from the perspective of Merleau-Ponty's later work.

8 It is thus immaterial here that "silence is still a modality of the world of sound" (PhP 516).

9 And this remained a recurrent theme for Merleau-Ponty—see, for example, EP 42/51, PNPH 275, 323, 333.

10 Although it is occasionally—albeit very seldom—*mentioned*, the theme of heroism is never actually *discussed* in the literature on Merleau-Ponty—but see Smyth (2010, 2011). Previously, the nearest thing to an exception is a now obscure article by Robert Campbell (1966), but even this is largely expository, offering little in the way of analysis, philosophical or otherwise. More recently, Flynn (2007, 136f) devoted a couple of paragraphs to the theme of heroism, but to little consequence. See also Dorfman (2007; cf. note 14 below).

11 Sartre attributed this expression to Merleau-Ponty in his tribute, "Merleau-Ponty vivant" (Sartre 1964, 191), a piece that was originally published in *Les Temps modernes* (October 1961). Merleau-Ponty used the expression frequently in *The Visible and the Invisible*, (an unfinished manuscript not published until 1964), but the idea is certainly already present in *Phenomenology of Perception*. But what exactly it should be taken to mean will be greatly enriched by consideration of the Exupérian ending of that text.

12 "Pour moi, voler ou écrire, c'est tout un. . . . L'aviateur et l'écrivain se confondent dans une égale prise de conscience. . . . C'est encore mal dire que l'un prolonge ou complète l'autre. Il s'agit d'une expérience totale." Interview with Luc Estang, in *Le Figaro littéraire* (27 May 1939), cited in Estang (1956, 167). See also Bernadie (1989, 128, 132).

13 As we shall see below, though, far from being merely *prima facie*, this incongruity actually runs quite deeply.

14 Eran Dorfman's recent effort (2007) to address the meaning of the lines cited from *Pilote de guerre* in terms of their connection with Merleau-Ponty's views concerning freedom and radical reflection is a potentially fruitful undertaking, and as such merits attention. But because Dorfman neglects to consider the context from which the lines were excerpted, and because he singles out, more or less arbitrarily, Saint Exupéry's term "invention" and focuses his discussion around it, Dorfman's take on the passage is skewed by the erroneous assumption that the Merleau-Pontian "hero" is Saint Exupéry *qua* individual, as literally invoked by the passage, whereas in fact it was Saint Exupéry *qua* "man" understood in universal terms. This assumption implies a misleading analogical likeness between Merleau-Ponty and the "hero" he invokes. For Dorfman regards the "hero" in question as someone "who invents his or her own life" (150) and, *for this reason*, as someone who exemplifies the freedom that Merleau-Ponty had discussed in the final chapter of *Phenomenology of Perception*, and thus as instantiating the same sort of creativity that occurs when radical reflection recovers its pre-reflective conditions. Yet, these claims sit badly with the fact that the heroism in question represents an existential coincidence of being and doing, since this would preclude the kind of reflective distance necessary for adopting an "inventive" attitude vis-à-vis oneself. And indeed, Dorfman does say that in the scenario depicted by Saint Exupéry there is no time for reflection (140). Hence if, as he claims, such action does nevertheless involve the creation of meaning, then heroism must be as much (or more) a matter of objective historical tendency as of individual freedom, however construed. A necessary condition of heroic action for Merleau-Ponty, after all, is that it contribute to the historical realization of freedom—being and doing may coincide in exactly the same way in the action and death of a fascist collaborator, for example, but he or she would *not* be a hero.

Moreover, though, there is in any case no sense in which Saint Exupéry is an exemplar of freedom in this context. As Merleau-Ponty made clear, the hero does not *live* but rather *gives* his or her freedom—this may be eminently laudable, but living one's relation to others and the world "to the limit" [*jusqu'au bout*] necessarily implies death, and the citation would be meaningless if Saint Exupéry had survived the war. (It is, in fact, surprisingly rare for a reference to the Exupérian ending of *Phenomenology of Perception* actually to mention that the words are presented as plainly being those of a dead man, someone recently and famously killed in the service of his country.) This clearly implies that, as invoked at the end of *Phenomenology of Perception*, Saint Exupéry could not possibly model the creativity inherent in radical reflection. It is thus problematic to claim, as Dorfman does, that Merleau-Ponty invoked *Pilote de guerre* as a work of *fiction* (140). It must not be overlooked that, however stylized it may be, at its core *Pilote de guerre* is presented as based on actual experiences that Saint Exupéry himself had as a reconnaissance pilot. And this ostensibly non-fictional status was crucial for Merleau-Ponty. For he invoked the lines from *Pilote de guerre* as a quasi-phenomenological description of what radical reflection would (*per impossibile*) disclose to the "hero." And it is for this reason alone that *Pilote de guerre*, or at least the relevant sections thereof, could be considered a "story" [*histoire racontée*] whose telling "can give meaning to the world with as much 'depth' as a philosophical treatise" (PhP xvi). It may certainly be granted that there is something akin to fiction in the claims that Merleau-Ponty would make on this basis. But that is not the business of the "hero" who, fully immersed in his or her action, is in no position to fictionalize. Rather, the relevant inventiveness pertains primarily to the rest of us, that is, the living—how we choose our heroes, if at all, how we portray them, and what meaning we assign to them. The hero *qua* hero has no hero.

15 And arguably, by extension, the entire subsequent development of Merleau-Ponty's *œuvre*. For this emerged largely on the basis of his self-critical attempt to resolve certain outstanding problems raised by his postwar formulations of existential phenomenology, fundamentally as concerns the spontaneity or productivity that makes the realization of concrete universality possible (cf. Pros. 42, 48/7, 11). To this extent, our understanding of Merleau-Ponty's later work will necessarily remain limited by any major lacunae in our understanding of his earlier work, and, as we shall see, the role of heroism in *Phenomenology of Perception* is one such lacuna— and arguably the single most significant one.

Chapter 1

1 This is not to deny that other implicit or explicit references in *Phenomenology of Perception* may similarly require careful and focused interpretive attention accurately to disclose their significance within the text, nor even that these may have a substantial impact on how the text is understood. But excepting the references to Fink's *Sixth Cartesian Meditation* discussed in the Preface (above), I would contend that any other such reference would be incomparably less significant.

2 It may be worthwhile briefly to consider the reasons for the lack of critical scrutiny of the ending of *Phenomenology of Perception*. A sufficient (but not necessary) condition for this lack would be a failure to discern the ending's outward incongruity with the rest of the text in the first place. And this condition may have been met variously over time. For instance, most early readers of *Phenomenology of Perception* (especially but not only) in France would have been very familiar with Saint Exupéry, and with *Pilote de guerre* in particular. In fact, in the immediate postwar years, Saint Exupéry was the focus of a considerable amount of overwhelmingly positive, even quasihagiographic, public attention (especially but not only) in France. But this would have tended to make Merleau-Ponty's invocation of him appear all the *less* significant—just one more expression of homage among so many others. At the same time, these contemporary readers would have been preoccupied with coming to terms with *Phenomenology of Perception* as a complex and highly original philosophical endeavor that drew upon and combined many sources that were not widely known in France at the time. Most early commentary on this work was thus largely expository—for example, Beauvoir (1945), Roland Caillois (1946), Guillaume (1946), which was, admittedly, primarily psychologically oriented, and Alquié (1947), which, although it was a critical discussion that did briefly touch on the idea of heroism in the context of the moral implications of Merleau-Pontian

existentialism (68), did not relate this to Saint Exupéry. See also Gurwitsch (1950) and De Waelhens (1951). The point here is that even if they were familiar with Saint Exupéry, early commentators on *Phenomenology of Perception* would have failed to notice the incongruity of its ending and thus passed over it without comment primarily because they were still engaged in the work of digesting and coming to terms with the philosophical content of Merleau-Ponty's work itself (a process which, it might be added, was initially slowed by the fact that in the late-1940s far more attention was paid to *Humanism and Terror*, a work which interested a much wider audience). Conversely, subsequent generations of commentators were (and still are) by and large in the opposite situation: enjoying the advantages of a more thorough and insightful perspective on Merleau-Ponty's phenomenology, they typically had (and have) a greatly diminished familiarity with Saint Exupéry (and more likely than not have not read *Pilote de guerre*). And inasmuch as he came to be viewed as an amateurish philosophical lightweight, much philosophical commentary probably preferred to disregard Saint Exupéry altogether in order to avoid sullying Merleau-Ponty's text with an embarrassing association which, anyway, seemed to add nothing to the text. In general, then, it seems safe to say that while recognition of the incongruity of the ending of *Phenomenology of Perception* requires appropriate knowledge of both Merleau-Ponty and Saint Exupéry, historically, there has tended to be an inverse relationship between these respective moments, such that by the time the relevant scholarship on *Phenomenology of Perception* had reached a mature stage, familiarity with Saint Exupéry had declined among commentators below the threshold required to appreciate properly the original significance of Merleau-Ponty's deference to him. (The unavailability of Fink's *Sixth Cartesian Meditation* was also a factor in this neglect—see above, Preface) The present book, of course, is intended as at least a partial remedy for this problematic interpretive situation.

3 There is an ongoing dispute among scholars as to the proper orthography of Saint Exupéry's surname—specifically, whether it is hyphenated or not. For while he himself did not hyphenate it, formally or informally, until residing in the United States, supposedly to avoid being called "Mr. Exupéry" (Schiff 1994, xi), it has become fairly conventional, even among scholars who are fully aware that this is not its original form, to insert a hyphen. There seems to be no good reason for this choice, and so, I will side with those who eschew the hyphen. In any quotation that refers to Saint Exupéry by name, however, I will retain the spelling used by the author in question.

4 On the early part of Saint Exupéry's life, see Schiff (1994, 31–118).

5 The details of his disappearance remained a mystery until relatively recently. Wreckage from his Lockheed P-38 Lightening was located in 2000 over a large area under the Mediterranean near Marseille. Some of this was recovered in 2003 and, in April 2004, it was officially confirmed to have come from Saint Exupéry's plane. The reasons for his fatal crash, however, remain unclear. Twice—in 1981 and then more recently in 2008—former Luftwaffe pilots have claimed that they had shot down a P-38 in that area on that date (31 July 1944). But these claims have proven unverifiable and are open to much doubt. It is perhaps just as likely that Saint Exupéry simply lost consciousness or that his aircraft suffered a mechanical failure of some kind. In addition, virtually since the time of his death, the possibility that he committed suicide has hovered in the background. On some of the aspects of this mystery, see Pradel and Vanrell (2008).

6 That is, with minimal instrumentation which, depending on the weather conditions, was often of little use anyway. To fly safely, experienced pilots relied heavily on the actual "feel" of the airplane as transmitted largely through the seat.

7 Mermoz fatally crashed in 1936, Guillaumet was shot down in 1940. To this day, they continue to arouse considerable interest—recent biographies include Chadeau (2000) and Migeo (1999), respectively. See also note 17.

8 "Le bonheur de l'homme n'est pas dans la liberté, mais dans l'acceptation d'un devoir" (Saint Exupéry 1931, 11). Cf. Merleau-Ponty's citation of this line in "Faith and Good Faith" (SNS 317/178).

9 In this, Saint Exupéry's work differed from that of other *engagé* writers from the 1930s with which it is often compared, as it structured his understanding of human action at once as both collective and constructive (cf. Ouellet 1971, 195; Losic 1965, 27). For example, it contrasted with Hemingway's usual portrayal of action in individualistic terms (see Smetana 1965, 77–129, *passim*; DeRamus 1990, 37ff). At the same time, it also differed from Malraux's work, where action tended toward adventure and rebellion (see Simon 1950, 127ff).

10 SV 179, originally in *Paris-Soir* (4 October 1938). Cf. SV 173: "the German finds in Hitler the opportunity to care intensely and to offer himself completely, because everything seems larger than life. *We must understand that the power of any movement rests on the man whom it liberates* [délivre]" (italics added). While Saint Exupéry thought the attractiveness of National Socialism lay in its offering a *prima facie* way out of the spiritual crisis of the time, he did also think that it exacerbated the problem. "When the Nazi respects only what resembles him, he respects nothing but himself. He rejects the creative contradictions, ruins all hope for ascent, and for the next thousand years replaces man with the robot of the termite mound" (EG 341).

11 "Do not try to explain to a Mermoz who is plunging toward . . . the Andes with victory in his heart that he's mistaken, that no letter – a merchant's perhaps – is worth risking his life for. Mermoz will laugh at you. *Truth is the man that is born in him as he passes over the Andes*" (SV 173, italics added).

12 SV 140, originally in *Paris-Soir* (3 July 1937).

13 Cf. McKeon (1974, 1087), who argues that Saint Exupéry gradually attenuated the élite character of the pilot as his writing developed, such that by *Pilote de guerre*, "the pilot, in spite of the plot, is present only as an intermediary to plead the cause of mankind."

14 The meharist whom Saint Exupéry had in mind was presumably a certain unnamed French officer who had been in charge of a colonial outpost in southern Morocco during the Rif War, and who, on the eve of being attacked by them, honorably repaid ammunition owed to the local Berber forces for once having come to their rescue. The idea is that even in waging war against one another, "we are all march toward the same promised lands" (SV 170).

15 Exactly what this "spiritual breath" amounts to for Saint Exupéry is not altogether clear; however, it is linked to freedom, which he appropriately described as being "like a favorable wind" (PG 227f).

16 Saint Exupéry made similar analogies involving "the call of the wild" as experienced by eels (SV 139f) and gazelles (TH 195f).

17 This episode was, incidentally, the basis for Jean-Jacques Annaud's 1995 movie *Wings of Courage (Guillaumet, les ailes du courage)*, which *cinéastes* know as the first dramatic feature to be shot in IMAX 3D.

18　For example, Guillaumet was concerned that in the absence of his corpse, his wife would be forced to wait several years before being able to collect his life insurance.

19　Sartre (1984, 54f): "I am reading *Terre des hommes* with a certain emotion. Yet I do not like the style very much: somewhat vatic, and in the Barrès, Montherlant tradition. . . . And above all," referring to the passage about Guillaumet, "I don't like that new humanism" (27 November 1939).

20　Nizan (1971, 308); originally in *Ce Soir* (30 March 1939).

21　Beauvoir (1992, 175, 190), letters dated 20 November 1939 and 1 December 1939, respectively. Sartre (1992, 370) did actually admit that it made him "feel homesick" (28 November 1939).

22　The "geography lesson" Saint Exupéry received from Guillaumet at the start of *Terre des hommes* (TH 16f) may be echoed in Merleau-Ponty's observation that geography is "abstract, signitive, and derivative . . . in relation to the countryside in which we have learned beforehand what a forest, a prairie, or a river is" (PhP iii). For a discussion of some of the possible social implications of this sort of aerial perspective, in particular in terms of the influence that Saint Exupéry had on the architect and urban planner Le Corbusier (Charles-Édouard Jeanneret), see Morshed (2002) and Amad (2012).

23　Marshal Henri Philippe Pétain (1856–1951), a World War I hero, was Head of State of Vichy France from 1940 to 1944; he was convicted and sentenced to death for treason, which was commuted to life imprisonment by Charles de Gaulle.

24　In a posthumously published letter, Saint Exupéry wrote: "France needs a common denominator that would enable it to renew its genuine qualities and diverse theories around a transcendental image"—also adding that "one can scarcely formulate this problem without posing the conceptual distinction between Intelligence and Spirit" (*Le Monde*, 29 July 1950, cited in Losic 1965, 86).

25　For example, in "The Fetish of Duty," a review of *Vol de nuit*, Clifton Fadiman had written: "This is no mere story of adventure – would that it were! – but a dangerous book. It is dangerous because it celebrates a pernicious idea by disguising it as a romantic emotion. . . . Saint Exupéry's admittedly eloquent deification of mere will and energy leads straight to Von Treischke and the megalomania of Il Duce" (Fadiman 1932, 215f; cf. Fay 1947, 93). But in "Beyond Defeat," a review of *Pilote de guerre*, Fadiman described Saint Exupéry's book, perhaps somewhat begrudgingly, as of unquestionable value, "a truly noble attempt to think out his war experiences as a philosopher would." It was like Hemingway's *For Whom the Bell Tolls*, but subtler and more anguished. *Pilote de guerre* was "an important work composed at a pitch of feeling to which, among those who have written about the war, few have attained." Fadiman claimed all this despite thinking that *Pilote de guerre* tended to be "lofty" and "extravagant," ultimately sermonistic and "even hysterical at times." For, in a sense, its lofty extravagance captured the conscience of the struggle against fascism (Fadiman 1942, 67f).

26　To some extent, this may well have been due to the fact that, with the landing of American troops in North Africa, Vichy had been dissolved shortly before, thus in effect obviating a key axis of factional disagreement.

27　Shortly after the defeat, Saint Exupéry had been unknowingly named a member of the National Council, an assembly of notables in Vichy. He vigorously repudiated this, but the issue continued to dog him (see Schiff 1994, 350).

28　"D'abord la France" ["An Open Letter to Frenchmen Everywhere"]. Various versions of this document exist. It was read as a radio appeal by Saint Exupéry at the end of November 1942; an English translation was published in the *New York Times Magazine* (29 November 1942), and in French in *Le Canada* (30 November 1942), which was reprinted in newspapers across North Africa. For a critical version, see EG 264–70.

29 The narrative actually combines that sortie (23 May 1940) with another (uneventful) one from 6 June 1940 (see EG 109 n1).

30 For example, Colin Smith (1980, 261) takes the liberty of assuming the existence of a Saint Exupéry "who is the author of *Pilote de guerre* minus the tiresomely didactic conclusion."

31 There are unexpected but important affinities between this view and Marcel Mauss' ethnological work on "potlatch," which showed that the social and economic life of certain human cultures was based on the preeminence of antiutilitarian sumptuary value over exchange value (see Mauss 2000). In fact, Saint Exupéry's notion of gift may be closer to Georges Bataille's more radical notion of "expenditure" [*dépense*] (Bataille 1933), which also drew on Mauss (see Bataille 1988, 63–77).

32 "Even pure destruction of wealth does not signify that complete detachment that one might believe to be found in it. Even these acts of greatness are not without egoism" (Mauss 2000, 74).

33 "Il n'est qu'un luxe véritable, et c'est celui des relations humaines" (TH 40). Note that Albert Camus all but quoted this in *Le mythe de Sisyphe*: "il n'y a qu'un seul luxe . . . et c'est celui des relations humaines" (1942, 120).

Chapter 2

1 François died on 10 July 1917. Interestingly, Saint Exupéry wrongly claimed that he was 15 at the time; rather, he was 17, while it was François who was 15.

2 Given that copies of the book—in either its original or clandestine forms—were somewhat scarce, and that it was not republished until 1947, it could be that some readers of *Phenomenology of Perception* shortly after its publication may have lacked immediate access to Saint Exupéry's text. But even if this is true, it is inconsequential. For surely it did not apply to *all* readers. And the relevant window for making the sort of observation in question was by no means closed by 1947.

3 There are some minor differences in punctuation between Merleau-Ponty's citation and the Gallimard text.

4 In addition to some minor differences in punctuation between Merleau-Ponty's citation and the Gallimard text, Saint Exupéry had written "conceive" [*conçois*] rather than "see" [*vois*].

5 It has been suggested that these references were added late, at the proofreading stage, given that "nothing in the body of the text directly mentions Saint Exupéry" (Saint Aubert 2004, 115 n2). But this is irrelevant. For even if it is true, it does not imply that the references in question are therefore somehow of lesser interest or philosophical significance. And as we shall see, when Merleau-Ponty's discussion is properly unpacked in terms of his claim that human history forms an existential totality, and that this claim alone is what validates methodologically taking a holistic approach to human *être-au-monde*, it becomes clear that the actual references to Saint Exupéry are in any case inessential to Merleau-Ponty's discussion. What

these references *do* do, though, is signal very clearly that and how this discussion is connected directly to climax of the book.

6 To this might be added the somewhat ironic fact that one of the earliest detailed discussions of Merleau-Ponty's political thought was a polemical critique from none other than Lukács himself (see Lukács 1948, 198–252).

7 In an address entitled "Fight Against 'Ultra-Lefts' and Theoretic Revisionism," in which he also named Antonio Graziadei and Karl Korsch, Zinoviev declared: "If we got a few more of these professors spinning out their Marxist theories, we shall be lost. We cannot tolerate such theoretical revisionism of this kind in our Communist International" (cited in Lukács 1967, 720f). The full text of this part of Zinoviev's speech is contained in Lukács (1967, 719–26).

8 The discovery of an unpublished manuscript (entitled *Chvostismus und Dialektik*) dating from 1925 or 1926, first published in 1996 and in English translation in 2000 (Lukács 2000), shows that at least privately, Lukács did not immediately capitulate at all to his Party critics. On this document, see Rees (2000); cf. Löwy (2011). I will draw from this text in discussing *History and Class Consciousness* below (Chapter 3).

9 In their introduction to a 1934 collection of texts and excerpts from Marx's philosophical and economic writings (Marx 1934), for example, Lefebvre and Guterman expressed views that had some substantial affinities with Lukács, even effectively affirming, with regard to the progressive development of Marxism, "method as the standard of orthodoxy" (Burkhard 2000, 208f; cf. Guterman and Lefebvre 1934, 29). The theme of their next joint work (Guterman and Lefebvre 1936), "la conscience mystifiée," has clear resonances with Lukács' critique of reification and "reified consciousness." And Lefebvre's very widely read introductory text, *Le matérialisme dialectique* (Lefebvre 1949), first published in 1940, was based explicitly on a notion of "concrete totality" (e.g. 77f, 120) and was oriented toward the idea of "the total man" [*l'homme total*] understood as "the subject and object of [historical] becoming" and the "disalienated' [« *désaliéné* »] man" (147). These could suggest a concealed influence on the part of Lukács, but it is also the case that the thought of Lefebvre and of others in the *Philosophies* circle were heavily influenced by Marx's *1844 Manuscripts*, a work with which *History and Class Consciousness* had a remarkable thematic overlap on a number of key points, for example, the Hegelian framework and the central role of alienation. This overlap was remarkable inasmuch as this early work from Marx was first published in 1932 and thus was not available to Lukács in the early 1920s. The 1934 volume of writings from Marx included translated excerpts from the *Manuscripts* (the philosophy portion of the book was edited by Nizan), although Guterman had already translated a portion of the Third Manuscript in 1928 (Burkhard 2000, 107), or possibly 1927 (Rabil 1967, 275 n110), which was published on the pages of the short-lived journal *Revue marxiste* in 1929 (Burkhard 2000, 106f). Prior to the 1930s, the only works from Marx that were available in French were *Capital* and *The Communist Manifesto*, along with some of his historical writings (see Zévaès 1947, 185–90). Jules Molitor edited and translated a multivolume edition of Marx's philosophical works (Marx 1927–37), but the *1844 Manuscripts* did not appear until 1937.

10 But we might note that he did intend to offer a course in early 1947 on Marxist and non-Marxist philosophy, and that he intended "to devote several lectures to Lukács"—the problem at the time was that the only text he had available was *History and Class Consciousness*. (Letter to György Szekeres, Lukács' literary

agent in Paris, n.d. (summer 1946), Magyar Tudományos Akadémia Filozófiai intézet, Lukács Archivum és Könyvtár (Philosophical Institute of the Hungarian Academy of Sciences, Lukács Archive and Library, Budapest), cited in Kadarkay (1991, 394f)).

11 Cf. Sartre's well-known claim to the effect that Merleau-Ponty was closest to Marxism in the years *before* World War II (Sartre 1964, 204). In general, Sartre's recollections about Merleau-Ponty may not be wholly reliable, and we should be cautious about putting too much stock in this claim, especially the implication that Merleau-Ponty's attachment to Marxism was *less* in the postwar than in the prewar period. But insofar as it suggests that Merleau-Ponty's interest in Marxism began earlier than is often thought, it is consistent with a number of suggestions that have been made over the years by commentators interested in Merleau-Ponty's political thought.

12 Cf. Whiteside (1988, 34f) where, with regard to Merleau-Ponty's statement, made in a 1959 interview, that he read Lenin, Marx, and Trotsky during the war, Whiteside claims that "[t]his is the only time [Merleau-Ponty] ever identified, however vaguely, the timing and sources of his political education" (1988, 35 n82). The point is not that this recollection on the part of Merleau-Ponty is accurate or even precisely decipherable, but rather that he was as a matter of fact quite reticent about discussing when and how he acquired his interest in and knowledge of Marxism.

13 This refers to Alexandre Kojève's famous lectures on Hegel's *Phänomenologie des Geistes* at the École Practique des Hautes Études, which were held between 1933 and 1939. There has always been some confusion as to who actually attended Kojève's lectures, and when they did so. According to the official records at the École Practique, Merleau-Ponty only attended in the 1937–38 academic year (Roth 1988, 225ff). Geraets suggested that his attendance began in 1935 when he returned to Paris (1971, 26). In a letter (30 March 1967) to George L. Kline, with regard to the latter's "The Existentialist Rediscovery of Hegel and Marx" (Kline 1967), Kojève stated that while neither Sartre nor Hyppolite had attended, contrary to what Kline had written, Merleau-Ponty had indeed "attended regularly" (Lee and Mandelbaum 1967, vii). As there was no strict requirement to officially register at the École Practique, it is entirely possible, and, I believe, probable, that Merleau-Ponty attended on a regular basis for three years (i.e., from 1935–36 to 1937–38).

14 Cooper needed this conclusion in order to buttress his claim that Merleau-Ponty's postwar political views, in particular as presented in *Humanism and Terror*, "float in a Hegelian ether" of Kojèvean extraction, and that they essentially express a "theoretical commitment to humanism learned at the feet [!] of Kojève" (Cooper 1979, 25; cf. 16f, 72f, 44). These claims on the part of Cooper have contributed significantly to legitimizing the widespread misconception among commentators that Merleau-Ponty was strongly and positively influenced by Kojève. Cooper's arguments cannot be refuted in detail here. But the key point was stated above (Preface, note 41), to wit, that in *The Structure of Behavior*, Merleau-Ponty precisely shows the human impossibility of the Kojèvean "Sage." In his sole explicit written reference to Kojève, Merleau-Ponty confirmed this in saying that his account of the end of history "is an idealization of death and could not possibly convey Hegel's core thought" (AD 277/206). Numerous other implicit claims make the same point. As to why Merleau-Ponty attended Kojève's lectures regularly, part of the answer may lie in the assiduous presence of Gaston Fessard, a Jesuit scholar who was no

less knowledgeable about Hegel than Kojève, but who countered the latter's reading with his own neo-Thomist interpretation. The contrast between the views presented respectively by Kojève and Fessard would have been quite productive for Merleau-Ponty in terms of working out his own position (see above).

15   It is worthwhile to note that Herbert Spiegelberg's claim (1984, 548) that there were "close personal contacts" between Merleau-Ponty and Kojève is essentially groundless. Spiegelberg had based this claim solely on that made by Rudolf Meyer to the effect that there were "close relations" [*enge Beziehungen*] between the two men (Meyer 1955, 138; cf. Spiegelberg 1984, 582 n20). But Meyer himself had based this on an earlier article by Iring Fetscher (1954). Spiegelberg evidently did not read this. Had he done so, he would have seen that no claim of "personal contacts" is made, beyond reporting Merleau-Ponty's attendance at Kojève's lectures (Meyer referred to p. 183 in Fetscher's article, but misidentified it as p. 181). But the point is that even this seemingly mundane disclosure broke new ground at the time. For it had not been previously known that Merleau-Ponty had attended Kojève's lectures. That this was the case is borne out by earlier reviews, which make no mention of it, even while jointly discussing the postwar works of Merleau-Ponty and Kojève. See, for example, Acton (1949), and Duhrssen (1953). Thus, in a footnote (138 n19), Meyer wrote: "Es ist das große Verdienst Fetschers, auf die engen Beziehungen zwischen Kojève und Merleau-Ponty erstmals hingewiesen zu haben" [It is Fetscher's great merit to have first pointed out the close relations between Kojève and Merleau-Ponty]. This is what Spiegelberg must have read. But because he took Merleau-Ponty's attendance at Kojève's lectures for granted, he inadvertently misinterpreted Meyer's statement as implying something much more significant. This does not mean that Merleau-Ponty and Kojève had no interpersonal relationship whatsoever. Obviously, they knew one another, and apparently Kojève even thought that Merleau-Ponty had Apollonian good looks (Rosen 1987, 106). But there is no evidence of anything in this regard that could serve legitimately to narrow the patent philosophical gap that separates the two.

16   On the idea of "second nature" [*zweite Natur*] in Lukács, cf. HCC (33f, 97, 142, 247/19, 86, 128, 240).

17   With regard to *The Structure of Behavior*, which was published on 30 November 1942 (Noble 2011, 73), one cannot pass over reference to Pierre Naville's robust defense of Watsonian behaviorism (Naville 1942). Although in theoretical terms quite opposed, one cannot but wonder whether the publication of Naville's text on 10 July 1942, under the title *La psychologie, science de la comportement*, accelerated in any way the publication—or even affected the title, which, until at least 1941 was *Conscience et comportement* (Noble 2011, 72)—of Merleau-Ponty's *thèse complémentaire*.

18   That is, the case of Alfred Dreyfus, a Jewish officer in the French Army who was wrongly convicted of espionage for Germany in 1894. After a long series of retrials, amid considerable anti-Semitic hysteria and polarizing views, Dreyfus was acquitted in 1906. Beginning in effect with Émile Zola's famous "*J'accuse . . . !*" in 1898, the Dreyfus Affair was "the epic genesis" of the self-consciousness of French intellectuals as a social category (Winock 1975, 9; cf. Schalk 1979, 5–17; Drake 2005, 8–34).

19   There is a virtual consensus that Sartre's recollection (1964, 205) suggesting that Merleau-Ponty had lost his faith by 1928 is simply wrong. It is self-evident that he maintained more than just a nominally Christian outlook well into the

1930s. According to Maurice de Gandillac, though, Merleau-Ponty had lost his faith temporarily sometime before 1926, but found it again when he visited the Benedictine abbey at Solesnes with de Gandillac "around 1926" (see Whiteside 1988, 28 n53).

20   There has been some dispute over the identity of the "young Catholic" to whom Merleau-Ponty refers in the first paragraph of "Foi et bonne foi" (SNS 305f/172), first published in *Les temps modernes* in February 1946. Although Kwant (1963, 139) suggested that this referred to Pierre Hervé, it is all but certain that Merleau-Ponty was simply referring to himself (although what he says may also happen to apply to Hervé as well). This would have some implications regarding the timing of his intellectual development. For the suppression in Austria to which he refers occurred in February 1934, and the journal he refers to is, no doubt, *Esprit*, founded by Emmanuel Mounier in 1932, which protested the Austrian government's actions (March 1934). Merleau-Ponty was interested in *Esprit* since its founding (Le Baut 2009, 136), but his association with it became much closer in 1934—perhaps motivated by the negative experience he described in this passage. The other religious order to which he refers is without a doubt the Dominicans, and the priest ("the Father") was Jean-Augustin Maydieu—Le Baut has claimed that Maydieu wrote to Merleau-Ponty in March 1946, wondering about the identity of the figure, and that in replying, Merleau-Ponty confirmed that it was indeed Maydieu (Le Baut 2009, 143f). As editor of *La vie intellectuelle*, Maydieu was responsible for soliciting the review articles that Merleau-Ponty published there in 1935 (on Scheler) and 1936 (on Marcel), and who went on to be an important figure in the Resistance (hence the claim: "a bold and generous man, as was seen later"). Of interest here is that for Merleau-Ponty, the movement *à gauche* first occurred *within* the context of social Catholicism, but also that in moving closer to *Esprit* around 1934, Merleau-Ponty was entering the epicentre of the Catholic "discovery" of the young Marx—this would surface on the pages of *La vie intellectuelle*, for example, a few years later (Curtis 1991, 174f)—something which further promoted his leftward movement. It is, however, also noteworthy that while Merleau-Ponty did publish those two reviews on the pages of Maydieu's journal, he did not publish anything in *Esprit*.

21   It may be possible to trace this back to 1932, to Merleau-Ponty's concluding "Discours d'usage" (13 July 1932) to students at the Lycée Beauvais, published in *Bulletin de l'Association amicale des anciens élèves du collège et du lycée de Beauvais* (pp. 20–8). According to Saint Aubert (2005, 61), Merleau-Ponty's speech at least in part echoed Paul Nizan's fiery Marxist polemic against the philosophical establishment, *Les chiens de garde*, especially as personified by Léon Brunschvicg, that dates from the same year. Compare this to Whiteside (1988, 20), who interpreted Merleau-Ponty's speech as expressing a sobering social conservatism that was categorically opposed to any sort of revolutionary change. But these views may be compatible. For while Whiteside thought that Merleau-Ponty expressed some agreement with Brunschvicg concerning the meaning and value of French civilization, he also admitted that the content of Merleau-Ponty's views was in tension with the philosophical education that he had received at the ENS. It thus seems reasonable to speculate that the sort of radicalism that Merleau-Ponty was most worried about had to do with the growing threat of Fascism in Europe, and in Germany in particular, and that he was concerned about the ability of mainstream French academic philosophy at the time to mount an effective defense of the

institutions and, especially, the universal values of liberal French society. In this way, his remarks may have expressed a certain affinity with Benda (1927).

22 The term "militant" derives from the Catholic theological trichotomy between (a) "the Church triumphant," denoting Christians in heaven, (b) "the Church suffering," denoting Christians in purgatory, and (c) "the Church militant," denoting Christians living on Earth, working—or *militating*—to establish the kingdom of God. Concerning the latter, see Merleau-Ponty's review of Scheler, for example, where he wrote that on account of the "substantial connivance of the 'spiritual person' and sensible consciousness. . . . Christianity in all its purity '*militates* against' sin, just as it *militates* to wrest the poor from their misery" (CR 31/99, citing Scheler, italics altered).

23 It is noteworthy that, in comments made in a review of Honnert (1937), Nizan's view of Fessard's argument and of his practical openness to dialogue was convivial and respectful, despite noting the insuperable theoretical irreconcilability of Catholicism and Marxism. For Nizan concurred with Fessard's statement that "the faith or loyalty inscribed in the heart of every man is the fundamental basis and cornerstone of every union" (*L'Humanité*, 3 April 1937; reprinted Nizan (1971, 254–9)). Rather differently, in a review of Fessard's book (1937), along with an earlier one (Fessard 1936), that he wrote in 1937 (but which was unpublished at the time), Kojève was critical of Fessard's effort to rethink Catholic theology on a Hegelian basis, and specifically, of his attempted rapprochement with Marxism, for being too indulgent of these other traditions, suggesting that Fessard's arguments could backfire in the sense of promoting atheism at the expense of Christianity. "In general, it is unwise when fixing something to make use of a tool that was made . . . expressly for its destruction" (in Fessard and Marcel (1985, 510–16); reprinted in Jarczyk and Labarrière (1996, 131–6)).

24 *Le Monde* (6 May 1961); cited in Geraets (1971, 26, italics added).

Chapter 3

1 Engels' *Dialectics of Nature*, an incomplete manuscript written between 1873 and 1883, with some additions around 1885/86, was not published until 1925.

2 And as mentioned earlier, in methodological terms, Merleau-Ponty once effectively identified the Lukácsian idea of "totality" with that of "incarnation" (EE 253).

3 Perhaps the most striking illustration of Merleau-Ponty's interest in Lukács stems from certain comments that he made at the inaugural Rencontres internationales de Genève, held in September 1946, a set of meetings between representative intellectuals originally intended to promote East-West dialogue. But this was not because these comments were wholly positive. Rather, Merleau-Ponty was critical of Lukács' proposal that the "democratic renewal" of Europe required the recovery of the 1941 anti-fascist alliance between Western democracies and the USSR. Although in agreement with Lukács methodologically with regard to totality (which Merleau-Ponty also glossed as "incarnation"), as well as with regard to his Marxist critique of formal democracy, which Merleau-Ponty basically took as a given, Merleau-Ponty claimed—or rather complained as politely as he could—that the conclusion Lukács presented was methodologically inconsistent and hence un-Marxist:

> Having offered a critique of formal democracy in the name of real democracy, I expected [Lukács'] conclusion to elaborate the ["classical"] Marxist solution.

This solution is to push liberalism from formal to real, . . . to realize . . . a concrete universality and a new humanity. . . . But Lukács did not present this solution. After his critique of formal democracy, he concluded that those formal democracies that remain should simply ally themselves . . . as they had done during the war, with the USSR, considered as at least a preliminary version of real democracy. . . . But if the first part of his presentation is correct, then how is this solution possible? If it is true that formal democracy has been withering for a century and has reached the height of its decay, and if it is true that it must be transformed into a real democracy, a proletarian democracy, then how can it be instructed to live on historically, when it has been condemned by history? . . . If Lukács believes that this persistence of formal democracy is possible, . . . and if we take seriously what he said at the end of his presentation, then are we not abandoning the classical Marxist perspective? (EE 253f)

Merleau-Ponty went on at some length and was clearly disappointed with Lukács— for not being the same Lukács who wrote *History and Class Consciousness*. It is not clear just how familiar Merleau-Ponty was with Lukács' biography and intellectual trajectory, although it may be the case that in terms of Lukács' published works, Merleau-Ponty was familiar only with *History and Class Consciousness* (see Chapter 2, note 10). In a letter to Lukács that was probably written after their encounter in Geneva, he wrote: "You should clarify to the French public your position on the Marxist method" (Merleau-Ponty to Lukács, n.d., Magyar Tudományos Akadémia Filozófiai intézet, Lukács Archivum és Könyvtár (Philosophical Institute of the Hungarian Academy of Sciences, Lukács Archive and Library, Budapest), cited in Kadarkay (1991, 394)).

4 And as we shall see, Merleau-Ponty anticipated later claims by Sartre when he wrote that "Marxism is not a philosophy of history; it is *the* philosophy of history" (HT 165/153).

5 In Merleau-Ponty's view, Marxism is not based on a futural projection of any sort, but rather on "the recognition of an impossibility, that of the current world understood as contradiction and decomposition" (HT 136/126). This would imply that alienating repression is ubiquitous in capitalist society inasmuch as this social form is taken as a privileged present, because its "impossible future," its crisis-prone unsustainability, is unrecognized.

6 "Harmony between the individual and history is a postulate of human existence. We cannot live without it. That does not mean that it will be—we can simply say that if it is not realized, then there will be no humanity" (NI 21 [9]).

Chapter 4

1 Given the importance of Scheler for the philosophy of personalism, and Merleau-Ponty's connection to *Esprit*, it is not insignificant that this review appeared in *La vie intellectuelle*.

2 Cf. Goldstein (1940, 229): "Some sacrifices are rightly to be considered an expression of an unusually high development of human nature. But self-sacrifice in itself is not of value. It is of value only if it is important for the actualization of the individual; it is of value only if the rescue of others is of such importance to the individual that his own self-realization demands this sacrifice. This is a border situation similar to one we have already discussed in which voluntary suicide is sometimes the last

way out in the attempt to preserve the personality. One has to be very careful in the evaluation of self-sacrifice, because it is often nothing more than an escape from the difficulties of normal self-actualization."

3 Delivered on 16 February 1946, this lecture was entitled "L'existence dans la '*Phénoménologie*' de Hegel." It is reprinted in Hyppolite (1971, 92–103).

4 SNS 117/68; cf. SC 136/126; PhP 249. In the conclusion to *Being and Nothingness*, Sartre had written that the for-itself "is nothing but the pure nihilation of the in-itself; it is like a hole in being at the heart of Being" (EN 711/617). Cf. Beauvoir (1945, 366f).

5 Merleau-Ponty may have been alluding to the character Katov in Malraux's *La condition humaine*, whose shadow cast on the wall as he proceeds to his execution stands as a sombre reminder to his comrades of one's ineluctable mortal involvement in politics.

6 There may be a productive comparison to be made between Merleau-Ponty's analysis and that of historian Marc Bloch (1946); cf. King (1971, 199).

7 The metaphor of *fulguration*, to which Merleau-Ponty resorted at other key points as well, involves a sense of *blindness* that is quite significant with regard to the limits of his existential phenomenology. It is thus of central importance to his project, yet it is unfortunately absent from Gill's study (1991) of metaphor in Merleau-Ponty's work.

8 This is not to imply that Merleau-Ponty had any sympathy for or even fascination with fascism. Rather, it points to the larger cultural fact that there were more than merely superficial similarities between the holism of Gestalt theory and that of the propaganda of National Socialism (see Ash 1995, 342–61; Harrington 1995; 1996, 175–206). As one Nazi supporter put it: "Wholeness and Gestalt, the ruling ideas of the German movement, have become central concepts of German psychology. . . . Present-day German psychology and the National Socialistic worldview are both oriented towards the same goal: the vanquishing of atomistic and mechanistic forms of thought: vanquishing through organic thinking, in the structure of völkisch life here, in the researching of psychological reality there" (Sander 1937, cited in Harrington 1996, 178).

9 Referenced in Sartre (1970, 110f). The document (five large typewritten pages) was originally thought to have been the work of Sartre. In Sartre (1970), however, the editors—Michel Contat and Michel Rybalka—made it clear that after the book had gone to press, new information and discussions with Sartre and Desanti convinced them that the text was, in fact, drafted by Merleau-Ponty. Although this text is seldom cited, its attribution to Merleau-Ponty is widely accepted (cf. Le Baut 2009, 142). It should be noted, though, that in a bibliographic discussion subsequent to the publication of Sartre (1970), Whiteside disputed the attribution to Merleau-Ponty, claiming that "[i]nquiries in Paris with the persons who had originally made [it] revealed no direct evidence to this effect" (1983, 196). What exactly would count as "direct evidence" with regard the authorship of an anonymous piece of writing is unclear. But as recently as 2012, Michel Rybalka reaffirmed that it was Sartre himself who indicated to Rybalka and Contat that Merleau-Ponty had written the document (personal correspondence with the author). It may be that Whiteside's doubts, which probably continue to have some currency, and his desire for "direct evidence," stem as much from the following additional concern that he expressed: "significant stylistic differences between this document and Merleau-Ponty's writings of this period argue against the hypothesis that he is its author." Regarding a text composed in 1941, it is unclear just what Whiteside could have

meant by "this period," and to which other of Merleau-Ponty's writings he could have been referring. If it is simply a claim that the sort of totalistic socialism that is advocated in the document is without precedent in Merleau-Ponty's published writing up to that point, then that would be a very weak claim. Given what we have discussed concerning the timing of Merleau-Ponty's attachment to Marxism, as well as the holism that characterized his prewar thought along with much of the relevant context, it would not be difficult at all to imagine that Merleau-Ponty was the author in question.

10 It was apparently slightly revised in 1944 before being sent to representatives of the French provisional government in Algiers. Owing to the nature of resistance activities, all of this was likely done without the original author's knowledge.

11 Concerning Merleau-Ponty's relation to other existentialists, Whiteside put it well: "At the heart of [Merleau-Ponty's] project is the belief that his theory is superior particularly in accounting for the political dimension of existence. He thinks that a wide range of 'existentializing' thinkers, including Marcel, Aron, Sartre, Beauvoir, Mounier, Malraux, Scheler, and Heidegger, have gone wrong when it comes to thinking politically. They misformulate their own existential insights in ways that either deprive their theories of political relevance or lead to tragically mistaken political commitments. He then modulates and reformulates their positions to explain how a theory can be both existential and political" (Whiteside 1988, 37).

12 In terms of the subheadings from the original table of contents, this discussion would thus span three successive sections, those entitled "Valuation of historical situations: class prior to class consciousness," "Intellectual project and existential project," and "The For-Itself and the For-Others, intersubjectivity."

13 I use this term—*generative*—to signal that Merleau-Ponty's idea of productivity may be instructively compared with Husserl's notion of "generativity," which Merleau-Ponty noted in Husserl's unpublished work (PhP 489), but which he did not adopt. Steinbock (1995; see also 1998) has developed this theme extensively and on the basis of much more unpublished material than that which was available to Merleau-Ponty.

14 Such would be how Merleau-Ponty's view differed from Kojève's claim that "man is not simply *mortal*; he is *death* incarnate; he *is* his own death," such that human existence is essentially "a *suicide*" (Kojève 1947, 569).

15 Lanzoni (2004) reports that archival records call into question quite forcefully Binswanger's view of just how much trust there really was on the part of the patient in this relationship.

16 In choosing the term "secrete," Merleau-Ponty no doubt had in mind to offset Sartre's rather different claim that "freedom is the human being putting his past out of play by secreting his own nothingness" [*la liberté, c'est l'être humain mettant son passé hors de jeu en sécrétant son propre néant*] (EN 65/28).

Chapter 5

1 Note that the bibliographic information given at the end of the English translation of *Sense and Non-Sense*, which claims that "Man, the Hero" was "especially written" for this volume, is false. Aside from the title, it was reprinted from <u>action</u> unchanged.

2 Ponge had become the literary editor of *action* after the Liberation, but resigned
   later in 1946, and left the Party in the following year on account of its dogmatism,
   in particular with respect to aesthetic issues. Interestingly enough, Ponge's
   "Notes premières de l'Homme," a series of notes from 1943 to 1944 for a projected
   (but never completed) work on "Man," was published in the inaugural issue of
   Les temps modernes (pp. 67–75), immediately after Merleau-Ponty's "La Guerre
   a eu lieu."

3 The following is the text and translation of the editorial preface that preceded
   Merleau-Ponty's essay (the two notes have been added):

> Maurice Merleau-Ponty est, avec Jean-Paul Sartre et Simone de Beauvoir, l'un
> des principaux représentants en France de la philosophie existentielle. Il a
> voulu remettre à *action* l'article qu'on va lire, dans lequel—selon les termes de
> sa lettre d'envoi—"l'attitude existentialiste (comme phénomène général de notre
> temps, et non comme attitude d'école) se trouve définie positivement et sur des
> exemples."
>
> Nous apprécions cette marque d'estime, et comme nous n'avons pas l'habitude
> de traiter dédaigneusement les problèmes qui intéressent authentiquement bon
> nombre de jeunes Français certainement sincères et certainement estimables,
> nous le publions aussitôt.
>
> Mais nous devons dire tout aussitôt que nous ne pouvons souscrire à
> ses conclusions. Sans vouloir longuement préluder aux réponses qu'une
> telle prise de position provoquera sans doute, affirmons déjà que beaucoup
> parmi nos lecteurs apercevront immédiatement et jugeront inadmissible le
> procédé (rhétorique) qui consiste à déclarer sans autre preuve—seulement
> parce que plusieurs héros de romans récents sont ainsi faits—que le "héros
> contemporain" "vit dans un tel chaos . . . qu'il ne peut apercevoir clairement
> ses devoirs et ses tâches . . . ni . . . conserver la certitude d'accomplir ce que
> l'histoire veut."[†]
>
> Gabriel Péri,[‡] à ce titre, et tous les héros marxistes ne devront-ils plus être
> comptés parmi les héros contemporains, eux qui n'ont pas cessé d'y voir clair,
> plus clair que jamais, dans le prétendu chaos de l'histoire contemporaine—et
> qui ont pris parti, ont combattu, ont défié la mort avec la même allégresse,
> sachant qu'ils agissaient dans le sens de l'histoire . . . et mouraient donc
> (puisqu'il fallait mourir) en entonnant les chants de l'espérance, mouraient
> certains, mouraient victorieux.

[†] As in the passage above signaled by Ponge, this text is presumably taken from
    Merleau-Ponty's letter, for it does not appear as such in the essay itself.

[‡] Gabriel Péri was a journalist and the Communist Deputy of Argenteuil in the French
    National Assembly from 1932. In virtue of his strong antifascist convictions, Péri
    was a leading figure in the PCF, especially among its militants. In 1941, he was
    denounced, arrested, and ultimately shot by the Nazis. In part due to Aragon's poetic
    tribute in "La légende de Gabriel Péri," at the time of the Liberation, he became a
    mythological figure of resistance and martyrdom.

> Along with Jean-Paul Sartre and Simone de Beauvoir, Maurice Merleau-Ponty
> is one of the principal representatives of existential philosophy in France.
> He wanted the following article—in which, according to his cover letter, "the

existential attitude (as a general phenomenon of our time, and not as a school of thought) is defined positively and on the basis of examples"—to be published in *action*.

We value this sign of respect. And as we are not in the habit of treating with contempt the problems that genuinely concern large numbers of young French people whose honesty and worthiness are not in doubt, we are publishing it immediately.

But we must also make clear that we cannot subscribe to its conclusions. Without wanting to give a lengthy anticipation of the responses that such a position will no doubt provoke, let us just assert that many of our readers will immediately notice and judge as unacceptable the (rhetorical) device that consists in declaring without further proof—solely because many heroes of recent novels are constructed in this way—that the "contemporary hero" "lives in such a chaos . . . that he cannot see his duties and his tasks clearly . . . nor . . . maintain the certainty of carrying out what history wants."

On this account, Gabriel Péri, and all Marxist heroes must no longer be counted as contemporary heroes—for they did not cease to see clearly, more clearly than ever, in the alleged chaos of contemporary history. They took a stand, they fought, and they braved death with the same elation, knowing that they were acting on the side of history. . . . They thus died (for they had to die) singing the songs of hope; they died sure of themselves, they died victorious.

4 Owing to its originality and nonconformist stance, "the influence of *action*, which militated very specifically for working class unity, [was] quite considerable for a long time" (Bellanger et al. 1975, 293).

5 Merleau-Ponty's essay "Foi et bonne Foi," also published in February 1946, refers positively to the relative openness and honesty of Hervé's Marxism (SNS 318–21/179ff), although he had criticized Hervé the previous month in his editorial article "Pour la vérité" (SNS 274f/155).

6 Without directly citing it, Merleau-Ponty paraphrases and quotes from the introduction to Hegel's *Lectures on the Philosophy of History* (see Hegel 1956, 30f; cf. NI 130 [64]).

7 Quoting Hegel: "die nächste Gattung, die im Innern bereits vorhanden war." In Sibree's rendering: "the species next in order . . . which was already formed in the womb of time" (Hegel 1956, 30).

8 This is expressed in "Letter to X, Lecturer on Hegel . . .," an incomplete letter (6 December 1937) addressed to Kojève (in Hollier 1988, 89–93). A revised version was published as an appendix in Bataille (1944).

9 Although Merleau-Ponty does not name Aron in his published work at this time, he did develop a direct critique of him, as Whiteside (1986) has convincingly shown.

10 The close triadic relation between the views of history held, respectively, by Kojève, Fessard, and Aron, along with Merleau-Ponty's relation to them, merits and would repay closer attention.

11 Cf. Bataille (1976, 651n): "A sovereignty which serves no purpose is at once the coming apart and the completion of the human being."

12 Although he does not reference this, Merleau-Ponty may have been referring to Saint Exupéry (TH 176): "It is not danger that I love. I know what I love. It is life." This line was also referenced by Gusdorf (1948, 247).

13 The classic article is Gelb and Goldstein (1918). However, it is noteworthy that beginning shortly after 1945, when *Phenomenology of Perception* was published, serious doubts began to be cast on this case. On the basis of a reexamination of the patient, the diagnosis of visual agnosia was questioned (Bay et al. 1949; cf. Jung 1949). And in general, it has been contended that Goldstein and Gelb exaggerated or simply misread the symptomatology of the case (Bay 1953; Tauber 1966). Goldenberg (2003) has claimed that in their eagerness to substantiate their theories, Goldstein and Gelb significantly embellished their findings, and that Schn. "learned how to be an ideal case study." Cf. Marotta and Behrmann (2004). This is significant in that unlike other philosophical interpreters of the case—Gurwitsch and Cassirer, for example—Merleau-Ponty never had direct contact with Schn.

14 For example, *Lucifer* was the original working title of Sartre's *Les chemins de la liberté* (see Sartre 1971, 27).

15 Reprinted as the conclusion to *Le mythe et l'homme* (Roger Caillois 1938), under the title "Pour une fonction unitaire de l'esprit."

16 Interview with Gilles Lapouge, June 1970 (cited in ES 142).

17 In his 1935 review of Scheler's *Ressentiment*, Merleau-Ponty wrote that Promethean humanism is based in hatred, "the hatred of the wisdom and goodness of God. . . . Nature immediately loses in value since man has worth only inasmuch as he separates himself from nature and distances himself from it" (CR 27f; cf. EP 36/43).

18 This was found in the first issue of *Cahiers d'action*, which was launched in part to offset the rising influence of existentialism.

19 This is significant with respect to Merleau-Ponty's rejection of Kojève's views concerning the end of History. Kojève had maintained that while the end of history marks the disappearance of humanity *qua* "subject *opposed* to the object," humans would remain alive in a time of peace and consensus, filled with "art, love, play . . . in short, everything that makes Man *happy*," and he portrayed this as equivalent to the "realm of freedom" envisioned by Marx at the end of the third volume of *Capital* (Kojève 1947, 434f n1). Following Marx, Merleau-Ponty held the contrary view that "human" history would *begin* with communism, that is, would follow the end of diremptive *pre*-history, and—lest it amount to a reversion to animality—would be a dynamic and open process admitting of no final synthesis. It is noteworthy that the only addition Kojève made to the second edition of the published form of his lectures on Hegel was to concede this point, which was clearly directed against him (he wrote that he rethought this around 1948). Here, we read that "after the end of History, men would construct their edifices and works of art as birds build their nests and spiders spin their webs, would perform musical concerts after the fashion of frogs and cicadas, would play like young animals, and would indulge in love like adult beasts" (1947, 436f n).

20 It is not a coincidence that the discussion of embodiment that first alludes to Saint Exupéry in *Phenomenology of Perception* occurs in the first chapter of Part I, "The Body as Object and Mechanistic Physiology," in the context of Merleau-Ponty's critique of mechanism.

21 To be sure, this had certain limited affinities with fascist thinking. But it is hardly the case that the discourses of holism and authenticity were intrinsically compromised in this way. And it should not be overlooked that such affinities were fairly widespread among those critical of bourgeois liberalism in France, applying as much to surrealism, sacred sociology, and Christian personalism as movements seeking spiritual-social renewal.

22 This is entirely consistent with Binswanger's *Daseinsanalyse*, which is centered on an account of "encounter" [*Begegnung*] as based in "love" [*Liebe*]. Moreover, it could be productively related to recent research that has brought to light the significance of the notion of "love" in Husserl's work, including Buckley (1996) and Melle (2002).

23 See also Major (1968, 63–105, especially 92), where Saint Exupéry's notion of "Esprit" is explicitly linked to Merleau-Ponty's invocation of the idea of "une raison élargie."

24 Robert Brasillach was a literary fascist who, on account of his editorship (until 1943) of the rabidly anti-Semitic and pro-Nazi Parisian newspaper *Je suis partout*, was tried for collaboration after the war (a one-day trial on 19 January 1945 that Merleau-Ponty, among others, attended) and executed on 6 February 1945. For a recent examination of his case, see Kaplan (2000).

25 This is not to align Merleau-Ponty nor Saint Exupéry with the nefarious Nazi rhetoric, especially of Karl Kötschau, of "machine-people" [*Maschinenmenschen*], those who could not survive without medical technology and outside institutions. But the broad affinities are noteworthy. For example, this statement from Kötschau: "Our time does not need externally controlled machine-people, but rather self-controlled people who have developed their own powers schooled in battles with a healthy Nature. *Our time needs the heroic man, the man who is up to the challenges of the time, and who does not have to rely on the doubtful protection of an all too artificial environment*" (cited in Harrington 1996, 186).

26 "C'est l'expérience . . . muette encore qu'il s'agit d'amener à l' expression pure de son propre sens" (PhP x). In the Peiffer and Levinas translation, the complete sentence reads: "Le début, c'est l'expérience pure et, pour ainsi dire muette encore, qu'il s'agit d'amener à l'expression pure de son propre sens" (Husserl 1931, 33; cf. PhP 253f). In Cairns' translation of the Husserliana edition: "Its beginning is the pure—and, so to speak, still dumb—psychological experience, which must now be made to utter its own sense with no adulteration" (Husserl 1960, 38f).

27 In his dispatches from the USSR, he did not use the word "'communism,'" and likewise with the word "'fascism'" in writing about Spain.

28 This is from Saint Exupéry's "Lettre au Général 'X'" [René Chambe] (July 1943), published posthumously in *Le Figaro littéraire* (10 April 1948).

29 This notion is clearly similar to, but not to be conflated with, Husserl's notion of *die lebendige Gegenwart*—Merleau-Ponty's notion is consequent to his intersubjective reinterpretation of transcendental subjectivity.

30 *Sense and Non-Sense* appeared in the same year as *Citadelle*, a work which laid bare Saint Exupéry's conservative moralism of "exchange." Reviewing the work in *Les temps modernes*, Jean-H. Roy (1948) was critical, not only of the book's poor organization, but also of the hierarchical, repressive monarchist model of society that it seemed to recommend. For Saint Exupéry's sake, he regretted its publication.

31 Although they did disagree somewhat about the successfulness of this event, concerning which Merleau-Ponty (1947a) was much more favorable (cf. Spender 1946c).

32 Certainly in March 1956 at the Rencontre Est-Ouest in Venice. It was apparently based on this that Spender, in his satirical novella *Engaged in Writing* (1958), caricatured Sartre and Merleau-Ponty as the disputative French philosophers "Sarret" and "Marteau" (cf. David 1992, 264).

33 This poem was originally published in the *New Yorker* magazine and was included as the final poem in Spender (1964, 80f).

34 This actually preceded its publication in English (Spender 1947).

35 Cf. Bachelard (1943, 296): "The realism of psychic becoming needs ethereal lessons. It even seems that, without aerial discipline, without apprenticeship in lightness, the human psyche cannot evolve. . . . Establishing a future always requires the values of flight."

36 Recall that Hegel ended this text with the final lines (slightly modified) from Friedrich Schiller's poem "Die Freundschaft" (1782): "aus dem Kelche dieses Geisterreiches/schäumt ihm seine Unendlichkeit" [from the chalice of this realm of spirits/foams forth for Him his own infinitude] (Hegel 1988, 531; 1977, 493).

Afterword

What I have discussed in this book, up to and including the Conclusion, seems to provide, at least in outline, a compelling answer to the question at hand. Numerous issues remain outstanding, and no doubt, the objections that might be posed are even more numerous. I am obviously not going to deal with any of that here. But there is one general implication of my overall argument that merits comment: the answer that I have given to the question as to why *Phenomenology of Perception* ends with Saint Exupéry does not remove the question mark that the initial problematization of the ending placed over the work. That is, if this answer holds, then it is not the case that a simple interpretive problem or anomaly has been ironed out such that we are returned to situation normal, so to speak. Rather, if the answer that I have given holds, then it would seem fair to say that *Phenomenology of Perception* is no longer quite the same book. For now, we need to come to terms with a unexpected set of contentious methodological issues.

This is important because inasmuch as the methodology of *Phenomenology of Perception* has not received very much critical attention, it has been relatively easy for scholars to mine the phenomenological descriptions and analyses that Merleau-Ponty laid out in that work, to abstract this or that result from its context, without worrying too much about the methodological commitments to which they are attached. If the answer that I have given holds, however, then it may turn out that such practices are unwarrantable. It belongs to another work to ascertain in detail how the account I have given impacts specific phenomenological analyses in *Phenomenology of Perception*. But based on the general approach to embodiment discussed earlier, it seems incontrovertible that the results of *Phenomenology of Perception*, inasmuch as they have philosophical validity, are firmly dependent upon and hence unabstractable from the methodological assumptions contained in Merleau-Ponty's view of history and historical change. In particular, they are "non-naturalizable," and this not because they are transcendental in some ontologically contrastive sense, but because they are bound up with the specific normativity of a dialectical logic of history that is, to borrow a phrase from Coole, "profoundly and intrinsically political" (Coole 2007, 123). One might attempt to recover the same results on a significantly different methodological basis, but reasons were given above to suggest that such attempts are unlikely to succeed.

What is especially important about coming to terms with Merleau-Ponty's conception of heroism, then, is that it serves to highlight the essential unity of his philosophical and political thought in the immediate postwar period. In particular, it brings to light the fact that his phenomenology has a deep *internal* need for the sort of framework that Marxism has to offer. To reiterate the key claim, it was only by conferring upon phenomenology a Marxist orientation that Merleau-Ponty was able to articulate a viable alternative to Fink. This implies that Merleau-Ponty's Marxism, however deficient or problematic it may appear today, is properly a concern of anyone with a serious interest in his philosophical work, and not just those who might just happen to an interest in his political thought. The point might be put as follows: in a fundamentally important and irreducibly philosophical way, *Phenomenology of Perception*—undeniably Merleau-Ponty's *magnum opus*, irrespective of his apparent subsequent critique thereof—must be approached and understood within the broad terms of *Humanism and Terror*, a text that many (if not *most*) philosophical commentators today would freely acknowledge as scarcely even registering on their Merleau-Pontian radar at all. The reason for saying this is not to defend Merleau-Ponty's Marxism (although as noted earlier, properly understood this may have greater merit than is often thought), but first of all simply to bring to light what is actually going on in his reinterpretation of phenomenology—how, existentially speaking, he could possibly present transcendental philosophy as a kind of embodied cognition.

Bibliography

Acton, H. B. (1949), "Philosophy in France." *Philosophy*, 24, 77–81.

Alquié, F. (1947), "Une philosophie de l'ambiguïté: L'existentialisme de Maurice Merleau-Ponty." *Fontaine: Revue mensuelle de la poésie et des lettres française*, 11(59), 47–70.

Amad, P. (2012), "From God's-eye to Camera-eye: Aerial Photography's Post-humanist and Neo-humanist Visions of the World." *History of Photography*, 36(1), 66–86.

Anderson, P. (1976), *Considerations on Western Marxism*. London: NLB.

Arato, A. and Breines, P. (1979), *The Young Lukács and the Origins of Western Marxism*. New York: Seabury Press.

Arbousse-Bastide, P. (1930), *Pour un humanisme nouveau*. Paris: Foi et Vie.

Aron, R. (1938a), *Essai sur la théorie de l'histoire dans l'Allemagne contemporaine, la philosophie critique de l'histoire*. Paris: Vrin. [Republished as Aron (1969)].

—(1938b), *Introduction à la philosophie de l'histoire: Essai sur les limites de l'objectivité historique*. Paris: Gallimard.

—(1946), *L'âge des empires et l'avenir de la France*. Paris: Éditions Défense de la France.

—(1955), *L'opium des intellectuels*. Paris: Calmann-Lévy.

—(1969), *La philosophie critique de l'histoire. Essai sur une théorie allemande de l'histoire.* [1938]. Paris: Vrin.

—(1981), *La sociologie allemande contemporaine* [1935], 4/e. Paris: Presses Universitaires de France.

—(1990), *Chroniques de guerre. La France libre, 1940-1945*. Paris: Gallimard.

Ash, M. G. (1995), *Gestalt Psychology in German Culture, 1890-1967: Holism and the Quest for Objectivity*. Cambridge; New York: Cambridge University Press.

Assouline, P. (1988), *Gaston Gallimard: A Half-Century of French Publishing*, trans. H. J. Salemson. San Diego: Harcourt, Brace, Jovanovich.

d'Astier de la Vigerie, E. (1971), "Écrivain engagé ou combattant solitaire?," in B. Vercier (ed.), *Les critiques de notre temps et Saint-Exupéry*. Paris: Éditions Garnier Frères, pp. 103–14.

Astre, G.-A. (1959), *Hemingway par lui-même*. Paris: Editions du Seuil.

Axelos, K. (1960), "Préface," in Lukács (1960), pp. 1–8.

Ayouch, T. (2008), "Lived Body and Fantasmatic Body: The Debate Between Phenomenology and Psychoanalysis." *Journal of Theoretical and Philosophical Psychology*, 28(2), 336–55.

Bachelard, G. (1943), *L'air et les songes. Essai sur l'imagination du mouvement*. Paris: José Corti.

Baldwin, T. (ed.), (2007), *Reading Merleau-Ponty: On Phenomenology of Perception*. London; New York: Routledge.

von Balthasar, H. U. (1947), *Prometheus: Studien zur Geschichte des deutschen Idealismus* [1937]. Heidelberg: F. H. Kerle. [Originally published as *Apokalypse der deutschen Seele: Studien zu einer Lehre von letzten Haltungen, I. Die Deutsche Idealismus*. Salzburg: Anton Pustet].

Bannan, J. F. (1967), *The Philosophy of Merleau-Ponty*. New York: Harcourt Brace & World.

Barbaras, R. (1991), *De l'être du phénomène: sur l'ontologie de Merleau Ponty*. Grenoble: Jérôme Millon.

—(2004), *The Being of the Phenomenon: Merleau-Ponty's Ontology*, trans. T. Toadvine and L. Lawlor. Evanston, IL: Northwestern University Press.

Barjon, L. (1945), "Un homme qui conquiert sa vérité: Fidelité de Saint-Exupéry." *Études*, 244 (February), 145–66.

—(1948), "Revue des livres." *Études*, 258, 277–8.

Barnacle, R. (2001), "Phenomenology and Wonder," in R. Barnacle (ed.), *Phenomenology*. Melbourne: RMIT University Press, pp. 3–15.

Barral, M. R. (1993), "Self and Other: Communication and Love," in K. Hoeller (ed.), *Merleau-Ponty and Psychology*. Atlantic Highlands, NJ: Humanities Press, pp. 155–80.

Bataille, G. (1930), "La mutilation sacrificielle et l'oreille coupée de Vincent Van Gogh." *Documents*, 8, 10–20. [Reprinted in Bataille (1970), pp. 258–70. Translated as Bataille (1985).]

—(1933), "La notion de dépense." *La critique sociale*, 7, 7–15. [Reprinted in Bataille (1970), pp. 302–20.]

—(1937), "Van Gogh Prométhée." *Verve*, 1(1) (December), 20. [Reprinted in Bataille (1970), pp. 497–500. Translated as Bataille (1986).]

—(1944), *Le coupable*. Paris: Gallimard. [Reprinted in Bataille (1973), pp. 235–392.]

—(1945), *Sur Nietzsche, volonté de chance*. Paris: Gallimard.

—(1955), "Hegel, la mort et le sacrifice." *Deucalion*, 5, 21–43.

—(1970), *Œuvres complètes I: Premiers écrits, 1922-1940*. Paris: Gallimard.

—(1973), *Œuvres complètes V: La somme athéologique, I*. Paris: Gallimard.

—(1976), *Œuvres complètes VIII: L'histoire de l'érotisme*. Paris: Gallimard.

—(1985), "Sacrificial Mutilation and the Severed Ear of Vincent Van Gogh" [1930], in A. Stoekl (ed.), *Visions of Excess: Selected Writings, 1927-1939*, trans. A. Stoekl (with C. R. Lovitt and D. M. Leslie, Jr.). Minneapolis: University of Minnesota Press, pp. 61–72.

—(1986), "Van Gogh as Prometheus," trans. A. Michelson. *October*, 36, 58–60.

—(1987), *Lettres à Roger Caillois, 4 août 1935-4 février 1959*, ed. J.-P. le Bouler. Romillé: Folle Avoine.

—(1988a), *The Accursed Share: An Essay on General Economy*, Vol. 1, trans. R. Hurley. New York: Zone Books.

—(1988b), *Guilty*, trans. B. Boone. Venice, CA: Lapis Press.

Bay, E. (1953), "Disturbances of Visual Perception and their Examination," *Brain*, 76, 515–30.

Bay, E., Lauenstein, O., and Cibis, P. (1949), "Ein Beitrag zur Frage der Seelenblindheit— der fall Schn. von Gelb und Goldstein," *Psychiatrie, Neurologie und medizinische Psychologie*, 1, 73–91.

de Beauvoir, S. (1945), "La Phénoménologie de la perception de Maurice Merleau-Ponty." *Les Temps modernes*, 2, 363–7.

—(1947), *Pyrrhus et Cinéas*. Paris: Gallimard.

—(1992), *Letters to Sartre*, trans. Q. Hoare. New York: Arcade Publishing.

Bellanger, C., Godechot, J., Guiral, P., and Terrou, F. (1975), *Histoire générale de la presse française, Tome 4: de 1940 à 1958*. Paris: Presses Universitaires de France.

Benda, J. (1927), *La trahison des clercs*. Paris: Bernard Grasset.

—(1937), *Précision (1930-1937)*. Paris: Gallimard.

Benda, J., Bernanos, G., Jaspers, K., Spender, S., Guéhenno, J., Flora, F., de Rougemont, D., de Salis, J.-R., and Lukács, G. (1947), *L'esprit européan. Textes in-extenso des conférences et des entretiens organisés par les Rencontres Internationales de Genève, 1946*. Neuchatel: Éditions de la Baconnière.

Bender, F. (1983), "Merleau-Ponty and Method: Toward a Critique of Husserlian Phenomenology and of Reflective Philosophy in General." *Journal of the British Society for Phenomenology*, 14(2), 176–95.

Berger, G. (1941), *Le cogito dans la philosophie de Husserl*. Paris: Aubier.

Bernadie, S. (1989), "Pour moi, voler ou écrire, c'est tout un." *Cahiers Saint-Exupéry*, 3, 123–32.

Besmer, K. M. (2008), *Merleau-Ponty's Phenomenology: The Problem of Ideal Objects*. London; New York: Continuum.

Besret, B. (1964), *Incarnation ou eschatologie?: Contribution à l'histoire du vocabulaire religieux contemporain, 1935-1955*. Paris: Éditions du Cerf.

Bigwood, C. (1991), "Renaturalizing the Body (with the help of Merleau-Ponty)." *Hypatia*, 6(3), 54–73.

Binswanger, L. (1930), "Traum und Existenz." *Neue Schweizer Rundschau*, 23, 673–85, 766–79. [Reprinted in Binswanger (1994), pp. 95–119.]

—(1935), "Über Psychotherapie." *Nervenarzt*, 8, 113–21, 180–9. [Reprinted in Binswanger (1994), pp. 205–30.]

—(1942), *Grundformen und Erkenntnis menschlichen Daseins*. Zürich: Niehans. [Republished as Binswanger (1993).]

—(1949), *Henrik Ibsen und das Problem der Selbstrealisation in der Kunst*. Heidelberg: Lambert Schneider.

—(1993), *Ausgewählte Werke*, Vol. 2, eds. M. Herzog and H.-J. Braun. Heidelberg: Roland Asanger.

—(1994), *Ausgewählte Werke*, Vol. 3, ed. M. Herzog. Heidelberg: Roland Asanger.

Blanc-Dufour, A., Vicaire, A., Delaigne, M., Meigniez R. (1946), "Correspondance à propos d'un article de Maurice Merleau-Ponty: 'Le Culte du Héros'." *Cahiers d'action*, 1 (May), 55–61.

Bloch, M. (1946), *L'étrange défaite: témoignage écrit en 1940*. Paris: Franc-Tireur.

Bloom, H. (1997), *The Anxiety of Influence: A Theory of Poetry*, 2/e. New York: Oxford University Press.

Boehm, R. (1965), "Basic Reflections on Husserl's Phenomenological Reduction." *International Philosophical Quarterly*, 5, 183–202.

Boivin, P. (1936), "Les catholiques découvrent Marx." *L'homme réel*, 28 (April), 13–19.

Bounin, P. (1999), "*Pilote de guerre*," in Saint Exupéry (1999), pp. 1300–41.

Brasillach, R. (1971), "Review of Saint-Exupéry, Terre des hommes," in B. Vercier (ed.), *Les critiques de notre temps et Saint-Exupéry*. Paris: Éditions Garnier Frères, 67–8. [Originally published in *L'action française*, 16 March 1939.]

Bruzina, R. (1995), "Translator's Introduction," in Fink (1995), pp. vii–xcii.

—(2002), "Eugen Fink and Maurice Merleau-Ponty: The Philosophical Lineage in Phenomenology," in T. Toadvine and L. Embree (eds), *Merleau-Ponty's Reading of Husserl*. Dordrecht: Kluwer, pp. 173–200.

—(2004), *Edmund Husserl and Eugen Fink: Beginnings and Ends in Phenomenology, 1928-1938*. New Haven: Yale University Press.

Buckley, R. P. (1996), "Husserl's Rational 'Liebesgemeinschaft'." *Research in Phenomenology*, 26, 116–29.

Burkhard, B. (2000), *French Marxism Between the Wars: Henri Lefebvre and the "Philosophies."* Amherst, NY: Humanity Books.

Butler, J. (1989), "Sexual Ideology and Phenomenological Description: A Feminist Critique of Merleau-Ponty's Phenomenology of Perception," in J. Allen and I. M. Young (eds), *The Thinking Muse: Feminism and Modern French Philosophy*. Bloomington: Indiana University Press, pp. 85–100.

Caillois, Roger. (1936), "Pour une orthodoxie militante: les tâches immédiates de la pensée moderne." *Inquisitions: Organe de recherche de la phénoménologie humaine*,1, 6–14. [Reprinted as the conclusion to Roger Caillois (1938), pp. 209–22, under the title "Pour une fonction unitaire de l'esprit."]

—(1937). "La naissance de Lucifer." *Verve*, 1, 150–71.

—(1938), *Le mythe et l'homme*. Paris: Gallimard.

—(1946), "Grandeur de Saint-Exupéry." *Valeurs* (Alexandrie) 4, 24–8.

—(1947), "Grandeur de l'homme." *Confluences* 7: 12–14, 244–51.

—(1953), "Préface," in Saint Exupéry (1953), pp. ix–xxv.

—(2003), *The Edge of Surrealism: A Roger Caillois Reader*, ed. C. Frank. Durham: Duke University Press.

Caillois, Roland. (1946), "Note sur l'analyse réflexive et la réflexion phénoménologique. À propos de la *Phénoménologie de la perception* de Maurice Merleau-Ponty." *Deucalion* 1, 125–39.

—(1947), "De la perception à la histoire: La philosophie de Maurice Merleau-Ponty." *Deucalion* 2, 57–85.

Campbell, R. (1947), "M. Merleau-Ponty et ses lecteurs." *Paru: l'actualité littéraire, intellectuelle et artistique*, 37 (December), 49–51.

—(1966), "De l'ambiguïté à l'héroïsme chez Merleau-Ponty." *Cahiers du Sud* 62(390/391), 273–84.

Camus, A. (1942), *Le mythe de Sisyphe*. Paris: Gallimard.

Carbone, M. (1998), "Le sensible et l'excédent: Merleau-Ponty et Kant," in R. Barbaras (ed.), *Notes de cours sur "L'origine de la géométrie" de Husserl, suivi de Recherches sur la phénoménologie de Merleau-Ponty*. Paris: Presses Universitaires de France, pp. 163–91.

—(2004), *The Thinking of the Sensible: Merleau-Ponty's A-Philosophy*. Evanston, IL: Northwestern University Press.

Carman, T. (2008), *Merleau-Ponty*. London; New York: Routledge.

—(2012), "Foreword," in Merleau-Ponty (2012), vii–xvi.

Carman, T. and Hansen, M. B. N. (eds) (2004), *The Cambridge Companion to Merleau-Ponty*. Cambridge: Cambridge University Press.

Cataldi, S. L. and Hamrick, W. S. (eds) (2007), *Merleau-Ponty and Environmental Philosophy: Dwelling on the Landscapes of Thought*. Albany: State University of New York Press.

Cate, C. (1970), *Antoine de Saint-Exupéry: His Life and Times*. London: Heinemann.

Chadeau, E. (2000), *Mermoz*. Paris: Perrin.

Chevrier, P. (1958), *Saint-Exupéry*. Paris: Gallimard.

Cohen, G. (1944), "Saint-Exupéry, poète et héros." *Les Lettres françaises*, 35 (23 December), 1.

Cohen-Solal, A. (with the collaboration of H. Nizan). (1980), *Paul Nizan: Communiste Impossible*. Paris: Grasset.

—(1987), *Sartre: A Life*. London: Heinemann.

Congar, Y. (1935), "Une conclusion théologique à la enquête sur les raisons actuelles de l'incroyance." *La vie intellectuelle*, 37, 214–49.

—(1937), *Chrétiens désunis*. Paris: Éditions du Cerf.

Coole, D. H. (1984), "The Aesthetic Realm and the Lifeworld: Kant and Merleau-Ponty." *History of Political Thought* 5(3), 503–26.

—(2003), "Philosophy as Political Engagement: Revisiting Merleau-Ponty and Reopening the Communist Question." *Contemporary Political Theory*, 2(3), 327–50.

—(2007), *Merleau-Ponty and Modern Politics After Anti-Humanism*. Lanham, MD: Rowman & Littlefield.

Cooper, B. (1975), "Hegelian Elements in Merleau-Ponty's *La structure du comportement*." *International Philosophical Quarterly*, 15, 411–23.

—(1976), "Hegel and the Genesis of Merleau-Ponty's Atheism." *Studies in Religion*, 6, 665–71.

—(1979), *Merleau-Ponty and Marxism: From Terror to Reform*. Toronto: University of Toronto Press.

—(1984), *The End of History: An Essay on Modern Hegelianism*. Toronto: University of Toronto Press.

Cornu, A. (1934), *Karl Marx, l'homme et l'œuvre: De l'hégélianisme au matérialisme historique (1818-1845)*. Paris: Alcan.

Crane, H. E. (1957), *L'humanisme dans l'œuvre de Saint-Exupéry*. Evanston, IL: The Principia Press of Illinois.

Crane, R. F. (2005), "Maritain's True Humanism." *First Things*, 150, 17–23.

Crowell, S. (2001), *Husserl, Heidegger, and the Space of Meaning: Paths Toward Transcendental Phenomenology*. Evanston, IL: Northwestern University Press.

Curtis, D. E. (1991), "Marx against the Marxists: Catholic Uses of the Young Marx in the Front Populaire Period (1934-1938)." *French Cultural Studies*, 2, 165–81.

—(2000), "True and False Modernity: Catholicism and Communist Marxism in 1930s France," in K. Chadwick (ed.), *Catholicism, Politics and Society in Twentieth-century France*. Liverpool: Liverpool University Press, pp. 73–96.

Daniélou, J. (1938), "La foi en l'homme chez Marx." *Chronique sociale de France*, 3, 163–71; 4, 275–82.

Dauenhauer, B. P. (1979), "The Teleology of Consciousness: Husserl and Merleau-Ponty," in A.-M. Tymieniecka (ed.), *Analecta Husserliana*, vol. 9. Dordrecht: D. Reidel, pp. 149–68.

David, H. (1992), *Stephen Spender: A Portrait with Background*. London: Heinemann.

Davis, D. H. (ed.), (2001), *Merleau-Ponty's Later Works and Their Practical Implications: The Dehiscence of Responsibility*. Amherst, NY: Humanity Books.

Depraz, N. (2002), "What about the *Praxis* of Reduction? Between Husserl and Merleau-Ponty," in T. Toadvine and L. Embree (eds), *Merleau-Ponty's Reading of Husserl*. Dordrecht; Boston: Kluwer, pp. 115–25.

DeRamus, B. (1990), *From Juby to Arras: Engagement in Saint-Exupéry*. Lanham, MD: University Press of America.

Desanti, D. (1997), *Ce que le siècle m'a dit: mémoires*. Paris: Plon.

Devettere, R. (1973), "Merleau-Ponty and the Husserlian Reductions." *Philosophy Today*, 17(4), 297–310.

De Waelhens, A. (1951), *Une philosophie de l'ambiguïté: l'existentialisme de Maurice Merleau-Ponty*. Louvain: Publications Universitaires de Louvain.

Devaux, A.-A. (1994), *Saint-Exupéry et Dieu*, 2/e. Paris: Desclée de Brouwer.

Dillard-Wright, D. B. (2009), *Ark of the Possible: The Animal World in Merleau-Ponty*. Lanham, MD: Lexington Books.

Dillon, M. C. (1987), "Apriority in Kant and Merleau-Ponty." *Kant-Studien*, 78(4), 403–23.

—(1988), *Merleau-Ponty's Ontology*, 2/e. Evanston, IL: Northwestern University Press.

Diprose, R. and Reynolds, J. (eds) (2008), *Merleau-Ponty: Key Concepts*. Stocksfield: Acumen.

Dorfman, E. (2007), "Perception, Freedom, and Radical Reflection," in T. Baldwin (ed.), *Reading Merleau-Ponty: On Phenomenology of Perception*. London; New York: Routledge, pp. 139–51.

Drake, D. (2005), *French Intellectuals and Politics from the Dreyfus Affair to the Occupation*. Basingstoke, UK: Palgrave Macmillan.

Drieu la Rochelle, P. (1941), *Notes pour comprendre la siècle*. Paris: Gallimard.

Duhrssen, A. (1953), "Some French Hegelians." *The Review of Metaphysics*, 7(2), 323–37.

Durkheim, E. (1995), *The Elementary Forms of Religious Life*, trans. K. E. Fields. New York: Free Press.

Edman, I. (1942), "A Frenchman Beyond Defeat or Despair. A Deeper, More Tragic Book than *Wind, Sand, and Stars*." *New York Herald Tribune Books* (22 February), 1–2.

Eliade, M. (1947), "Le 'dieu lieur' et le symbolisme des nœuds." *Revue de l'histoire des religions*, 134(1–3), 5–36.

Engels, F. (1940), *Dialectics of Nature*, trans. C. Dutt. New York: International Publishers.

—(1969), *Anti-Dühring: Herr Eugen Dühring's Revolution in Science* [1878]. Moscow: Progress Publishers.

Esprit. (1935), "Notre humanisme. Déclaration collective." *Esprit*, 37, 1–24.

Estang, L. (1956), *Saint-Exupéry par lui-même*. Paris: Éditions du Seuil.

Evans, F. and Lawlor, L. (eds) (2000), *Chiasms: Merleau-Ponty's Notion of Flesh*. Albany: State University of New York Press.

Fadiman, C. (1932), "The Fetish of Duty." *The Nation* (7 September), 215–16.

—(1942), "Beyond Defeat." *The New Yorker* (21 February), 67–8.

Fargue, L.-P. (1947), "Un homme complet." *Confluences* 7(12–14), 38–43.

Fay, E. G. (1947), "The Philosophy of Saint Exupéry." *The Modern Language Journal*, 31(2), 90–7.

Feenberg, A. (1981), *Lukács, Marx, and the Sources of Critical Theory*. Totowa, NJ: Rowman and Littlefield.

Fessard, G. (1936), « *Pax nostra* »: *Examen de conscience international*. Paris: Bernard Grasset.

—(1937), *La main tendue? Le dialogue catholique-communiste est-il possible?*. Paris: Bernard Grasset.

Fessard, G. and Marcel, G. (1985), *Gabriel Marcel – Gaston Fessard: Correspondance, 1934–1971*, eds. H. de Lubac, M. Rougier and M. Sales. Paris: Beauchesne.

Fetscher, I. (1954), "Der Marxismus im Spiegel der französischen Philosophie." *Marxismus-Studien,* 1, 173–213.

Feuer, L. (1969), *Marx and the Intellectuals: A Set of Post-Ideological Essays*. Garden City, NY: Anchor Books.

Fielding, H. (1996), "Grounding Agency in Depth: The Implications of Merleau-Ponty's Thought for the Politics of Feminism." *Human Studies*, 19(2), 175–84.

Fife, A. (1959), "Saint-Exupéry and Fascism." *The French Review*, 32(2), 174–6.

Fink, E. (1930), "Vergegenwärtigung und Bild: Beiträge zur Phänomenologie der Unwirklichkeit." *Jahrbuch für Philosophie und phänomenologische Forschung*, 11, 239–309. [Reprinted in Fink (1966), pp. 1–78.]

—(1933), "Die phänomenologische Philosophie Husserls in der gegenwärtigen Kritik." *Kant-Studien*, 38, 319–83. [Reprinted in Fink (1966), pp. 79–156.]

—(1934), "Was will die Phänomenologie Edmund Husserls? (Die phänomenologische Grundlegungsidee)." *Die Tatwelt*, 10, 15–32. [Reprinted in Fink (1966), pp. 157–78.]

—(1939), "Das Problem der Phänomenologie Edmund Husserls." *Revue internationale de Philosophie*, 1, 226–70. [Reprinted in Fink (1966), pp. 179–223.]

—(1966), *Studien zur Phänomenologie, 1930-1939*. The Hague: Martinus Nijhoff.

—(1970), "The Phenomenological Philosophy of Edmund Husserl and Contemporary Criticism" [1933], trans. R. O. Elveton, in R. O. Elveton (ed.), *The Phenomenology of Husserl: Selected Critical Readings*. Chicago: Quadrangle Books, pp. 73–147.

—(1976a), "Die Idee der Transcendentalphilosophie bei Kant und in der Phänomeno-logie" [1935], in Franz Anton Schwarz (ed.), *Nähe und Distanz: Phänomenologische Vortäge und Aufsätze*. Freiburg: Karl Alber, pp. 7–44.

—(1976b), "Operative Begriffe in Husserls Phänomenologie," in Franz Anton Schwarz (ed.), *Nähe und Distanz: Phänomenologische Vortäge und Aufsätze*. Freiburg: Karl Alber, pp. 180–204.

—(1988a), *VI. Cartesianische Meditation, Teil 1. Die Idee Einer Transzendentalen Methodenlehre*, eds. H. Ebeling, J. Holl, and G. van Kerckhoven. Dordrecht; Boston: Kluwer.

—(1988b), *VI. Cartesianische Meditation, Teil 2. Ergänzungsband: Texte aus dem Nachlass Eugen Finks (1932) mit Anmerkungen und Beilagen aus dem Nachless Edmund Husserls (1933/34)*, ed. G. van Kerckhoven. Dordrecht: Kluwer.

—(1995), *Sixth Cartesian Meditation: The Idea of a Transcendental Theory of Method*, trans. R. Bruzina. Bloomington: Indiana University Press.

—(2006), *Gesamtausgabe 3.1. Phänomenologische Werkstatt: Die Doktorarbeit und erste Assistenzjahre bei Husserl*, ed. R. Bruzina. Freiburg: Karl Alber.

—(2008), *Gesamtausgabe 3.2. Bernauer Zeitmanuskripte, Cartesianische Meditationen und System der phänomenologischen Philosophie*, ed. R. Bruzina. Freiburg: Karl Alber.

Flynn, B. (2007), "The Development of the Political Philosophy of Merleau-Ponty." *Continental Philosophy Review*, 40, 125–38.

Flynn, B., Froman, W., and Vallier, R. (eds) (2010), *Merleau-Ponty and the Possibilities of Philosophy: Transforming the Tradition*. Albany: State University of New York Press.

Fouchet, M.-P. (1945), "Le plus court chemin." *Les lettres françaises* 38(13 January), 4.

Frank, C. (2003), "Introduction," in Roger Caillois (2003), pp. 1–53.

Froman, W. (2005), "Merleau-Ponty and the Relation Between the *Logos Prophorikos* and the *Logos Endiathetos*," in A.-T. Tymieniecka (ed.), *Analecta Husserliana*, vol. 88. Dordrecht: Kluwer, pp. 409–16.

Fukuyama, F. (1992), *The End of History and the Last Man*. New York: The Free Press.

Furter, P. (1961), "La pensée de Georges Lukács en France." *Revue de Théologie et de Philosophie*, 11(4), 353–61.

Gascht, A. (1947), *L'humanisme cosmique d'Antoine de Saint-Exupéry*. Bruges: A. G. Stainforth.

Gelb, A. and Goldstein, K. (1918), "Psychologische Analysen hirnpathologischer Fälle auf Grund von Untersuchungen Hirnverletzer," *Zeitschrift für die gesamte Neurologie und Psychiatrie*, 41, 1–142.

Gendlin, E. T. (1992), "The Primacy of the Body, Not the Primacy of Perception." *Man and World*, 25, 341–53.

Geneste, Y. R. (1968), "L'authenticité de Saint-Exupéry." *The French Review*, 41(4), 518–23.

George, A., Maldinet, H., Hervé, P., Marcel, G., Archambault, P., and Boisselot, R. P. (1946), *Les grands appels de l'homme contemporain: six conférences prononcées au Centre de culture de l'amitié française (janvier-avril 1946)*. Paris: Éditions du temps présent.

Geraets, T. F. (1971), *Vers une nouvelle philosophie transcendantale: La genèse de la philosophie de Maurice Merleau-Ponty jusqu' à la Phénoménologie de la perception*. The Hague: Martinus Nijhoff.

—(1989), "The Return to Perceptual Experience and the Meaning of the Primacy of Perception," in H. Pietersma (ed.), *Merleau-Ponty: Critical Essays*. Washington, DC; Lanham, MD: Center for Advanced Research in Phenomenology; University Press of America, pp. 31–43.

Giddens, A. (1981), *A Contemporary Critique of Historical Materialism*. Berkeley: University of California Press.

Gide, A. (1945), "Saint-Exupéry." *France-Amérique* (25 March), 3.

Gill, J. H. (1991), *Merleau-Ponty and Metaphor*. Atlantic Highlands, NJ: Humanities Press.

Goldenberg, G. (2003), "Goldstein and Gelb's Case Schn: A Classic Case in Neuropsychology?," in C. Code, C. W. Wallesch, Y. Joanette, and A. R. Lecours (eds), *Classic Cases in Neuropsychology*, Vol. 2. Hove: Psychology Press, pp. 281–300.

Goldmann, L. (1948), "Matérialisme dialectique et l'histoire de la philosophie." *Revue philosophique de la France et l'Étranger*, 138(4–6), 160–79. Reprinted in Goldmann (1959), pp. 26–44.

—(1959), *Recherches dialectiques*. Paris: Gallimard.

Goldstein, K. (1934), *Der Aufbau des Organismus: Einführung in die Biologie unter besonderer Berücksichtigung der Erfahrungen am kranken Menschen*. The Hague: Martinus Nijhoff.

—(1940), *Human Nature in the Light of Psychopathology*. Cambridge, MA: Harvard University Press.

—(1995), *The Organism: A Holistic Approach to Biology Derived from Pathological Data in Man*. New York: Zone Books.

Gordon, H. and Tamari, S. (2004), *Maurice Merleau-Ponty's Phenomenology of Perception: A Basis for Sharing the Earth*. Westport, CT: Praeger.

Gramsci, A. (1990), *Selections from Political Writings, 1910-1920*, ed. Q. Hoare, trans. J. Mathews. Minneapolis: University of Minnesota Press.

Grier, M. (2001), *Kant's Doctrine of Transcendental Illusion*. Cambridge: Cambridge University Press.

Guillaume, P. (1946), "Review of *La structure du comportement* and *Phénoménologie de la perception*." *Journal de la psychologie normale et pathologique*, 39, 489–94.

Gurwitsch, A. (1950), "Review of *Phénoménologie de la perception*." *Philosophy and Phenomenological Research*, 10(3), 442–5.

—(1957), *Théorie du champ de la conscience*, trans. M. Butor. Paris: Desclée de Brouwer.

Gusdorf, G. (1948), *L' expérience humaine du sacrifice*. Paris: Presses Universitaires de France.

Guterman, N. and Lefebvre, H. (1934), "Introduction," in Marx (1934), pp. 7–30.

—(1936), *La conscience mystifiée*. Paris: Gallimard.

Gutting, G. (2001), *French Philosophy in the Twentieth Century*. Cambridge, UK; New York: Cambridge University Press.

Hamrick, W. S. and Van der Veken, J. (2011), *Nature and Logos: A Whiteheadian Key to Merleau-Ponty's Fundamental Thought*. Albany: State University of New York Press.

Harrington, A. (1995), "Metaphoric Connections: Holistic Science in the Shadow of the Third Reich." *Social Research*, 62(2), 357–85.

—(1996), *Reenchanted Science: Holism in German Culture from Wilhelm II to Hitler*. Princeton, NJ: Princeton University Press.

Harris, J. R. (1990), "The Elusive Act of Faith: Saint-Exupéry's Sacrifice to an Unknown God." *Christianity and Literature*, 39(2), 141–59.

—(1999), *Chaos, Cosmos, and Saint-Exupéry's Pilot-Hero: A Study in Mythopoeia*. Scranton: University of Scranton Press.

Hass, L. (2008), *Merleau-Ponty's Philosophy*. Bloomington: Indiana University Press.

Hass, L. and Olkowski, D. (eds) (2001), *Rereading Merleau-Ponty: Essays Beyond the Analytic-Continental Divide*. Amherst, NY: Humanity Books.

Hatley, J., Mclane, J., and Diehm, C. (eds) (2006), *Interrogating Ethics: Embodying the Good in Merleau-Ponty*. Pittsburgh: Duquesne University Press.

Hegel, G. W. F. (1956), *The Philosophy of History*, trans. J. Sibree: New York: Dover.

—(1967), *The Philosophy of Right*, trans. T. M. Knox. New York: Oxford University Press.

—(1977), *Phenomenology of Spirit*, trans. A. V. Miller. Oxford: Oxford University Press.

—(1988), *Phänomenologie des Geistes,* eds. H.-F. Wessels and H. Clairmont. Hamburg: Felix Meiner Verlag.

Heidegger, M. (1957), *Sein und Zeit* [1927]. Tübingen: Max Niemeyer.

—(1962), *Being and Time* [1927], trans. J. Macquarrie and E. Robinson. Oxford: Blackwell.

Heinämaa, S. (1999), "Merleau-Ponty's Modification of Phenomenology: Cognition, Passion and Philosophy." *Synthese*, 118, 49–68.

—(2002), "From Decisions to Passions: Merleau-Ponty's Interpretation of Husserl's Reduction," in T. Toadvine and L. Embree (eds), *Merleau-Ponty's Reading of Husserl*. Dordrecht; Boston: Kluwer, pp. 127–46.

Heller, G. (1981), *Un Allemand à Paris: 1940-1944*. Paris: Éditions de Seuil.

Hellman, J. (1976), "French 'Left-Catholics' and Communism in the Nineteen-Thirties." *Church History*, 45(4), 507–23.

—(1981), *Emmanuel Mounier and the New Catholic Left, 1930-1950*. Toronto: University of Toronto Press.

Hemingway, E. (1940), *For Whom the Bell Tolls*. New York: Charles Scribner's Sons.

Henriot, E. (1948), "Citadelle." *Le Monde* (26 May), 3.

Herbenick, R. (1973), "Merleau-Ponty and the Primacy of Reflection," in G. Gillan (ed.), *The Horizons of the Flesh: Critical Perspectives on the Thought of Merleau-Ponty*. Carbondale: Southern Illinois University Press, pp. 92–113.

Hervé, P. (1946), "Sommes-nous tous des coquins?" *action: Hebdomadaire de l'indépendance française*, 76 (15 February), 3.

Hoeller, K. (ed.), (1993), *Merleau-Ponty and Psychology*. Atlantic Highlands, NJ: Humanities Press.

Hollier, D. (1986), *The Politics of Prose: Essay on Sartre*, trans. J. Mehlman. Minneapolis: University of Minnesota Press.

—(ed.), (1988), *The College of Sociology (1937-39)*, trans. B. Wing. Minneapolis: University of Minnesota Press.

Honnert, R. (1937), *Catholicisme et communisme*. Paris: Éditions sociales internationales.

Hughes, H. S. (1968), *The Obstructed Path: French Social Thought in the Years of Desperation, 1930-1960*. New York: Harper & Row.

Husserl, E. (1931), *Méditations cartésiennes: Introduction à la phénoménologie*, trans. G. Peiffer and E. Levinas. Paris: A. Colin.

—(1956), "Kant und die Idee der Transzendentalphilosophie," in R. Boehm (ed.), *Erste Philosophie (1923/24), Erster Teil*, The Hague: Martinus Nijhoff, pp. 230–87.

—(1960), *Cartesian Meditations: An Introduction to Phenomenology*, trans. D. Cairns. The Hague: Martinus Nijhoff.

—(1969), *Formal and Transcendental Logic*, trans. D. Cairns. The Hague: Martinus Nijhoff.

—(1970), *The Crisis of European Sciences and Transcendental Phenomenology*, trans. D. Carr. Evanston, IL: Northwestern University Press.

—(1980), *Ideas Pertaining to a Pure Phenomenology and to a Phenomenological Philosophy. Third Book: Phenomenology and the Foundation of the Sciences*, trans. T. Klein and W. Pohl. Dordrecht: Kluwer.

—(1982), *Ideas Pertaining to a Pure Phenomenology and to a Phenomenological Philosophy, First Book*, trans. F. Kersten. Dordrecht: Kluwer.

—(2002), *Zur phänomenologischen Reduktion, Texte aus dem Nachlass (1926-1935)*, ed.
   S. Luft. Dordrecht: Kluwer.
Hyppolite, J. (1971), *Figures de la pensée philosophiques*, vol. 1. Paris: Presses Universitaires
   de France.
Ishaghpour, Y. (1990), *Paul Nizan: l'intellectuel et le politique entre les deux guerres*. Paris:
   La Différence.
Jarczyk, G. and Labarrière, P.-J. (1996), *De Kojève à Hegel: cent cinquante ans de pensée
   hégélienne en France*. Paris: Albin Michel.
Jay, M. (1984), *Marxism and Totality: The Adventures of a Concept from Lukács to
   Habermas*. Berkeley: University of California Press.
John, S. B. (1985), "Saint-Exupéry's *Pilote de guerre*: Testimony, Art and Ideology," in
   R. Kedward and R. Austin (eds), *Vichy France and The Resistance: Culture and Ideology*.
   Totowa, NJ: Barnes & Noble, pp. 91–105.
Johnson, G. A. (2009), *The Retrieval of the Beautiful: Thinking Through Merleau-Ponty's
   Aesthetics*. Evanston, IL: Northwestern University Press.
Judt, T. (1992), *Past Imperfect: French Intellectuals, 1944-1956*. Berkeley: University of
   California Press.
Jung, C. (1949), "Über eine Nachuntersuchung des Falles Schn. von Goldstein und Gelb."
   Psychiatrie, Neurologie und medizinische Psychologie, 1, 353–62.
Kadarkay, A. (1991), *Georg Lukács: Life, Thought and Politics*. Oxford: Basil Blackwell.
Kant, I. (1998a), *Critique of Pure Reason* [1781/1787], ed./trans. P. Guyer and A. W. Wood.
   Cambridge; New York: Cambridge University Press.
—(1998b), "What Does it Mean to Orient Oneself in Thinking?" [1786], trans. A. Wood,
   in A. Wood and G. di Giovanni (eds), *Religion within the Boundaries of Mere Reason,
   and Other Writings*. Cambridge; New York: Cambridge University Press.
—(2000), *Critique of the Power of Judgment* [1790], ed. P. Guyer, trans. P. Guyer and
   E. Matthews. Cambridge; New York: Cambridge University Press.
Kaplan, A. (2000), *The Collaborator: The Trial and Execution of Robert Brasillach*. Chicago:
   University of Chicago Press.
Kaushik, R. (2011), *Art and the Institution of Being: Aesthetics in the Late Works of
   Merleau-Ponty*. London; New York: Continuum.
Kelly, M. (1982), *Modern French Marxism*. Oxford: Basil Blackwell.
—(2004), *The Cultural and Intellectual Rebuilding of France After the Second World War*.
   Houndmills, UK; New York: Palgrave Macmillan.
Kern, I. (1964), *Husserl und Kant: Eine Untersuchung über Husserls Verhältnis zu Kant und
   zum Neukantianismus*. The Hague: Martinus Nijhoff.
—(1977), "The Three Ways to the Transcendental Phenomenological Reduction
   in the Philosophy of Edmund Husserl," in F. Elliston and P. McCormick (eds),
   Husserl: Expositions and Appraisals. Notre Dame: University of Notre Dame Press,
   pp. 126–49.
Kersten, F. (1995), "Notes from Underground: Merleau-Ponty and Husserl's [*sic*] Sixth
   Cartesian Meditation," in S. G. Crowell (ed.), *The Prism of the Self: Essays in Honor of
   Maurice Natanson*. Dordrecht: Kluwer, pp. 43–58.
King, J. H. (1971), "Philosophy and Experience: French Intellectuals and the Second
   World War." *Journal of European Studies*, 1(3), 198–212.
Kingwell, M. (2000), "Husserl's Sense of Wonder." *The Philosophical Forum*, 31(1), 85–107.
Kline, G. L. (1967), "The Existentialist Rediscovery of Hegel and Marx," in E. N. Lee and
   M. Mandelbaum (eds), *Phenomenology and Existentialism*. Baltimore: Johns Hopkins
   Press, pp. 113–38.

Knight, E. W. (1957), *Literature Considered As Philosophy: The French Example*. London: Routledge & Kegan Paul.

Kojève, A. (1947), *Introduction à la lecture de Hegel: Leçons sur La Phénoménologie de l'Esprit, professées de 1933 à 1939 à l'École des Hautes-Études*, ed. R. Queneau. Paris: Gallimard.

Kolakowski, L. (1978), *Main Currents of Marxism*. New York: Oxford University Press.

Kruks, S. (1981), *The Political Philosophy of Merleau-Ponty*. Atlantic Highlands, NJ: Humanities Press.

Kwant, R. C. (1963), *The Phenomenological Philosophy of Merleau-Ponty*. Pittsburgh: Duquesne University Press.

Lagneau, J. (1928), *Célèbres leçons*. Nîmes: Imprimerie coopérative La Laborieuse.

Landsberg, P.-L. (1936), *Essai sur l'expérience de la mort*. Paris: Desclée de Brouwer.

— (1937), "Réflexions sur l'engagement personnel." *Esprit*, 62, 179–97.

Langer, M. M. (1989), *Merleau-Ponty's Phenomenology of Perception: A Guide and Commentary*. Tallahassee: The Florida State University Press.

Lanzoni, S. (2004), "Existential Encounter in the Asylum: Ludwig Binswanger's 1935 Case of Hysteria." *History of Psychiatry*, 15(3), 285–304.

Lawrence, C. and Weisz, G. (1998), *Greater than the Parts, Holism in Biomedicine, 1920-1950*. New York: Oxford University Press.

Le Baut, H. (2009), "Merleau-Ponty entre Mounier et le Père Maydieu." *Transversalités*, 112, 131–45.

Leduc, V. (2006), *Les tribulations d'un idéologue*. Paris: Galaade Editions.

Lee, E. N. and Mandelbaum, M. (eds) (1967), *Phenomenology and Existentialism*. Baltimore: Johns Hopkins Press.

Leeming, D. (1999), *Stephen Spender: A Life in Modernism*. New York: Henry Holt.

Lefebvre, H. (1945), "Existentialisme et Marxisme: réponse à une mise au point." *action: Hebdomadaire de l'indépendance française*, 40 (8 June), 8.

—(1949), *Le matérialisme dialectique*, 3/e. Paris: Presses Universitaires de France.

Leiner, J. (1970), *Le destin littéraire de Paul Nizan et ses étapes successives: contribution à l'étude du mouvement littéraire en France de 1920 à 1940*. Paris: Klincksieck.

Lenkowski, W. J. (1978), "What is Husserl's *Epoche*? The Problem of the Beginning of Philosophy in a Husserlian Context." *Man and World*, 11(3–4), 299–323.

Lhermitte, J. (1939), *L'image de notre corps*. Paris: Nouvelle Revue Critique.

Lloyd, C. (2003), *Collaboration and Resistance in Occupied France: Representing Treason and Sacrifice*. Houndmills, UK; New York: Palgrave Macmillan.

Losic, S. (1965), *L'idéal humain de Saint-Exupéry*. Paris: A. G. Nizet.

Low, D. B. (1987), *The Existential Dialectic of Marx and Merleau-Ponty*. New York: Peter Lang.

—(2002), *Merleau-Ponty's Last Vision: A Proposal for the Completion of "The Visible and the Invisible."* Evanston, IL: Northwestern University Press.

Löwy, M. (2011), "Revolutionary Dialectics Against 'Tailism': Lukács' Answer to the Criticisms of *History and Class Consciousness*," in M. J. Thompson (ed.), *Georg Lukács Reconsidered: Critical Essays in Politics, Philosophy and Aesthetics*. London; New York: Continuum.

Luft, S. (1998), "Husserl's Phenomenological Discovery of the Natural Attitude." *Continental Philosophy Review*, 31, 153–70.

—(2004), "Husserl's Theory of the Phenomenological Reduction: Between Life-world and Cartesianism." *Research in Phenomenology*, 34(1), 198–234.

Lukács, G. (1948), *Existentialisme ou Marxisme?*, trans. E. Keleman. Paris: Nagel.

—(1960), *Histoire et conscience de classe: Essais de dialectique marxiste* [1923], trans. K. Axelos and J. Bois. Paris: Editions de Minuit.

—(1967a), *Geschichte und Klassenbewußtsein: Studien über Marxistische Dialektik* [1923]. Amsterdam: Thomas de Munter.

—(1967b), *Schriften zur Ideologie und Politik*, ed. P. Ludz. Neuwied: Luchterhand.

— (1971), *History and Class Consciousness: Studies in Marxist Dialectics* [1923], trans. R. Livingstone. Cambridge, MA: MIT Press.

—(2000). *A Defence of History and Class Consciousness: Tailism and the Dialectic*, trans. E. Leslie. London; New York: Verso.

Madison, G. B. (1981), *The Phenomenology of Merleau-Ponty: A Search for the Limits of Consciousness* [1973]. Athens, OH: Ohio University Press.

—(1992), "Did Merleau-Ponty Have a Theory of Perception?," in T. W. Busch and S. Gallagher (eds), *Merleau-Ponty, Hermeneutics, and Postmodernism*. Albany: State University of New York Press, pp. 83–106.

Major, J.-L. (1968), *Saint-Exupéry, l'écriture et la pensée*. Ottawa: Éditions de l'Université d'Ottawa.

Mallin, S. B. (1979), *Merleau-Ponty's Philosophy*. New Haven: Yale University Press.

Malraux, A. (1933), *La condition humaine*. Paris: Gallimard.

Maritain, J. (1936), *Humanisme intégral: Problèmes temporels et spirituels d'une nouvelle chrétienté*. Paris: Aubier.

—(1941), *À travers le désastre*. New York: Éditions de la Maison Française.

—(1942), "Il faut parfois juger (À propos d'une lettre ouverte de Saint-Exupéry)." *Pour la victoire* (12 December 1942). [Reprinted in Saint Exupéry (1982), pp. 275–81.]

Marotta, J.J. and Behrmann, M. (2004), "Patient Schn: Has Goldstein and Gelb's Case Withstood the Test of Time?" *Neuropsychologia* 42, 633–8.

Marshall, G. J. (2008), *A Guide to Merleau-Ponty's Phenomenology of Perception*. Milwaukee: Marquette University Press.

Marx, K. (1927–37), *Œuvres philosophiques*, 6 vols., trans. J. Molitor. Paris: Alfred Costes.

—(1934), *Morceaux choisis de Karl Marx*, eds, P. Nizan and J. Duret. Paris: Gallimard.

—(1975a), "Difference Between the Democritean and Epicurean Philosophy of Nature" [1840/41], in K. Marx and F. Engels (eds), *Collected Works*, vol. 1. Moscow: Progress Publishers, pp. 25–105.

—(1975b), "Contribution to the Critique of Hegel's Philosophy of Law. Introduction" [1843–44], in K. Marx and F. Engels (eds), *Collected Works*, vol. 3. Moscow: Progress Publishers, pp. 175–87.

—(1976), *The Poverty of Philosophy. Answer to the* Philosophy of Poverty *by M. Proudhon* [1847], in K. Marx and F. Engels (eds), *Collected Works*, vol. 6. New York: International Publishers, pp. 105–212.

Massonet, S. (1998), "Lucifer en 1938: Incandescence et mal à l' œuvre chez Bataille, Klossowski et Caillois," in M. Watthee-Delmotte and M. Zupancic (eds), *Le mal dans l'imaginaire littéraire français (1850-1950)*. Paris: Éditions L'Harmattan, pp. 67–75.

Matthews, E. (2002), *The Philosophy of Merleau-Ponty*. Montréal: McGill-Queens University Press.

—(2006), *Merleau-Ponty: A Guide for the Perplexed*. London; New York: Continuum.

Maublanc, R. (1935), *Le philosophie du marxisme et l'enseignement officiel*. Paris: Bureau d' éditions.

Maurois, A. (1942), "Meditation of a French Aviator." *The Yale Review*, 31(4), 819–21.

Mauss, M. (2000), *The Gift: The Form and Reason for Exchange in Archaic Societies*, trans. W. D. Halls. New York; London: W. W. Norton & Company. [Originally published in 1925 in *L'année sociologique*, n.s. 1, 30–186.]

Mauss, M. and Hubert, H. (1964), *Sacrifice: Its Nature and Function*, trans. W. D. Halls. Chicago: The University of Chicago Press.

Mayer, H. (1949), *Literatur der Übergangszeit*. Wiesbaden: Limes.

McKeon, J. T. (1974), "Saint-Exupéry, the Myth of the Pilot." *PMLA* 89(5), 1084–9.

Mehlman, J. (2000), *Emigré New York: French Intellectuals in Wartime Manhattan, 1940-1944*. Baltimore: Johns Hopkins University Press.

Melle, U. (1992), "Consciousness: Wonder of all Wonders." *American Catholic Philosophical Quarterly*, 66(2), 155–73.

—(2002), "Edmund Husserl: From Reason to Love," in J. J. Drummond and L. Embree (eds), *Phenomenological Approaches to Moral Philosophy: A Handbook*. Dordrecht; Boston: Kluwer, pp. 229–48.

Menninger-Lerchenthal, E. (1934), *Das Truggebilde der eigene Gestalt*. Berlin: Karger.

Merleau-Ponty, M. (unpublished), "Notes inédites de Maurice Merleau-Ponty, 1946-1949." Transcribed by K. Whiteside.

—(1935), "Christianisme et ressentiment." *La vie intellectuelle*, 7(36), 278–306. [Reprinted in Merleau-Ponty (1997), pp. 9–33.]

—(1942), *La structure du comportement*. Paris: Presses Universitaires de France.

—(1945), *Phénoménologie de la perception*. Paris: Gallimard.

—(1946), "Le Culte du héros." <u>action</u>: *Hebdomadaire de l'indépendance française*, 74 (1 February) 12–13.

—(1947a), "Pour les Rencontres Internationales." *Les temps modernes*, 19 (April), 1340–4.

—(1947b), *Humanisme et terreur: Essai sur le problème communiste*. Paris: Gallimard.

—(1948), *Sens et non-sens*. Paris: Nagel.

—(1953), *Éloge de la philosophie: leçon inaugurale faite au Collège de France, le jeudi 15 janvier 1953*. Paris: Collège de France.

—(1955), *Les aventures de la dialectique*. Paris: Gallimard.

—(ed.) (1956), *Les philosophes célèbres*. Paris: L. Mazenod.

—(1960), *Signes*. Paris: Gallimard.

—(1961), "Réponse à Olivier Todd." *France Observateur*, (2 March), 17–18. [Reprinted in Merleau-Ponty (2000), pp. 305–9.]

—(1962a), "Un inédit de Maurice Merleau-Ponty." *Revue de métaphysique et de morale*, 67(4), 401–9. [Reprinted in Merleau-Ponty (2000), pp. 36–48.]

—(1962b), *Phenomenology of Perception*, trans. C. Smith. London; New York: Routledge & Kegan Paul.

—(1963), *The Structure of Behavior*, trans. A. L. Fisher. Boston: Beacon Press.

—(1964a), *Le visible et l'invisible*, ed. C. Lefort. Paris: Gallimard.

—(1964b), *The Primacy of Perception, And Other Essays on Phenomenological Psychology, the Philosophy of Art, History and Politics*, ed. J. M. Edie. Evanston, IL: Northwestern University Press.

—(1964c), *Sense and Non-Sense*, trans. H. L. Dreyfus and P. A. Dreyfus. Evanston, IL: Northwestern University Press.

—(1964d), *Signs*, trans. R. C. McCleary. Evanston, IL: Northwestern University Press.

—(1964e), *The Visible and the Invisible*, trans. A. Lingis. Evanston, IL: Northwestern University Press.

—(1968), *Résumés de cours. Collège de France, 1952-1960*. Paris: Gallimard.

—(1969), *Humanism and Terror: An Essay on the Communist Problem*, trans. J. O'Neill. Boston: Beacon Press.

—(1973), *Adventures of the Dialectic*, trans. J. Bien. Evanston, IL: Northwestern University Press.

—(1988), *In Praise of Philosophy, and Other Essays*, trans. J. Wild, J. M. Edie and J. O'Neill. Evanston, IL: Northwestern University Press.

—(1992), *Texts and Dialogues: Maurice Merleau-Ponty*, eds. H. J. Silverman and J. Barry Jr., trans. M. B. Smith et al. Atlantic Highlands, NJ: Humanities Press.

—(1996a), *Le primat de la perception et ses conséquences philosophiques, précédé de Projet de travail sur la nature de la perception, 1933, La Nature de la perception, 1934*, ed. J. Prunair. Lagrasse: Verdier.

—(1996b), *Notes de cours, 1959-1961*, ed. S. Ménasé. Paris: Gallimard.

—(1997), *Parcours, 1935-1951*, ed. J. Prunair. Lagrasse: Verdier.

—(2000), *Parcours deux, 1951-1961*, ed. J. Prunair. Lagrasse: Verdier.

—(2012), *Phenomenology of Perception*, trans. D. A. Landes. London; New York: Routledge.

Mersch, E. (1936), *Le corps mystique du Christ: études de théologie historique*. Paris: Desclée; Bruxelles: L'Edition Universelle.

Meyer, R. (1955), "Merleau-Ponty und das Schicksal des französischen Existentialismus." *Philosophische Rundschau* 3, 129–65.

Michel, H. (1962), *Les courants de pensée de la Résistance*. Paris: Presses Universitaires de France.

Migeo, M. (1999), *Henri Guillaumet, pionnier de l'Aéropostale*. Grenoble: Arthaud.

Miller, J. (1979), *History and Human Existence: From Marx to Merleau-Ponty*. Berkeley: University of California Press.

Milligan, E. E. (1955), "Saint Exupéry and Language." *The Modern Language Journal*, 39(5), 249–51.

de Montherlant, H. (1935), *Service inutile*. Paris: Gallimard.

Moré, M. (1934), "Notes sur le marxisme." *Esprit*, 21, 453–70.

—(1935), "Les années d'apprentissage de Karl Marx (à propos d'un livre récent)." *Esprit*, 31, 15–30; 33, 355–72; 36, 752–72; 37, 47–70.

—(1936), "La pensée de Marx et nous." *Esprit*, 40, 552–68.

Morgan, C. (1944), "Hommage à Saint-Exupéry." *Les lettres françaises*, 19 (August), 4.

Morshed, A. (2002), "The Cultural Politics of Aerial Vision: Le Corbusier in Brazil (1929)." *Journal of Architectural Education*, 55, 201–10.

Mounier, E. (1937), "Chrétiens et communisme." *Esprit*, 56, 306–12.

—(1938), *A Personalist Manifesto*, trans. Monks of St. John's Abbey. London; New York; Toronto: Longmans, Green and Co.

Murphy, R. (1966), "A Metaphysical Critique of Method: Husserl and Merleau-Ponty," in F. J. Adelmann (ed.), *The Quest for the Absolute*. Chestnut Hill: Boston College; The Hague: Martinus Nijhoff, pp. 175–207.

Nagel, C. (2000), "Knowledge, Paradox, and the Primacy of Perception." *The Southern Journal of Philosophy*, 38, 481–97.

Naville, P. (1942), *La psychologie, science du comportement. Le behaviorisme de Watson*. Paris: Gallimard.

Nizan, P. (1933a), "Sur un certain front unique." *Europe*, 121, 137–46. [Reprinted in Nizan (1971), pp. 51–65.]

—(1933b), "Les enfants de la lumière." *Commune*, 2, 105–12. [Reprinted in Nizan (1967), pp. 219–25.]

—(1939), "Review of Saint-Exupéry, Terre des hommes." *Ce Soir* (30 March), 2. [Reprinted in Nizan (1971), pp. 307–9.]

—(1960), *Aden Arabie* [1931] (with a Preface by J.-P. Sartre). Paris: Maspero.

—(1967), *Paul Nizan, intellectuel communiste, 1926-1940. Articles et correspondance inédite*, ed. J.-J. Brochier. Paris: Maspero.

—(1969), *Les chiens de garde* [1932]. Paris: François Maspero.

—(1971), *Pour une nouvelle culture*, ed. S. Suleiman. Paris: Bernard Grasset.

Noble, S. A. (2011), "Maurice Merleau-Ponty, Or The Pathway Of Philosophy: Desiderata for an Intellectual Biography." *Chiasmi International*, 13, 63–122.

Olkowski, D. and Morley, J. (eds) (1999), *Merleau-Ponty, Interiority and Exteriority, Psychic Life and the World*. Albany: State University of New York Press.

Olkowski, D. and Weiss, G. (eds) (2006), *Feminist Interpretations of Maurice Merleau-Ponty*. University Park, PA: Pennsylvania State University Press.

Ouellet, R. (1971), *Les relations humaines dans l'œuvre de Saint-Exupéry*. Paris: Minard.

Park, J. Y. and Kopf, G. (eds) (2010), *Merleau-Ponty and Buddhism*. Lanham, MD: Lexington Books.

Pax, C. (1982), "Social Encounters and Death: Hermeneutical Reflections," in R. Bruzina and B. Wilshire (eds), *Phenomenology: Dialogues and Bridges*. Albany: State University of New York Press, pp. 195–201.

Pietersma, H. (1988), "Merleau-Ponty and Spinoza." *International Studies in Philosophy* 20(3), 89–93.

—(1989), "Merleau-Ponty's Theory of Knowledge," in H. Pietersma (ed.), *Merleau-Ponty: Critical Essays*. Washington, DC: University Press of America; Lanham, MD: Center for Advanced Research in Phenomenology, pp. 101–31.

—(2000), *Phenomenological Epistemology*. New York; Oxford: Oxford University Press.

Politzer, G. (1928), *Critique des fondements de la psychologie*. Paris: Rieder.

Poster, M. (1975), *Existential Marxism in Post-War France: From Sartre to Althusser*. Princeton: Princeton University Press.

Pradel, J. and Vanrell, L. (2008), *Saint Exupéry: l'ultime secret. Enquête sur une disparition*. Paris: Rocher

Price, R. H. (1957), "Saint-Exupéry and Fascism." *Modern Language Forum*, 42(2), 141–5.

—(1960), "Saint-Exupéry and Fascism: A Clarification." *The French Review*, 34(1), 81.

Priest, S. (2003), *Merleau-Ponty*. London; New York: Routledge.

Rabil, A. (1967), *Merleau-Ponty: Existentialist of the Social World*. New York: Columbia University Press.

Ragache, G. and Ragache, J.-R. (1988), *La vie quotidienne des écrivains et des artistes sous l'Occupation, 1940-1944*. Paris: Hachette.

Rauch, R. W. (1971), *Politics and Belief in Contemporary France: Emmanuel Mounier and Christian Democracy, 1932-1950*. The Hague: Martinus Nijhoff.

Rees, J. (2000), "Introduction," in Lukács (2000), pp. 1–38.

Rémond, R. (1960), "Les catholiques et le Front Populaire (1936-1937)." *Archives des sciences sociales des religions*, 10(10), 63–9.

Revel, J.-F. (1965), *En France: La fin de l'opposition*. Paris: Julliard.

Reynolds, J. (2004), *Merleau-Ponty and Derrida: Intertwining Embodiment and Alterity*. Athens, OH: Ohio University Press.

Richman, M. (2002), *Sacred Revolutions: Durkheim and the Collège de Sociologie*. Minneapolis: University of Minnesota Press.

—(2003), "Myth, Power, and the Sacred: Anti-Utilitarianism in the Collège de Sociologie, 1937-39." *Economy and Society* 32(1), 29–47.

Rickman, H. P. (1996), "A Philosophic Fairy Tale: Existentialist Themes in St. Exupéry's *The Little Prince*," in *Philosophy in Literature*. Madison, NJ: Fairleigh Dickinson University Press, pp. 129–41.

Romdenh-Romluc, K. (2010), *Routledge Philosophy GuideBook to Merleau-Ponty and Phenomenology of Perception*. London; New York: Routledge.

Bibliography

Rosen, S. (1987), *Hermeneutics as Politics*. Oxford: Oxford University Press.

Roth, M. S. (1988), *Knowing and History: Appropriations of Hegel in Twentieth-Century France*. Ithaca: Cornell University Press.

Roy, J.-H. (1948), Review of *Citadelle*, *Les temps modernes*, 35 (August), 364–7.

Rude, F. (1978), "Éditions clandestines." *Icare: Revue de l'aviation française*, 84, 130–9.

de Saint Aubert, E. (2004), *Du lien des êtres aux éléments de l' être: Merleau-Ponty au tournant des années 1945-1951*. Paris: Vrin.

—(2005), *Le scénario cartésien: Recherches sur la formation et la cohérence de l'intention philosophique de Merleau-Ponty*. Paris: Vrin.

de Saint Exupéry, A. (1929), *Courrier sud*. Paris: Gallimard.

—(1931), *Vol de nuit*. Paris: Gallimard.

—(1939), *Terre des hommes*. Paris: Gallimard.

—(1942a), *Pilote de guerre*. New York: Éditions de la Maison Française.

—(1942b), *Flight to Arras*, trans. L. Galantière. New York: Reynal & Hitchcock.

—(1942c), *Pilote de guerre*. Paris: Gallimard.

—(1946), *Le petit prince*. Paris: Gallimard.

—(1953), *Œuvres*. Paris: Gallimard.

—(1956), *Un sens à la vie. Textes inédits*, ed. C. Reynal. Paris: Gallimard.

—(1975), *Carnets, édition intégrale*. Paris: Gallimard.

—(1981), "Le marxisme anti-marxiste." *Cahiers Saint-Exupéry (Textes réunis et présentés par le Comité de l'Association des Amis d'Antoine de Saint-Exupéry)* 2, 11–21.

—(1982), *Écrits de guerre, 1939-1944, avec Lettre à un otage, et des témoignages et documents*. Paris: Gallimard.

—(1999), *Œuvres complètes II: Ecrits de guerre, œuvres littéraires*, eds. M. Autrand and M. Quesnel. Paris: Gallimard.

Sander, F. (1937), "Deutsche Psychologie und nationalsozialistische Weltanschauung." *Nationalsozialistisches Bildungswesen*, 2, 641–61.

Sartre, J.-P. (1943), *L'être et le néant*. Paris: Gallimard.

—(1944), "À propos de l'existentialisme: mise au point." *action: Hebdomadaire de l'indépendance française*, 17 (29 December), 11.

—(1946), "Matérialisme et révolution." *Les temps modernes*, 9, 1537–1563; 10, 1–32. [Reprinted in Sartre (1949), pp. 135–228.]

—(1948), *Situations II*. Paris: Gallimard.

—(1949), *Situations III*. Paris: Gallimard.

—(1956), *Being and Nothingness: An Essay on Phenomenological Ontology*, trans. H. E. Barnes. New York: Philosophical Library.

—(1964), *Situations IV*. Paris: Gallimard.

—(1970), *Les écrits de Sartre: Chronologie, bibliographie commentée*, eds. M. Contat and M. Rybalka. Paris: Gallimard.

—(1983), *Cahiers pour une morale*. Paris: Gallimard.

—(1984), *The War Diaries of Jean-Paul Sartre: November 1939/March 1940*, trans. Q. Hoare. New York: Pantheon Books.

—(1992), *Witness to My Life: The Letters of Jean-Paul Sartre to Simone de Beauvoir, 1926-1939*, ed. S. de Beauvoir; trans. L. Fahnestock and N. MacAfee. New York: Charles Scribner's Sons.

Schalk, D. L. (1973), "Professors as Watchdogs: Paul Nizan's Theory of the Intellectual and Politics." *Journal of the History of Ideas*, 34(1), 79–96.

—(1979), *The Spectrum of Political Engagement: Mounier, Benda, Nizan, Brasillach, Sartre*. Princeton: Princeton University Press.

Schiff, S. (1994), *Saint-Exupéry: A Biography*. New York: A.A. Knopf.

Schilder, P. (1923), *Das Körperschema: Ein Beitrag zur Lehre vom Bewusstsein des Eigenen Körpers*. Berlin: Springer.

Schmidt, J. (1985), *Maurice Merleau-Ponty: Between Phenomenology and Structuralism*. Basingstoke, Hampshire: Macmillan.

Scriven, M. (1988), *Paul Nizan: Communist Novelist*. New York: St. Martin's Press.

Seebohm, T. M. (2002), "The Phenomenological Movement: A Tradition Without Method? Merleau-Ponty and Husserl," in T. Toadvine and L. Embree (eds), *Merleau-Ponty's Reading of Husserl*. Dordrecht; Boston: Kluwer, pp. 51–68.

Semonovitch, K. and DeRoo, N. (eds) (2010), *Merleau-Ponty at the Limits of Art, Religion, and Perception*. London; New York: Continuum.

Sheasby, W. (1999), "Anti-Prometheus, Post-Marx: The Real and the Myth in Green Theory." *Organization & Environment*, 12(1), 5–44.

Sheets-Johnstone, M. (1999), *The Primacy of Movement*. Amsterdam; Philadelphia: John Benjamins.

Simon, P.-H. (1950), *L'homme en procès: Malraux, Sartre, Camus, Saint-Exupéry*. Neuchatel: À La Baconnière.

Singer, L. (1981), "Merleau-Ponty on the Concept of Style." *Man and World*, 14, 153–63.

Smetana, J. (1965), *La philosophie de l'action chez Hemingway et Saint-Exupéry*. Paris: La Marjolaine.

Smith, C. (1964), *Contemporary French Philosophy: A Study in Norms and Values*. London: Methuen.

—(1980), "Saint-Exupéry and the Problem of Embodiment," in C. E. Pickford (ed.), *Mélanges de littérature française moderne offerts à Garnet Rees, Professor à l'Université de Hull*. Paris: Librairie Minard, pp. 261–74.

Smith, J. (2005), "Merleau-Ponty and the Phenomenological Reduction." *Inquiry*, 48(6), 553–71.

Smith, M. A. (1956), *Knight of the Air: The Life and Works of Saint-Exupéry*. New York: Pageant Press.

Smyth, B. (2010), "Heroism and History in Merleau-Ponty's Existential Phenomenology." *Continental Philosophy Review*, 43(2), 167–91.

—(2011), "The Meontic and the Militant: On Merleau-Ponty's Relation to Fink." *International Journal of Philosophical Studies*, 19(5), 669–99.

Spender, S. (1946a), *European Witness*. London: Hamish Hamilton.

—(1946b), "Pensées dans un avion au-dessus de l'Europe," trans. M. Sibon. *Les temps modernes*, 13, 65–78.

—(1946c), "Meeting at Geneva." *Time and Tide*, 27(42) (19 October), 996, 998; 43 (26 October), 1020.

—(1947), "Thoughts in an Aeroplane over Europe." *Polemic: A Magazine of Philosophy, Psychology, and Aesthetics*, 8, 55–67.

—(1958), *Engaged in Writing*. London: Hamish Hamilton.

—(1964), *Selected Poems*. New York: Random House.

Spiegelberg, H. (1972), *Phenomenology in Psychology and Psychiatry: A Historical Introduction*. Evanston, IL: Northwestern University Press.

—(1973), "Is the Reduction Necessary for Phenomenology? Husserl's and Pfänder's Replies." *Journal of the British Society for Phenomenology*, 4, 3–15.

—(1974), "Epoché without Reduction: Some Replies to My Critics." *Journal of the British Society for Phenomenology*, 5, 256–61.

—(with the collaboration of K. Schuhmann). (1984), *The Phenomenological Movement: A Historical Introduction*, 3/e. The Hague: Martinus Nijhoff.

Spurling, L. (1977), *Phenomenology and the Social World: The Philosophy of Merleau-Ponty and Its Relation to the Social Sciences*. London; Boston: Routledge and Kegan Paul.

Steeves, J. B. (2004), *Imagining Bodies: Merleau-Ponty's Philosophy of Imagination*. Pittsburgh: Duquesne University Press.

Steinbock, A. (1995), *Home and Beyond: Generative Phenomenology after Husserl*. Evanston, IL: Northwestern University Press.

—(1998), "Spirit and Generativity: The Role and Contribution of the Phenomenologist in Hegel and Husserl," in N. Depraz and D. Zahavi (eds), *Alterity and Facticity*. Dordrecht: Kluwer, pp. 163–203.

Stoekl, A. (1992), *Agonies of the Intellectual: Commitment, Subjectivity, and the Performative in the Twentieth-Century French Tradition*. Lincoln: University of Nebraska Press.

Stoller, S. (2000), "Reflections on Feminist Merleau-Ponty Skepticism." *Hypatia*, 15(1), 175–82.

Sullivan, L. (1980), "L'image de la mort chez Saint-Exupéry." *The French Review*, 54(1), 78–84.

Sullivan, S. (1997), "Domination and Dialogue in Merleau-Ponty's *Phenomenology of Perception*." *Hypatia*, 12(1), 1–19.

Taminiaux, J. (2004), *The Metamorphoses of Phenomenological Reduction*. Milwaukee: Marquette University Press.

Tane, P. D. (1998), *The Ideological Hero: The Novels of Robert Brasillach, Roger Vailland, and André Malraux*. New York: Peter Lang.

Tauber, H. L. (1966), "Kurt Goldstein's Role in the Development of Neuropsychology," *Neuropsychologia*, 4, 299–310.

Ton-That, Thanh-Vân. (2000), "Images et voix de l'enfance dans *Pilote de guerre*." *Roman 20/50*, 29, 51–63.

Thuillier, G. (1957), "Saint-Exupéry, poète politique." *La Revue administrative*, 10(60), 572–80.

Toadvine, T. (ed.) (2006), *Merleau-Ponty (Critical Assessments of Leading Philosophers)*, 4 vols. London; New York: Routledge.

—(2009), *Merleau-Ponty's Philosophy of Nature*. Evanston, IL: Northwestern University Press.

Toadvine, T. and Embree, L. (eds) (2002), *Merleau-Ponty's Reading of Husserl*. Dordrecht; Boston: Kluwer.

Todd, Olivier. (1961), "Nizan et ses croque-morts." *l'Observateur littéraire* (23 February), 15–16.

Trân Dúc Tháo. (1946), "Marxisme et phénoménologie." *La Revue internationale*, 2, 168–74.

—(1949), "Existentialisme et matérialisme dialectique." *Revue de métaphysique et de morale*, 54, 317–29.

—(1951), *Phénoménologie et matérialisme dialectique*. Paris: Minh-Tân.

Vailland, R. (1945), *Drôle de jeu*. Paris: Corréa.

Van Breda, H. L. (1962), "Maurice Merleau-Ponty et les Archives-Husserl à Louvain." *Revue de métaphysique et de morale*, 67(4), 410–30.

van den Berghe, C. L. (1985), *La pensée de Saint-Exupéry*. New York: Peter Lang.

Van-Huy, P. N. (1982), "*Pilote de guerre*, ou la conscience cosmique de St.-Exupéry." *The USF Language Quarterly*, 21(3)–4, 33–8.

Vercier, B. (ed.) (1971), *Les critiques de notre temps et Saint-Exupéry*. Paris: Éditions Garnier Frères.

Vignaux, P. (1935), "Retour à Marx ." *Politique*, 11, 900–14.

de Waelhens, A. (1967), *Une philosophie de l'ambigüité: l'existentialisme de Maurice Merleau-Ponty*, 2/e. Louvain: Nauwelaerts.

Wagner, W. (1996), *La conception de l'amour-amitié dans l'œuvre de Saint-Exupéry*. Frankfurt am Main; New York: Peter Lang.

Waldenfels, B. (1991), "Vérité à faire: Merleau-Ponty's Question Concerning Truth." *Philosophy Today*, 35(2), 185–94.

—(1997), "L'auto-référence de la phénoménologie," in N. Depraz and M. Richir (eds), *Eugen Fink: Actes du Colloque de Cérisy-la-Salle, 23.07-30.07.1994*. Amsterdam: Rodopi, pp. 63–74.

Weldon, T. (2011), *Faring Homewards: The Philosophy of Antoine de Saint-Exupéry*. Montgomery, AL: E-Book Time.

Welton, D. (2000), *The Other Husserl: The Horizons of Transcendental Phenomenology*. Bloomington: Indiana University Press.

Wessell, L. P., Jr. (1984), *Prometheus Bound: The Mythic Structure of Karl Marx's Scientific Thinking*. Baton Rouge; London: Louisiana State University Press.

Whiteside, K. (1983), "The Merleau-Ponty Bibliography: Additions and Corrections." *Journal of the History of Philosophy*, 21(2), 195–201.

—(1986), "Perspectivism and Historical Objectivity: Maurice Merleau-Ponty's Covert Debate with Raymond Aron." *History and Theory*, 25, 132–51.

—(1988), *Merleau-Ponty and the Foundation of an Existential Politics*. Princeton, NJ: Princeton University Press.

Winock, M. (1975), *Histoire politique de la revue 'Esprit', 1930-1950*. Paris: Seuil.

Zévaès, A. (1947), *De l'introduction du marxisme en France*. Paris: M. Rivière.

Index